Legal Aspects of
Foodservice Management

Legal Aspects of Foodservice Management

John E. H. Sherry, J.D.

Associate Professor of Law
School of Hotel Administration
Cornell University

A NIFI Textbook

William C. Brown Publishers
in cooperation with the
National Institute for the Foodservice Industry

*On behalf of the
people in our industry
who will benefit, the Institute
is pleased to thank*

COCA-COLA USA

*for the financial support
which has made possible the
development of this book and
related course materials.*

Contents

Appendixes 289

A Message from the Institute

The National Institute for the Foodservice Industry is proud to present *Legal Aspects of Foodservice Management,* a law book for foodservice operators. This book, written by Professor John E. H. Sherry, is designed to be read and used as a management tool by supervisors and managers of foodservice businesses and by students of foodservice management.

Managing a foodservice operation is a many-faceted job, requiring skills in different fields such as marketing, supervision, and purchasing. These skills are necessary tools used in the process of maintaining a business and making it grow. Too often, operators are not aware of the legal aspects of management until it is too late.

Employee relations, food liability, liquor liability, patron civil rights, and federal regulations are subjects that concern foodservice operators, who know that preventing legal problems is the best way to keep profits from being siphoned off into expensive legal hassles. This book is designed to give readers an opportunity to look at foodservice operations from a legal standpoint and to develop management strategies to prevent legal problems.

Professor Sherry attacks head-on the common reaction of businesspersons that (1) the law is too complex to understand, and (2) ignorance of the law will somehow protect operators from legal pitfalls. He debunks both reactions in the first chapter and carries this theme throughout the rest of the book.

Legal Aspects of Foodservice Manage-ment is a *practical* book, designed for those seeking a down-to-earth explanation of legal subjects relevant to food service. It is a *read-able* book. For students and teachers, it con-tains outlines, chapter objectives, cases, review questions, and footnotes for further study. For operators and students alike, the explanations are thorough and the concepts are illustrated with examples.

Once read, this book should be kept as part of the foodservice operator's personal library. Its chapters and the glossary and appendixes can be referred to as specific questions arise. questions arise.

A few words are in order about the Na-tional Institute for the Foodservice Industry (NIFI), the educational foundation. NIFI is dedicated to the advancement of profession-alism in the foodservice industry, fostering and nurturing it through education. NIFI pro-vides vital services to the industry through the development of educational programs and materials and the administration of scholar-ships and work-study grants, and by promot-ing industry careers. We at NIFI feel the quality of the foodservice industry is only as good as the quality of its trained personnel, and that the healthy growth of either is tied to education.

It is our hope that *Legal Aspects of Food-service Management* will contribute to your professional growth.

Richard J. Hauer
Executive Director
National Institute for the Foodservice Industry

Preface

"Don't bother me with a legal headache, I have a business to run. Let my lawyer handle it." This often heard plea illustrates two common fallacies people believe about the law: (1) that the law is the enemy; and (2) that all legal problems are a lawyer's problems.

The objective of this book is to put to rest the notion that law is a necessary evil intended to undermine foodservice operators in the conduct of their businesses.

First, the book's premise is that foodservice operators need help in preventing avoidable legal problems, and in minimizing the harmful effects of unavoidable legal situations. Second, this book takes the position that the law works best when it is used as a management tool, and not as a last resort. Those in the foodservice industry, as well as students about to enter it, need to know the legal basics of how to run a business. The law is not something that intrudes when something goes wrong; it is an ongoing factor in running a foodservice operation, or any business.

The traditional limitation of current business law texts is their stress on legal concepts without practical examples of law in action. Moreover, such texts are so general in scope that they lack relevance to the everyday operational needs of the foodservice manager. The pressurized demands of running a food service do not afford managers the luxury of extensive business law training. This book is designed to teach problem solving, not the niceties of legal knowledge for its own sake, unrelated to the give and take of foodservice management.

Why do we need a business law text for foodservice managers and students about to enter the industry? The answer is that the foodservice industry is representative of the small businessperson in general, as well as a specialized industry, some of whose members cannot afford continuous legal services or costly legal hassles. This book is intended to serve both students about to enter the industry and those who are already running a business.

This is not a theoretical text, although students and operators should be able to determine what legal pitfalls are possible, through both comprehensive explanation and the legal cases presented. To anticipate and prevent problems, and to obtain the best use of this book, the reader must bring a thinking framework into play. The objective is not to have the reader think like a lawyer, but like a businessperson who (1) is aware of the law regarding major foodservice issues, (2) knows what is needed to prevent serious legal problems, and (3) knows how to make the law work in his or her favor, whether on the job or in a courtroom.

Legal Aspects of Foodservice Management is organized into 15 chapters covering the areas of law most likely to confront those managers who are new to business as well as more experienced managers. One chapter has been developed to help businesspersons choose and work with lawyers, a subject neglected in most business law texts. This chapter enables small businesspersons to put scarce legal funds to the best use.

Specific topics include those usually essential to business law texts, such as forms of business organization and property law. In addition, there is material on foodservice contracts, liability, labor, civil rights, foodservice regulations, and security, all topics of particular relevance to the foodservice industry. The purpose of this coverage is to provide an overview of common business transactions, while examining those areas most likely to confront foodservice managers in their daily activities.

This practical, operational approach to business law for foodservice managers fits the overall theme of the book, which is *early detection and prevention of legal problems,* rather than reaction to those problems later—in court.

Specific learning aids are included to provide students, managers, and teachers with a ready means of understanding foodservice law in action. Chapter outlines highlight the major topics. A "case in point" appears at the beginning of each chapter to put the subject matter into a practical management context. Each chapter also contains objectives, summaries, questions, and excerpts from court decisions relevant to foodservice operators. Foodservice law educators and lawyers are provided with an extensive set of footnotes at the end of each chapter. Figures and legal forms also aid learning. Various state-by-state charts are contained in the appendixes to provide operators with state provisions on key issues. Finally, although any critical legal terms are explained in the text at first mention, a glossary provides a ready reference for the reader.

The preparation of this book was greatly aided by the diligence, perseverance, and constructive criticisms of Marlene R. Chamberlain, Managing Editor, National Institute for the Foodservice Industry. Her eye for the practical, commonsense approach to the legal side of foodservice management made my task much easier.

Dean John J. Clark, Jr., School of Hotel Administration, Cornell University, was generous in his support of this undertaking. Special thanks are due him for his interest and encouragement.

Anthony Marshall, Dean of the School of Hospitality Management at Florida International University, contributed his technical expertise in reviewing the manuscript.

Teresa A. Manheim, my secretary, devoted long hours to the final typing of my manuscript.

Finally, my wife, Margaret Linger Sherry, requires special mention. Her patience and devotion throughout my period of authorship was responsible for making this manuscript a reality.

John E. H. Sherry

Note to Students and Teachers
Use of Footnotes

The footnotes at the end of each chapter are included to enable you to find and read the actual statute or opinion referred to.

The reasoning of the court is as important as the principle of law the court states or adopts. Under our common law legal system, the reasoning of the court may serve as a guide to determining the outcome of future cases. In legal language, such a case is called a *precedent.* Teachers and students of foodservice law may find these footnotes helpful for further research.

Very few trial court decisions are published. Rather, they are filed with the clerk of the court, where they are available for inspection. Appellate or appeals court decisions are published in book form. These decisions contain principles of law and help you find trends that may affect foodservice business decisions. This fact holds true whether or not the problem presented to the court involves a foodservice dispute, since reviewing courts often apply general common law principles to solve specific issues. Only where a statute or specific common law rule governing foodservice operators is involved is the court called upon to use that statute or rule to settle such a dispute.

How then does one find a law decision? These decisions are published in volumes, called Reports, that are numbered in order, starting with volume 1. The West Publishing Company publishes state reports for all states in a National Reporter System: Atlantic (A. or A 2d), Northeastern (N.E. or N.E. 2d), Pacific (P. or P 2d), Southeastern (S.E. or S.E. 2d), Southern (So. or So. 2d), and Southwestern (S.W. or S.W. 2d). For each case, the title of a decision is *cited,* meaning reported. Let us use the case of *Kauffman v. Royal Orleans, Inc.,* cited as 216 So. 2d 394 (La. 1968), to illustrate how to find such a report.

After the name of the parties, normally plaintiff (the party suing) v. (meaning versus or against) the defendant (the party being sued), the opinion is found in Volume 216 of the Southern Reporter, Second Series (the most recent series) on page 394. The state court is abbreviated (La., for Louisiana, which, standing alone, means the Supreme Court of Louisiana), and the year 1968 (the year the decision was filed).

The majority of federal court decisions are reported in the Federal Supplement (F. Supp. for District Courts) and the Federal Reporter (F. or F 2d, for Circuit Courts of Appeal). The United States Supreme Court Reports (U.S.), Supreme Court Reporter (S. Ct.), and the Lawyer's Edition (L. Ed.) each contains all United States Supreme Court opinions. The same procedure is followed in finding a particular federal opinion. First, the name, then volume number, page number, District, Circuit, or Supreme Court designation (S.D.N.Y., meaning U.S. District Court for the Southern District of New York), and the date.

In some cases, the names of the parties are switched to reflect the fact that the appellant (party appealing) is bringing an appeal against the respondent (the party against whom the appeal is taken). Therefore, to avoid confusion, you must sort out the parties by reading the opinion carefully. By doing so you will understand which of the parties ultimately prevailed or won the appeal.

1
Law for Foodservice Operators
Introduction

Objectives

The purpose of this chapter is to:
1. Define foodservice law.
2. Review the kinds of foodservice
   establishments the law governs.
3. Outline the rights and responsibilities the
   law creates to protect both foodservice
   operators and customers.

Case in Point

Paul Rourke knew he would have a bad day when he came into the restaurant to open up. First, he had all weekend to think about the shortage in the cash register drawer last week. Then, when he arrived, he found that his order for ten cases of tomatoes was one case short and the weekend inventory clerk had already signed for the order. Also, the safety inspector was coming, and Paul had been cited for a safety violation the week before by the fire inspector. But the day was just beginning.

When he went through his mail, Paul noticed that the credit card company had refused to pay an overcharge on a credit card account after Paul's cashier failed to phone the company regarding the credit limit.

The seafood restaurant down the street was being picketed by local representatives of a national restaurant workers' union, and Paul was worried that he was next on their list, and wondered what his rights were if he was. Paul had bought the empty lot next door for parking, but the city said the lot, only a few yards from his restaurant, was not zoned for business.

Later that night, while Paul was away making a deposit at the bank, a patron became unruly and began verbally to attack other patrons. Not only did the bartender fail to oust the patron, but he leaped into the resulting fray, breaking a bottle over the head of another customer who had only been trying to leave the premises. The next day, the injured patron had his lawyer call Paul, asking him if he wanted to settle out of court or in.

Do you think Paul needs a lawyer?

Paul does need a lawyer, but a lot of his problems could have been prevented with only rudimentary knowledge about how the law affects his foodservice operation. Such knowledge would allow him to supervise his employees better, stand up for his rights as a businessperson, and prevent future pitfalls

from affecting his operation. However, even if Paul gets a lawyer, odds are he won't know how to work with one to obtain the most effective help. Finally, going to an attorney and saying, "Get me out of this," is not much different from closing the barn door after the horse has escaped, and is twice as costly.

It's fairly obvious that Paul didn't use his head in every instance. However, it's even more obvious that he isn't using the law to work for him, but allowing it to work against him. Instead of using the law as a management tool to operate his foodservice business properly, he's going to use it as adhesive to patch up some problems he could have prevented.

FOODSERVICE LAW IN PERSPECTIVE

Law is a body of rules that apply to given situations, exist to maintain order in society and in business and personal dealings, and balance your rights with the rights of those with whom you deal. These rules are backed up by an enforcement system to interpret them, mete out punishment for violations, and settle disputes arising out of alleged violations.

Foodservice law is the area of consumer law that governs the legal rights of owners and operators of foodservice establishments and their responsibilities to consumers of their products or services. It includes the following duties and corresponding rights: (1) the duty to admit and the legal right to refuse admission to a prospective customer; (2) the duty to construct, maintain, and supervise the premises in a proper manner so as to protect customers and their property against harm, and the right to remove a customer who threatens the person or property of others; and (3) the duty to sell the product or service in a manner fit for the intended purpose and the right to impose lawful restrictions on sales of the product or service.

Types of Laws Which Apply to Foodservice Operators

There are different types of laws. Laws vary in the way they come into being, how they are administered, and how they apply to certain segments of the population. Several kinds of laws make up the body of foodservice law. As a foodservice operator, you are concerned with the following types:

1. *Common law* or *case law* refers to rules of law that originate in court decisions rather than in statutes. Common law is judge-made law. American common law is inherited from the English common law, and in many states remains in effect unless altered or repealed by the state legislature.[1] In practice, the common law is usually the law formulated by the highest reviewing court, and these appellate courts have the authority to make legal rules binding on all other courts within that state or federal system.
2. *Statutory law* originates in the lawmaking bodies of the United States. *Statutes* are rules created by legislation at either the local, state, or federal level.
3. In the foodservice business, you are also affected by *administrative law*. Administrative law includes rules created by various federal and state regulatory agencies, has the force of law, and is subject to court interpretation. For foodservice operators, administrative law appears in the form of consumer laws and employer laws. In some cases the system passing out punishment is not the court system but the regulatory agency itself.

The Expansion of Consumer Law and the Foodservice Operator[2]

Today U.S. consumers in increasing numbers are using the law to recover compensation for wrongs inflicted by manufacturers or sellers of a product or service that has caused them personal injury or economic harm.[3]

The foodservice industry is not exempt from this trend. On the contrary, it is always a possibility, considering the nature of the product sold. Food services deal in foods and beverages, and while the potential for economic harm to a customer is not as serious as with some other products, the potential to cause injury or illness to patrons is always there, and with it the accompanying potential for legal snarls.

Patrons may also seek legal compensation for injuries that occur to themselves or their property on your premises and are caused by foodservice managers or employees, directly or indirectly.[4]

The traditional approach is for the victim to sue the wrongdoer and obtain a money judgment. However, when the amount involved is inadequate to justify hiring an attorney, or the wrongs are widespread within a particular industry, consumers may lobby for a broad legislative solution. The result of consumer lobbying may be a regulatory agency, created to license industry members, set standards of conduct, and punish violators by fine or license revocation. Whether through a regulatory agency or by statute, the objective of consumer law is to protect the legal rights of consumers.[5] As the next chapter will illustrate, the foodservice industry is a highly regulated industry.

Types of Operations Affected by Foodservice Law

Many types of foodservice operations exist; all are affected, to varying degrees, by foodservice law.

Commercial foodservice operations are units that compete with each other in the private marketplace for profits from selling food and beverages. The vast majority of such establishments are privately owned by individual proprietors or corporate chains. Commercial operations include sit-down restaurants, fast-food establishments, cafeterias, drive-ins, and vending operations. Contract feeding is also commercial in that a contract feeder will contract with an institution such as a hospital to feed patients or with a recreational facility such as a racetrack to feed the patrons. Another type of food service that falls into the commercial category is transportation food service, that found on planes and trains. Although the food service may be incidental to the main service (transportation), it is nonetheless a commercial, and competitive, part of the industry. Recreational food service, such as that in ballparks, may be run by a contract feeder or may be privately run by an individual entrepreneur.

Noncommercial operations make up the rest of the foodservice industry. A profit motive is *not* a legal requirement for entry into the foodservice field, and every establishment that provides foods and beverages that are prepared, served, sold, or provided for consumption, on or off the premises, is a foodservice operation.

Noncommercial operations include institutional facilities such as hospitals and nursing homes, which provide food for patients; military clubs and messes, which provide food for the men and women serving in the armed forces; schools and universities, which prepare and serve food to students; and correctional facilities, which feed prisoners. Other noncommercial operations might include companies that offer dining rooms for the convenience of both owners and employees and are not intended to operate for profit. Similarly, hospitals and schools, while they may charge for foods in different types of operations, do so at such low cost to the patrons as only to recover the costs of labor and supplies.

These operations do have in common at least two things: (1) They are all affected, in varying degrees, by the law. They are affected in the areas of labor relations, liability, and security, and by regulations affecting food services in particular and small businesses in general. (2) Whether or not they operate for profit, many foodservice operations operate close to the bottom line, particularly in the beginning, and cannot afford legal snarls that are easily preventable.

Why You Need to Know Foodservice Law

Because of the complexity of modern law and the day-to-day struggle of trying to stay competitive in an unpredictable economy, it should come as no surprise that most businesspeople instinctively shy away from the subject of law and justify this attitude with the excuse: "Legal problems? Call my lawyer. That's none of my concern. My lawyer will take care of it. The law is for lawyers, not for me." If this refrain sounds familiar, don't be surprised. Few of us want to shoulder responsibility for legal problems. It may seem easier to shift the burden to a lawyer, with the expectation that he or she can work miracles while we continue to mind the store.

Like most expectations, this one is wishful thinking.

1. The excuse, "The law is for lawyers, not for me," is dangerous because it rests on the premise that ignorance of the law is a defense to a civil lawsuit or criminal prosecution. The contrary is the rule. Ignorance of the law is usually *not* a defense;[6] nor are good intentions that fail to satisfy the requirements of the law. The absence of intent to inflict harm does not excuse responsibility.[7] It may serve merely to lessen the damages or punishment.

2. An understanding of foodservice law is essential to help you *prevent* as well as cope with legal problems that may arise out of your foodservice management responsibilities.

3. A good understanding of foodservice law will help improve the performance of your management responsibilities. You will be able to adjust your daily management responsibilities to fit within a legal framework. Knowing foodservice law will sharpen your management skills by causing you to look before you leap into a legal snare. By expanding your knowledge of the law's requirements, you will be on guard as to how the law may affect your operation in particular circumstances. For example, if you know that a parcel of land you wish to buy may require rezoning for foodservice use, you will be able to negotiate the purchase with a better appreciation of the risks. What might have first appeared to be a once-in-a-lifetime offer may, on closer examination, seem less desirable.

4. Knowledge of foodservice law will enable you to carry out your responsibilities effectively regarding government regulations. Growers, producers, and *preparers* of foods and beverages are subject to strict health and sanitary standards imposed by all levels of government. The aim of government regulation is to stop unhealthy or unsanitary practices and to prevent harm to the public. In extreme cases, a regulatory agency may close down a foodservice operation until violations have been corrected. Such a shutdown may be reported in the local news media. The result not only may mean an immediate revenue loss to you, but the bad publicity may drive away patrons. When you maintain the standards required by law, *you are less likely to violate regulations and so ruin an otherwise profitable operation.*

5. Your understanding of foodservice law will better equip you to work with an attorney, when one is needed. Knowledge of your own needs makes it more likely that an attorney can take action that will prevent or remedy a legal snarl. Ignorance of the legal consequences of your actions or omissions usually results in unnecessary, time-consuming, and expensive legal steps.

Ultimately, failure to prevent or minimize legal risks will jeopardize your ability to operate successfully. For commercial operations, success means profitability and customer goodwill. For noncommercial establishments, it means operating within a budget. For both types of operations, success can be staying in business. In a word, your foodservice business depends on good legal management—yours and your lawyer's.

An Overview of How the Law Affects Foodservice Operators

For purposes of the law, the foodservice manager who does not own the business that occupies the premises is considered responsible if he or she is in direct, continuous contact with patrons. As such, the foodservice manager has duties that the law imposes regarding the protection of patrons the business is intended to serve. The manager cannot ignore these responsibilities by pleading that they are solely owner responsibilities. The foodservice manager is *directly responsible* to patrons, as well as to regulatory agencies concerned with public safety and welfare.[8] Additional duties may also be imposed by the operating agreement with the owner. However, the manager cannot ignore statutory responsibilities, such as not serving alcoholic beverages to minors, just because they were not included in the owner-manager agreement.[9] The law is not something that can be ignored when it is convenient to do so. Any agreements operators make with others must be made within a legal framework.

The foodservice manager not only is responsible for his or her own legal wrongs, *but may also be held responsible for the acts or omissions of employees who injure someone or who damage a patron's property* while on the job.[10] This general rule, referred to by its legal name, *respondeat superior,* makes the employer liable for an employee's conduct when that conduct occurs in the course of the employment and is intended to benefit the employer.[11] This means that foodservice managers not only have a responsibility to know the laws that affect their own business relations with patrons, but also to *train employees* to avoid legal pitfalls that might result in costly litigation with patrons or regulatory agencies.

Benefits of Law

The law benefits you as well. *For every legal duty you are required to perform, a corresponding legal duty is required of the persons or parties with whom you do business.* Anyone on whom the law imposes a legal duty or for whom it creates a legal right is responsible for the performance of that duty or the exercise of that right. The law does not operate in a vacuum. An individual claiming to have been injured or a regulatory agency claiming a violation must initiate legal action. By the same token, you are responsible for initiating legal action if you feel you have been wronged.

Foodservice law, like law in general, attempts to balance two interests. One is your *business interest* in maximizing your profitability and minimizing your liability to your patrons, your employees, your competitors, and the government. The other is the interests of all these groups, or *governmental interest* in protecting their legal rights, health, welfare, and safety. You are responsible to all of these groups for physical or economic injuries or losses caused by your failure or refusal to obey the law. Your responsibility to individuals is usually to compensate them for the cost of such injuries or losses. Your responsibility to government is to halt acts found illegal, to pay fines for violations, or to pay damages either to the regulatory body established to police your activities or to your victims.

Since the law usually attempts to strike a reasonable balance between the economic needs of the foodservice industry and the welfare of the industry's patrons, it is important to recognize that awareness and compliance with the law is not a necessary evil, but rather a positive good. Protection of your patrons enhances your credibility and supports the objective of the law—that is, to provide for the well-being of the consuming public as well as your own.

The law affects you in almost every phase of your business. The following is just a capsule view of the areas of your foodservice business that have legal implications.

1. As the seller of products to the public, you are obligated by the government to provide a warranty and to see to it that your food and beverage products are in a fit condition for consumption.
2. As an operator of a business, you occupy premises and are obligated by federal, state, and local statutes to maintain the premises in a safe condition. The degree to which you are obligated for this varies from locality to locality, but generally minimal standards are enforced for older buildings and more rigorous standards for newer ones.
3. You are obligated to conform to laws and ordinances enforced for businesses.
4. You are obligated both to yourself and to the law to keep your premises and customers reasonably secure from crime by patrons, third parties, and employees.

5. You are obligated to obey the consumer protection laws and civil rights laws of the federal government, and, increasingly, those of state and local governments.
6. As an employer, you are obligated to obey the laws regarding employment of adults and minors.

These are just some of the areas where the law affects you. Far from being a bane to foodservice operations, the law is a boon. Along with the obligations outlined, you also have corresponding rights as an employer, as a salesperson, and as the operator of a business serving the public. You have the right to make contracts and see that they are enforced. You have the right to buy, maintain, and sell property to operate your business. You have the right to set up your business in a form appropriate to your financial situation and your future plans. You have the right to operate your business to maintain its class, turnover, and profitability. Should you encounter serious financial difficulties, you have the right to file for bankruptcy within established guidelines. Finally, to make the law work for you and to defend your rights, you have the court system as a recourse. You have the right, but not the obligation, to go to court well prepared, with a good understanding of the facts and an attorney who can manage your case competently.

7. If you feel the law is not working for you but against you, you have the option of telling your local, state, or federal representative through petitions, telephone calls, and letters asking to have the laws changed. First, however, you have to know what the law says on a specific issue.

A final note: Without respect for and voluntary compliance with the law, there would be no mechanism other than brute force with which to settle disputes and maintain stability and certainty in business. Such a state of affairs would ultimately jeopardize the rights of all of us.

SUMMARY

It is a major premise of this book that *prevention* of legal pitfalls, consistently practiced, not only protects the public but also *enhances* your credibility as a foodservice operator, and ultimately the credibility of the entire foodservice industry. Foodservice owners and managers must recognize those aspects of food service that have legal implications, train themselves and their staffs to comply with regulations, and, most important, prevent needless exposure to liability.

A foodservice operator cannot usually prevent patrons from filing a lawsuit or complaining to a regulatory agency once they are determined to do so. However, obedience to statutory requirements and the use of reasonable care will, in many cases, allow the foodservice operator to prevail in any litigation, contain legal costs, and remain competitive.

QUESTIONS

1. How is the law an aid to foodservice owners and operators?
2. Describe the differences between statutory law, common law, and administrative law.
3. How does consumer law affect foodservice operators?
4. What is the common attitude of businesspersons regarding the law? Why is this attitude faulty?
5. A patron is injured in Steve Kelly's restaurant by a careless employee and decides to sue. Who may be held responsible and why?

NOTES

1. The 1895 Revised Statutes, originally enacted in 1840 by the Texas Republic, contain the following representative language: "The common law of England so far as it is not inconsistent with the Constitution and laws of this State shall, together with such Constitution and laws, be the rule of decision and shall continue in force until altered or repealed by the Legislature."

2. See generally J. McCall, *Consumer Protection: Cases, Notes and Materials* (1977); D. Epstein and S. Nickles, *Consumer Law in a Nutshell* (2d ed. 1981).

3. See generally D. Noel and J. Phillips, *Cases on Products Liability* (1977); D. Noel and J. Phillips, *Products Liability in a Nutshell* (2d ed. 1981).

4. See J. Sherry, *The Laws of Innkeepers* sec. 11:13 (Restaurant Keeper's Duty to Protect Patrons), secs. 15:1–15:7 (Responsibility Arising from the Sale of Food [and] Beverages), secs. 19:1–19:8 (Responsibility of Restaurant Keeper for Patron's Property) (rev. ed. 1981).

5. See R. Anderson, *Social Forces and the Law* 1–31 (2d ed. 1981), E. Tucker, *Adjudication of Social Issues* Chapters 19–20, 296–331 (2d ed. 1977).

6. See W. LaFave and A. Scott, *Criminal Law* 356 *et seq.* (1972).

7. This rule is illustrated by the offense of selling liquor to minors by those licensed to traffic in alcoholic beverages. This crime does not recognize the defense that the licensed vendor believed the minor was of age; or that the minor appeared to be of age; or that the minor represented himself or herself as having reached the required age; or that the minor produced false credentials showing that he or she was of age. See LaFave and Scott, *supra* note 6, at 359 nn.23–27.

8. See *Fitzgerald v. 667 Hotel Corp.,* 103 Misc. 2d 80, 426 N.Y.S.2d 368 (Sup. Ct. 1980). (Both owner and occupier held liable to injured residential and commercial tenants. Owner's statutory duty to keep building in repair held *nondelegable* to occupier of building.)

9. Statutory duties such as these operate independently of the agreement between owner and occupier of the premises. This is so because these duties were enacted to protect the public, whose rights cannot be diminished by a contract to which the public was not a part.

10. *Block v. Sherry,* 43 Misc. 342, 87 N.Y.S. 160 (1904). (Restaurant owner held liable for waiter's negligence in spilling water on patron's wearing apparel.)

11. *Fruit v. Schreiner,* 502 P.2d. 133 (Sup. Ct. Alaska 1972). (Employer responsible for intoxication of employee causing harm to third party.) See also *Riviello v. Waldron,* 47 N.Y.2d 297, 391 N.E.2d 1278, 418 N.Y.S.2d 300 (1980). (Operator of tavern liable for injuries inflicted by employee upon patron.)

2
Foodservice Operators and the Government
Federal, State, and Local Regulations

Objectives

The purpose of this chapter is to:
1. Describe the various federal agencies and their powers.
2. Discuss areas where foodservice operators may be affected by state and local regulations.

Case in Point

You open a restaurant in a retail district in your community and secure a liquor license. The community then enacts a zoning ordinance prohibiting the sale of alcoholic beverages by restaurants in that district. Can you be forced to surrender your liquor license because your district has been zoned to ban liquor sales in restaurants? No. Only the State Liquor Authority has the right to regulate traffic in alcoholic beverages. Having granted you a liquor license, the Authority's decision overrides the community zoning ordinance.[1]

TYPES OF REGULATIONS

The foodservice industry is highly regulated, with regulations appearing at the federal, state, and local levels. You are likely to be more immediately affected by the state and local regulations; however, you should be familiar with the federal regulatory agencies as a few of them have broad powers that can affect your business.

FEDERAL REGULATIONS

Federal regulations affect the preparation and sale of food and beverage products, as well as such nonfood areas as advertising, labor, and even the organization of a business. Federal regulations often result in federal agencies being set up to enforce or amend the rules. Enforcement may range from an agency with tight controls and harsh punishments to a laissez-faire agency that serves as a federal "watchdog," and not a policing organization.

History helps to explain much federal regulation. Federal regulations tend to be the result of abuses in certain areas of business over a period of time. For example, turn-of-the-century conditions in meat packing resulted in much of our modern-day federal regulation of meat processing and packing. Abuses of immigrants and children by employers in some textile industries resulted in stiff labor laws for all employers. Some federal regulations historically have fallen by the wayside as the abuses that prompted them have ceased. Others continue, and are even expanded or amended as new situations arise.

The main thing for you to know is that there are a number of federal agencies that directly or indirectly affect the operation of your business. You should be familiar with their broader powers.

Federal Agencies Regulating Sales of Foods and Beverages

From the time of the industrial revolution and the related development of a complex, highly diversified food and beverage production and distribution system, the federal government has attempted to protect the public against unwholesome products.[2] Since food products are necessary for human survival, and the risk of contagious diseases that unfit foods and beverages might cause is so great, a number of regulatory bodies have been created to eliminate or minimize risks to consumers.

The role of federal regulatory agencies in the food products field is twofold: (1) to prevent unsafe food products from reaching the marketplace, and (2) to maintain a minimum level of food quality, to furnish adequate and reliable descriptions of foods, and to provide standard measures and descriptions of food quantities.[3] The first aims to regulate the food production industry and has little direct effect on the foodservice business. The second role is broader. It covers all foods produced for human consumption. The following federal agencies regulate the sale of foods and beverages.

The Food and Drug Administration (FDA)

First and foremost among the federal regulatory agencies is the Food and Drug Administration (FDA). Created in 1906 by the Food, Drug, and Cosmetic Act, and established in its present form in 1938, the FDA is empowered to: (1) require truthful and informative labeling and proper packaging of foods and beverages; (2) protect against commercial misrepresentations by enforcement of food and beverage standards; and (3) provide for food safety. It enforces these objectives in the federal district or trial courts by seizure of unfit products, criminal prosecution of violators, and obtaining of court orders barring further distribution or sale.

The FDA regulations are aimed mainly at food growers, producers, and processors rather than at retailers, and apply only to products prepared for *interstate commerce.* (Interstate commerce occurs when a food product prepared or grown in one state is shipped to another state for sale. The commerce is between two separate states.) Since most foodservice operators have a single place of business within one state and obtain most of their food items from local markets, they are usually not subject to FDA regulations. However, where Maine lobsters, for instance, are ordered by a New York restaurant for service to New York consumers, the commerce is *interstate* rather that *intrastate,* and FDA regulations apply.

Local commerce, however, is often covered by *state* food and drug acts patterned on the federal model. These laws may be stricter, but cannot be more lenient, than the federal law.

The Food and Drug Administration regulates the materials used in the manufacture and processing of foods to ensure wholesomeness and to eliminate *misbranding* (false and misleading advertising) and *adulteration* (preparing, packing, or holding food products in unsanitary conditions whereby the product may become contaminated with filth).

These forms of federal regulation normally apply only to growers, producers, and processors who originate food products, and only to those products sold in interstate commerce. Hence the end result should be that foods are safe when you purchase them for use in your operation. However, foodservice operators are indirectly subject to FDA regulations.

The FDA has the power to step in and seize harmful products, irrespective of the fact that the buyer did not cause or contribute to the seller's conduct.[4] An operator may be completely innocent of any violation of the Food, Drug, and Cosmetic Act, yet subject to the drastic remedies the FDA can enforce.

The Federal Food, Drug, and Cosmetic Act provides for severe criminal penalties for violations of the Act.[5] The only effective self-help measure is to sue the suppliers for any losses suffered because of them. Normally, the person or business against whom the enforcement action is taken has the right to contest the action in a court hearing, conducted by the federal district trial court where the action was taken by the FDA.[6]

The Federal Trade Commission (FTC)

Another area of federal regulation concerns deceptive or unfair advertising of foods and beverages. The Federal Trade Commission (FTC), established in 1914, has authority over this area in cooperation with the Food and Drug Administration. This authority applies only to interstate commerce, or false and misleading advertising claims for food products originating in one state for distribution in another state. Such advertising claims include those found on labels on food and beverage products, in television and radio commercials, and in advertisements in newspapers and magazines.[7] It may also regulate the wording on menus shipped by a foodservice chain from its home office to out-of-state retail outlets.[8]

The Federal Trade Commission has the power to stop false food advertising, including ads that fail to reveal that products are dangerous or that their use under certain conditions can cause harm.[9]

A false advertisement for food, when the use of the product may injure health or where the ad is intended to defraud or mislead the buyer, is a *misdemeanor.*[10] The FTC requires that advertisers make no statements that are *materially misleading,* meaning that consumers might not have purchased the food product if they had known the facts.[11] The deception may be *implied;* that is, it need not be expressly stated.

As a foodservice operator, you could violate this federal law if you share in or underwrite the cost of out-of-state advertising by your supplier, and the advertising contains materially false and misleading statements. The fact that you did not cause or contribute to the false statements is no defense to an FTC action. If you own a chain of restaurants in different states, and prepare the advertising for all of them, the FTC rules apply.

The United States Department of Agriculture (USDA)

The U.S. Department of Agriculture establishes and enforces standards, and inspects and grades a variety of food products, including meats and poultry. This agency generally works in favor of foodservice operations by enforcing standards that affect your buying of food products. In the case of fish, inspection is voluntary. Inspection services are provided by the Department of Commerce. Meat and poultry inspection is required by law. *Grading* is voluntary. These functions enable foodservice buyers to evaluate and select meat and poultry products with reasonable assurances of quality and safety, and to obtain the right cuts of meat for the style and class of their operations.

Federal Control in Practice

Federal law will directly govern multi-state chain or franchise operators who obtain food ingredients from central stores or commissaries outside their own state that are owned or licensed by the home office. It will also apply to any out-of-state food and beverage purchases operators make. State and local laws will apply to commerce within a single state or city.

In cases of conflict between federal, state, and local regulations, *the federal regulations are controlling.* When federal acts do not prohibit state and local legislation on the same subject, the state and local acts *may strengthen, but may not weaken, the federal laws.* As between state and local laws, the same general principles apply. Some cities are authorized to enact their own laws, independently of the state, but they may not weaken the state's regulations. They are also free to adopt the state codes.

The threat to public health and welfare that lack of uniformity would cause in the area of foods and beverages sold for human consumption explains why federal law governs interstate sales. The states are free to adopt their own standards within their own borders. State standards vary, as does the amount of money provided for enforcement. The penalties for violations also vary. However, a degree of cooperation and unity may yet emerge.

Nonfood Areas of Federal Regulation

Among the nonfood areas regulated by the federal government are those related to employment practices and safety. The following federal agencies affect foodservice operators.

The Department of Labor (DOL)

The Department of Labor affects all employers. This federal department sets hour guidelines and labor standards, defines workweeks, and regulates child labor. The DOL also sets the minimum wage. Each state is free to set its own guidelines, which may be higher than, but not lower than the federal minimum.

The Equal Employment Opportunity Commission (EEOC)

The Equal Employment Opportunity Commission was set up as the enforcement agency for the employment section of the Civil Rights Act of 1964. This agency's authority was further broadened by the Equal Employment Opportunity Act of 1972.

The EEOC enforces equal opportunity laws regarding race, color, religion, national origin, sex, and pregnancy. All employers with 15 or more employees *or* who engage in interstate commerce are regulated by the EEOC.

Where this agency differs from other federal agencies is that it may *initiate* lawsuits on behalf of employees against employers. It will investigate discrimination complaints of employees. This agency has the power to request company records as part of an investigation.

The EEOC may directly affect employers who fail to comply with federal civil rights laws. In addition, many states have their own civil rights laws, which may require even stricter compliance. Chapter 6 on labor law will cover employment civil rights laws.

The Federal Occupational Safety and Health Administration (OSHA)[12]

OSHA is responsible for enforcing measures protecting the on-the-job health and safety of employees.[13] The goal of this agency is to prevent industrial health hazards and injuries, the costs of which are ultimately paid by operators and their customers for products and services.

Department of Justice

The foodservice industry must comply with federal and state laws that forbid certain types of activities the laws broadly define as *antitrust*.[14] The Department of Justice is the arm of the executive branch of government, which, among other things, enforces the federal antitrust laws. These laws are designed to prevent trade monopolies. For example, foodservice operators may not cooperate or agree to cooperate with competitors to fix the prices or the products and services provided to customers. History demonstrates that such actions cause prices to go up, since free competition is not present to influence prices downward. Antitrust laws also prevent groups of competitors from monopolizing the industry to prevent others from entering.[15] This hurts two groups: the competitor, who is frozen out of the market; and the consumer, who must pay higher prices not justified by the normal forces of supply and demand.

Severe criminal and civil fines, as well as other forms of enforcement, are provided to the U.S. Department of Justice and similar state agencies.[16] Ignorance of the law or good intentions are not usually valid defenses to prosecution in this area.[17]

The Federal Trade Commission— Franchises

The Federal Trade Commission also is interested in franchising agreements for hotels, motels, and restaurants, and regulates certain aspects of this form of business.[18] Chapter 11 on franchising will discuss this type of regulation in more detail.

The Federal Model

Federal regulations affect foodservice operators in another way as well. Federal laws and agencies often serve as models for similar state laws and agencies. One such model is the FDA Food Service Sanitation Ordinance, which has been adopted by a number of states (Figure 2.1). Some states, including New York, go

Figure 2.1
FDA Model Ordinance Outline

Many state and local ordinances are patterned on the Model Food Service Sanitation Ordinance recommended by the federal Food and Drug Administration. The following outline of the main provisions of that ordinance will illustrate the range of interests of all levels of government:

- Food Care: Supplies, protection, storage, preparation, display and service, transportation.
- Personnel: Health, personal cleanliness, clothing, practices.
- Equipment and Utensils: Materials, design, and fabrication, equipment installation and location.
- Cleaning, Sanitization, and Storage of Equipment and Utensils.
- Sanitary Facilities and Controls: Water supply, sewage, plumbing, toilet facilities, lavatory facilities, garbage and refuse, insect and rodent control.
- Construction and Maintenance of Physical Facilities: Floors, walls and ceilings, cleaning facilities, lighting, ventilation, dressing rooms and locker areas, poisonous materials.
- Mobile Units.
- Temporary Units.
- Compliance Procedures: Issuance and suspension of permits.
- Examination and Condemnation of Food.

Reproduced by permission from Applied Foodservice Sanitation Certification Coursebook, *by the National Institute for the Foodservice Industry, copyright 1978. All Rights Reserved.*

beyond the FDA model and enforce stricter compliance of sanitation standards. State governments are encouraged, but not required, to use federal guidelines in lawmaking. This results in state health and sanitary codes, agriculture and marketing laws, state or city truth-in-menu laws, indoor clean air laws, and other consumer protection measures that *do* have an impact on your foodservice business.

STATE AND LOCAL REGULATION

Foodservice operators are most likely to feel the regulatory pinch not at the federal level, but at the state and local levels. Here is where the cost of regulation, in time and money, is most often felt by owners and operators of foodservice businesses. State and local governments regulate your business in a number of areas and with varying degrees of enforcement, so that you may not always know by whom and to what extent you are being regulated. Some states regulate more than others. However, one area where states are consistently strict and have broad enforcement powers is in the regulation of the sale of alcohol.

The Regulation of Alcohol Sales

The sale of alcoholic beverages is heavily regulated. Many food services offer alcohol to patrons in order to increase profits. The production of alcohol is closely regulated by the federal government, *but its retail sale for on or off premises consumption is regulated primarily by the states.*[19]

A Historical Perspective

History explains the reason for such heavy regulation. Liquor has often been viewed as a moral evil to be stamped out. The Temperance Movement, promoted politically by the Temperance Party that flourished in the nineteenth century, eventually brought about Prohibition. This was accomplished by ratification of the federal Volstead Act, outlawing commercial traffic in liquor, beer, and related beverages, as the Eighteenth Amendment to the Constitution on January 16, 1919.

Because of the demand for alcohol by many Americans, and the denial of consumption through legal channels, organized criminal elements saw the opportunity to intervene and profit. From 1919 until 1933, criminal gang members executed rival gang members to gain control over the lucrative black market in alcohol.

When Prohibition ended in December 1933 by ratification of the Twenty-First Amendment, there were strong fears that notorious criminal syndicates, collectively called "the mob," would retain their grip over the liquor traffic to further their other criminal enterprises. Such fears, together with renewed public clamor for temperance, caused most states to create regulatory agencies to license and police the commercial sale of alcohol at all levels, including retail sales by hotels, restaurants, taverns, clubs, and other authorized outlets.[20]

Modern Regulation

You have the option to offer or not to offer your patrons alcohol, as you choose, but once you opt to sell, your state regulates your entry into the field and your ongoing conduct *for as long as you choose to market such beverages.*

Each of the 50 states has a liquor authority or liquor commission to regulate the sales of alcoholic beverages. The states set up the regulations *and* the enforcement apparatus. The authority may be very broad, overlapping into gray areas such as regulation or restriction of prostitution and loitering, or it may be limited simply to regulating liquor sales to adults and minors.

One note: Although every state has the authority to regulate traffic in liquor, some states have a "dry option," meaning that some communities may opt to be dry and prohibit the sale of liquor completely. In these cases, you would be under the umbrella of the local regulation and would be expressly prohibited from selling alcohol at all. Once the city or community opts to allow the sale of alcohol, however, the state standards take precedence over any local laws regarding liquor. (Some communities only allow sales of beer and wine. Even so, these limited sales are still controlled by the state.)

Operators in a "wet" area must usually apply for a liquor license from the state, which will enable them to sell alcohol. (Foodservice businesses usually come under slightly different regulations than package liquor stores. In some areas, the standards are stricter than for sales of packaged liquor.)

License requirements vary from state to state, with some states more lenient than others. The following factors are considered in New York, a strict state: (1) operating experience; (2) financial assets and source of financing; (3) good character and freedom from organized criminal activity; (4) compliance of premises with all building code requirements; (5) no interest in any wholesale liquor business, brewery, winery, or distillery; (6) physical location of premises within proscribed distance from church or school; (7) number of liquor licenses within predetermined area in which premises are located; (8) environmental factors—potential noise and traffic that might be created by your operation.[21]

Of these requirements, the most sensitive and most open to interpretation is the "good character and freedom from organized criminal activity" condition. New York and most other states frown on any criminal record but are usually concerned only with criminal convictions involving *moral turpitude,* meaning immoral criminal conduct, unsavory business dealings, or more serious crimes. New York does not permit any *association* with organized criminal elements, either directly or indirectly through financial support. This also holds true in most states. Any past or present dealings with crime syndicates in whatever form will automatically disqualify an applicant.

The courts have the power to review the denial of any liquor license application, either when such application is first made or at the time of license renewal. The test used is whether the liquor authority or board acted arbitrarily in denying the license. This means that the reviewing court must find in the record (the facts and circumstances on which the denial was based) no reasonable basis on which the authority could have acted. Otherwise, the authority's or board's actions are presumed valid and such bodies are given wide discretion in denying a new license or renewal of a current license.[22]

The second major regulatory power of liquor control bodies is license revocation or suspension. Regulatory agencies have the power to regulate the conduct of license holders, once their licenses are granted. All of the grounds for disciplinary action against violators apply equally to all license holders, irrespective of the type of license held.[23] The kinds of liquor licenses vary from state to state, but the grounds for suspension or revocation are fairly uniform. The following activities can result in license suspension or revocation in most states:

1. *Disorderly Conduct.* Most states interpret this term to include allowing fights or assaults by either patrons or employees, creating a disturbance or nuisance, or otherwise violating public order. Threats to the peace and safety of the surrounding neighborhood would fit the definition of a nuisance. Disorderly conduct may also include public displays of and attempts to satisfy sexual urges. One single or isolated incident will not establish such a violation.

2. *Gambling.* Gambling is any game of chance where people pay for the opportunity to receive any property offered in return for their payment. It is illegal in many states. Some states make exceptions for charitable raffles, bingo games, parimutuel betting, and sales of lottery tickets in licensed operations. Gambling is typically prohibited on licensed premises except in states that allow casino gambling.

As in the case of disorderly conduct, there must be proof that the license holder allowed gambling. This means proof that the license holder knew or should have known that gambling was in progress. An isolated, onetime instance of gambling is normally insufficient for revocation of a liquor license.

3. *Homosexual Activity.* The traditional view, still followed in some states, prohibited the presence of homosexuals on licensed premises. The fact that homosexual patrons did not openly solicit customers or commit indecent acts was immaterial. Today there is a growing trend to require proof of *objectionable conduct* to sustain the revocation of a liquor license. In many states, the mere presence of homosexuals where no misbehavior is involved is not enough to jeopardize a license. A pattern of misbehavior known to the license holder must be established first.

4. *Prostitution.* Prostitution and related forms of sexual misconduct, such as soliciting and inducing minors to commit sexual acts, are uniformly prohibited. Proof that the solicitation of customers took place only once is usually not sufficient reason for revocation of a liquor license. More than one isolated incident is usually required to justify license revocation. The license holder must have consistently *tolerated* the misconduct.

5. *Adult Entertainment.* Traditionally the courts made a distinction between partially or completely nude entertainment and lewd, indecent, or obscene entertainment. However, the Supreme Court of the United States has ruled that the states are free to ban all forms of nude dancing, including topless entertainment, and that the

First Amendment right to free speech and expression must bow to the Twenty-First Amendment, which gives states very broad powers to regulate conduct on premises licensed to serve alcohol.[24]

If you intend to include some form of adult entertainment, and your operation is licensed to serve alcohol, you must comply with state regulations on that subject. *All* state liquor control statutes ban lewd or indecent performances. If you do not serve alcohol, then you have more leeway to include sexually explicit entertainment, at least topless dancing, to attract patrons.

6. *Narcotics Traffic.* The sale or distribution of narcotic drugs by employees or patrons is disorderly conduct under most liquor control laws and is forbidden. A license holder will not be held responsible for the criminal sale of narcotics by employees unless the sale forms a pattern or practice for a long enough time to put the proprietor on *constructive notice*—meaning that he or she *should have known what was happening had he or she exercised reasonable diligence to supervise the premises.*

The following case is an example of how poor management almost cost an operator a liquor license; moreover, it is a rare example of a successful appeal of a state liquor authority decision.

Show Boat of New Lebanon, Inc. v. State Liquor Authority
Supreme Court of New York, Appellate Division
33 A.D.2d 954, 306 N.Y.S.2d 850 (1970)

Facts. The State Liquor Authority canceled the restaurant operator's liquor license after it was proved that drug trafficking was taking place on the premises, thus causing the operation to become disorderly and in violation of the license agreement. The operator

appealed and the court upheld the Authority's determination, but decided that the cancellation was excessive punishment and that a three-month suspension would be more appropriate.

Reasoning. The court said that (1) the decision as to whether a licensed operation has become disorderly and is supported by substantial evidence is up to the State Liquor Authority; (2) a single act of disorder with no proof showing the licensee knew or should have known of the disorder is insufficient for cancellation; (3) the alleged disorder need not have been known to the licensee, but it is sufficient if he or she should have known (the court noted that the operator "had knowledge or had the opportunity through the exercise of reasonable diligence to acquire knowledge" about trafficking in narcotics and drugs occurring and allowed it to take place); (4) police officers obtained narcotics from two of the licensee's employees on separate occasions, and this was enough to determine that there was drug traffic on the premises that the licensee should have been aware of; but, nonetheless, (5) the cancellation was excessive punishment and suspension of three months was more appropriate.

Conclusion. In noting that the operator could or should have been aware of the trafficking through "reasonable diligence," the court made an interesting observation. The operator must make sure that he or she or a supervisor is aware of what the employees are up to on the job—and during on-premises break time—and guard against liquor law violations. This also holds true for patrons who may carry on a little illegal (or illicit) business on poorly managed premises—at the operator's expense.

7. *Sales to Minors.* In virtually all states a sale of alcohol by a license holder to any person under the state's legal drinking age is both a crime and a violation of the liquor

control statutes (see Appendix B). Each liquor authority has the right to suspend or revoke the license, irrespective of whether the minor concealed or lied about his or her age. In most localities it is a *misdemeanor* (a lesser crime than a felony, but more serious than a traffic violation) to serve a minor alcohol.[25]

The law does not require proof that the operator intended to serve a minor alcohol. Moreover, the fact that he or she is found not guilty of the crime *does not prevent the liquor authority from suspending or revoking the liquor license.* The two types of cases are not the same. One is a criminal trial, before a court of law; the other is an administrative hearing before an officer employed by the state authority. A finding of not guilty by the criminal court does not require the administrative officer to dismiss the authority's charges at the hearing. A single finding of a sale to a minor is normally insufficient to justify revocation. A pattern or practice of such sales would justify it.

Consistently serving minors is a certain, proven way to lose a liquor license, or at least have it suspended.

The practical problem for the foodservice operator and employees is to know how to verify age. Liability may also be imposed for a failure to verify age or for inadequate verification of age, if a minor injures someone. This is discussed in Chapter 4. It is not enough just to ask for the required forms of identification. They may be phony and must be verified by careful observation of the person to whom they allegedly belong. As the following case illustrates, being in a hurry or otherwise ignoring the statutory requirements regarding service to minors carries a heavy penalty.

5501 Hollywood v. Department of Alcohol Beverage Control
Court of Appeals of California
155 Cal. App. 2d 48, 318 P.2d 820 (1957)

Facts.   After being found guilty of selling liquor to a minor in violation of California statute, the defendant, a tavern owner, had his liquor license suspended. He appealed the Alcohol Beverage Control Board's decision. A superior court reversed the Board's decision. Then the Board appealed, the defendant arguing that he had met the requirements of a companion statute authorizing acceptance upon demand of a valid driver's license, Selective Service certificate, or similar form of identification. His defense was that he acted in good faith to obtain proper identification. The court of appeals rejected the argument, on the grounds that the identification must be *checked* against the physical characteristics of the holder, and that her appearance in this case did not match the age stated on the driver's license she presented to the defendant.

Reasoning.   The court noted that (1) the defendant had failed to adhere to the present demands of the statute requiring bona fide evidence of identity. Merely producing a driver's license was not enough because the person bearing the card may not be the person described on the card; (2) the girl, Peggy, was ". . . too young in appearance to be 21; she weighed 19 pounds more than the person to whom the license was issued; she was three and one-half years younger, and had blue eyes instead of hazel." The referee who had acted for the Board in making the initial decision had said that the discrepancies between the license and Peggy's appearance, ". . . were such that a reasonable, prudent licensee or employee in premises licensed for the sale of alcoholic beverages would not in good faith accept said driver's license as a bona fide documentary evidence of the identity of or the majority of . . . Peggy . . . The apparent discrepancies between the driver's license presented and the minor presenting it were sufficient to put appellant's employee on guard and to indicate that further inquiry was in order."

Conclusion. This case illustrates the fallacy of assuming that mere demand of identification is enough to satisfy liquor control laws. Identification must be verified by checking the appearance of the presenter. (1) Virtually all states authorize suspension or revocation of a liquor license, independently of criminal penalties, for sales of alcohol to minors. (2) Any statutory defense, such as good faith reliance upon a false driver's license or other authorized proof of age, is strictly interpreted in favor of the minor, even though the minor may have sought purposely to mislead the operator. (3) Operators must act reasonably in accepting any otherwise valid proof of age. If the proof of age accepted deviates in any degree from the appearance of the patron, it is a risk to serve that person. (4) The law imposes an affirmative non-delegable duty of reasonable care to check proof of age on licenses. The carelessness of employees is treated as the licensee's carelessness, whether or not he or she is present at the time.

The following are guidelines for verifying drinking age:

- Know what your state law requires as acceptable proof of age and demand to see that proof.
- Do not accept any proof of age other than items specifically mentioned in your state statute.
- Do not serve anyone who cannot provide acceptable proof of age, no matter how above age he or she appears nor how authentic the proof may seem.
- Always check the required proof of age against the physical appearance and characteristics of the person presenting it. If any discrepancies exist, either demand other acceptable proof or do not serve that person.
- Instruct and supervise your bar staff and table servers to follow the above rules.

8. *Sales to Intoxicated Persons or to Persons Actually or Apparently Under the Influence of Liquor.* Sales to intoxicated patrons or persons believed to be under the influence of alcohol are forbidden by most states. Such sales are also crimes in many states, as well as violations of the beverage control laws. However, unlike the prohibited sales to minors, the license holder is given some objective leeway in determining whether or not the patron is *actually* or *apparently* intoxicated. If the patron, on the basis of speech, walk, and manner, appears sober, he or she may be served without running afoul of the law. This is called the *objective appearance test*. A few states refuse to apply the objective appearance test. This means that you may jeopardize your license even if you honestly believe a patron to be sober and serve him or her.

9. *Sales to Known Alcoholics or Habitual Drunkards.* The same factors that govern responsibility for sales to intoxicated persons apply to sales to known habitual drunkards. The critical factor is the word *known*. If the person serving alcohol does not know that an otherwise sober person is an alcoholic, then the server does not violate the law by serving that patron.

Judicial Review

Judicial review is usually available to an applicant whose license has been denied, suspended, or revoked. In the case of initial denial, the courts are generally more liberal in reviewing the agency's grounds, especially if they feel the agency has overstepped its powers.[26]

In cases of suspension or revocation, it is generally more difficult to have the agency's decisions overturned.[27] An exception would be a court finding inadequate evidence to support an agency decision.[28]

Since the existence or profitability of an operation is at stake in many cases, adverse decisions by alcohol control agencies are appealed more frequently than are those for health violations.

The scope and regulation of liquor laws are fairly uniform, but each state is free to add or drop provisions or to interpret its liquor laws strictly or liberally. Usually the courts, in reviewing liquor law violations, are especially concerned with sales to minors, and this is the area of greatest risk to your liquor license.

Dramshop Liability

The other area of concern to foodservice operators is *dramshop liability*. Dramshop is the term used for the state laws that govern operator liability for liquor service to patrons that results in injuries or death to third persons. In many states, operators may be directly responsible to third parties or their families for injuries or death caused by liquor service to patrons. This and other areas of liquor liability are covered in Chapter 4.

OTHER AREAS OF STATE AND LOCAL REGULATION

Sanitation

As you learned earlier, the regulation of the foodservice field in the area of sanitation begins at the federal level, where uniform standards and enforcement mechanisms are set. These regulations, however, are generally aimed at the source or the originator of the food product, not necessarily foodservice operators. These relatively few, but highly complex, laws are supplemented by state and local

health sanitary codes, with their own enforcement schemes, and usually less uniformity. State health and sanitary codes are enforced by municipal health departments.[29] Larger cities will usually set up their own agencies for health enforcement. Smaller communities and rural areas often come under the state umbrella, with regulation and enforcement handled by the county. It is these regulatory agencies that supervise the day-to-day operations, investigate violations, and prosecute violators. Local regulation is the cutting edge of the regulatory apparatus regarding sanitation.

Since you deal in food and beverage sales, you must comply with state and local health and sanitary codes. These codes usually regulate all aspects of the storage, preparation, and handling of food products from the time you receive the basic ingredients until you serve the prepared dish. Sanitation regulations are often strict, since poor sanitation and unhealthy conditions could lead to the outbreak of disease in the local community as well as injury to individual patrons.

Regulation begins with the licensing of the operation. A health or foodservice permit is issued after an inspection and approval by the local regulatory body. A new permit must be obtained whether you open a new foodservice operation or purchase or lease your business from someone else.

Inspections may be held without prior warning after you open to ensure that you are maintaining health and sanitary standards throughout your ownership or occupancy period. Many local agencies pattern their inspections and their inspection forms on the federal model. Figure 2.2 is a typical inspection form. Violations are treated either as offenses (minor) or as crimes (major), and if proven in court, may result in a fine or imprisonment or both. Regulatory bodies are not bound by any court decision as to whether or not an offense was criminal, and may still suspend or revoke the operating permit.

Figure 2.2
Typical Inspection Form

DEPARTMENT OF HEALTH AND HUMAN SERVICES
PUBLIC HEALTH SERVICE · FOOD AND DRUG ADMINISTRATION

FOOD SERVICE ESTABLISHMENT INSPECTION REPORT

Based on an inspection this day, the items circled below identify the violation in operations or Facilities which must be corrected by the next routine inspection or such shorter period of time as may be specified in writing by the regulatory authority. Failure to comply with any time limits for correction specified in this notice may result in cessation of your Food Service operations.

OWNER NAME

ESTABLISHMENT NAME

ADDRESS

ZIP CODE

ESTABLISHMENT I.D.				CENSUS TRACT	SANIT CODE	DATE			INSPECT TIME (Min)	PURPOSE	29
COUNTY	DISTRICT	TYPE	EST. NO.			YR.	MO.	DAY			

PURPOSE:
Regular .... 1 Complaint 3
Follow-up .... 2 Investigation 4
Other 5

ITEM	WT	COL	ITEM	WT	COL	ITEM	WT	COL
FOOD			18 PRE-FLUSHED, SCRAPED, SOAKED	1	47	**GARBAGE AND REFUSE DISPOSAL**		
*01 SOURCE; SOUND CONDITION, NO SPOILAGE	5	30	19 WASH, RINSE WATER: CLEAN, PROPER TEMPERATURE	2	48	33 CONTAINERS OR RECEPTACLES, COVERED ADEQUATE NUMBER, INSECT/RODENT PROOF, FREQUENCY, CLEAN	2	62
02 ORIGINAL CONTAINER: PROPERLY LABELED	1	31	*20 SANITIZATION RINSE: CLEAN, TEMPERATURE, CONCENTRATION, EXPOSURE TIME, EQUIPMENT, UTENSILS SANITIZED	4	49	34 OUTSIDE STORAGE AREA ENCLOSURES PROPERLY CONSTRUCTED, CLEAN; CONTROLLED INCINERATION	1	63
FOOD PROTECTION			21 WIPING CLOTHS: CLEAN, STORED, RESTRICTED	1	50	**INSECT, RODENT, ANIMAL CONTROL**		
*03 POTENTIALLY HAZARDOUS FOOD MEETS TEMPERATURE REQUIREMENTS DURING STORAGE, PREPARATION, DISPLAY, SERVICE, TRANSPORTATION	5	32	22 FOOD CONTACT SURFACES OF EQUIPMENT AND UTENSILS CLEAN, FREE OF ABRASIVES, DETERGENTS	2	51	*35 PRESENCE OF INSECT/RODENTS — OUTER OPENINGS PROTECTED, NO BIRDS, TURTLES, OTHER ANIMALS	4	64
*04 FACILITIES TO MAINTAIN PRODUCT TEMPERATURE	4	33	23 NON-FOOD CONTACT SURFACES OF EQUIPMENT AND UTENSILS CLEAN	1	52	**FLOORS, WALLS AND CEILINGS**		
05 THERMOMETERS PROVIDED AND CONSPICUOUS	1	34	24 STORAGE, HANDLING OF CLEAN EQUIPMENT/UTENSILS	1	53	36 FLOORS: CONSTRUCTED, DRAINED, CLEAN, GOOD REPAIR, COVERING INSTALLATION, DUSTLESS CLEANING METHODS	1	65
06 POTENTIALLY HAZARDOUS FOOD PROPERLY THAWED	2	35	25 SINGLE-SERVICE ARTICLES, STORAGE, DISPENSING, USED	1	54			
*07 UNWRAPPED AND POTENTIALLY HAZARDOUS FOOD NOT RE-SERVED	4	36	26 NO RE-USE OF SINGLE SERVICE ARTICLES	2	55	37 WALLS, CEILING, ATTACHED EQUIPMENT CONSTRUCTED, GOOD REPAIR, CLEAN SURFACES, DUSTLESS CLEANING METHODS	1	66
08 FOOD PROTECTION DURING STORAGE, PREPARATION, DISPLAY, SERVICE, TRANSPORTATION	2	37	**WATER**					
09 HANDLING OF FOOD (ICE) MINIMIZED	2	38	*27 WATER SOURCE, SAFE: HOT AND COLD UNDER PRESSURE	5	56	**LIGHTING**		
10 IN USE, FOOD (ICE) DISPENSING UTENSILS PROPERLY STORED	1	39	**SEWAGE**			38 LIGHTING PROVIDED AS REQUIRED, FIXTURES SHIELDED	1	67
PERSONNEL			*28 SEWAGE AND WASTE WATER DISPOSAL	4	57	**VENTILATION**		
*11 PERSONNEL WITH INFECTIONS RESTRICTED	5	40	**PLUMBING**			39 ROOMS AND EQUIPMENT VENTED AS REQUIRED	1	68
*12 HANDS WASHED AND CLEAN, GOOD HYGIENIC PRACTICES	5	41	29 INSTALLED, MAINTAINED	1	58	**DRESSING ROOMS**		
13 CLEAN CLOTHES, HAIR RESTRAINTS	1	42	*30 CROSS-CONNECTION, BACK SIPHONAGE, BACKFLOW	5	59	40 ROOMS CLEAN, LOCKERS PROVIDED, FACILITIES CLEAN, LOCATED, USED	1	69
FOOD EQUIPMENT AND UTENSILS			**TOILET AND HANDWASHING FACILITIES**			**OTHER OPERATIONS**		
14 FOOD (ICE) CONTACT SURFACES DESIGNATED, CONSTRUCTED, MAINTAINED, INSTALLED, LOCATED	2	43	*31 NUMBER, CONVENIENT, ACCESSIBLE, DESIGNED, INSTALLED	4	60	*41 NECESSARY TOXIC ITEMS PROPERLY STORED, LABELED, USED	5	70
15 NON-FOOD CONTACT SURFACES, DESIGNED, CONSTRUCTED, MAINTAINED, INSTALLED, LOCATED	1	44				42 PREMISES MAINTAINED, FREE OF LITTER, UNNECESSARY ARTICLES, CLEANING MAINTENANCE EQUIPMENT PROPERLY STORED, AUTHORIZED PERSONNEL	1	71
16 DISHWASHING FACILITIES: DESIGNED, CONSTRUCTED, MAINTAINED, INSTALLED, LOCATED, OPERATED	2	45	32 TOILET ROOMS ENCLOSED, SELF-CLOSING DOORS, FIXTURES, GOOD REPAIR, CLEAN. HAND CLEANSER, SANITARY TOWELS/TISSUE/HAND-DRYING DEVICES PROVIDED, PROPER WASTE RECEPTACLES	2	61	43 COMPLETE SEPARATION FROM LIVING/SLEEPING QUARTERS, LAUNDRY	1	72
17 ACCURATE THERMOMETERS, CHEMICAL TEST KITS PROVIDED, GAUGE COCK (¼" IPS VALVE)	1	46				44 CLEAN, SOILED LINEN PROPERLY STORED	1	73

FOLLOW-UP		74	RATING SCORE ("100" Less Weight of Items Violated)
YES 1			▐▐▐▐▐▐▐▐ ➔
NO 2			

* CRITICAL ITEMS REQUIRING IMMEDIATE ACTION

RECEIVED BY (Name and Title)

INSPECTED BY (Name and Number and Title)

FORM FD 2420 (2/76) PREVIOUS EDITIONS ARE OBSOLETE.

Use reverse for remarks. (80-1)

U.S. Department of Health and Human Services, Food and Drug Administration

A violation of a health or sanitary code may be proof of negligence (a legal wrong where the victim is exposed to an unreasonable risk of harm), which can give an injured customer the right to sue and recover damages. In some states, such a violation of a statute is in itself conclusive proof of such wrongdoing. In other states, the violation creates a *prima facie* (on the face of it—held to be true unless disputed) case of wrongdoing, meaning that the victim will recover *unless* the foodservice operator can prove that he or she did not cause or contribute to the violation.[30]

There is one more weapon in the arsenal of the regulators. Many foodservice operators naturally try to avoid bad publicity, especially regarding sanitation. This concern is understandable. The consumer complaint or claim may or may not be justified, yet the attendant publicity may injure an otherwise good reputation. Some large metropolitan newspapers publish the sanitary and health code violations of foodservice establishments and a list of forced closings.[31] Although not printed in banner headlines on the front page, such publicity has the effect of warning customers away, which provides an additional reason to comply with local sanitation guidelines.

Each state may establish its own sanitation standards, so long as they do not weaken or dilute the FDA model. In other words, states may improve upon the federal model for sanitation but may not limit or curtail its scope and effectiveness. The states are not required to adopt any standards, since the federal Food, Drug, and Cosmetic Act will serve in the absence of any state legislation.[32] (The same is true of agricultural and marketing requirements governed by federal law, such as the Federal Meat Inspection Act of 1906 and the Poultry Products Inspection Act, enacted in 1957, administered by the U.S. Department of Agriculture.)[33]

Criminal Trespass and Disorderly Conduct

Independently of liquor law violations, most local legislatures have written laws to protect private property from trespassers or intruders who have no legitimate interest in being on your property and whose conduct infringes on your rights, and on the rights of your patrons and of others on the premises. The Supreme Court, in a landmark decision, ruled that the United States Constitution only protects government action, or private action on public property, not action on private property.[34]

You have a right to keep intruders out of your private business premises, or remove them, as long as you use no more force than absolutely necessary under the circumstances.[35]

Blue Laws

Under common law, business activity was legal on Sunday. Many states, however, have statutes called *blue laws,* which modify this "business as usual on Sunday" common law rule. They prohibit any nonreligious business transactions on Sunday. Some states modify the rule to allow communities to choose which day business must close. Other states prohibit the sale of merchandise other than for "necessity" and "charity" on Sunday. The most typical sales prohibited by blue laws are sales of alcoholic beverages. Each state is permitted to define sales of "necessity" and "charity," and to include as well as exclude alcohol from the scope of such laws.

Works of charity are those acts that involve religious worship or helping persons in distress. Works of necessity include acts that must be done to save life, health, or property. Some courts have interpreted the "works of necessity" exception very broadly to permit sales where their prohibition would cause serious economic loss to the seller or inconvenience to the buyer.

Some communities do not enforce their blue laws at all, others do so strictly, and in many states such laws have been declared unconstitutional.

Truth-in-Menu

In line with federal regulations on food and beverage advertising and packaging, a number of states have authorized local health departments to enforce their own similar regulations and to investigate and fine violators. Some states have enacted their own "truth-in-menu" or "truth-in-dining" acts (Figure 2.3) as well. These acts are the result of complaints filed by consumers who were served products advertised as originating from a particular locality, or as prepared in a certain manner, in a certain condition, or as representing a certain portion size or weight, when in fact the claims were untrue. (See also Appendix C for menu guidelines.)

The most serious customer complaints deal with product substitutions, where the product served differs materially from the one advertised. For example, if a restaurant advertises prime rib of beef on the menu and the waiter brings a beef shoulder cut instead without telling the customer about the substitution, then that patron may feel justified in making a complaint. The substitution is often inferior in quality and less costly, and may signal the patron that he or she is being ripped off.

The reason for the expansion of such regulations is to protect consumers against economic losses suffered when they do not get the product they pay for—a loss of the benefit of the bargain a consumer makes with the foodservice operator. The lack of consumer protection against this form of loss encourages less honest foodservice operators to benefit by such "substitutions," to the detriment of consumers as well as more honest operators. This

Figure 2.3
State Regulations

Truth-in-Menu Acts
Colorado, Connecticut, Hawaii, Idaho, Michigan, Minnesota, Missouri, Montana, Nebraska, New Jersey, Oregon, Utah, Washington.

Indoor Clean Air Acts
California, Colorado, Connecticut, Michigan, Minnesota, Montana, Nebraska, Nevada, North Dakota, Rhode Island, Utah, Vermont.

practice has been enough to justify truth-in-menu regulations in some states.[36]

Kosher Food

Some local governments go a step further than state truth-in-menu regulations and make it illegal for restaurants to advertise falsely that a food is prepared in the Jewish orthodox kosher manner when it is not.[37] These regulations make the misrepresentation a crime, regardless of whether there was any intent to defraud.

No Smoking

Another form of regulation involves the controversial issue of segregation of smokers in dining facilities. With increasing medical evidence to support the connection between smoking and the risk of lung cancer as well as other health hazards to smokers and nearby nonsmokers, indoor clean air acts have been adopted in a few states.[38]

The first state to do so was Minnesota, which adopted its Indoor Clean Air Act in 1975. Twelve states have followed this pattern (Figure 2.3).

The Minnesota Act, the most comprehensive of its type, prohibits smoking in eating establishments, except in designated smoking sections. At least 25 percent of restaurant tables must be set aside for nonsmokers, who must be advised that they have the right to be seated and served in such a section. Bars and taverns—that is, establishments serving alcoholic beverages without food service—are exempt, but signs to that effect must be posted. Violators are usually subject to a civil fine.[39]

The clean air doctrine represents a legislative compromise between the competing interests of smokers and nonsmokers. As the old refrain goes, one person's pleasure is another person's poison. In practice, it may be good business to provide separate seating for nonsmokers, who make up the majority of the population. Voluntary action may serve to forestall legal regulation of yet another aspect of foodservice management.

Zoning Laws

Local governing bodies have the power to regulate land use within their boundaries. Almost every local government exercises this power to some extent.

Usually the objective is to allow for both business and residential needs without one land use conflicting with another. A secondary goal of land-use regulations is to protect certain institutions, especially churches and schools, from being exposed to business activities, such as the sale of alcohol or adult books, that might be perfectly acceptable elsewhere.

Most local governments regulate land use through *zoning.* Zoning is dividing up land for specific uses. One area may be a residential zone, another a commercial zone, and another mixed residential and commercial. These laws have the effect of regulating *both* private and public land. In other words, if you buy a piece of property in a residential area,

although you have full ownership rights, the local government may still prevent you from opening a restaurant there, or even from conducting a catering business in your home. This should serve to warn you that private property is not always all that private. This topic will be explored in detail in Chapter 10 on property law.

Building and Safety Codes

In addition to regulating land use, most local governments regulate what you may do to your restaurant building to improve or expand it. Many local governments have building and safety codes to guide you. Business owners will encounter more building and safety regulations than owners of private homes, and foodservice operators will have even more regulations to deal with.

The purpose of building and safety codes is to protect the surrounding area—and, in the case of a restaurant, the patrons—from poor building or safety practices.

Building codes usually specify requirements for building a new structure or for adding to an existing one. At some point in your business, you may want to add to your restaurant building. Before you go to an architect with grand plans for a scenic pool bar surrounded by a trilevel walkway, you must stop at your local building commission office. It may have specific regulations for installing your pool, and may prohibit your trilevel walkway altogether. Always, before you spend *any* money on building materials and advice, consult the local building authorities.

Safety codes are designed to prevent accidents to the public and your employees. These codes usually concern fire regulations. Along with a visit from the health inspector, you will probably be inspected by the local fire department, which usually is looking for faulty wiring, unsafe lighting, and other fire hazards. Get a copy of the local codes so you can be sure that you stay within the requirements. Violating safety codes is not only illegal and may cost you a fine, but if a patron is injured due to a code violation, he or she is one step closer to holding you liable. (Building and safety codes will be discussed further in Chapter 10 on property law.)

LIVING WITH REGULATIONS

Each state has the power to create regulatory agencies independently of the federal government, as long as the state does not override federal authority to regulate interstate commerce, in which federal law is supreme. State and local commerce are within the power of state and local bodies to regulate. However, federal regulations often provide models for state and local regulations and cooperative state and local guidelines are often written into federal laws.

Normally, the regulatory maze does not create conflicting rules for the single-operation foodservice operator. However, the multi-establishment operator within a single state may find that regulations vary from locality to locality, thus adding to the overall cost of doing business. This problem is substantially greater for the multi-state chain operator, who must comply with more federal regulations as well as state and local rules.

Regulation increases the individual operator's cost of doing business. The operator usually passes these costs on to consumers, and may suffer the consequences of lost patronage because of more expensive products. To the extent that costs associated with regulation are uniform, and affect each operator equally, consumers are not directly affected, since the costs of regulation are equalized for operators in that market. However, when the regulations overlap and are inconsistent, then the costs of doing business also vary, making the operator suffer or benefit, depending on the locality. If regulations are made much

tougher, the manager/owner may find it difficult, if not impossible, to continue operating at a profit.

When regulations involve the preservation of patrons' lives and health, they must be accepted as a cost of entering into, or continuing in, the foodservice business, since the benefit to the public clearly outweighs any economic detriment to the foodservice operator.

When a regulation does not involve any threat to life or health, we in industry must examine it to see if it meets reasonable public expectations at a reasonable cost. When the costs of regulation unreasonably exceed the benefits to the public, you have the power to help eliminate such regulations through the political process.

The foodservice industry as a whole should educate the public to promote useful regulation and to do away with regulation that is costly but of little benefit. The form, content, and scope of regulations prepared by legislatures are based upon input from consumers *and* foodservice industry representatives, so that a proper compromise may be reached when those interests differ. The role of the courts is to interpret statutes to suit the collective values of the individual judges. Ultimately, the legislatures control the process of adoption and change, and so it is to the lawmakers that you must address your concerns.

Wherever possible, a voluntary plan of action is always superior to legally compelled compliance. This holds true for everyone in the industry. The more foodservice operators can do to prevent consumer abuses, the less likely will be the need for legislation. Cooperative efforts are not only good business, but reflect a pride in the foodservice profession and a resolve to weed out those few operators who would tarnish the reputation of the industry as a whole. On the other hand, indifference to consumer desires or attempts to cut corners in the proper operation of business can only invite governmental regulation.

SUMMARY

A number of federal agencies regulate the processing and distribution of food products. Most of those will not affect the foodservice operator directly, but will provide standards for sources of food products, and hence buying guides.

Foodservice operators will encounter federal regulations in the area of employment. These federal regulations are supplemented by state guidelines as well.

Where operators will really feel the regulatory pinch is at the state and local levels. The states generally have some apparatus to regulate employment practices in the area of civil rights, and local metropolitan governments may also.

State regulation is heaviest with regard to liquor sales. Operators who wish to sell alcohol are regulated from the time they apply for a license through the entire time they sell liquor on their premises. The severity of alcohol regulations and enforcement will vary from state to state, but all states are uniformly strict in the area of liquor sales to minors, and such sales pose the greatest threat to a liquor license.

Local regulations usually deal with building codes, sanitation regulations, and fire and safety inspections. Preferably, operators should know these regulations before building or opening a foodservice establishment. Generally, preventive medicine is the best way to avoid problems with local regulations.

QUESTIONS

1. Why are federal inspection and grading of meat products important to the foodservice operator?
2. What effect do federal regulations have on the lawmaking bodies at the state and local levels?
3. A state sanitation law prohibits employees from smoking in food preparation and service areas. A city law prohibits employees from smoking in food preparation areas, but not in service areas. Which law will control city restaurants and why?
4. What are some on-premises activities that may threaten a liquor license? Which activity is most closely regulated by every state?
5. How may a violation of a sanitation code leave you open to liability?

NOTES

1. *Tad's Franchises, Inc. v. Incorporated Village of Pelham Manor,* 42 A.D.2d 616, 345 N.Y.S.2d 136 (2d Dep't 1973), *aff'd* 35 N.Y.2d 672, 319 N.E.2d 202, 360 N.Y.S.2d 886 (1974).
2. H. Schultz, *Food Law Handbook* 1–30 (1981); Regier, *The Struggle for Federal Food and Drugs Legislation* in Law & Contemp. Probs. 3 (1933).
3. Schultz, *supra* note 2, at 196.
4. 21 U.S.C. secs. 302, 304(a), (b), (d), 306, 704, 705 (1976).
5. 21 U.S.C. sec. 303(a) and (b). Each violation of the Act is a *misdemeanor,* a criminal offense punishable by a maximum $1000 fine, or up to a year in jail, or both. Repeat offenders are subject to a maximum three-year prison term and a maximum $10,000 fine, or both, for *each* violation. *Willful* violations of prohibited acts (including adulteration, misbranding of product, refusal to permit inspection of premises, introduction or receipt of any adulterated or misbranded product, and the like) with intent to defraud or mislead, can result in a maximum three-year prison term, or a maximum fine of $10,000, or both, for each violation.
6. 21 U.S.C. secs. 304(b), 333, 335. A right to be heard is afforded any person subject to criminal prosecution after the FDA has notified the federal Attorney General to prosecute. The burden of proof is on the FDA, but will be satisfied by the weight of credible evidence. See also Christopher, *Cases and Materials on Food and Drug Law* (1966), Chapter 8, sec. 9 (Burden of Proof),

pp. 577–78 citing food cases. Either side may appeal to a higher reviewing court, and with that court's permission, to the U.S. Supreme Court. Administrative Procedure Act, 5 U.S.C. secs. 701(a), 702. Either side may file for a *writ of certiorari,* a procedure giving the Supreme Court the right to grant review or not, as the High Court sees fit.

7. The Federal Trade Commission Act, 15 U.S.C. secs. 12(a), 12(b), 13, 14, 15, 16, 41–58 (1976).

8. To date, the FTC has not exercised its authority to regulate chain restaurant menu advertising in interstate commerce.

9. 15 U.S.C. secs. 12(a), 13(a), 14(a) (1976). The "affirmative failure to reveal" rule has been most frequently applied to drug advertisements by the FTC. FTC cease and desist orders that made the "failure to reveal" itself a deceptive act have been affirmed in *Wybrant System Products Corp. v. Federal Trade Commission,* 266 F.2d 571 (2d Cir.), *cert. denied* 361 U.S. 883 (1959) and in *Erickson and Scalp Specialists v. Federal Commission,* 272 F.2d 318 (7th Cir. 1959), *cert. denied* 362 U.S. 940 (1960). Contra *Alberty v. Federal Trade Commission,* 182 F.2d 36 (D.C. Cir.), *cert. denied* 340 U.S. 818 (1950). *Federal Trade Commission v. Merck & Co.,* 69 FTC 526 (1966) (drugs); *in re* Porter and Deitsch, Inc., noted in *Legal Developments in Marketing,* 42 J. Mkting. 90 (Oct. 1978) (weight-loss pills).

10. 15 U.S.C. sec. 54(a) (1976).

11. *Id.* sec. 55(a)(1). Section 55(b) defines "food" to mean "(1) articles used for food or drink for man or other animals, (2) chewing gum, and (3) articles used for components of any such articles."

12. 29 U.S.C. secs. 651–78 (1976).

13. Section 651 of the Act sets forth a Congressional statement of findings and declaration of purposes and policy. See 29 U.S.C. sec. 651 (1976).

14. See J. Sherry, *The Laws of Innkeepers,* secs. 12:1–12:19 (rev. ed. 1981).

15. Sherry, *supra* note 14, sec. 12:2.

16. Sherry, *supra* note 14, secs. 12:12–12:14.

17. *Per se* violations of the federal Sherman Antitrust Act are immune from such defenses. Sherry, *supra* note 14, secs. 12:4–12:9.

18. The FTC issued a trade regulation, effective October 21, 1979, having the force and effect of law, entitled Disclosure Requirements and Prohibitions Concerning Franchising and Business Opportunity Ventures, 16 C.F.R. sec. 436 (1982).

19. The Federal Alcohol Administration Act, 27 U.S.C. secs. 201–12 (1976) controls traffic in distilled spirits, wine, and malt beverages in interstate (between-the-states) commerce and between states and foreign nations. The United States Constitution, Twenty-First Amendment, grants the states power over the sale and distribution of liquor within their borders.

20. The powers and duties of alcohol beverage control boards or commissions vary from state to state. Essentially, they license, police, and discipline distillers, wholesalers, and retailers who are subject to their respective rules and regulations.

21. N.Y. Alcoholic Beverage Control Law, sec. 1 *et seq.* (McKinney 1970 & Supp. 1982); Rules and Regulations Promulgated by The New York State Liquor Authority. See *Show Boat of New Lebanon, Inc. v. State Liquor Authority,* 33 A.D.2d 954, 306 N.Y.S.2d 859 (3d Dep't), *aff'd,* 27 N.Y.2d 676, 262 N.E.2d 211, 314 N.Y.S.2d 2 (1970).

22. *Show Boat of New Lebanon, supra* note 19; *Circus Disco Ltd. v. State Liquor Auth.,* 51 N.Y.2d 24, 409 N.E.2d 963, 431 N.Y.S.2d 491 (1980).

23. Section 65, N.Y. Alcoholic Beverage Control Law, states: No person shall sell, deliver or give away or cause or permit or procure to be sold, delivered or given away any alcoholic beverage to:

    1. Any minor, actually or apparently, under the age of nineteen years;
    2. Any intoxicated person or to any person, actually or apparently, under the influence of liquor;
    3. Any habitual drunkard known to be such to the person authorized to dispense any alcoholic beverages.

    Neither such person so refusing to sell or deliver under this section nor his employer shall be liable in any civil or criminal action or for any fine or penalty based upon such refusal, except that such sale or delivery shall not be refused, withheld from or denied to any person on account of race, creed, color or national origin.

24. In New York, operators may provide topless dancing without jeopardizing their license. *Bellanca v. State Liquor Auth.,* 54 N.Y.2d 228, 429 N.E.2d 765, 445 N.Y.S.2d 87 (1981). Other states, however, are free to outlaw such entertainment. *Cianci v. Division of Liquor Control, Department of Business Regulation,* 50 U.S.L.W. 3798 (April 4, 1982), *cert. denied,* 102 S. Ct. 1769 (1982).

25. See sec. 65(1), (2) and (3) of the N.Y. Alcoholic Beverage Control Law, *supra* note 21.
26. See *Circus Disco, supra* note 22.
27. *Show Boat of New Lebanon, supra* note 21.
28. See *Circus Disco, supra* note 22.
29. See Schultz, *supra* note 2.
30. See Chapter 4, *infra.*
31. The *New York Times* does so regularly.
32. Schultz, *supra* note 2, at 4–5, 1–30.
33. 21 U.S.C. secs. 541–570 (1976). Section 661 of the Federal Meat Inspection Act and sec. 451 of the Poultry Products Inspection Act provide federal and state cooperative guidelines.
34. *Lloyd Corp. v. Tanner,* 407 U.S. 551 (1972). See also *Hudgens v. National Labor Relations Board,* 424 U.S. 507 (1976) (peaceful picketing of retail store).
35. Trespassing members of the news media are liable in damages to foodservice operators. *Le Mistral, Inc. v. Columbia Broadcasting,* 61 A.D.2d 491, 402 N.Y.S.2d 815 (1st Dep't 1978).
36. See Sherry, *supra* note 14, sec. 14:10.
37. Florida and New York make it a crime to represent falsely that food sold is kosher when, in fact, it is nonkosher.
38. See Sherry, *supra* note 14, sec. 14:11.
39. *Id.*

3
Patron Civil Rights

Objectives

The purpose of this chapter is to:

1. Outline the rights of foodservice operators to admit or refuse patrons and their duties to avoid discrimination against patrons.
2. Discuss the scope and effect of civil rights laws as related to operator admission policies.
3. Define *house rule* and provide guidelines for formulating such a rule.

Case in Point One

The Golden Nugget Saloon is located in a small community in the Pacific Northwest. Twenty percent of the total population consists of Mexican-Americans, most of whom are native-born U.S. citizens. The owner of the saloon has issued a rule that directs his bartenders not to allow a foreign language to be used at the bar, "if it interferes with the regular trade." If a problem arises, employees are to turn the jukebox up (using house money) and then ask the "problem" people to move to a table.

One night, three Mexican-Americans went to the saloon where the bartender served them beer. While drinking, the three men began to speak Spanish. Other customers, also sitting at the bar, became irritated and complained to the bartender. The bartender told the three that if they persisted in speaking Spanish, they would have to sit at a table or leave. An argument broke out, the police were called, and the three Mexican-Americans left peacefully. Two days later the scene was reenacted with different Mexican-Americans. The bartender "pulled" the beers of these customers, and they left. This time, however, they were followed out of the tavern and assaulted by three English-speaking customers.

The Mexican-Americans sued, charging a violation of their civil rights *not to be discriminated against because of their race and national origin. Were their civil rights violated? Yes, according to the court.*

The court found that the tavern management had violated the civil rights of the plaintiffs, namely, a federal statute that allows all persons to make and enforce contracts—and to enjoy the full and equal benefits of all laws and proceedings for the security of person and property as enjoyed by white English-speaking citizens.[1] The rule, the court said, deprived Spanish-speaking Mexican-Americans of their rights to drink their purchases and enjoy equal hospitality with English-speaking customers.[2]

The tavernkeeper's excuse that the policy was adopted simply to avoid trouble and not to arouse the anger of the "preferred" English-speaking customers was rejected. The equal protection of the laws guaranteed by the Fourteenth Amendment of the Federal Constitution cannot be ignored when patrons enter in a fit and proper condition, conduct themselves in a peaceful manner, and are provoked by other patrons.[3]

Case in Point Two

Fred Fineburg and Gloria Goodfrank operate a foodservice establishment, which caters to families with preteen children who are served a cafeteria-style selection of fast foods and soft drinks. No alcoholic beverages are sold. Fred and Gloria make every effort to accommodate families in clean, pleasant surroundings at low cost, and the operation's profitability depends upon high turnover.

Lately Fred and Gloria have experienced a loss of family patronage due to the presence of a large number of town toughs who smell of alcohol, are boisterous, and generally disrupt normal business. These unsavory types usually occupy tables and chairs for a longer time than needed to eat their food, verbally harass other customers, and threaten to "cause trouble" if anyone complains about their aggressive behavior. Fred and Gloria wish either to deny admission to these punks or to remove them. Do they have the legal right to do so?

Yes. In contrast to innkeepers, who are generally required by law to admit all who appear in a fit condition and able to pay, the foodservice operation has more freedom to pick and choose customers. The only restrictions the law imposes are civil rights laws that prohibit discrimination in all places of public accommodation, including restaurants, on the basis of race, creed, color, or national origin, and in some states, on the basis of sex or physical handicap.

In this case, Fred and Gloria can legally deny access to the unpleasant patrons or remove those who overstay their welcome and disrupt business by annoying or vocally abusing other customers. Can you determine the difference between the two cases? After reading this chapter you should be able to do so.

ADMISSION OF CUSTOMERS

The first contact you or your employees have with customers is at the front door. Your rights to admit or refuse patrons are limited by your own standard admission policies and by federal and state civil rights laws prohibiting discrimination.

No one usually intends to violate another's civil rights, including restaurant operators. It is not easy for operators, subjected to other business pressures, always to recognize where their business rights end and patrons' civil rights begin. It is important that you be able to differentiate between those rights, so that you can develop admissions policies that are in keeping with the civil rights of patrons and your own rights as a businessperson.

COMMON LAW ADMISSION POLICIES: ENGLISH ROOTS

From the earliest recorded evidence, places of public hospitality have been a fact of life in the development of modern civilized societies. Our present-day common law reflects the early English recognition of hospitality businesses as places of public refuge, entertainment, and accommodation.

However, medieval English law made a sharp distinction between innkeepers and proprietors of restaurants or taverns as to their respective duties to admit patrons or guests.

These distinctions were based on the different functions of each establishment.

The innkeeper was required to admit and receive all travelers, as long as a prospective guest was in a fit condition and able to pay for the lodging. This was so because a traveler was assumed to be a stranger to the locality, and thus a person in need of shelter and protection as well as food and lodging. Travel during the Middle Ages was dangerous. The roads were infested with outlaws who would prey upon unwary travelers, especially at night. The only places of refuge were the wayside inns, but these were few in number and located sporadically along the way. As a result, admission was a serious matter because of the threat of loss of life as well as of property that confronted the traveler if shelter could not be found. It was for these reasons that common law required innkeepers to admit all travelers—with very few exceptions.[4]

The tavernkeeper—although, like the innkeeper, also a provider of food and drink—was not under the same duty to admit everyone. The English common law gave the proprietor of a tavern the right to discriminate as to customers, because the function of the tavern was to serve local inhabitants who knew the risks of venturing out at night and who did not require shelter and protection.[5]

MODERN ADMISSION POLICIES: HOUSE RULES AND CIVIL RIGHTS

The law does not require foodservice operators, tavernkeepers, and others who invite the public on their premises to admit everyone.[6] Only innkeepers and public transportation carriers must do so.[7] In all cases the potential patron, guest, or passenger must be in a fit condition to be received and be prepared and able to pay for food and services provided.[8]

As a foodservice operator, you are limited only by civil rights laws and your own admissions policies.

The modern trend is to require all operators of public businesses to base any denial of access on a *house rule,* which is a policy adopted voluntarily and used consistently to protect the reputation and class of that establishment, as well as the safety and welfare of other patrons.[9]

In practice, most courts allow you a good deal of discretion in deciding whether or not to admit patrons.

For you, the foodservice manager, the first test of your admissions policy that must stand up in court is whether or not a house rule exists, whether it is reasonable, whether it is adequately communicated to patrons, and whether a prospective patron has violated the rule.

The term "house rule" is relative, since there is no standard that uniformly fits every proprietor. Generally the courts view *reasonableness* in terms of your circumstances, that is, the size, class, and nature of your operation. For example, a coat and tie for a man and an appropriate dress for a woman might be a reasonable requirement for admission to a first-class French restaurant. However, less formality would be expected in a fast-food establishment or a family restaurant. Likewise, the management of a family restaurant might reasonably refuse to admit or serve an underdressed person because other customers might object to a life-style that would be totally acceptable in a singles resort dining area.

In some cases the force of statutory health codes will override any discretion you may wish to exercise. The admission of people in bare feet or who are accompanied by pets other than seeing eye dogs is often forbidden irrespective of your own more liberal admission standards.

Under no circumstances are you required to admit anyone who is drunk, disorderly, filthy, or acting in a threatening manner. Here you and your employees must use relatively consistent powers of observation *at the door.* You may have more trouble ejecting these types once they are admitted.

The following example illustrates the application of the reasonable house rule concept in a typical restaurant setting.[10]

> A young woman, age 26, and her male escort, upon leaving a fraternity house party, went to a fast-food establishment. Both went through the cafeteria line, selected and paid for their food, and sat at a table. When she started to eat, the woman was approached by the foodservice manager, who told her to leave because she was not wearing shoes. The manager informed her that it was company policy not to serve anyone not wearing shoes, although there was no sign to that effect posted. She replied that she would leave when she was through eating. An argument started, and she told the manager to "go to hell." The manager called a police officer, who informed the patron that she was violating the city's unlawful-entry criminal statute. When she persisted in refusing to leave, the officer arrested her. Later the criminal charge of unlawful entry was dropped, but not until she had been fingerprinted, photographed, and placed in a police lineup. She then sued the owner of the restaurant for false arrest. Was the arrest justified?

The court held that the arrest was lawful and dismissed her suit, noting that she unlawfully refused to leave after being properly ordered to do so by the manager.

The court reasoned that the restaurant manager had the common law right to refuse service to any patron, and that there was no violation of the woman's civil rights (a refusal based on race, creed, color, or national origin) that would establish an exception to this rule. The court said that while it is unlawful for a foodservice operator to refuse to serve any "quiet and orderly person," the statute did not prevent an operation from establishing a reasonable dress requirement. A rule that all patrons must wear shoes as a condition of admission and service is typically viewed as reasonable.

Today, as in the Middle Ages, a restaurant patron's legal status is not the same as that of a guest at an inn, who, once admitted, has a right to remain until proven guilty of misconduct. The restaurant patron merely has revocable permission to remain, and cannot lawfully remain once ordered to leave. In this example, the patron's only legal remedy was to sue the foodservice owner for the breach or violation of her contract for the food she purchased. Obviously she should not have been admitted at all, since she was in violation of the dress code to begin with.

Dress codes have to be clear and consistently enforced, however. In the following California case a house rule regarding dress codes was too vague.

Hales v. Ojai Valley Inn and Country Club
Court of Appeals of California, Second District
73 Cal. App. 3d 25, 140 Cal. Rptr. 555 (1977)

Facts. With his family, Mr. Hales went into the inn's restaurant to buy some food and drink. Mr. Hales had made room reservations for the facility, using information from a brochure he had obtained before his vacation. Referring to its three dining facilities, the brochure said:

> Sports and casual clothes are in order during the day. A warm sweater or wrap is suggested for the evenings which are frequently cool. Gentlemen are requested to wear jackets and ties to dinner.

When Mr. Hales tried to order, however, he was told he could not be served because he was not wearing a tie. He alleged that, at the time, female patrons who were similarly attired in leisure suits without ties were being

served. On this basis, he sued the inn for sex discrimination and false advertising. The trial court dismissed his complaint and he appealed. The trial court order dismissing the complaint by the guest, which claimed sex discrimination and false advertising, was reversed.

Reasoning. According to the California Unruh Civil Rights Act, all members of the public of lawful age have a right to patronize a public restaurant as long as they are acting properly and are not committing unlawful or illegal acts. Further, proprietors have no right to eject patrons "without good cause," and may be liable otherwise. The appeals court found that, while the plaintiff should provide more information, there appeared to be enough facts to justify a cause of action (suit) for sex discrimination.

As for false advertising, the appeals court determined that there was enough information to uphold the complaint. The court said that the advertising indicated that a suit and tie were preferred, *but not required.* The defendant said that he intended the advertising to indicate that jackets and ties were required. The plaintiff said if he had known that to be the case, he would not have made reservations at the inn for himself and his family.

Conclusion. (1) Rules regarding dress codes have to be specific and not arbitrary or open to confusion by either patrons or employees. In this case the dress preference could have been interpreted either way by a would-be patron. A dress code should not be made up of "maybes" but clear, consistent standards. (2) The court pointed to a California Supreme Court decision that prohibits owners of public establishments from refusing to admit persons because they wear their hair long or dress unconventionally, in the absence of proof of illegal or immoral conduct.

(3) This ruling was based on a violation of the California Civil Rights Act. A denial of admission on the grounds of violation of a reasonable dress code would be permissible in common law. The California Civil Rights Act, as interpreted, alters the common law rule. In a similar case, the New York Supreme Court ruled in favor of a patron who complained that he was denied admission because he had long hair, whereas women with even longer hair were served. (4) State civil rights laws vary from state to state, and these laws may be stricter than the federal civil rights laws.[11]

Civil Rights Legislation

The history of access to places of public accommodation and entertainment in the United States reveals a clear-cut pattern of refusals to admit certain groups of people, particularly racial minorities.[12] Even innkeepers practiced such discrimination, in clear violation of the common law.

Some states, applying the common law duty to admit all, passed special legislation prohibiting whites and nonwhites from occupying space within the same hotel, restaurant, or other facilities open to the public, thereby legalizing discrimination.[13]

The U.S. Supreme Court adopted a "separate but equal" accommodations doctrine, which was ignored by all states, including those that did not have discriminatory public access statutes.[14] *Separate but equal* meant that the product or service offered to a member of a minority must be equal in all ways to that offered to a white person. Although more commonly applied to schools, this doctrine also included restaurants and inns. In other words, an inn could have separate rooms for minorities as long as they were equal in class, decor, and services provided to rooms offered to nonminorities. However, innkeepers in some states ignored the doctrine. In restaurants

there could be a separate entrance and separate seating, as long as the food and service were equal. Restaurant owners and tavernkeepers, never under any common law duty to admit everyone, did as they pleased. In each case, as the Supreme Court decided regarding schools in 1954, separate was not usually equal.[15]

Federal Laws

The federal Civil Rights Act of 1964 drastically changed these common law and statutory rules. Title II of the Act, called the *public accommodations section,* outlaws discrimination by all businesses serving the public, including foodservice operators, on the basis of race, creed, color, and national origin (Figure 3.1). No state statute to the contrary is enforceable.[16] Only sex-based discrimination in public accommodation remains outside the scope of the Civil Rights Act.

State Laws

The majority of states have passed their own civil rights acts governing public accommodations. Some have also outlawed sex-based discrimination in public places.[17]

State civil rights acts often cover areas not mentioned under the federal act. Not only may sex-based discrimination be prohibited, but discrimination based on such matters as sexual preference, marital status, age, and physical or mental handicap may also be prevented by state laws (see Appendix D).[18] In addition, some large cities have passed their own civil rights laws.[19]

You may refuse to admit potential patrons on neutral grounds, such as for abusive conduct or their use of your premises for drug sales or other illegal activities.[20] In the first situation, the misconduct is open and obvious. In the second situation, it is hard to detect the illegal act until the drug sale is attempted on

Figure 3.1
Establishments Covered by Title II of the Civil Rights Act

Section 201. *Establishments Covered*

(a) All persons shall be entitled to the full and equal enjoyment of the goods, services, facilities, privileges, advantages, and accommodations of any place of public accommodation, as defined in this section, without discrimination or segregation on the ground of race, color, religion, or national origin.

(b) Each of the following establishments which serves the public is a place of public accommodation within the meaning of this title if its operations affect commerce, or if discrimination or segregation by it is supported by State action:

(1) any inn, hotel, motel, or other establishment which provides lodging to transient guests, other than an establishment located within a building which contains not more than five rooms for rent or hire and which is actually occupied by the proprietor of such establishment as his residence;

(2) any restaurant, cafeteria, lunchroom, lunch counter, soda fountain, or other facility principally engaged in selling food for consumption on the premises, including, but not limited to, any such facility located on the premises of any retail establishment; or any gasoline station;

(3) any motion picture house, theater, concert hall, sports arena, stadium or other place of exhibition or entertainment; and

(4) any establishment (A)(i) which is physically located within the premises of any establishment otherwise covered by this subsection, or (ii) within the premises of which is physically located any such covered establishment, and (B) which holds itself out as serving patrons of such covered establishment.

(c) The operations of an establishment affect commerce within the meaning of this title if (1) it is one of the establishments described in paragraph (1) of subsection (b); (2) in the case of an establishment described in paragraph (2) of subsection (b), it serves or offers to serve interstate travellers, or a substantial portion of the food which it serves, or gasoline or other products which it sells, has moved in commerce; (3) in the case of an establishment described in paragraph (3) of subsection (b), it customarily presents films, performances, athletic teams, exhibitions, or other sources of entertainment which move in commerce; and (4) in the case of an establishment described in paragraph (4) of subsection (b), it is physically located within the premises of, or there is physically located within its premises, an establishment the operations of which affect commerce within the meaning of this subsection. For purposes of this section, "commerce" means travel, trade, traffic, commerce, transportation, or communication among the several States, or between the District of Columbia and any State, or between any foreign country or any territory or possession and any State or the District of Columbia, or between points in the same State but through any other State or the District of Columbia or a foreign country.

(d) Discrimination or segregation by an establishment is supported by State action within the meaning of this title if such discrimination or segregation (1) is carried on under color of any law, statute, ordinance, or regulation; or (2) is carried on under color of any customer or usage required or enforced by officials of the State or political subdivision thereof; or (3) is required by action of the State or political subdivision thereof.

(e) The provisions of this title shall not apply to a private club or other establishment not in fact open to the public, except to the extent that the facilities of such establishment are made available to the customers or patrons of an establishment within the scope of subsection (b).

the premises. Only if the patron was known by you to have sold or attempted to sell drugs in your place of business on previous occasions would you be within your legal rights to bar access to that person.

Penalties

What penalties does the common law provide for unlawful discrimination? Usually a damage award is imposed to compensate the victim. Damages include humiliation, emotional harm, and mental suffering.[21]

The federal Civil Rights Act of 1964 permits federal courts to stop discriminatory practices against prospective and admitted patrons. However, the courts lack the power to award compensatory or punitive damages.[22] Only when a restaurant operator violates a court order to stop discriminating may that court impose a fine or jail sentence.

However, state civil rights laws can and do provide penalties for violators. New York, for example, authorizes its courts to fine violators up to $500 and to imprison them for up to 90 days, as well as to award compensatory damages to the victims not to exceed $500 for each violation.[23] New York also empowers its State Commission on Human Rights to halt future violations and fine violators up to $500 and to impose a maximum one-year jail sentence.[24]

Exemptions to Civil Rights Act

Clubs not open or advertised to the public are exempt from the 1964 Civil Rights Act. The general guidelines are that a club that calls itself private, maintains selectivity in the admission of members, does not advertise for members or does so selectively, does not operate strictly for profit, and has a history of membership selectivity is deemed private.

Public clubs, however, which advertise for members and are less arbitrary in their selection, are not usually exempt from either federal or state antidiscrimination laws.

There is disagreement in U.S. courts as to whether clubs that refer to themselves as private but operate on public land, have unclear admissions policies, or advertise may be held liable for violations of civil rights or other discriminatory statutes.

There is one exception to this. *Guests of members are protected by civil rights laws during their stay on the premises.* The following case, based on a New York civil rights statute, illustrates this issue.

Batavia Lodge No. 196 v. Division of Human Rights
Court of Appeals of New York
35 N.Y.2d 143, 316 N.E.2d 318, 359 N.Y.S.2d 25 (1974)

Facts.   Plaintiffs, black persons invited by club members to private Moose Lodge club premises to attend a fashion show, sued to recover damages for the club's refusal to serve them at the bar and for verbal abuse inflicted by club members. White nonmembers were served at the same bar without incident. The Commissioner of the Human Rights Division awarded each claimant $250 in compensatory damages. On appeal, the intermediate reviewing court, the Appellate Division, affirmed the finding of discrimination but eliminated (struck out) the damage award as not permissible, since the claimants suffered no actual out-of-pocket expenses. The plaintiffs appealed to have the damages reinstated. The modification by the intermediate reviewing court striking out the damage award to black guests of the private lodge was *reversed* and the award made by the Commissioner of the Human Rights Division was reinstated.

Reasoning.   The appeals court upheld the damage award to the guests, and based that decision on the weight New York State gave to its antidiscrimination policy as proof that an individual did not need to produce large amounts of evidence to prove discrimination.

The court said that the evidence was ample to support the Commissioner's determination of damages.

Conclusion. Private clubs are not totally exempt from civil rights laws, especially when it comes to members' guests. Some state and city civil rights commissions may prescribe a punitive damage award to the wronged party in addition to a compensatory one.

Sex Discrimination

Many states have laws prohibiting sex discrimination, particularly in employment (see Appendix D). Some of these laws are also aimed at protecting women from being denied admission to public places or being subjected to discriminatory action once they are admitted. However, the law also recognizes some forms of reverse discrimination, where males may be discriminated against.

The more common form of sex discrimination is against women. For states that have sex discrimination laws, their general guidelines regarding public accommodations apply to foodservice operations open to the public. In states without sex discrimination laws, the high court is left to rule on each case.

Age Discrimination

According to common law, a minor, usually a person 18 years of age or younger, who is otherwise fit and able to pay is entitled to admission and service by an *innkeeper*.[25] Foodservice operators are free to admit or reject minors.[26]

Once a minor is admitted, however, he or she is entitled to the same consideration and protection as an adult patron, with the caution that the minor may be entitled to the benefit of the doubt as to the ability to assume risks that might lessen your legal liability to an adult.[27]

Mostly, where you will come into contact with age discrimination laws is in the area of employment, specifically regarding persons over 50. However, age discrimination laws can affect public businesses, and are usually meant to protect both minors and the elderly.

What effect do current civil rights laws prohibiting age discrimination have on your right to refuse a minor access or service? You may not discriminate against minors solely because of their age. Only in the case of liquor service to minors, a crime in all states, would an exception exist.

The nature of your business will serve as an appropriate guide to admission of minors. Common sense dictates that a minor of tender years, 12 or under, should be treated as a special case. If you operate an ice cream parlor that caters to children, you will naturally want to allow a young child to enter and be served. However, when adult entertainment is provided, combined with alcoholic beverage service, you would be on fairly solid legal ground to deny access to a minor.

Physically or Mentally Handicapped Patrons

The rights of the handicapped in public places are covered by federal law. You are prohibited from discriminating against these persons as long as they are otherwise in a fit condition to be served and able to pay.

In addition, a number of states have laws protecting the handicapped.

The general rule is to accommodate all handicapped persons, unless their admission would work an undue hardship in the normal conduct of your business.

Sexual Preference

Most states do not have laws specifically protecting homosexuals from discrimination. The common law is your guide to your limitations. The general common law rule is that unless these patrons are engaging in openly offensive acts or otherwise acting unruly, they should be admitted and served along with other patrons.[28]

Discriminatory Action Once on Premises

Once patrons have been admitted, they should not be subjected to discriminatory action as long as they behave in a proper manner and are prepared to pay. Patrons of atypical race, color, or religion should be served and treated with the same respect as your most typical patrons. Abusive language, rude treatment, a failure to serve, or extremely slow service to patrons who are not your idea of "preferred" customers only make your operation look bad to all of your patrons. Be as even in your treatment as you are in your admissions.

GENERAL GUIDELINES

The laws regarding admission to places of public accommodation are generally not as strict as those regarding employment discrimination; however, it is to your own advantage to standardize your admissions procedure, *not to prevent* admission of certain groups of people, but only to exercise your right to maintain the class of your operation, whether it is a first-class restaurant or a fast-food operation. You should develop an admissions policy, including dress codes, that will best suit the economic needs and type of your operation.

Keep in mind that some dress codes shift from midday to the evening. You should be specific about your dress code, and place signs specifying what it is at the outer entrance to your operation, or in the lobby, or both. Relying on employees to "enforce" your dress code by observation alone often leads to arbitrary decisions by them and bad feelings, or even legal action, on the part of disgruntled patrons.

It is not enough just for you, the manager, to be aware of the potential for legal pitfalls regarding discrimination or anything else. You must, in turn, train your employees to enforce house rules fairly—and quietly. Embarrassing patrons in the process of enforcing house rules by speaking loudly and carrying on unnecessarily lengthy discussion will only aggravate them further. Having a sign to which you or your employees can point, or even, as some restaurants do, a few ties on hand, or at least making a polite suggestion to return properly dressed, can appease an otherwise disgruntled patron, *and* maintain your good business reputation.

SUMMARY

Foodservice managers are given more leeway to deny admission to prospective patrons under the common law than are innkeepers to prospective guests. These rights are not unlimited, though, and the best practice is to establish reasonable house rules and enforce them in a consistent way.

The common law has been supplemented by federal and state civil rights statutes prohibiting discrimination in public restaurants, bars, taverns, and other food and beverage establishments, and in hotels and motels. These federal statutes cover more types of establishments, but are limited to forbidding discrimination based on race, creed, color, or national origin. Refusals to admit on the basis of sex, sexual preference, age, and handicap may be prohibited at the state and local levels, if at all. Neither the federal nor state acts prevent you from excluding or removing from your operation people who are drunk, disorderly, abusive, or in violation of reasonable dress and appearance codes. This law recognizes that your management policies are your own, and that the courts were not created to supervise your daily business responsibilities.

QUESTIONS

1. What criteria will the courts usually use in reviewing a house rule?

2. How may private clubs be exempt from the Civil Rights Act of 1964? What requirements must they meet to be exempt? Describe a situation in which such clubs would not be exempt.
3. The following is an example of a sign posted in a restaurant lobby: *We prefer our gentlemen patrons to wear dress suits. Ladies must wear dresses.* What is wrong with this sign?
4. Aside from a house rule, give an example where a person might be denied admission on legal grounds.
5. What is the general common law rule regarding the admission of homosexuals?

NOTES

1. Civil Rights Act of 1866, 42 U.S.C.A. sec. 1981 (1976).
2. *Hernandez v. Erlenbusch,* 368 F. Supp. 752 (D. Or. 1973).
3. There was, however, no violation of the common law duty of tavern owners to protect their patrons from assaults within the premises, since the defendant had no reason to anticipate the assault that took place outside the tavern.
4. Wyman, *The Law of the Public Callings as a Solution of the Trust Problem,* 17 Harv. L. Rev. 156, 159 (1903).
5. *Id.* See also J. Sherry, *The Laws of Innkeepers,* secs. 1:1–1:6 (rev. ed. 1981).
6. *Jacobson v. New York Racing Ass'n, Inc.,* 33 N.Y.2d 144, 305 N.E.2d 765, 350 N.Y.S.2d 639 (1975); *Rockwell v. Pennsylvania State Horse Racing Comm'n,* 15 Pa. Commw. Ct. 348, 327 A.2d 211 (1974), and authorities cited therein.
7. The original English common law duty to admit is noted in 21 *Halsbury's Laws of England* 445–46 (3d ed. 1957). The New Jersey Supreme Court cited and followed this rule, which is uniform throughout the United States, in *Doe v. Bridgeton Hospital Ass'n, Inc.,* 71 N.Y. 478, 483, 366 A.2d 641, 646 (1976), *cert. denied,* 433 U.S. 914 (1977). See Sherry, *supra* note 5 at sec. 3:3.
8. *Doe v. Bridgeton Hospital Ass'n, Inc., supra* note 7.
9. Sherry, *supra* note 5, at sec. 16:1.
10. *Feldt v. Marriott Corp.,* 322 A.2d 913 (D.C. App. 1974) (Junior Hot Shoppe fast-food operation).
11. *Braun v. Swiston,* 72 Misc. 2d 661, 340 N.Y.S.2d 468 (1972).
12. See J. Sherry, *The Laws of Innkeepers,* sec. 6:5 (1972). The public accommodations section of the Civil Rights Act of 1875 was struck down by the Supreme Court in the *Civil Rights Cases,* 109 U.S. 3 (1883).
13. *Peterson v. City of Greenville,* 373 U.S. 244 (1963).
14. The initial doctrine applicable to innkeepers and common carriers was enunciated by Judge Dick in his charge to the grand jury in North Carolina. *Charge to the Grand Jury—The Civil Rights Act,* 30 F. Cas. 999, 1001 (W.D.N.C. 1875). Also see Sherry, *supra* note 5.
15. *Brown v. Board of Education,* 347 U.S. 483 (1954).
16. 42 U.S.C. secs. 2000(a), (d), 2002 (1976).
17. Sherry, *supra* note 5, at sec. 4:13.
18. N.Y. Exec. Law sec. 291 *et seq.* (McKinney Supp. 1982) is a representative state civil rights law extending prohibited discrimination beyond the federal Act, to include sex, disability, marital status, and extension of credit.
19. New York City and Chicago have adopted such legislation.
20. Sherry, *supra* note 5, at sec. 4:5.
21. *Id.* at sec. 3:7. *Cornell v. Huber,* 102 A.D. 293, 92 N.Y.S. 434 (2d Dep't 1905).
22. Sherry, *supra* note 5, at sec. 4:7.
23. N.Y. Civ. Rights Law, sec. 41 (McKinney 1976).
24. N.Y. Exec. Law secs. 297(9), 299 (McKinney Supp. 1982).
25. Sherry, *supra* note 5, at sec. 3:5.
26. See note 7 *supra.*
27. See, as representative legal authorities, *Young v. Caribbean Assoc., Inc.,* 358 F. Supp. 1220 (D.V.I. 1973) (resort dining room); *Peterson v. Haule,* 304 Minn. 160, 230 N.W.2d 51 (1975) (fast-food establishment); *Baker v. Dallas Hotel Co.* 73 F.2d 825 (5th Cir. 1934) (hotel).
28. The state of California is the only state thus far to outlaw discrimination in public places based on sexual preference. *Stoumen v. Reilly,* 37 Cal. 2d 713, 234 P.2d 969 (1951).

4
Liability I
Liability for the Sale of Foods and Beverages

Objectives

The purpose of this chapter is to:
1. Define areas of liability created by sales of foods and beverages.
2. Explain the role of the consumer law and the Uniform Commercial Code in the development of food liability law.
3. Contrast the theories for food liability claims.
4. Discuss liability to patrons and third parties created by the service of alcohol.
5. Discuss the various defenses to liability claims for the service of foods and beverages.
6. Identify management action to avoid liability.

Case in Point

Nancy Merrill orders a Super Sub in Gwynn's Gourmet, a sit-down delicatessen. The sandwich includes bologna, sausage, turkey, olive loaf, ham, and tomato, with either mustard or mayonnaise, served on a buttered French roll. She bites into the sandwich, and promptly breaks a tooth on what is discovered to be a section of the spatula used to butter the bread. Is the owner of Gwynn's liable to Nancy?

Probably. A section from a spatula is not naturally expected to be found in a submarine sandwich or any other food product. However, if the object Nancy broke her tooth on was found to be a sausage casing, the court might apply a different interpretation, saying that the casing, which is natural to the sausage, might occur in a sandwich despite the best efforts of the preparer to keep it out.[1]

LIABILITY

According to the law, *liability* is an enforceable responsibility one person has to another. Liability is not just there. It is *created*. Foodservice operators create liability by the careless preparation and service of food, poor judgment in the service of alcohol, and unsafe conditions in the operation. The good news is that since liability is created, it can be *prevented*.

FOOD LIABILITY: THREE THEORIES

There are three approaches a patron can take to recover for injuries suffered as a result of eating or drinking unfit foods or beverages. These three legal theories form the backbone of liability law for the service of foods and beverages.

The first is the *negligence theory,* a theory used under the common law. In its most basic form, this theory requires that the injured patron be able to prove that negligence on the part of the foodservice operator resulted in the food being unfit to eat, and in turn resulted in the illness. The common law negligence theory is still available as a recourse to consumers, and, if proven in court, can result in liability for the operator.

The second theory, and the most commonly used, is the *breach of warranty* theory applied under the Uniform Commercial Code. Here the patron is not required to prove that the foodservice operator was negligent in the storage, preparation, or service of the product, but only that the product caused the illness and that the seller breached the contract of sale by serving unfit food. Depending on which alternative of the Uniform Commercial Code your state has adopted, the operator may be held liable not only to the buyer of the food, but also to third parties who ate the food after the buyer brought it home. An advantage of the breach of warranty theory for foodservice operators is that they have recourse against the grower, producer, or packer of the food item if it was contaminated or unwholesome and the operator lost profits because it had to be thrown out.

Finally, *strict liability* is the most recent common law theory. This theory has evolved via a number of court decisions and is most favorable to the consumer, if not the seller. Strict liability does not require that negligence or breach of warranty be established, but simply that the unfit food caused the person to become ill. This theory rests on the assumption that the consequences of eating unfit food are so threatening to human health and life that the law requires that *someone* be held responsible for injury to a patron. That someone could be the grower, the processor, the foodservice operator, or all three.

COMMON LAW ROOTS: THE NEGLIGENCE THEORY

From its early development in England, the common law has been criticized for its lack of uniformity.

In the United States each local judge or court was given wide discretion to mold the common law to fit the particular needs of the locality.[2] These officials had control over the content of the law, subject only to the state appellate courts. Under our multi-state legal system, this meant that each high state court was free to formulate its own legal principles, subject only to that state's constitution and statutes.[3] Since the high courts of individual states were not required by law to confer with each other, the law in one state could, and often did, differ from the laws of other states.[4]

Nowhere was the lack of uniformity less desirable than in the area of commercial transactions, that is, sales of foods between merchants, and sales by merchants to consumers. In early England commercial transactions were dealt with through the *law merchant,* a system of rules and customs used by sellers of goods. The law merchant was the businessperson's law for handling business transactions and for the resolution of controversies. English common law ultimately absorbed the law merchant, and the common law was transferred to the American colonies in the seventeenth century.[5]

In its formative period the common law honored the widest degree of freedom of contract between sellers and buyers of products and services. Products and services were exchanged on a one-to-one basis, and the law adopted the maxim of *caveat emptor* (let the buyer beware) because every product was available for inspection.

The common law did not suffer the foolish or careless buyer lightly.[6] Each state applying the common law could treat the sale of foods as a *service* or as a *sale.* If a transaction was classified as a sale, there was an *implied warranty,* or unspoken guarantee that the product was fit for consumption. However, if it was a service, no warranty was implied.

Most often the transaction was a service. In the absence of deceit or fraud on the part of the seller, the buyer assumed all the risks of a purchase, and had legal recourse only if the product was defective or deficient and the defect or deficiency caused the buyer physical harm.[7] The *negligence theory* of common law required that the injured patron prove fault or intentional harm on the part of the food-service operator for the injury.[8] No warranties of product fitness were implied, because the courts, applying the common law, treated the transaction as a service and not as a sale.[9] The buyer was at the mercy of the seller unless the latter expressly (orally or in writing) guaranteed the fitness of the product.[10] For obvious reasons, very few express warranties were offered, since no one wished to guarantee product performance against all risks.

The law of the state where the foodservice establishment was situated governed the rights of the patron and the foodservice operator.[11] This meant that in each state the highest court was free to adopt the theory of service, for which no contract liability existed, or to treat the transaction as a sale with an implied warranty or guarantee that the food sold was reasonably fit for human consumption.[12] Under this *warranty theory,* the liability of the foodservice operator was extended to include members of the immediate family, and not just the patron who purchased the food.[13]

In terms of protection, the negligence theory left the consumer somewhere out in left field. Obviously it was difficult for the patron to prove that the foodservice operator was negligent in the storage, preparation, or service of the food. If the food had been contaminated at the source—by the processor or grower—the patron was out of luck, because the common law required that *privity of contract,* a direct contractual relationship, exist between the parties to a sale for the buyer to recover for injuries.[14] Second, the common law made the seller responsible only to the buyer of unfit foods and beverages, and not to any other injured person, such as a family member who ate the food later after receiving it from the buyer.[15]

These two common law elements of the negligence theory made it difficult for consumers with justifiable complaints. First, they only had recourse to the seller of the product, the foodservice operator, even though he or she might not have been the source of the problem. Second, negligence, even if it existed, was difficult to prove. As for the foodservice operator, the unhappy consumer was another lost customer.

The negligence theory may still be used by anyone bringing suit as a result of injuries from eating unfit food, especially if there is strong proof of negligence. However, the Uniform Commercial Code breach of warranty theory eliminated most of the problems consumers had with the negligence theory. The strict liability theory, which is applied by some courts, goes even further.

THE UNIFORM COMMERCIAL CODE: BREACH OF WARRANTY THEORY

After the Civil War, the industrial revolution took the United States into a new economic era. The transformation of an agricultural society into a vast industrial and commercial society added to the problems consumers already had with the common law. This was true because previously the producer and the seller of food products were often the same person. The seller dealt directly with the consumer, and the consumer who had a complaint knew where to take it—directly back to the seller.

Now, foods and beverages are sold through a complex system of middlemen, often with processing of the product at each stage from manufacturer to retailer. With the advent of a more advanced food distribution system, the common law was far too inadequate to protect the greater numbers of consumers who lacked the bargaining power to protect themselves.

During the nineteenth century, the need for uniformity in the commercial area was finally recognized. Legislation was enacted to supplement the common law and to overcome its limitations. With the coming of the industrial revolution, many states adopted more uniform laws, including sales acts. However, these laws were not collectively adopted by every state.[16]

Finally, in 1942 the Uniform Commercial Code project was set in motion by the American Law Institute and the National Conference of Commissioners on Uniform State Laws. Various official texts were adopted, the latest being the 1972 Official Text.[17] The Uniform Commercial Code is the most integrated and uniform law governing commercial transactions, and has been adopted by all states except Louisiana.[18]

The Uniform Commercial Code is the vehicle which unified the law on foodservice liability. Every food sale automatically comes with an implied warranty that the food is fit for consumption. It also extended the scope of liability to protect others in addition to the buyer. The importance of the Uniform Commercial Code is that *it imposes a stricter standard of foodservice operator responsibility than did the common law negligence theory.* Patrons no longer need to prove negligence or intentional misconduct to recover in unwholesome-food cases. Rather, they need only prove that the unfit food *caused* the injury or illness, and that by selling the unfit food the operator breached the warranty of the sale. Patrons can sue either the foodservice operator, the grower, or the producer. Privity of contract is not required.

The Code also offered some protection to the foodservice operator by recognizing the right of the retailer to sue growers or producers to recover any losses sustained because of their negligence.[19] This principle, called *equitable risk distribution,* was adopted by the drafters of the Code when their work began in 1942.

The Applicable Code

Section 2–314 of the Uniform Commercial Code (UCC), uniformly enacted into law in *all* states except Louisiana, specifically provides:

> (1) Under this section the serving for value of food or drink to be consumed either on the premises or elsewhere is a sale.

Section 2–314 also provides that:

> (1) A warranty that the goods shall be merchantable is implied in a contract for their sale if the seller is a merchant with respect to goods of that kind.
> (2) Goods to be merchantable must be at least such as . . .
>> (c) are fit for the ordinary purposes for which such goods are used.

Under this provision, the service of food or drink consumed either on the foodservice premises or elsewhere creates a warranty or guarantee that the items are fit. The service itself is a sale.

The UCC imposes an *implied warranty,* a guarantee independent of any express guarantees made by the seller to the buyer or to third parties. An *express warranty* is an oral or written guarantee made by the seller to the buyer.

However, *UCC section 2–318* provides three alternative provisions regarding who other than the purchaser (i.e., a third party)

may obtain the protection of the implied or express warranty. The states are not required to adopt this section, or its alternatives. The states may substitute their own language in place of this section, or they may do nothing, allowing the courts to decide the issue. Once the choice is made, however, the state courts are bound to apply the alternative selected in all appropriate cases (see Appendix E).

Alternative A. A seller's warranty, whether express or implied, extends to any natural person who is in the family or household of his or her buyer, or who is a guest in the home, if it is reasonable to expect that such person may use, consume, or be affected by the goods and who is injured by breach of the warranty. A seller may not exclude or limit the operation of this section.

Alternative B. A seller's warranty, whether express or implied, extends to any natural person who may reasonably be expected to use, consume, or be affected by the goods and who is injured in person by breach of the warranty. A seller may not exclude or limit the operation of this section.

Alternative C. A seller's warranty, whether express or implied, extends to any person who may reasonably be expected to use, consume, or be affected by the goods and who is injured by breach of the warranty. A seller may not exclude or limit the operation of this section with respect to injury to the person of an individual to whom the warranty extends.

These two sections of the UCC, when read together, make up the subject of product liability for foodservice operations.

Under alternative A, all guarantees by the seller, whether express or implied by law, extend to any person in the buyer's family or household, or to anyone who is a guest in the home, when it is reasonable to expect that they will use, consume, or be injured because of a breach of the guarantee that the product is fit. For example, John buys hamburgers, fries, and soft drinks at Sam's Hams and takes them home to his family. His daughter Fran eats one hamburger and gives another to her guest, Betty, who is having dinner with the family.

Both Fran and Betty can recover if the hamburgers turn out to be unfit for human consumption, and they become ill from eating them. However, Betty must be in the home of the purchaser, John, in order to recover. If she eats the hamburger outside the home (i.e., on her way to the home or after leaving), she may not recover. Alternative A is most favorable to the foodservice industry.

Alternative B eliminates the restriction on liability that the guest must eat the product in the home of the purchaser to recover from the seller. All persons are included, not just family or household members. So Betty could recover regardless of where she ate the hamburger. She would not have to prove that she ate it in John's home. This alternative strikes a balance between alternatives A and C.

Neither alternative A nor B permits corporations or other business entities to recover. Nor do they permit individuals to recover property damages or lost profits resulting from a violation of a guarantee of food fitness. In other words, Sam, the fast-food operator, could not recover from the meat manufacturer for profit losses associated with meat he purchased for preparation and service to his patrons, if that meat were found to be unwholesome and subsequently seized by the local health board. He could, however, recover for liability suffered when sued by John.

Alternative C provides virtually unlimited protection to third parties, and permits recovery for either personal injury or property damage. However, the seller may exclude or limit the operation of that liability for property damage or losses, but may not limit or exclude liability for individual personal injuries.

The reason for the three alternatives is to give each state a wide range in choosing the provision that best meets its commercial needs and policies *vis-à-vis* the competing interests of growers and producers, retail vendors, and consumers.

Alternative A is most restrictive in terms of remedies available to a third party beneficiary who sues a retail vendor. Only *natural persons,* and not artificial legal entities such as corporations, may sue, and the person must be a family member or guest who eats the food or beverage in the buyer's home. The majority of states have adopted alternative A (see Appendix E). Alternative A appears to offer more protection to growers, producers, and foodservice vendors, in that restrictions are placed on who can recover in terms of buyer status, on the location where the product was consumed, and on damages.

Alternative B widens the scope of alternative A by permitting any person to sue for personal injuries irrespective of where the unfit food or beverage was consumed. Alternative B opens the door to recover further by eliminating the requirements of buyer status and location of consumption, but maintains the other restrictions contained in alternative A.

Alternative C offers the widest scope of recovery because it applies to all persons, and includes artificial entities such as corporations. It permits recovery for both personal injuries and property damage, and allows sellers, including growers, producers, and retail foodservice operators, to exclude or limit liability for economic or property losses, but not for personal injuries. For example, a corporation may recover for a loss of profits associated with unfit foods, unless the seller limits or expressly excludes his or her liability.

For these reasons, alternative C appears favorable to growers, producers, retail vendors, individuals, and beneficiaries suing for personal injuries. The three sellers can protect themselves against property losses. The individual buyer or beneficiary can sue the grower, producer, and foodservice operator without being bound by any express or implied warranty restrictions. Each group of potential plaintiffs and defendants gets some degree of protection.

The Code in Practice

The need for proof of negligence or intentional misconduct on the part of the seller was eliminated by the UCC. The seller is now required to guarantee the fitness of every food and beverage product.[20] This places a heavy burden on the retail foodservice operator, who must guarantee the performance of food growers and producers, even though not involved in these activities. Obviously, as a foodservice operator you are not in control of what happens at the source of the food distribution system. However, you and your employees must exercise great care in inspecting incoming foods and beverages. You are the final link in the distribution chain, and your role should be to make sure the product is fit when you receive it and that it stays that way up to service to your customer (Figure 4.1).

A few courts have carved out an exception to the Code by judicial interpretation; that is, the implied warranty of fitness does not extend to products sold in sealed containers for resale to consumers.[21] Since most retailers further process foods for resale to consumers, the exception, even if applicable to food growers and producers, is not usually available to retail foodservice vendors. The only time you might encounter this exception is if you sell canned or bottled products directly to patrons.

Relief is not automatically granted consumers under the UCC, but is determined by the courts on a case-by-case basis. Either a jury or a judge decides on the facts presented in court.

Figure 4.1
The Ten Commandments of
Safe Food Service

1. When refrigerating potentially hazardous foods, make certain an internal product temperature of 45°F (7.2°C) or less is maintained.
2. Use extreme care in storing and handling food prepared in advance of service.
3. Cook or heat-process food to recommended temperatures.
4. Relieve infected employees of food-handling duties and require strict personal hygiene on the part of all employees.
5. Make certain that hot-holding devices maintain food at temperatures of 140°F (60°C) or higher.
6. Give special attention to inspection and cleaning of raw ingredients that will be used in foods that require little or no cooking.
7. Heat leftovers quickly to an internal temperature of 165°F (73.9°C).
8. Avoid carrying contamination from raw to cooked and ready-to-serve foods via hands, equipment, and utensils.
9. Clean and sanitize food-contact surfaces of equipment after every use.
10. Obtain foods from approved sources.

Reproduced by permission from Applied Foodservice Sanitation Certification Coursebook, *by the National Institute for the Foodservice Industry, copyright 1978. All Rights Reserved.*

The judge or jury basically has to decide three issues: (1) whether the food was unfit; (2) whether the unfitness caused the illness or injury; and (3) whether there was a breach of warranty under the state's UCC section by the seller.

Fitness under the Uniform Commercial Code

What is "fit" for human consumption? Normally any ingredient or object which is natural to the food product is considered "fit."

Two court tests are used to determine food fitness under the breach of warranty theory: the *foreign or natural test* and the *reasonable expectations test*.

The Foreign or Natural Test

The courts, in applying the applicable section of the UCC, usually apply the "foreign or natural" test to determine whether the food-service operator is liable to the injured patron. What would establish liability under this test? A stone or piece of glass embedded in a dinner roll would do so, since such objects are totally foreign to the food.[22] A cherry pit, however, *might* be expected in a cherry pie, and the restaurant operator might not be held liable if the court applied the "foreign or natural" test. In *Musso v. Picadilly Cafeterias, Inc.*, the court held that the vendor did not breach the implied warranty of the UCC because the cherry pit might naturally be present in a cherry pie.[23]

The following case gives one example of a court interpretation of the foreign or natural test.

Webster v. Blue Ship Tea Room, Inc.
Supreme Judicial Court of Massachusetts
347 Mass. 421, 198 N.E.2d 309 (1964)

Facts. Webster, a patron of the Blue Ship Tea Room, swallowed a piece of fish bone while eating a dish of fish chowder. As a result she required medical treatment for removal of the fish bone. She sued for injuries she suffered as a result of the bone getting caught in her throat. She argued that the fish chowder was unfit for human consumption and violated the applicable warranty of food fit for consumption established under the Massachusetts version of the Uniform Commercial Code (alternative A adopted). After a jury trial, the jury found for Webster. The restaurant proprietor made a motion for a directed verdict (a verdict made by the judge), which was denied. The order of the Supreme Court, denying the defendant's motion for a directed verdict, based on a jury verdict for the plaintiff, was *reversed* by the Supreme Court, and judgment entered in favor of the restaurant owner.

Reasoning.　The court said:

> We must decide whether a fish bone lurking in a fish chowder, about the ingredients of which there is no other complaint, constitutes a breach of implied warranty under applicable provisions of the Uniform Commercial Code, the annotations to which are not helpful on this point. As the judge put it in his charge, "Was the fish chowder fit to be eaten and wholesome? . . . (N)obody is claiming that the fish itself wasn't wholesome . . . But the bone of contention here—I don't mean that for a pun—but was this fish bone a foreign substance that made the fish chowder unwholesome or not fit to be eaten?"

By applying the foreign or natural test, the court found for the defendant, the owner of the Blue Ship. In doing so, the court pointed to the historical value of the chowder dish in New England and to several traditional fish chowder recipes, none of which mentioned fish bones or advised the preparer to check for or remove same. The court said that someone sitting down to eat a bowl of fish chowder might be expected to have to remove a fish bone.

> We are not inclined to tamper with age-old recipes by any amendment reflecting the plaintiff's view of the effect of the Uniform Commercial Code upon them. We are aware of the heavy body of

case law involving foreign substances in food, but we sense a strong distinction between them and those relative to unwholesomeness of the food itself, e.g., tainted mackerel (Smith v. Gerrish, 256 Mass. 183, 152 N.E. 318), and a fish bone in a fish chowder. Certain Massachusetts cooks might cavil at the ingredients contained in the chowder in this case in that it lacked the heartening lift of salt pork. In any event, we consider that the joys of life in New England include the ready availability of fresh fish chowder. We should be prepared to cope with the hazards of fish bones, the occasional presence of which in chowders is, it seems to us, to be anticipated, and which, in the light of a hallowed tradition, do not impair their fitness or merchantability. While we are buoyed up in this conclusion by *Shapiro v. Hotel Statler Corp.,* 132 F. Supp. 891 (S.D. Cal.), in which the bone which afflicted the plaintiff appeared in "Hot Barquette of Seafood Marnay," we know that the United States District Court of Southern California, situated as are we upon a coast, might be expected to share our views. We are most impressed, however, by *Allen v. Grafton,* 170 Ohio St. 249, 164 N.E. 2d 167, where in Ohio, the Midwest, in a case where the plaintiff was injured by a piece of oyster shell in an order of fried oysters, Mr. Justice Taft (now Chief Justice) in a majority opinion held that "the possible presence of a piece of oyster shell in or attached to an oyster is so well known to anyone who eats oysters that we can say as a matter of law that one who eats oysters can reasonably anticipate and guard against eating such a piece of shell . . ." (P. 259 of 170 Ohio St., p. 174 of 164 N.E. 2d).

Thus, while we sympathize with the plaintiff who has suffered a peculiarly New England injury, the order (denying defendant's motion for a directed verdict) must be (reversed).

Conclusion.   This is a classic foodservice case involving an alleged breach of an implied warranty of fitness under the Uniform Commercial Code. The Massachusetts decision (called the Massachusetts rule) established that unfitness, the key to liability, can be determined by the foreign or natural test. The unfit object must be foreign to the food product to impose liability.

However, the court was careful to point out that a breach of implied warranty of fitness would exist had the food itself been found *unwholesome*. In other words, when a food product is tainted, diseased, or putrid, the foreign or natural test has no application.

The Reasonable Expectations Test

The Massachusetts rule is still followed by the majority of states, but a growing number apply the reasonable expectations test. This test is applied to food in its final, processed form, and not in its original form.[24]

Under this test, the condition of the product served must be reasonable in terms of the expectations of the patron.[25] This means that a patron might expect a chicken bone in a serving of fried chicken, but would not expect to find a bone in a serving of chicken salad.

Under the foreign or natural test, the determination of fitness is made by the courts as a matter of law.[26] Under the reasonable expectations test, the determination is made by the jury as a question of fact.[27] Since juries are not consistent, the outcome of cases applying the second test is always less predictable.

STRICT LIABILITY

There is a growing trend for patrons seeking compensation for injuries from unfit food to ask the courts to apply strict liability. This judge-made legal theory, applied in some states, is generally easier for patrons, because it does not require that they prove negligence or breach of warranty on the operator's part. Patrons only have to prove that the food they ate made them ill. The law imposes a guarantee of food purity to the consumer without the need to determine whether an express or implied warranty between seller and buyer exists.

Where this theory differs slightly from the UCC breach of warranty theory is this: The UCC generally provides that patrons must prove breach of warranty and that the food purchased made them ill. Strict liability does not require patrons to prove a breach, only that the food made them ill. Once a victim has been established—that is, the injured patron has proved that the food was the source of the illness—the patron has legal grounds to recover.

The difference is one in law and not of fact. In other words, the law *imposes* liability, once the plaintiff has proved damages. The plaintiff does not have the burden of proving negligence or breach of warranty, using the two tests given for the latter theory. The thinking behind strict liability is that someone in a better position to pay should be held liable for injuries.

The Uniform Commercial Code is still the dominant product liability theory, with strict liability a growing one. The negligence theory is seldom used, but is available for patrons who can prove negligence.

THE THEORIES IN CONTRAST

Suppose that you purchase chicken salad from a well-known national distributor. Unknown to you, the salad contains chicken bones, which you cannot detect in the course of normal preparation. You prepare your dishes, using the product in your usual prudent manner and using your most sanitary preparation procedures. A patron orders and eats a chicken salad sandwich and the bones get caught in his throat, requiring his hospitalization. The patron sues you for medical and hospital expenses, lost wages, pain, and suffering. Can the patron recover under either the negligence, breach of warranty, or strict liability theory?

Under the negligence theory, the patron cannot recover against you. Why? Because you did not violate your legal duty to exercise reasonable care. You did not know, nor could you have known, that the chicken salad contained tiny bones and would cause the patron injury. Nor did you contribute in any way to the harm suffered. You complied with all reasonable sanitary standards.

According to the negligence theory, you are not liable for risks caused by the grower, producer, or packager of the product served in its original container, unless you cause or contribute to those risks.[28] You cause or contribute to a risk by knowing of the chicken bones and failing to warn your patrons or to remove the bones from the food. Since many food products you purchase for your restaurant are served "as is," except for heating and refrigeration, you would escape liability for any unfitness in the original product that caused harm to a patron. The injured patron would have to prove that your heating or refrigeration was negligently maintained, or that you allowed the chicken salad with bones to be served. It would not be enough to prove that the distributor was negligent in processing or packaging the product. In that case the patron would have to sue the distributor and not you.

Under the breach of warranty theory, all the members of the distribution chain, starting with the producer or processor, the distributor, and you, the foodservice operator, are liable to the patron if he or she (1) can prove that the food caused injury, and (2) can prove breach of warranty, using the reasonable expectations test. The law does not require the patron to prove negligence. None of the parties sued can defend on the grounds that they exercised all the care required of them under the circumstances, and were not at fault. Why? Because negligence is equated with a finding of fault. Breach of warranty does not depend on any finding of fault, only on the breach, since each party guarantees the fitness of the product for human consumption.[29]

The breach of warranty theory rests on a contract of sale between the patron and the foodservice operator. How then can the theory apply to the producer or distributor of the chicken salad, since neither party sold or served anything to the patron? It applies because the producer advertises the product for *ultimate* use by foodservice patrons, and is held to the same *implied* representation of fitness as is the retail foodservice operator.

One more important note: A service of a food or beverage is deemed a sale, regardless of *who* pays the bill.

Under the strict liability theory, both the chicken salad distributor and the foodservice operator could be liable to the patron. The strict liability theory imposes a guarantee of product fitness, regardless of any express or implied guarantee imposed by the Uniform Commercial Code, and does not require proof of breach of warranty. If the food is found to be unfit to eat, someone will pay, either you or the chicken salad distributor.[30]

DEFENSES FOR FOOD LIABILITY CLAIMS

There are four general defenses you may use if a patron brings a liability suit against you; however, not all these defenses can be used in every situation. The defenses are privity of contract, proximate cause, contributory negligence, and assumption of risk (Figure 4.2).

Privity of Contract

This defense limits your liability to the proper plaintiff or proper defendant. According to the negligence theory, only the buyer can take action against you, and not a family member who may eat the food after the buyer brings it home. In most states, third parties usually

can take action against you. In some states, however, there is still some confusion as to whether the UCC extends or limits who may seek compensation from the retailer.

The proper defendant must also be established. According to the negligence theory, privity of contract is required. The plaintiff whose only contract was with you, the seller, can take action only against you and not the manufacturer. In addition, they must prove that you were the *source* of the negligence. Patrons trying to prove breach of warranty would have to prove that you breached the warranty of implied or express fitness. However, in some states you would then have recourse to sue the manufacturer or processor to recover your losses.

Proximate Cause

Under all of the liability theories we have examined, the patron must prove that your unfit (unwholesome) product caused the illness or injury. This means that the patron must eliminate alternative causes equally likely to be the cause of the illness.[31]

The burden rests on the victim to demonstrate that (1) the food or beverage was unfit to eat; and (2) the unfit product was the cause of illness or injury.[32]

For example, if a patron went to another restaurant for dessert after having dinner at your place and had a French pastry, that patron must prove that it was your creamed chipped beef and not the pastry that caused the illness. Or if a patron is taking a prescription or nonprescription drug, there is a very good question as to whether the drug and not your food caused the problem. In *all* cases of liability the patron must be able to prove that the illness or injury was the result of your food or beverage product, and not from some other cause.

Figure 4.2
Typical Defenses Against Liability Claims for Foodservice Sales

Liability Theory		
Negligence	*Breach of Warranty*	*Strict Liability*
Privity	Privity*	Proximate cause
Proximate cause	Proximate cause	
Assumption of risk	Assumption of risk	
Contributory negligence	Contributory negligence†	

*Some states have different requirements as to who the plaintiff may be.
†In some states.

Assumption of Risk

According to this defense, the courts expect that the patron assumes risks when eating certain types of foods. For example, in *Webster v. Blue Ship Tea Room, Inc.,* the plaintiff should have assumed that a fish bone might naturally be found in a soup dish containing chunks of fish. The plaintiff would not expect that the dish contained a chemical contaminant. *This defense may not be used in strict liability cases* (Figure 4.2).

Contributory Negligence

This defense is only good against a negligence claim and is seldom used. Here the operator can try to prove that the patron contributed to the risk, by exposing the food to contamination, improper storage, or poor reheating.

Since these defenses are not all available for every liability claim, your lawyer should advise you (1) which type of claim the plaintiff is filing against you, and (2) what the prevailing judicial defense is in your state.

Every one of the defenses in this chapter is useful only *after the fact.* Your best defense is to exercise reasonable care by instituting and maintaining good sanitation practices and employee training procedures.

GENERAL MANAGER GUIDELINES: TRAINING AND FOOD SAFETY

The development of the law from English common law to the Code demonstrates a shift away from *caveat emptor,* let the buyer beware, to *caveat vendor,* or let the seller beware. This places a heavy responsibility on you to educate yourself, *and your employees,* to minimize liability.

Almost every foodservice operator will encounter some form of local regulation concerning sanitation. These regulations vary. Some may be so complete that if the operator follows the standards, he or she may be less open to liability. Others may keep operators out of trouble with the government, but since they do not provide maximum standards, still can result in liability.

It is up to the manager to adopt the *maximum* sanitation standards justified by cost and training. At the bottom line, operators should enforce sanitary procedures concerning time and temperature, and safe food handling (Figure 4.1). Food can be contaminated from the time it enters the restaurant until it is served to the patron. Sanitary procedures all along that route can prevent contamination.

Since you must guarantee the fitness of your food products, you are under a continuing legal duty to exercise the standards of *reasonable care*. You must anticipate, warn, and/or remove unreasonable risks of harm. You must regularly inspect your entire food-service operation to protect your patrons against disease due to impurities, contamination, and spoilage.

The "law" of logic maintains that you exercise reasonable care in the management of your operation and in the sanitary preparation of your food products. There are a couple of reasons for this: (1) You are less likely to encounter liability in the first place if you institute good sanitation and inspection procedures. (2) According to the doctrine of *respondeat superior,* or "let the master answer," you are legally responsible not only for your own actions, but also for the actions of your employees in the course of their employment.

LIABILITY FOR THE SALE OF ALCOHOLIC BEVERAGES

Alcoholic beverage sales have occupied a unique place in our social and economic development. Our puritanic social heritage makes drinking alcohol a vice and temperance a virtue. Our experience with organized crime during the Prohibition era of the late 1920s reinforced this historic social concern by associating the commercial sale of alcohol with criminal profiteering. When Prohibition ended, the combination of fears of mob control and persistent calls for temperance resulted in state regulation of alcohol sales through adoption of the Twenty-First Amendment to the federal Constitution.

Public attention recently has shifted from the specter of organized crime to spiraling drunk driving death and injury statistics.

Consumer groups are seeking to impose stricter control over alcoholic beverage sellers. Tougher dramshop and liability laws are being sought to compensate for injuries caused to both patrons and third persons by inebriation resulting from illegal alcohol sales by licensees.

Our purpose is to review what legal duties and liabilities licensed foodservice operators have to patrons and third parties as a result of liquor sales.

Common Law Liability

The common law placed the entire responsibility for intoxication on the consumer, and not the seller of alcoholic beverages. The theory behind this was that it was the *voluntary consumption* of alcohol by an able-bodied person that caused intoxication, and not the sale or service of alcohol.[33] Therefore, since the person knew or should have known the consequences of drinking, he or she voluntarily assumed the risks of intoxication, including any injuries suffered as a result.[34] In practice, neither the intoxicated patron nor any innocent third person injured by that patron, such as a child run down by the drunk's car, could recover from a licensed seller of alcohol.

A number of states have reversed this policy, either by court decision or by their legislatures passing statutes governing alcohol-related injuries.[35]

Statutory Liability to Patrons

Mostly, liability is covered through state "dramshop" acts or by court interpretation of state liquor laws. Disobeying state laws regarding the sale of alcohol leaves operators not only open to criminal prosecution, but to liability to injured parties as well, since persons bringing suit are often able to use the violation of the law as a support for their claim.

State laws especially pertinent to operator liability are those involving sales of alcohol to minors, intoxicated persons, or known alcoholics. However, the common law of most states still excuses operator responsibility to the so-called able-bodied patron.[36]

A minor is not presumed to be an able-bodied patron. Sales of alcohol to minors, forbidden by all states, may make operators liable to the minor or to the minor's survivors for injury or death claims. The law presumes that a minor does not have the maturity or drinking experience to know the risks of intoxication.[37]

The able-bodied definition does *not* usually include alcoholics or known drunkards either, and operators may be liable for injuries to these patrons, as well as any third parties they may injure. This is so because many states recognize alcoholism as a sickness. Some states even allow relatives of an alcoholic to give written notice to licensed operations, ordering them not to serve liquor to an alcoholic relative.

Liability to Third Parties: Dramshop Acts

Many state statutes do make operators responsible in damages to innocent third persons who suffer as the result of illegal sales of alcohol.[38] These statutes, called "dramshop acts," make operators liable to third parties injured because of an illegal sale of alcohol to a patron. They may be sued by third parties, or by relatives or friends acting on their behalf, for injuries, death, and, in some states, even for loss of support in cases where a spouse is killed or permanently disabled.

Increasingly, states are toughening dramshop laws in the face of public concern over high fatality rates caused by people who drink and drive. These laws and the public outcry that precipitates them place greater responsibility on foodservice operators to exercise prudent judgment in the service of alcohol, and to train employees to do the same.

Dramshop acts typically require the injured third party to prove the following: (1) an illegal sale of alcohol by a licensed seller; (2) that the seller caused or contributed to the intoxication; and (3) that the sale resulted in injury to the victim (see Appendix F).[39]

Injured third parties may have a choice of legal remedies to support their claim: (1) common law negligence for failure to foresee the effects of lack of good supervision of the premises; (2) dramshop act liability; (3) common law negligence for failure to comply with statutes designed to curb illegal sales of alcohol.[40]

The common law rule exempting licensed operators from liability to able-bodied patrons is not altered by dramshop acts unless the statute specifically creates such liability.[41] In a few states, the common law of negligence is applied whether or not the sale to the patron is made illegal by statute. These states hold that you must *foresee* that any sale to an obviously intoxicated patron whom you know intends to drive a motor vehicle creates a *reasonably foreseeable* risk of harm to other highway drivers or pedestrians.[42]

Liability can be expensive. Some states permit recovery of compensatory as well as punitive damages. Other states permit recovery of compensatory damages, and death claims to compensate the estate of the deceased third person.[43] A few states place a monetary ceiling on liability.[44]

Defenses against Liability for the Sale of Alcohol

There are few defenses to liquor liability to third parties.

As for liability to patrons, if the patron is an adult, and is not an alcoholic, then there are the defenses of *contributory negligence* or *assumption of risk*. Contributory negligence

Figure 4.3
To Serve or Not To Serve: That Is the Question!

The Basics

Keep count of the number of drinks consumed.

Keep close watch on behavior patterns after each drink is served.

Quite often you can sense or feel that the customer is becoming high. Don't hesitate—decline further service. There is always the problem of a negative response from the patron—but better obviously insulted than obviously intoxicated.

The key: When in doubt, don't serve.

Twenty Basic Signs of Intoxication

1. Becoming drowsy.
2. Drinking too fast.
3. Becoming loud, argumentative, mean, obnoxious.
4. Becoming entertaining, animated, boisterous.
5. Being careless with money at the bar or table.
6. Complaining about drink prices or check.
7. Spilling a drink—all or part of it.
8. Complaining about drink strength or preparation.
9. Being overly friendly to customers and/or employees.
10. Evidencing altered speech pattern.
11. Slurring words.
12. Annoying other customers.
13. Losing eye contact, concentration, focus.
14. Lighting more than one cigarette.
15. Letting cigarette burn without smoking it.
16. Having difficulty in lighting cigarette and/or pipe.
17. Losing muscular control, becoming clumsy.
18. Changing gait/walk.
19. Becoming detached; brooding.
20. Making too many comments about other people in lounge.

NOTE: Attorneys report that the signs of intoxication mentioned most often in liquor liability trials are loud voices, arm waving, and furniture knocked over.

Courtesy of the California Restaurant Association.

is based on the premise that an adult patron should know when he or she is getting "high" and should stop drinking.

Assumption of risk is a similar defense; patrons should assume risks if they consume too much alcohol. However, what is too much for an already drunk patron? After a certain point the patron might not be able to determine that, and it might be up to the manager, the bartender, or other service employees to do so (Figure 4.3).

In one landmark case, *Ewing v. Cloverleaf Bowl,* the California Supreme Court ruled that a liquor dispenser was liable for willful misconduct for serving a patron who had just turned 21, could not fully appreciate the danger of drinking large quantities of liquor, and died from acute alcohol poisoning.[45] In this case the court pointed out that the bartender (1) knew the patron had just turned 21 and was an inexperienced drinker; but (2) despite that, served him 10 shots of 151-proof rum, as well as several other drinks; and (3) exercised willful misconduct in his actions.

There are virtually no defenses to knowingly serving alcohol to minors. At the least, you may encounter a lawsuit or lose your liquor license; at worst, you may encounter a criminal penalty, including jail. Do not hesitate to ask for several forms of identification when in doubt. You have the right and the duty!

The following cases illustrate liquor liability under certain conditions.

Grasser v. Fleming
Court of Appeals of Michigan
74 Mich. App. 338, 253 N.W.2d 757 (1977)

Facts. A tavern owner served alcohol to an intoxicated, elderly compulsive alcoholic contrary to an agreement with his family not to serve him. After leaving the tavern, the alcoholic suffered injuries, which caused his death when he lost his balance and fell eight feet to the ground while walking on an unguarded, narrow concrete projection to a bridge. A wrongful death claim was brought on behalf of the alcoholic. The tavern owner moved to dismiss the claim on the grounds that Michigan's Dramshop Act was the exclusive remedy, and no action by an adult drinker was recognized at common law by the Michigan courts. The trial court denied the motion to dismiss, and this decision was appealed and upheld.

Reasoning. In this case the court said that the state's dramshop act did not prohibit "common law cause of action for gross negligence or willful, wanton and intentional misconduct in the sale of alcoholic beverages under the circumstances of this case."

The court pointed to an exception to the general rule of a patron's liability for his or her own actions, when "the customer was in such a helpless state as to have lost his free will . . ." The court said there was no reason to dismiss the case under the circumstances and that the plaintiff had "a cause of action for gross negligence and willful, wanton, and intentional misconduct independent of the dramshop act . . ."

Conclusion. This case illustrates the rule that you may be liable for selling liquor to

known alcoholics. Alcoholics are often given the same special consideration as minors, because of their inability to control their drinking.

1. Any willful (deliberate), wanton (reckless), grossly negligent (indifferent to the consequences), or intentional misconduct, which intoxicates the person, may give that person or his or her family the right to sue you.
2. Involuntary intoxication, when established, will also impose liability, even though the drinker is normally not able to recover for his or her own injuries.
3. Involuntary intoxication will not allow you to escape liability automatically as a matter of law by using the defenses of contributory negligence and assumption of risk. Contributory negligence and assumption of risk remain jury questions.

Chausse v. Southland Corp.
Court of Appeals of Louisiana
400 So. 2d 1199 (1981)

Facts. Three teenage female passengers were riding in a vehicle driven by a drunk, 16-year-old male who was sold alcohol at the defendant's licensed tavern. A two-car collision resulted in the death of one of the girls, injuries to two other passengers, and injuries to two persons in the second car. The passengers from the second car sued and were awarded damages. Plaintiffs also sued on behalf of the three teenage girls, but damages were denied them because the court found that the girls, by getting drunk and driving with someone they knew, or should have known, was drunk, contributed to their own injuries and assumed the risk of riding with a drunk driver. The plaintiffs for the three girls appealed that decision. The appeals court reversed the lower court's decision regarding the three teenage girls.

Reasoning. The appeals court found that minors served illegally do not contribute negligently to their own injuries or deaths. In such cases the law does not prohibit recovery by survivors or the minors themselves. The court pointed to the state's prohibition of liquor sales to minors as evidence of the legislature's intent to prevent risks like the one associated with the accident, and said that even in the absence of a dramshop act in Louisiana, recovery could be obtained on behalf of a minor, if not an adult.

Conclusion. This case illustrates the rule of the common law, that licensed operators who sell liquor to minors are responsible for injuries or deaths inflicted upon patrons and third parties, whether or not a dramshop act exists.

The key issues dealt with are the defenses by the tavern operator of contributory negligence and assumption of risk on the part of the female participants. The violation of the Louisiana statute making it a crime to sell liquor to minors imposes strict or absolute liability, making those defenses unavailable to the tavernkeeper or restaurateur. A Louisiana high court ruling that makes these defenses valid in cases involving adult drinkers does not apply to minors.

General Manager Guidelines to Prevent Alcohol Liability

In most states it is a crime to serve minors and intoxicated persons. This, coupled with the potential liability for illegal service of alcohol, should alert you to the fact that there is little room for error in selling liquor.

You are not expected to anticipate a patron's actions after leaving your operation. You are expected to try and recognize the danger signals and determine when not to serve.

Poor judgment in the service of alcohol is a serious source of liability, not to mention criminal prosecution for foodservice operators. *If you want to sell alcohol to increase your profitability, make sure you and your service employees use educated judgment on who to serve, when to serve, and when to refuse service.* Figure 4.3 gives some guidelines to help you recognize when a person has had too much. What may seem like an extra bill in the cash register or a tip to the employee might be one too many for the patron. Your service employees need to be trained in this aspect of their jobs. They need to be trained in how to refuse as well as when to refuse.

Refusing Service

When a patron has had enough, you have the right, even the duty, to refuse him or her more alcohol. There are ways to refuse service without offending the patron. With a combination of tact and common sense, you and your employees can refuse an intoxicated patron service politely, but firmly: (1) Do not say "you're drunk" or words to that effect. Do say "I can't give you any more alcohol. Would you like a cup of coffee instead?" If the patron asks why, say you are concerned about his or her safety. (2) Do keep calm and remain firm when refusing. Do not be swayed. (3) Do promote public transportation or offer to call a taxi when you know the patron has already had one too many. (4) Do, if a patron becomes loud, obnoxious, and/or abusive, politely ask the patron to leave. (5) Do not embarrass the patron. Many people can tell when they are drunk. If you make a big deal of it, you will probably offend other patrons. A patron who has been refused gently will be more likely to return—and stay sober.

One note of caution: Do not reverse an employee's refusal of service. If you feel an employee misjudged a patron, tell the employee later, but not in front of the person. Patrons may "bait" or challenge the reversed employee, making it even more difficult for the employee to maintain authority. More important, reversing such an employee decision will only make him or her less firm the next time, and any laxity could backfire in liability for you.

Serving liquor can increase your profitability and enhance your food sales, and once you obtain a liquor license, you are in business. Limiting your liability will help you stay there.

One final word: The following chapter discusses liability insurance. You need to request coverage for liquor liability, as it is not automatic in every policy.

SUMMARY

As a foodservice manager you are confronted with a variety of laws that govern the day-to-day conduct of your business. This chapter deals with one of the most critical in terms of your economic survival—your legal liability to patrons and others with respect to the service of foods and beverages.

Training is the key to prevention of liability for the service of both foods and alcohol. Knowledge must be shared with employees directly responsible for serving food and alcohol.

Today you are liable for personal injuries to whomever eats or drinks your products in the buyer's household. This liability is the *minimum liability* provided by the Code. Also, you may be liable for personal injuries to persons or to corporations for economic losses, such as lost profits. However, the patron may now sue the grower or producer. You need to adopt and maintain sanitation standards for your operation. Employee training is vital to such a program.

Alcoholic beverage sales by licensed dispensers can result in liability for injuries caused by illegal transactions in many states. As a manager of licensed premises you are duty bound to avoid sales to minors, persons apparently or actually under the influence of alcohol (or any intoxicated person), and known alcoholics or habitual drunkards. You may be liable to third persons who are injured or killed by patrons as a result of such sales.

QUESTIONS

1. Grant Mooney buys two chocolate malteds at Diane's for himself and his friend Karen. The malteds are contaminated with a chemical Diane used to clean the mixer, and which is not designed for that purpose. Both Grant and Karen become ill. Grant sues on the basis of the negligence theory and wins damages. If Karen sues on the basis of this theory, she would be unlikely to get far. Why? What theory should she use instead? Why?
2. What protection does the Uniform Commercial Code give to foodservice operators?
3. How would you suggest foodservice operators prevent liability for the service of food?
4. In what cases might you be held liable for *patron* injuries due to the service of alcohol?
5. Sheila Longyear was walking down the street near her home in California when she was hit by a car driven by Richard Pettit, who had been served one too many at Earl's restaurant and bar. Richard was (a) 16, (b) intoxicated, and (c) as he let it be known, was driving to a party from Earl's. What grounds does Sheila have for suing Earl? What would you suggest to Earl to prevent this problem in the future?

NOTES

1. *Webster v. Blue Ship Tea Room, Inc.,* 347 Mass. 421, 198 N.E.2d 309 (1964).

2. For example, Kentucky, in an early statute, prohibited the reading of English common law cases and reliance upon such cases as legal authority in any of its courts. Act of February 12, 1808, reprinted in 3 *The Statute Law of Kentucky* 457 (Littell 1811). The New Hampshire judges declined to listen to citations (of cases) from "musty old worm-eaten (English) books," and stated that "not (English) Common Law—but common sense" would control their decisions. Warren, *A History of the American Bar* 227 (1911). Also see *Wagner v. Bissell,* 3 Iowa 396 (1857), a representative decision where Judge Trumbull said: "However well adapted the rule of the common law may be to a densely populated country like England, it is surely but ill adapted to a new country like ours."

3. What these statements indicated is that the common law, unless adopted as the controlling law by state statute, was American common law based on the customs, condition, and usage of the people of each state.

4. See N. Dowling, E. Patterson, R. Powell, *Materials for Legal Method* 5–7 (2d ed. 1952) (Judicial Decisions and Persuasive Authority of Precedents from Other Jurisdictions).

5. The *law merchant* was a specialized court, originating in Roman civil law, that heard commercial cases only, for the benefit of persons engaged in commercial businesses in which the prevailing customs of merchants were recognized and enforced. The body of laws developed by the law merchant was international in scope, administered and enforced in France, Italy, Spain, and other trading nations, as well as in England. As early as 1543, the English common law courts absorbed the law merchant into the common law. As a general rule, the law merchant concepts were applied by the English common law judges in all law cases, unless the concepts were found to be unreasonable, in which case the common law judges refused to accept or apply them. In those cases the applicable common law rule was substituted. W. Walsh, *A History of Anglo-American Law* 362–68 (2d ed. 1932).

6. *Seixas v. Woods,* 2 Caines 48, 2 Am. Dec. 215 (1804) (sale of wood).

7. *Id.*

8. Intentional wrongdoing or negligence was the traditional common law tort theory of recovery. *Seixas v. Woods, supra* note 6, stresses the rule that absent proof of fraud or other misconduct, "the purchaser purchases at his peril." Negligent preparation of foods and beverages imposes liability upon a seller to a consumer of such products.

9. *Merrill v. Hodson,* 88 Conn. 314, 91 A. 533 (1914) (sale of food).

10. See Dowling, *et al., supra* note 4, at 167 nn.14 & 15 (synthesis of cases on the liability of a seller or manufacturer of goods).

11. Under a legal theory called Conflicts of Law, the place of injury traditionally determines the applicable law of liability. However, the rule favored by a growing number of courts is to apply the law of the place having the greatest *contacts* involving the injured party and the occurrence for which that party seeks to recover. See M. Levine, *Business and the Law* 8–11 (1976).

12. *Chysky v. Drake Bros. Co.,* 235 N.Y. 468, 139 N.E. 576 (1923).

13. *Greenberg v. Lorenz,* 9 N.Y.2d 195, 173 N.E.2d 773, 213 N.Y.S.2d 39 (1961).

14. R. Covington, E. B. Stason, J. Wade, E. Cheatham, T. Smedley, *Legal Methods* 159–61 (1969) (noting *Chysky v. Drake Bros. Co., supra* note 12).

15. The traditional rule is contained in *Chysky v. Drake Bros. Co., supra* note 12.

16. See Covington *et al., supra* note 14, at 260–63, quoting Schnader, *The New Uniform Commercial Code: Modernizing Our Uniform Commercial Acts,* 36 A.B.A.J. 179 (1950).

17. *Id.* at 264–67.

18. Louisiana has adopted only Articles 1, 3, 4, and 5.

19. This rationale is noted in *Matthews v. Campbell Soup Co.,* 380 F. Supp. 1061 (S.D. Tex. 1974), and by the New York Court of Appeals in *Randy Knitwear, Inc. v. American Cyanamid Co.,* 11 N.Y.2d 5, 181 N.E.2d 399, 226 N.Y.S.2d 363 (1962) (a nonfood case), citing and following *Greenberg v. Lorenz, supra* note 13.

20. See J. Sherry, *The Laws of Innkeepers* sec. 15:2 (rev. ed. 1981). See also *Matthews v. Campbell Soup Co., supra* note 19.

21. See D. Noel and J. Phillips, *Products Liability in a Nutshell,* 25–28 (1974).

22. *Spencer v. Good Earth Restaurant Corp.*, 164 Conn. 194, 319 A.2d 403 (1972) (glass particles in chow mein); *Cushing v. Rodman*, 82 F.2d 864 (D.C. Cir. 1936) (pebble in roll).

23. *Musso v. Picadilly Cafeterias, Inc.*, 178 So. 2d 421 (La. App. 1965).

24. See Sherry, *supra* note 20.

25. See *Matthews v. Campbell Soup Co., supra* note 19.

26. See *Webster v. Blue Ship Tea Room, Inc., supra* note 1 (liability based on negligence as well as breach of warranty).

27. *Matthews v. Campbell Soup Co., supra* note 19.

28. Restatement (Second) of Torts sec. 402, representing the rule adopted by the majority of state courts. A minority of state courts, including California and Texas, reject this negligence rule and apply the strict liability rule.

29. See Noel and Phillips, *supra* note 21.

30. *Matthews v. Campbell Soup Co., supra* note 19.

31. *Wintroub v. Abraham Catering Service*, 186 Neb. 450, 183 N.W.2d 741 (1971).

32. Sherry, *supra* note 20, secs. 15:4–15:5.

33. See *Vesely v. Sager*, 5 Cal. 3d 153, 486 P.2d 151, 95 Cal. Rptr. 623 (1971) in which the Supreme Court of California overruled its prior common law decisions exonerating the commercial seller or dispenser of alcohol from all responsibility arising out of the patron's intoxication.

34. See Recent Developments, *Common-Law Negligence Action Held to Lie Against Tavern Owners for Injuries Resulting from Illegal Sales of Liquor*, 60 Colum. L. Rev. 554 (1960).

35. *Vesely v. Sager, supra* note 33, abrogated the common law rule by its authority to alter its prior decisions. Other states, such as New York, have adopted dramshop acts making a licensed owner or operator liable to third persons injured as a result of the owner or operator's illegal sales to a patron. See N.Y. Gen. Oblig. Law secs. 11–101 (McKinney 1978 & Supp. 1982).

36. *Mitchell v. Shoals, Inc.*, 19 N.Y.2d 338, 227 N.E.2d 21, 280 N.Y.S.2d 113 (1967).

37. *Ewing v. Cloverleaf Bowl*, 20 Cal. 3d 389, 572 P.2d 1155, 143 Cal. Rptr. 13 (1978) (patron had just attained 21, legal drinking age). The court ruled that the victim could have assumed the risks of voluntary intoxication, but not alcoholic poisoning resulting in his death.

38. Sherry, *supra* note 20, at sec. 15:8, noting that Illinois, Iowa, Minnesota, New Jersey, Ohio, Oregon, and Washington impose common law liability on commercial vendors of alcohol. Nebraska and Wisconsin reject common law liability.

39. *Id.* interpreting the New York Dramshop Act. Each state is free to establish its own legislation, but these factors are representative of what the courts would require to sustain liability.

40. See *Paul v. Hogan*, 56 A.D.2d 723, 392 N.Y.S.2d 766 (4th Dep't 1977) (discussing the three theories and applying New York law).

41. *Robinson v. Bognanno*, 213 N.W.2d 530 (Iowa 1973).

42. *Grasser v. Fleming*, 74 Mich. App. 338, 253 N.W.2d 757 (1977); *Vesely v. Sager, supra* note 33; *Rappaport v. Nichols*, 31 N.Y. 188, 202–3, 156 A.2d 1, 9 (1959); *Berkeley v. Park*, 47 Misc. 2d 381, 262 N.Y.S.2d 290 (Sup. Ct. 1965).

43. See N.Y. Gen. Oblig. Law, secs. 11–101(1) (McKinney 1978 & Supp. 1982) (any injured party); *id.* 11–101(2) (specifying surviving husband, wife or child); *id.* 11–101(4) (specifying surviving father or mother).

44. A few states place a monetary ceiling on liability. Only California insulates licensed operators from liability, except in the cases of illegal sales to minors who injure someone or kill third persons [Cal. Bus. & Prof. Code sec. 25692(a), (b), and (c) (West 1978)].

45. *Ewing v. Cloverleaf Bowl, supra* note 37.

5

Liability II
Liability for Patron Safety and Property

Objectives

The purpose of this chapter is to:

1. Explain potential operator liability
   caused by unsafe conditions that lead to
   patron injury, or to loss or damage to
   property.
2. Outline the duty owed to patrons to
   maintain safe premises.
3. Discuss the defenses for liability claims
   for injuries to patrons or their property.

Case in Point

Laura Lee, a patron of your dining room, went up the stairs to your restroom located on the mezzanine level of your premises. On returning down the stairway, she slipped on the fourth step from the bottom and fell the remaining four stairs, lacerating her right leg on one of the lower stairs.

She sues, claiming that you owed her a legal duty to maintain the stairway in a reasonably safe condition, and that you violated that duty because of the presence of a raised metal strip on the stair which caught her shoe heel, causing her to fall and to be injured. However, during court testimony she admits she cannot remember what caused her fall.

Is this claim sufficient to result in a decision in Laura Lee's favor? No. It is not enough for Laura Lee to state facts, which, if proven, might *give rise to liability. In every lawsuit for liability the victim must prove that a cause-and-effect relationship existed between the incident causing injury and your responsibility. The mere fact that Laura Lee tripped and fell will not make you liable. As the owner or operator of a business, you are not an ensurer against all accidents occurring to patrons on your premises. Laura Lee admitted during her testimony that she could not remember what caused her to fall. This compels a finding of no liability on your part.*[1]

LIABILITY FOR SAFETY

As you read in Chapter 4, liability is the responsibility one person has to another that is enforceable in court.

For you, the foodservice operator, your liability consists of the duties and obligations you owe your patrons for safe premises, a safe environment, and safe food.

This chapter will concentrate on *your* liability and not that of your patrons, since it is your liability that can get you into hot water.

However, mention will be made of similar examples where you would be the wronged party and could consider legal action against someone else.

Some lawsuits arise out of statutory duties imposed by government regulatory agencies. However, many legal duties are created by the common law and enforced by the courts independently of any statute. We will deal with these common law duties.

TORT LAW

In common law, *tort* is a legal wrong caused by one person which harms another's person, reputation, or property. The tort arises from the responsibility one person owes to another. For example, restaurant operators are responsible for patron safety while the guests are in the restaurant. If an operator violates that duty, either intentionally or through negligence, the operator has committed a legal wrong, a tort, and the patron may hold him or her liable. A tort may or may not be a crime, depending on state and local laws.

Tort law rests on two foundations: a legal wrong has been committed and *compensation* is owed to the person who is injured as a result of the wrong.

THEORIES OF RESPONSIBILITY AND LIABILITY: INTENTIONAL TORTS, NEGLIGENCE, STRICT LIABILITY

There are three types of torts, and these three types of torts also constitute the theories for the nonfood area of foodservice operator liability, including liability for your own acts, those of your employees, and those of other patrons for injuries and property losses or damage suffered by your customers.

The first two types are classified by the circumstances in which a person deliberately wishes to harm another. A tort caused by *negligence* is one in which the wrongdoer, through ignorance or neglect, failed to prevent harm to another. If a bartender throws a glass at a patron and injures the patron, an intentional tort has been committed. If a patron slips on a glass and is injured, the foodservice operator may be liable for negligence, since the glass should not have been on the floor.

The third type, strict liability, is imposed by law, regardless of whether the incident was caused by negligence or was intentional. Strict liability applies only to extraordinary circumstances and is rarely used in nonfood cases.

Intentional Tort

An *intentional tort* is one whereby the wrongdoer deliberately wants to inflict harm or recognizes that the actions might result in harm to another person. The degree of damage or harm inflicted makes no difference. If you intentionally strike a patron, the fact that you did not intend to break his or her arm does not excuse you from compensating the patron for the broken arm. The intentional striking is the tort, not the *amount* of harm (the broken arm) you intended to inflict.

There are two kinds of intentional torts: (1) wrongs against a person and (2) wrongs against property.

Torts against Persons

The most typical wrongs are assaults and batteries against people.

1. An *assault* is any act or threat that creates a reasonable likelihood of harmful or offensive contact. The completion of the harmful act toward someone is a *battery*. A threat to strike a patron is an assault, whereas the act of striking the patron is a battery. A typical case is an incident in which two patrons have a go at each other in a bar.

2. *False imprisonment.* Another personal tort, false imprisonment, is interference with someone's right to move without restraint. Threats, as well as use of physical force, are included within the definition. You have a right to detain a patron who tries to leave without paying. This wrongdoing on the patron's part justifies the restraint. But if a patron is innocent of the attempt to skip, then he or she may sue you.[2]

3. *Mental distress.* This is another personal tort, and is defined as any intentional act, outrageous and extreme, that causes emotional harm.[3] Canceling a wedding reception without any notice would be an example.

4. *Defamation.* This tort involves injury to a person's reputation. It is a false statement or one made in reckless disregard of the truth. The statement must be given to a third person, either in writing or by word of mouth. Your shouting of the words "child molester" in your crowded dining room is an illustration of this wrong. A written defamation is called *libel.* An oral defamation is called *slander* and proof of damage to the victim is usually essential.[4] The common law definition of slander includes statements that another person has committed improprieties or engaged in serious criminal misconduct while operating a business or a profession. Statements by a disgruntled patron that you are selling narcotics to patrons in your restaurant is an example.

5. A tort similar to defamation, called *slander of title* or *disparagement of goods,* consists of false statements uttered about one's product, business, or property. Statements by a competitor that you use tainted or putrid food items in your restaurant is

one example. Communication to a third person and proof of damage caused by the false statements must be proved.

6. *Misrepresentation* (fraud, deceit) involves deliberate false statements or concealments of the truth for personal gain.[5]

7. *Defamation by computer.* This is a fairly new tort and involves false information disseminated either by a computer company or by the company that owns the information, such as a credit collection agency, or both. The company at fault is responsible. Erroneous computer printouts calling you a deadbeat would fit this category.

8. *Invasion of a right of privacy* includes the use of a person's name or picture for commercial purposes without permission, and public disclosure of private facts about another.[6] If the person is a private citizen and not a public figure, liability is more likely for this tort.

Property Torts

1. *Trespasses to land.* A trespass is wrongfully interfering in or invading another's property rights. No damages need be proven, since the tort is the invasion or interference itself. An example of a trespass to land would be your neighbor extending his or her business onto your restaurant operation. You need only prove ownership or the legal right to occupy the land to obtain relief.

2. *Conversion.* A taking, use, or retention of another's property without legal justification is called a *conversion* of that property—for example, if you borrowed an automobile for personal use and then used it, without permission, in your restaurant business. The injured party may recover the fair market value of the property.[7] An *intentional trespass* may be justified, however. Many states, for example, permit a garage owner who is not paid for work done

on a car to keep the vehicle until the bill is paid, and even to sell it if no payment is made. A similar right is provided innkeepers to ensure payment of guest charges. They may keep a guest's property until the room charge is paid.

3. *Interference with another's contract relations.* For this property tort there must be proof that you caused the violation of a contract for your own personal gain. For example, suppose you persuade a famous chef to breach an employment contract with your competitor. This would establish the tort of interference with another's contract, and any losses suffered by your competitor could be recovered from you. But if you did not interfere with the contract, but merely benefited from a contract broken by either the chef or your competitor, you are not liable.[8]

Tort Requirements

For a tort to exist there must be court determination that someone suffered an injury as a result of the failure of another person to meet a required standard of care. The following criteria must be established:

1. There must be a *legal duty* of care owed by the party causing the harm to the injured party. Tort law equates a duty of care with the *standard of reasonable care owed under the circumstances of each case.* In other words, what would a reasonable person expect another to do under the particular circumstances?

2. The person accused of wrongdoing (the tortfeasor) has done or failed to do something, thereby violating the duty of care owed to the injured party. For example, you may commit a tort by striking a patron yourself, *or* by failing to break up a fight between two patrons in which one patron

is injured, who then sues you for your failure to act.[9] Liability under the circumstances may rest on a number of factors: the nature of the act (how serious or morally wrong); how the act is performed (intentionally or accidentally); the nature of the injury (serious or slight); and the ability of the wrongdoer to pay.[10]

3. There must be *causation.* The wrongful act or failure to act *must* cause the harm for which the victim seeks compensation. If there is any other reasonable explanation for the injury that does not involve you in any violation of a legal duty, then you cannot be held liable. Sometimes the cause of the harm is beyond your control, and normally this fact will excuse you from responsibility. But if you contribute in any substantial way to someone's injuries by your misconduct, you may still be held liable to that person. For example, if an arsonist were suddenly to set several of your booths on fire, and a patron were injured, only the arsonist would be liable to the victim. *But* if your failure to report the fire contributed to the victim's injury, then some courts would impose liability on you as well. The fact that you did not cause the fire does not excuse you from liability for your failure to report it, if that failure to act aggravated or worsened the injury or harm.[11]

4. Legal *damages* must exist, or a loss or injury that would justify recovery for that loss. Without damages, there can be no compensation, *and no liability.* The scope of damages which justify recovery is broad. Physical injury, loss of physical security, and loss of freedom of movement, as well as loss or injury to property, are *tangible* forms of damage. *Intangible* forms of damage include interference with the right to privacy and damage to one's good reputation and to personal dignity. The law

changes in step with changes in society, by creating new legal interests and areas of liability.[12]

The victim is required to state and prove *all* of the four essential elements of a tort to recover under the tort theory of liability.[13]

Negligence Theory of Liability

Negligence is the most common liability theory. Negligence is actually an *unintentional tort,* and is usually the result of carelessness. Negligence liability applies to your liability for either property damage or personal injury. Most legal claims for injuries are based on this theory, since we do not usually intend to cause others harm.

To prove negligence for injuries, a patron must meet four conditions:

1. The patron must prove that the restaurant operator had a legal duty to protect him or her from injury. For example, someone who is trespassing on your property after hours or is there for illegal purposes is likely to be unable to prove you owed him or her a legal duty. However, a patron who slips on catsup in your restaurant might be able to meet this element.

2. The patron must prove that actions or failures to act on the part of the operator or the employees created an unreasonable risk. If a waiter spills salad oil on the floor, he creates an unreasonable risk for any patron passing by, and you might be liable.

3. The patron must prove that the negligence was proximately caused or contributed to by the operator. In the "case in point," Laura Lee could not prove proximate cause, because the mere presence of a raised metal strip and the fact that she fell were not enough to establish the owner's liability.

4. The patron must prove legal damages. A patron who is injured enough to require medical attention has suffered legal damages. A patron who is embarrassed but not physically injured by a fall will more than likely be unable to prove legal damages.

If your waiter knocks over a pot of hot coffee, which was too close to the edge of the table to begin with, and the coffee scalds a patron, you may be liable for negligence. Just because your waiter did not intend the coffee to spill does not excuse your responsibility to prevent it. An example of negligence for property damage would be carelessly spilling grape juice on a patron's clothing and ruining it. Carelessness can result in liability, despite your or your employees' best intentions.

The negligence theory of liability covers every possible type of event, including injuries caused by improperly maintained carpeting; defective doors, windows, furniture, and fixtures; and violations of statutory safety standards governing fire doors, flammable materials, and exterior and interior lighting.[14]

Strict Liability

Strict liability is the third major category of torts. This liability theory makes operators responsible for certain acts regardless of whether they were at fault. The fact that they acted reasonably under the circumstances does not matter.[15] This theory is not usually used in liability claims in nonfood areas, as only a few state courts will apply it for that use.

Strict liability normally applies to extraordinary, hazardous activities, such as the use of fireworks at a Fourth of July celebration. In nonfood cases, the theory involves three findings: (1) the activity is potentially extremely harmful; (2) the activity involves a degree of risk that cannot be avoided or minimized by reasonable care; and (3) the activity is not commonly performed in the locality.

Compensation for the Victim under the Three Theories

The common law negligence doctrine only requires compensation to the victim. No punitive damages are required.

The purpose of the intentional tort doctrine is to compensate the injured party *and* punish violators, making them think twice before undertaking the same activity again.[16] This is similar to the purpose of the criminal law: to punish and to deter misconduct.[17] The punishment for liability takes the form of punitive damages, similar to a criminal fine, which are awarded in addition to compensatory damages. In other words, you make two payments. First, you pay the victim punitive damages because of your wrongful act. Second, you pay the victim the court-fixed cost of the injury suffered. Crimes are punished by society for the benefit of society, whereas punitive damages are paid only to the injured victim.

The negligence doctrine and the strict liability theory allow only for compensatory, not punitive, damages.

Sometimes proof of negligence or of an intentional tort is not readily available, yet the law wishes to impose liability on you for your actions. The law does this by applying the doctrine of *res ipsa loquitur* (the thing speaks for itself); and uses circumstantial evidence of negligence in place of specific evidence.[18] For example, should a mirror fall from a wall of your foodservice premises and injure a patron, the patron, unable to prove you were at fault, might still win the suit if able to prove that (1) the mirror was within your exclusive control and supervision, (2) the injury suffered would normally not have happened but for your fault, and (3) the patron did not voluntarily cause or contribute to his or her own injury.[19] Another example would be that circumstantial evidence exists that the mirror was not sufficiently attached to the wall. This rule shifts the burden of proof to you to prove that the injury was caused by circumstances beyond your control. You are given the opportunity to dispute the presumption of fault this rule creates. Proof that the mirror fell as the result of an earthquake might be ample. If you fail to provide such proof, you will be held liable.[20]

DUTY TO PROVIDE SAFE PREMISES

In general, the law requires you to exercise reasonable care to protect patrons from personal injuries or harm to property caused by poorly maintained premises or lack of safety precautions. You must protect patrons against injuries due to defective, improperly constructed, or improperly supervised premises.[21]

You are required to obey local statutes regarding building codes, fire regulations, and safety. Not only will you avoid fines or criminal prosecution if you keep your premises up to standard, but you can usually avoid liability as well. Taking shortcuts with regard to building materials and safety precautions may seem attractive to your operating budget, but will hurt your bottom line if you (1) are fined for a safety violation or (2) are sued by a patron.

You are not required to take extreme and expensive measures to guard against each and every accident. You are only expected by the law to exercise *reasonable care* in the supervision of your employees and the management of your premises to help ensure patron safety. For example, if you notice that a rug in your lobby needs to be tacked down, and you do nothing about it, you may be liable if someone trips over it. However, if you do tack it down tightly and someone still falls, you are less likely to be held responsible. You performed the minimum duty the law requires.

Your only other option would have been to rip out the rug and start over, but the expense would probably not have justified such an action. If you know that your waiter dropped a bottle of catsup and swept the area before going back to work but did not mop it all up, you may be liable if a patron slips on it.

The test courts often use to determine a standard of care is called *foreseeable risk*. If you can foresee a risk and yet do nothing about it, you can be held liable for a patron's injury as a result of the risk. In other words, if you did absolutely nothing about the spilled catsup, you may be in trouble. On the other hand, if you swept up the broken glass carefully, mopped up the catsup thoroughly, and put up a sign warning patrons that the area was still slippery, you might escape liability to someone who ignores the sign, walks through the area, and falls.

A word of caution: What would be a reasonable standard for an adult patron might not apply to a child, since a child might lack the intelligence or experience to appreciate danger and avoid it.[22] For example, if you equip your premises with sliding clear-glass doors and do not mark them as required by statute, an adult patron still might be barred from recovering for injuries sustained in walking into the doors. Why? On the commonsense theory that the adult did not look where he or she was going, should have known better, and thereby contributed to the accident. But a minor might recover because of a lack of experience with such doors.[23] However, if the minor were old enough to understand the risk, or had been warned previously about it, then you might prevail.[24]

To establish negligence, the patron must prove the violation of a legal duty. Legal duties for safety include exercising ordinary care to protect patrons against unreasonable risks of harm.[25] The patron must prove both (1) that the operator knew or should have known of the unreasonable risk you or your employees caused, such as failing to clean up a spill; and (2) that the operator failed either to warn the patron, or to remove the risk, that is, the operator did nothing to prevent or curb the risk. The *reasonable person* test is applied to both requirements. The law only requires the operator to do what a reasonable person could do under the circumstances. In practice, this burden of proof excuses the operator from liability when he or she had too little time to anticipate the risk and do something about it.[26]

The following cases resulted in different outcomes for the restaurant owner/operator and will help to illustrate the reasonable care doctrine.

Kauffmann v. Royal Orleans, Inc.
Court of Appeals of Louisiana
216 So. 2d 394 (1968)

Facts. Kauffmann, a luncheon patron of the defendant's Rib Room, fell after being escorted to her table by the headwaiter and suffered injuries. Kauffmann sued. She claimed that the headwaiter was negligent in not warning her of the presence of an orange or lemon peel on the floor beside her table, on which she fell. The presence of the peel was disputed, and no one else could explain the cause of the fall. The trial court gave a judgment in favor of the hotel owner after hearing the evidence. Kauffmann appealed. The appeals court upheld the lower court's judgment.

Reasoning. The court said:

> We quite agree with the argument of counsel for plaintiff that Mrs. Kauffmann had every reason to believe that the headwaiter would not conduct her through an aisle that was dangerous or on which there was some foreign object on which she might slip and fall . . . That argument does not relieve plaintiff of the burden of proving there was negligence on the part of any hotel employee in carelessly dropping the foreign object on the floor, or that the employee had actual knowledge that such an object was on the floor at the time, or, if the employees had no actual knowledge of the object being on the floor, that the object had gotten on the floor by some other means and had been there long enough to constitute constructive notice or knowledge of its presence. We also agree that Mrs. Kauffmann was not required under these circumstances to keep her eyes constantly on the floor when she was following the headwaiter on that occasion . . .

> The issue before this court now is: Do these facts prove that the hotel employees failed to exercise reasonable care in its floor cleaning and inspection system and did Mrs. Kauffmann slip on a foreign object, the presence of which on the floor the employees had actual or constructive knowledge . . . ?

> We find that the testimony in our case is convincing that the hotel employees were instructed to keep the floors free of any foreign objects and that the system followed in the Rib Room was sufficient to enable the court to find and hold that the premises were kept in a reasonably safe condition. There is no evidence that the waiters, busboys, and porters did not perform the duties assigned them. The time lapse between observations and inspections of the floor make it reasonable to assume that the small piece of peel found on the floor could have been there only a very short time, probably only a very few minutes or few seconds. No one had seen it and we believe that there was no knowledge or notice of it and there was no negligence proven on the part of these employees. We are not even sure that Mrs. Kauffmann's foot slipped on the peel. It was not near her feet and it still had a fresh appearance. If her foot had slipped on it, it is most likely that it would have been crushed . . .

> Plaintiff has failed to carry her burden of proof; plaintiff has failed to show that the alleged extraneous substance on the floor of the Rib Room of The Royal Orleans was placed there by the owner or one of his employees, or if placed there by someone else, that the owner or his employees had actual knowledge of the presence of the substance

or that it remained in such a position of danger for such a length of time that the owner or his employees should have had knowledge of the presence of the substance . . .

For these reasons the judgment appealed from is affirmed with costs to be paid by plaintiff.

Conclusion.   This case represents the "slip and fall" variety of lawsuit lodged against restaurants, hotels, motels of all kinds, and other places of public accommodation and entertainment. What makes this case unusual is that it illustrates the point that unless a plaintiff can *convince* the jury that the injuries were caused by the carelessness of the owner, the defendant may prevail and avoid liability. Here the patron failed to prove that the owner was negligent in maintaining the dining room floor. Since the patron's accident could just have easily been caused by circumstances beyond the owner's control, she was not entitled to recover.

Ott v. Faison
Supreme Court of Alabama
287 Ala. 700, 255 So. 2d 38 (1971)

Facts.   Ott, a patron of a licensed nightclub, slipped and fell to the floor of the club while walking to a table. Sober at the time, Ott was burned by a thick sulfuric acid liquid substance found on the floor. The sulfuric acid was used for cleaning drains. She sued the owner of the club for damages, claiming that the owner failed to exercise reasonable care by leaving the liquid on the floor without removing it or warning her of its presence. The owner appealed a judgment given in Ott's favor. The appeals court upheld the lower court's judgment.

Reasoning.

There was introduced into evidence a red bottle marked plaintiff's Exhibit 2. There is evidence to the effect that in the bottle was a liquid substance containing sulfuric acid used for cleaning drains,

that defendant purchased the bottle, that defendant had stated to plaintiff that she fell in liquid drain cleaner which had been in the men's rest room and defendant had forgotten and left it there that afternoon, that the rest room was open to patrons of the night club and people who get intoxicated use the rest room, that the red bottle was on a table outside the rest room about an hour before plaintiff was injured, that after the injury there was liquid on the floor where plaintiff had fallen and the red bottle was found in a corner on the other side "of the table" next to the wall, that after the fall the clothes plaintiff was wearing smelled like sulfuric acid . . . There was conflicting evidence.

We are of the opinion that the evidence supports a finding that plaintiff was an invitee at defendant's place of business, that defendant breached the duty owed by a proprietor to a business invitee, and that defendant's breach of duty proximately caused plaintiff's injury.

Conclusion.   In this "slip and fall" case, all of the essential elements of negligence were established by the patron. There was enough proof of negligence to allow the jury to find for the patron.

The duty the defendant owed the plaintiff was to exercise reasonable care to provide for safety. Leaving a bottle of a substance containing sulfuric acid, a dangerous chemical, lying around the restaurant is not an example of reasonable care.

DUTY TO POLICE CONDUCT OF PATRONS, EMPLOYEES, AND THIRD PARTIES

Every foodservice operator, as an owner or occupier of business premises, is under a duty to exercise reasonable care for the safety of patrons. This general duty includes the duty to protect patrons from intentional injuries or other harm inflicted by other patrons, employees, or third parties.[27]

Third Party Actions

The foodservice operator is not totally responsible for the safety of patrons with regard to acts of third parties or other patrons. In a liability case involving a third party, the common law requires the patron to prove that the operator knew or should have known that the misconduct of a third party would cause the patron injury. If a restaurant manager knows or should have known that a sequence of events can cause others harm, then the law requires him or her to make every reasonable effort, as soon as possible, either to prevent the misconduct, or to stop it and remove the offending person. At the least, calling the police or summoning other help is required, especially in situations involving knives or firearms.[28]

Service of Alcohol

If you serve liquor, you must furnish a sufficient number of guards, bouncers, or security personnel to control the actions of others on the premises. No minimum number of security personnel has been established by the courts. Each case is examined on its own merits. One factor may be the existence of prior incidents calling for better security measures, which, if ignored, leave operators open to liability.

The risks of assaults, fights, and general misconduct are known to increase where alcoholic beverages are sold. This is due to the effects of intoxication on normally reasonable persons. Your duty to protect patrons is viewed by most courts as coinciding with such known risks.[29] The greater the risks you create, or allow to continue, the greater is the likelihood of your liability.

Employee Misconduct

The intentional misconduct or negligent actions of employees who injure patrons is governed by the same rules that apply to third party misconduct. The employee is always liable for his or her own torts.

To make the employer liable, there must be proof that the employee was acting within the scope of the operator's authority.[30] This legal rule is called *respondeat superior,* which means, "let the employer respond for the torts of his or her employees." This doctrine is critical to those bringing legal action, since without proof that the employee was acting with the employer's authority and knowledge, the latter may escape liability.[31]

However, employers have an independent legal duty to select competent and responsible employees. Those hired must meet both the physical and mental qualifications of the job. If the manager knew or should have known that a job applicant was unfit, and the unfitness causes injury or harm to a patron, the patron can sue on that basis.[32] In such cases, it makes no difference whether or not the employee was acting within the scope of the manager's authority.

Because foodservice owners and operators are assumed to be better able to pay for injuries inflicted by their employees than the employees are, some courts tend to stretch the rule to its outer limits.[33] This means that there is a greater potential for liability, as the following case illustrates.

Baldwin v. Wiggins
Court of Appeals of Kentucky
289 S.W.2d 729 (1956)

Facts.   The court stated the facts as follows:

> George Pope, a counterman in a Cynthiana restaurant called "The Lunch Box," owned and operated by D. C. Baldwin, sprayed or poured a flammable fluid used in automatic cigarette lighters on the shirt of Nelson Wiggins, a patron, and set it afire. Wiggins had dozed off while seated at a counter where he had drunk a cup of coffee. Pope testified that Wiggins had been drinking intoxicants, but Wiggins denied it. Wiggins suffered

burns that necessitated hospitalization for nine days. In his action for damages, the jury returned a verdict for the plaintiff for $1,274.50, with the added provision that the defendant, Baldwin, should pay $1,200 and Pope, the counterman, should pay $74.50. The plaintiff had incurred doctor and hospital expenses of $174.50 . . .

The proprietor, Baldwin, was not present on this occasion and Pope was in charge of the restaurant. This sort of vicious and savage horseplay had been going on for about four years. Baldwin admitted he had personally engaged in it. He stated that this was the first time any harm had resulted and attributed the plaintiff's injury to the fact that he had run in front of a fan.

The jury found for the plaintiff, Wiggins. The trial court denied the defendant's motion for a new trial and entered judgment for the plaintiff. The defendant appealed. The judgment for the plaintiff (Wiggins) was affirmed by the appeals court.

Reasoning.   The court said:

This case is not within the principle, as the [defendant] contends it is, that a master is not legally liable for a wrongful act of his servant which was outside of the scope of his employment or not within the contemplation or the service of his employment. The case is under the rule that where an employer leaves one in charge of his business during his absence and that one wrongfully does something to injure a patron, which the employer has reason to know he may do, the employer is liable therefor. He is deemed to have delegated his obligation to protect and not to harm the patron. The [defendant's] liability clearly comes within the latter rule . . .

In *Bauman's Adm'r v. Brown & Williamson Tobacco Corp.,* 305 Ky. 344, 204 S.W. 2d 327, an employee, as a prank, threw alcohol inside a fellow workman's trousers. Another man, in a spirit of fun, threw a lighted match on the floor and it ignited the alcohol. The flames spread and caused the victim's death. We held there was no liability on the employer because it had had no notice that its workmen had been engaging in any such prank or horseplay that would endanger life or cause injury. But in the present case the proprietor had set

the example for his employees to follow and knew they were doing it. He had thereby countenanced and sanctioned such vicious horseplay as a distorted sense of fun in his restaurant. Its inherent danger presaged injury . . . The court properly overruled the defendant's motion for a peremptory instruction . . . The liability for all damages is inseparable as between the employer and the employee.

Conclusion.   This case is a novel example of criminal misconduct on the part of an employee resulting in injury to a patron where the restaurant owner/employer was forced to compensate the victim. Even though the owner was not on the premises at the time of the injury, *he was held legally responsible for the actions of his counterman, Pope, who was the person in charge.* The fact that the infliction of injury was bizarre was held not to be a defense, since the owner knew of, and in fact had engaged in, similar past "pranks."

The court applied the common law doctrine of *respondeat superior,* which makes employers liable for the negligence of their employees, even though the employer may not be directly at fault.

The case alerts foodservice operators to train and supervise employees, and to place only competent, responsible people in charge when the managers must be absent.

In the following similar case, the court applied a different interpretation and reversed the original trial court judgment against the owner and operator of the tavern. Can you determine the difference?

Schwingler v. Doebel
Supreme Court of Minnesota
309 N.W.2d 760 (1981)

Facts.   Schwingler, a patron at the Earl and Dorothy Tavern, sued Doebel individually, the owning corporation, and the sole shareholder and bartender, Earl McQuiston, for Doebel's assault upon Schwingler while Doebel was employed as a liquor server. The assault took place outside the tavern. Schwingler claimed that all defendants were responsible, either because Doebel was acting within the scope of his employment or, independently, because as owners and operators of the tavern they failed to maintain a reasonably safe place for their patrons. The trial court awarded a default judgment—a judgment awarded where the defendant fails to appear and defend the action—for Schwingler against Doebel, and at the next trial, found for Schwingler against the remaining defendant, McQuiston. He appealed.

> The testimony of plaintiff, McQuiston, and Doebel is in sharp conflict. According to plaintiff, he entered the tavern shortly after midnight July 18, 1975, and sat between a couple at one end of the L-shaped bar. Doebel was then standing near a bartender's stool at that end of the bar, and plaintiff assumed Doebel was an employee when he served the three beers for which the couple paid. Doebel again waited on the three when plaintiff ordered a second round. After serving the couple, he suddenly threw the beer in the glass he brought the plaintiff in plaintiff's face. Plaintiff tossed the remaining beer in his first glass at Doebel and left the tavern immediately, telling his companions that he would not buy beer there. McQuiston was working at the bar about five feet away when this incident occurred.
>
> Plaintiff then crossed the street and entered his parked automobile. As he started it, Doebel approached, thrust his arm through the window on the driver's side of the vehicle, and struck plaintiff several times on the head. Doebel then opened the door and attempted to drag plaintiff from the automobile, striking him on the shoulder and left arm. When he could not remove plaintiff from the automobile, Doebel then cracked the steering wheel and broke some switches on the dash. Plaintiff was bruised and dazed as a result of the incident, subsequently sought medical attention, and still suffers headaches. He testified that Doebel was intoxicated that evening and generally was "known for trouble."

> Doebel testified that he was not working for the other defendants but had served plaintiff a beer because McQuiston, the only bartender, was busy and plaintiff was impatient. He said that some of the second beer was accidentally spilled on plaintiff's shirt whereupon plaintiff threw the rest of it in Doebel's face and subsequently "antagonized" him further before leaving. Doebel denied following plaintiff from the tavern and said they met across the street and plaintiff then called him bad names and hit him, in response to which Doebel walked plaintiff to his automobile and slapped him. He said also that plaintiff was intoxicated and had started fights on other occasions.
>
> McQuiston testified that Doebel had been employed as a bartender in 1970 but not since then and was not employed that evening. McQuiston admitted that he knew Doebel had been convicted of aggravated assault and was quick tempered. He also said that Doebel had never been violent while in the tavern and was not intoxicated that evening. He knew that Doebel had occasionally taken drinks while employed and that after his employment terminated he would occasionally go behind the bar to make himself drinks. He denied seeing Doebel serve himself or others that evening, although he stated that it was possible Doebel might "grab a beer." McQuiston said he heard no loud remarks by either Doebel or plaintiff, did not see the beer-throwing incident, did not see plaintiff leave the building, and knew nothing that evening about the assault across the street. A customer who had sat at the bar much of the evening said she did not see or hear any confrontation between plaintiff and Doebel.
>
> A disinterested witness . . . who was seated in a parked automobile near the tavern, corroborated plaintiff's testimony concerning the assault outside the tavern. She testified that Doebel emerged from the tavern a few minutes after plaintiff had done so and that plaintiff had entered and started his automobile when Doebel approached and began striking him. Another witness who had been in plaintiff's company until 10:45 p.m. that evening said that plaintiff had nothing to drink during that time.

The judgment of the trial court in favor of the plaintiff (Schwingler) against the bartender and the owner/operator of the tavern was *reversed* and *remanded* (sent back) to the trial court for entry of judgment in favor of the defendant.

Reasoning. The appeals court said that simply because Doebel had waited on the plaintiff with the knowledge of the other defendants, did not justify imposing liability on McQuiston and the owner. The court pointed out that Doebel had acted out of a "deep personal animosity" toward the plaintiff, and not within the scope of this "volunteer employment." They further pointed out that Doebel was outside of the tavern. The court said that while Doebel had an assault record, he had, according to testimony, never been unruly at the tavern either previously or on the night of the incident, and the bartender had no way of foreseeing the incident. Finally, there was no evidence that the bartender could have stopped the incident, as there was no verbal threat inside the tavern.

Conclusion. The case is important because it illustrates a situation in which the appeals court refused to apply the doctrine of *respondeat superior,* sparing the owner substantial liability.

1. The case upholds the rule that both the employee, as the wrongdoer, and employer, under *respondeat superior,* may be responsible for injuries inflicted by the employee upon a patron, if, in fact, the employee was liable and *was acting within the scope of the employment.*
2. The case establishes that neither the employee nor the employer was liable because (a) the person making the assault was not a regular, full-time employee; (b) the assault took place off the premises; and (c) the bartender was motivated by personal animosity toward the patron.

3. The case applies the rule of *foreseeable* unreasonable risks and concludes that the sudden, violent assault of the patron off the premises was not foreseeable by the owner/operator, requiring the conclusion that the premises were not unsafe or disorderly.

Removing Unruly Patrons

There are times, especially in operations with bars, when unruly patrons will have to be removed. *Do not use physical force.* When removing a bothersome patron, your employee must use only such reasonable force as required. The use of unnecessary force will expose both employee and employer to liability. If you or your employees have trouble removing a patron through vocal persuasion or by gently guiding him or her out, call the police and let them handle it. Unless the patron is harming or threatening to harm either yourself, your employees, or other patrons, you could be liable for unnecessary force used in removing the person. If you err, do so on the side of caution.

Liability for Inaction

One more thing that should serve to alert: You are just as responsible for your *failures to act* as for your actions. If you do nothing after a patron is injured, or watch a patron being hurt by another person, you may be held liable for your inaction. At minimum, if you are unable to provide help directly, you should summon help quickly and make the injured patron as comfortable as possible.

At the least, you should make sure you and your employees know how to obtain help. Post emergency numbers, including yours, near the telephone and near service work stations.

Taking appropriate action quickly can make a difference between no liability, low liability, and going to the cleaners.

What the Law Expects

In a public service business, you are expected by the law to anticipate and react to trouble much more rapidly than the usual business-person.[34] You deal with many people and many types of people in the operation of your business. This fact requires you to stop any disturbance by removing the people responsible or summoning help quickly.[35] If you sell alcohol, you must be constantly on the lookout for trouble. Not all patrons will misbehave, but you must deal with those who do. Since risks are more likely to be present because of the nature of your business, you must foresee them.

Patrons are entitled to assume that your premises are and will remain reasonably safe and that your supervision of the premises will foster congenial surroundings and good food and drink.[36] The law does not expect you to anticipate every risk. It does require you to remove or warn of such risks once they are known to you.[37] No set formula exists for doing so. The best rule of thumb is: At the first sign of trouble, call for help.

DEFENSES AGAINST LIABILITY CLAIMS FOR INJURIES

The only defense you have against strict liability claims is to prove that the injury did not take place on your premises, but somewhere else.

There are three general defenses to liability claims based on torts or negligence. These defenses may be used simultaneously or alone. The critical thing to remember is that the burden of proving the defense is on you, the defendant.

The first defense is that the original negligence was not the cause of the harm because it was followed by an *unforeseeable cause* that was the direct cause of the harm. For example, if you store flammable materials in your fast-food operation, it is foreseeable that a patron might be injured if the materials are ignited by a careless employee, and you might be liable. However, if the materials are ignited by an act of God, such as lightning, which you cannot reasonably foresee, you might escape liability. When you either create a foreseeable and unreasonable risk of harm *or* contribute to an unforeseeable risk by careless conduct, such as failing to call the fire department or installing flammable furnishing in violation of the building code, then you may be held liable. The test of the liability is whether your careless conduct made the harm more serious.[38] Since each case is judged on its own facts, no general rule is available that will cover every situation.

A second defense to liability claims for intentional torts or negligence is that of *contributory negligence* or *comparative negligence*. At common law everyone was expected to use reasonable care in looking out for one's own well-being. If the victim contributed at all to his or her injuries or losses, the common law made the defendant's proof of that contribution a complete defense to the claim. This was true regardless of the degree of negligence.[39] To balance the law between the injured party and the defendant, most states have passed statutes that create a *comparative negligence rule*. Under this rule, a jury must assign a percentage to the victim's carelessness in comparison with your carelessness and then reduce the victim's total recovery by the dollar amount of that percentage.[40] For example, if a patron won a judgment of $1000 against you, but the jury found that the patron was 10 percent negligent, the patron would recover only $900 ($1000 less 10 percent = $900) from you.

The third defense is called *assumption of risk*. When a patron knows that a risk of harm exists *and* voluntarily takes that risk, that patron assumes that risk and may not recover.

For example, if an adult patron walks up a stairway you have blocked with a rope and a sign, you may not be held liable because the patron ignored the sign and assumed the risk. If a child walks up the same stairs, however, you may be held liable, because the child could not be expected to recognize a risk. You must prove the patron knew of a risk and took voluntary action based on that knowledge.[41] There are exceptions, however. If you force a risk on a person by your own fault, such as your unlawful blocking of a fire exit, and a fire forces the use of that exit, you are responsible. This result occurs even though under normal circumstances the exit was adequate.[42] In emergencies assumption of risk is not considered a defense.[43] Nor does it apply to situations involving a violation of statutes intending to protect patrons from the risks, such as one requiring an adequate number of fire exits.[44] The knowledge of possible risks is evaluated by courts on the basis of the patron's particular age, maturity, and general intelligence.[45] If your restaurant caters to families with young children, the sign and the rope to warn people away from the stairs would be inadequate. You would have to take stronger steps to protect yourself against liability and your small patrons against injury.

All of the defenses described above must be set up and proved by you in court. They are not automatically granted. If you fail to plead and prove these defenses, the plaintiff will win the lawsuit.[46]

DUTY TO SAFEGUARD PROPERTY OF PATRONS

Unlike innkeepers, foodservice operators are only required to exercise reasonable care in protecting patron property handed over to them for safekeeping.[47] Innkeepers must ensure guest property against virtually all risks, subject only to ceilings imposed to protect them against excessive liability.[48] Only the hotel guest is entitled to strict liability for the loss of or damage to property.[49]

To protect patron property, you should:

1. Supervise the premises to prevent thefts or other losses of property.[50]
2. Supervise the service of foods and beverages by employees and try to halt careless actions that might result in damage to patron property.[51]
3. Guard carefully property deposited with you for safekeeping. You have the additional responsibility to return the property in the same condition as when deposited.[52]

The third form of responsibility is called a *bailment,* meaning a voluntary transfer of personal property to another for safekeeping. The checking of a coat with your checkroom attendant is a typical bailment. You are under no legal duty to accept any property for safekeeping. Once you do so, however, you are liable for loss or damage unless you can prove that the loss of or damage to the property under your care was caused by circumstances beyond your control, such as a flash flood or nearby fire.[53]

Unlike innkeepers, foodservice operators do not have to accept patron property just because they admit the patron. Once they have admitted the patron, however, *and* accepted the coat, wrap, or briefcase, the restaurant is liable for the full established price of the item at the time it was lost.[54]

The distinction between innkeepers and foodservice operators regarding property is this: Foodservice operators are not responsible for patron property, *unless* they voluntarily accept the responsibility, such as through a check system, *or,* in the absence of such a system, the patron can prove that the restaurant operator or the employees did not exercise reasonable care in protecting the property from damage or loss.

Your responsibility depends in part on the nature of your operation. A first-class French restaurant is expected to exercise more care in safeguarding patron property than is a fast-food operation. Patrons of the former would expect to have a coat checkroom, whereas patrons of the fast-food operation would expect to keep their coats with them.

When patrons keep property under their own supervision, you are not liable for loss of or damage to the property unless the patron can prove that you failed to exercise *reasonable* care in safeguarding it.[55] In every case where the disappearance of or damage to the property cannot be explained, the party having the burden of proof loses that case.[56] If a patron keeps the coat while eating, and the coat is lost, the patron loses. When the coat is left with an attendant, in the bailment case, the operator loses.

The key element in the creation of a bailment is your *voluntary acceptance* of the property for the purpose of exercising *exclusive* supervision and control. Simply stated, a bailment cannot be imposed on you without your consent. (An exception: Your consent is *implied* when an employee finds patron property left behind and turns it over to you for return to the patron.)[57]

What about bailment for the *contents* of a bag, briefcase, or similar container? If you are told the nature of the contents and/or their value, and you voluntarily accept the contents, as well as the bag, for safekeeping, you are liable for the value of bag and its contents. When you are not told of the contents or their value, you are only liable for the value of those items which you may reasonably expect to be present—a scarf and gloves in an overcoat, but not a $1 million negotiable stock certificate. This commonsense rule varies in its application with the size, kind, and class of establishment you operate. The larger the size, the higher the class or nature of your business, the greater is the potential liability

for property losses. This means that you may expect your wealthy clientele to carry larger amounts of valuables than patrons of a more modest establishment.[58]

Is a bailment created when you permit patrons to hang their own coats and leave other articles on open racks? No, since the requirement of exclusive control and supervision by you is not present.[59] However, to protect yourself, you should always put up a prominent sign or notice as follows: "Not responsible for property unless checked with the Management." This will not ensure you against liability, but will go far toward strengthening your case should the patron sue you.[60]

If an employee takes a patron's property and hangs it or deposits it out of sight of the patron, a bailment may be created.[61] Why? Because the patron is unable to exercise control and supervision over the property. Only you and your employees can see it and supervise it.

If you voluntarily accept patron property for deposit in a checkroom or cloakroom, can you issue a claim check or stub conditioning acceptance of the article on the patron releasing you from a liability claim? No. Public policy in some states forbids those who make bailments in the normal course of their business to waive liability.[62]

Many first-class operations park their patrons' cars for them. This is considered a bailment, and the restaurant owner may be liable not only for the loss of the car itself, but for any property in it.

Diplomat Restaurant, Inc. v. Townsend
Court of Appeals of Georgia
118 Ga. App. 694, 165 S.E.2d 317 (1968)

Facts.   The court stated the facts as follows:

Dr. Robert Townsend, Dianne Townsend, and Sherry Fitts brought this suit against Diplomat Restaurant, Inc., to recover the value of personal property stolen while they were guests in the defendant's restaurant. The property was taken from an automobile which one plaintiff had delivered to defendant's employee to be parked in facilities operated by the defendant.

An earlier judgment was in favor of the plaintiff and held the defendant responsible for loss of the property. Defendant contended on appeal that the judgment for each plaintiff was excessive because its liability to each was limited to $100 by Code sec. 52–111.

The judgment for the plaintiff without any limitation of liability was *affirmed* on appeal.

Reasoning: Bell, P. J.:

> The pertinent portions of Code sec. 52–111 (Ga. L. 1922, p. 52) are: "The liability of the innkeeper for loss or for injury to personal property placed by any guest under his care . . . shall not exceed the sum of $100: Provided . . . that the innkeeper shall post a copy of this section printed in distinct type on the inside of the door of the guest's room." We think it clear from the quoted proviso that the Act of 1922 was intended to apply only to houses of public entertainment furnishing lodging to a guest. See *Walpert v. Bohan,* 126 Ga. 532, 534, 55 S.E. 181, 6 L.R.A., N.S., 828. Obviously, as defendant merely operated a restaurant and a bar for serving liquors, it could not introduce evidence of the notice required by Code sec. 52–111. This Code section was not effective to limit defendant's liability.

Conclusion.   This case illustrates the common law rule that innkeeper's liability statutes limiting liability for the loss of guest property are intended to benefit innkeepers only. Restaurant keepers are not included, irrespective of the fact that both restaurants and inns serve members of the public.[63]

Defenses against Liability Claims for Property

The most significant defense to liability claims for property is to establish whether or not a bailment was created. If a bailment was created, the operator must prove that he or she exercised reasonable care to protect the property.

Where no bailment is created, the patron has the burden of proving negligence. However, the operator must still prove that reasonable care was used and that he or she did nothing to place the property in a risky situation. If an employee sees someone taking a coat known to be another patron's and does nothing, the operator may be liable for the loss.

COMMON LAW EXCEPTIONS TO LIABILITY

Foodservice operators and operators of most other types of business are not liable for events over which they have absolutely no control. Such acts include acts of God, or natural catastrophes such as a flood, tornado, or hurricane. Also included are acts of a public enemy, either through war, civil disorder, or martial law, over which the foodservice operator has no control.[64] Another general category would include airplane crashes or spilled dangerous gases or liquids—other humanly caused acts—for which others, not the foodservice operator, would be liable.

INSURANCE GOVERNING PUBLIC LIABILITY

You can buy liability insurance to protect your business against the legal claims of patrons. There are four types of importance to foodservice operators:

1. *Fire insurance* is intended to protect your property against the risks of fire and other related perils, such as windstorms, lightning, or earthquakes caused by natural elements or in case of fires caused by arson or other human activity.
2. *Casualty insurance* is intended to protect your personal property from acts other than

fire and the elements. These acts are usually caused by humans, and include strikes and robberies.

3. *Dramshop liability insurance* may be sold in those states which have dramshop acts to protect you against claims of this type (see Chapter 4).
4. *Liability insurance* shifts the costs of defending a lawsuit and the value of any judgment against you to the insurance carrier (insurer).

To qualify for liability coverage, you must have an *insurable interest* in the premises to be insured. Insurable interest is defined as whether the insured will suffer any loss in the event the risk insured against happens. This means that you must either own or lease the property to qualify for coverage. This is a protective device to both the insured and the carrier, and helps prevent unethical or illegal "accidents." For example, a competitor cannot take out a policy on your restaurant in order to burn it down and collect on the claim.

Insurance: Know What You're Getting

It is important that you allocate your resources intelligently to avoid excessive liability in any one area. You must understand what coverage you are buying.

Insurance is a contract, which means that both sides, the carrier and the operator, must agree on all terms and conditions. The fact that most insurance policies are enforced as written[65] places an especially heavy responsibility on you to understand all the terms and conditions.

In all types of insurance, the carrier assumes the risk of the covered situations in exchange for payment of a *premium*. The size of the premium is usually based on the nature of your premises and volume of business, the frequency of legal claims made, and the size of such claims.

The insurer is not obligated to provide liability insurance, and you should only purchase the amount of insurance you can afford.

The *policy* is the contract between you and the carrier containing the terms and conditions by which the agreement is governed. The *face amount* of the policy is the maximum payable on a claim, irrespective of your economic loss. If you have a claim, the insurer is only obligated to pay you the amount of the economic loss you suffered, *not the total face amount of the policy*. The insurer is not obligated to pay any claim in excess of the face amount of the policy.

Because your understanding of insurance terms may be limited, the law usually applies the *reasonable person* standard to insurance language.[66] This means that any vague language in the policy may be interpreted most strongly against the carrier.[67]

In case of a dispute between you and your carrier over the coverage of the policy you purchased, you must prove that (1) there was a liability claim, (2) the claim occurred while your policy was in force, and (3) the claim was of a kind covered by your policy.[68]

Exclusions

The carrier always has the right to *exclude,* or refuse to cover, certain types of liability claims from your policy. The most obvious exclusion is your intentional injury to the person or property of a patron. Your criminal misconduct against a patron or patron's property also falls into this area.[69]

However, your negligent, unintentional acts or those of your employees, which might result in a liability claim, should be covered. In practice, when the carrier denies your claim, you have the burden of proving that it was covered in the language of the policy.[70]

Exceptions

An *exception* in the policy means that, although the claim is otherwise covered, an exception exists that excuses the carrier from paying you under certain circumstances. For example, dramshop act liability is generally covered by insurance available in those states that recognize such liability (see Chapter 4). However, these policies may contain a provision that the insured must have a valid liquor license in effect at the time the incident resulting in a claim takes place. Without such a license, the carrier excepts itself from coverage on that claim. However, the carrier must prove the existence of the exception and the insured's failure to comply with the policy terms. Usually the courts view exceptions strictly against the carrier. This means that if the exception is unclear, it will not be enforced.[71]

Carrier Defenses to Claims

False, material representations incorporated in your policy are treated as warranties or guarantees and relied upon by your carrier in issuing the policy. On discovery of such false statements, the carrier may elect to cancel the policy without further liability. The seriousness of the misrepresentation is tested with the question: Would the policy have been issued *but for* the falsehoods? If the statements are false but not serious, then the carrier may not avoid some payment. All paid-up premiums must be returned to you when the carrier cancels on this basis.[72]

Concealment is another carrier defense in liability insurance disputes. Here your failure to disclose relevant facts must be fraudulent as well as serious enough to justify denial of your claim. The test in such a case is as follows: (1) Is there reason to think that the fact concealed was material? (2) Would the carrier have issued the policy had the truth been known?[73]

Another kind of defense that might excuse performance of the carrier would be a policy requirement that a health permit be in effect when a patron sues to recover on the grounds of food unfitness. If it isn't, you could be out of luck.

Notice of a claim is often an express condition written into your contract. This means that you must give notice of a claim to your carrier within a reasonable time. You must notify your carrier of any occurrence that *might* give rise to a legal action and forward to them any legal summons and other papers served on you as soon as possible.[74]

How Many Policies?

Unless your insurance policy prohibits your doing so, you may obtain more than one policy from different carriers covering the same liability claims. This does not permit you to recover the full or face amount of the claim on every policy. You can only recover once for the full amount of that claim, limited to the maximum amount stated in your policy.

You may carry a *basic* public liability policy *and* an *excess liability* policy, which would protect you in the event the basic policy money limits were insufficient to cover the liability claim in full. You cannot obtain full payment of the same claim under all the insurance policies. So it will not pay you to buy more than one policy for the same liability risk.

LIABILITY PREVENTION

All liability in a foodservice operation is traceable to risks, most of which can be prevented. If you take steps to *minimize* your risks, you will be more likely to *prevent* costly liability, and *maximize,* or at least *maintain,* your profitability.

You should be aware of *where* your potential risks are. If your premises are potential gold mines for would-be liability claims, you should consider getting some work done. (There is an additional factor in this: You must provide your employees with a safe place to work—see Chapter 7).

At the least, you must regularly inspect your premises for dangerous conditions and repair them. If local building or fire inspectors point out violations, take steps to correct them immediately. These inspections may prevent liability, as well as a fire.

In every type of business it is important to keep costs down and profits up, and the two are related. You should try to keep your business costs to a minimum, but this does not necessarily mean leaving yourself wide open to liability claims by failing to keep your food products and your premises safe.

SUMMARY

Foodservice operators owe patrons a safe environment, free from threats of harm to themselves or their property. Failure to provide a safe operation may result in a tort, or legal wrong, which, in turn, may result in costly liability.

There are three types of torts: *intentional* torts, torts caused by *negligence,* and torts created by the courts, which may impose *strict liability.*

The damages for torts due to negligence or strict liability are compensatory. Damages for intentional torts can be both compensatory and punitive.

The duty the law imposes on foodservice operators to provide safe premises is one of *reasonable care.* The law expects operators to do only what is reasonable under the circumstances and what customers can reasonably expect. It is also important to obey local laws regarding building and fire safety, since an injured patron may use violation of such a law as grounds for a lawsuit.

Foodservice operators are to exercise reasonable care in the selection and supervision of employees and in supervision of patrons' activities while on the premises. The doctrine of *respondeat superior* makes operators liable for the misdeeds of employees, if the actions take place in the course of employment.

There are several defenses to negligence claims: unforeseeable cause, contributory negligence, and assumption of risk.

Foodservice operators have more leeway when it comes to protecting patron property. Generally, they must supervise employees to prevent careless actions that might damage patron property and supervise the premises to prevent theft. Greater care must be taken to safeguard property accepted as a bailment.

Foodservice operators must shop carefully for insurance and select only what is necessary to prevent substantial losses arising from liability claims.

QUESTIONS

1. What is an intentional tort? How does this type of tort differ from injury due to negligence? Provide an example of an intentional tort.
2. A patron strikes another patron in a restaurant, injuring him. The manager does not summon help or try to stop the unruly patron. Can the manager be held liable? Why or why not?
3. How does the law hold a manager responsible for employee actions that injure patrons? Give an example where a manager may be held liable for an employee's action against a patron. Name the principle that applies here.

4. What must a patron establish to prove negligence? Give a foodservice example in which all the elements of negligence are present.

5. A patron puts a fur coat on her chair and leaves it there to go to the rest room. It is gone when she returns. Another patron leaves her fur coat with the attendant in the coat checkroom. It disappears. In which instance would the operator probably be held liable? Why?

NOTES

1. *Campbell v. Bozeman Community Hotel,* 160 Mont. 327, 502 P.2d 1141 (1972) (stairway to hotel dining room).

2. *Keys v. Sambo's Restaurant, Inc.,* 398 So. 2d 1083 (La. 1981).

3. *Cacares v. Anthony's Villa,* File No. 65063 (County Court, York District of Toronto, Ontario, Feb. 23, 1978). See also *Counce v. M.B.M. Co.,* 266 Ark. 1064, 597 S.W.2d 92 (1980) (wrongful firing of restaurant employee).

4. *Mid-America Food Service, Inc. v. ARA Services, Inc.,* 578 F.2d 691 (8th Cir. 1978).

5. *Whipp v. Iverson,* 43 Wis. 2d 166, 168 N.W.2d 201 (1969).

6. *Nader v. General Motors Corp.,* 25 N.Y.2d 560, 255 N.E.2d 765, 307 N.Y.S.2d 647 (1970).

7. *Staub v. Staub,* 37 Md. App. 141, 376 A.2d 1129 (1977).

8. *Wear-Ever Aluminum, Inc. v. Townecraft Industries, Inc.,* 75 N.Y. Sup. Ct. 135, 182 A.2d 387 (1962). See also *Imperial Ice Co. v. Rossier,* 18 Cal. 2d 31, 112 P.2d 631 (1941).

9. *Eastep v. Jack-in-the-Box, Inc.,* 546 S.W.2d 116 (Tex. Civ. App. 1977) (fast-food establishment); *Kimple v. Foster,* 205 Kan. 415, 469 P.2d 281 (1970) (tavern).

10. See J. Sherry, *The Laws of Innkeepers,* sec. 9:4 (rev. ed. 1981).

11. *Northern Lights Motel, Inc. v. Sweaney,* 561 P.2d 1176, *reh'g* 563 P.2d 256 (Alaska 1977).

12. *Sunday v. Stratton Corporation,* 136 Vt. 293, 390 A.2d 398 (1978). (Vermont Supreme Court disallowed assumption of risk doctrine in downhill ski-slope injury to skier.)

13. Sherry, *supra* note 10, sec. 9:5.

14. *Id.* secs. 9:8–9:17.

15. H. Lusk, C. Hewitt, J. Donnell, A. J. Barnes, *Business Law and the Regulatory Environment* 76–77 (1982).

16. W. Prosser, *Law of Torts* 15–16 (4th ed. 1972).

17. W. LaFave and A. Scott, *Criminal Law* 21–25 (1972).

18. Sherry, *supra* note 10, sec. 9:7.

19. *Deming Hotel Co. v. Prox,* 142 Ind. App. 603, 236 N.E.2d 613 (1968).

20. Sherry, *supra* note 10, sec. 9:7.

21. All owners and occupiers of land who invite the public to use their facilities are subject to this rule of law, since injury due to carelessness is most likely to occur in such facilities. Foodservice establishments are for the most part open to the public, but private clubs are also governed by this rule. The Restatement (Second) of Torts, sec. 343 (1977), which states this rule, has been repeatedly applied to hotels and restaurants. See *Winkler v. Seven Springs Farm, Inc.,* 240 Pa. Super. 641, 359 A.2d 440 (1976), *aff'd per curiam,* 477 Pa. 445, 384 A.2d 241 (1978) (resort); *Dillman v. Nobles,* 251 So. 2d 210 (La. App. 1977) (bar lounge); *Withrow v. Woozencraft,* 90 N.M. 48, 559 P.2d 425 (1976) (motel); *Bauer v. Saginaw County Agricultural Society,* 349 Mich. 616, 622–23, 628, 84 N.W.2d 827, 833–34, 839 (1957) (private fairground); *Deming Hotel Co. v. Prox, supra* note 19 (hotel restaurant); *Afienko v. Harvard Club of Boston,* 365 Mass. 320, 312 N.E.2d 196 (1974) (defective window-washing hooks and bolts; club liable to employee of independent contractor).

22. *Gault v. Tablada,* 400 F. Supp. 136 (S.D. Miss. 1975), *aff'd,* 526 F.2d 1405 (5th Cir. 1976); *Haft v. Lone Palm Hotel,* 3 Cal. 3d 756, 478 P.2d 465, 91 Cal. Rptr. 745 (1970).

23. *Peterson v. Haule,* 304 Minn. 160, 230 N.W.2d 51 (1975) (fast-food establishment).

24. *Williamson v. Travelers Ins. Co.,* 235 So. 2d 600 (La. 1970) *reh'g denied,* 256 La. 818, 239 So. 2d 345 (1970) (private swimming club).

25. Sherry, *supra* note 10, sec. 9:5.

26. *Winkler v. Seven Springs Farm, Inc., supra* note 21; *Campbell v. Bozeman Community Hotel,* 160 Mont. 327, 502 P.2d 1141 (1972) (hotel dining room).

27. *Eastep v. Jack-in-the-Box, Inc., supra* note 9. Authorities are noted in Sherry, *supra* note 10, sec. 11:13.

28. Sherry, *supra* note 10, sec. 11:13.

29. *Alonge v. Rodriquez,* 89 Wis. 2d 544, 279 N.W.2d 207 (1979) (bar lounge).

30. *Riviello v. Waldron,* 47 N.Y.2d 297, 391 N.E.2d 1278, 418 N.Y.S.2d 300 (1980) (tavernkeeper).

31. Sherry, *supra* note 10, sec. 11:8.

32. *Bradley v. Stevens,* 329 Mich. 556, 46 N.W.2d 382 (1951); *Tobin v. Slutsky,* 506 F.2d 1097 (2d Cir. 1974) (liability predicated upon violation of innkeeper's contractual duty to guest).

33. *Riviello v. Waldron, supra* note 30.

34. See *Eastep v. Jack-in-the-Box, Inc., supra* note 9; *Alonge v. Rodriquez, supra* note 29. See also Sherry, *supra* note 10, sec. 11:13.

35. *Heathcoate v. Bisig,* 474 S.W.2d 102 (Ky. 1971) (barroom).

36. *Alonge v. Rodriquez, supra* note 29.

37. *Eastep v. Jack-in-the-Box, Inc., supra* note 9.

38. *Ford v. Jeffries,* 474 Pa. 588, 379 A.2d 111 (1977) (residential fire).

39. *Karna v. Byron Reed Syndicate #4,* 374 F. Supp. 687 (D. Neb. 1974) (dangerous condition known to hotel guest).

40. *Peterson v. Haule, supra* note 23.

41. *Hunn v. Windsor Hotel Co.,* 119 W.Va. 215, 193 S.E. 57 (1937); *Scott v. John H. Hampshire, Inc.,* 246 Md. 171, 227 A.2d 751 (1967).

42. *Montes v. Betcher,* 480 F.2d 1128 (8th Cir. 1973) (hotel lakefront dock).

43. *Darby v. Checker Co.,* 6 Ill. App. 3d 188, 285 N.E.2d 217 (1972) (hotel fire).

44. *Northern Lights Motel, Inc. v. Sweaney, supra* note 11.

45. *Gault v. Tablada, supra* note 22.

46. See *Bazydlo v. Placid Marcy Co.,* 422 F.2d 842 (2d Cir. 1970) (ski toboggan).

47. *Shamrock Hilton Hotel v. Caranas,* 488 S.W.2d 151 (Tex. Ct. Civ. App. 1972) (loss of purse from hotel restaurant caused by negligent misdelivery to unauthorized third person).

48. Sherry, *supra* note 10, sec. 16:2; *Minneapolis Fire & Marine Ins. Co. v. Matson Navigation Co.,* 44 Hawaii 59, 61, 352 P.2d 335, 337 (1960); *Hulett v. Swift,* 33 N.Y. 570, 572–75 (1865).

49. *Summer v. Hyatt Corp.,* 153 Ga. App. 684, 266 S.E.2d 333 (1980). (Hotel guest does not lose guest status by using hotel restaurant. As such, guest may not recover for loss of purse containing valuables because guest did not comply with statutory requirements for deposit of valuables.) *Diplomat Restaurant, Inc. v. Townsend,* 118 Ga. App. 694, 165 S.E.2d 317 (1968).

50. *Montgomery v. Ladjing,* 30 Misc. 92, 61 N.Y.S. 840 (1899), cited and followed in *Kuchinsky v. Empire Lounge, Inc.,* 27 Wis. 2d 446, 134 N.W.2d 436 (1965).

51. *Block v. Sherry,* 43 Misc. 342, 87 N.Y.S. 160 (1904).

52. *Wentworth v. Riggs,* 159 A.D. 899, 143 N.Y.S. 955 (1st Dep't 1913); *Johnston v. B. & N., Inc.,* 190 Pa. Super. 586, 155 A.2d 232 (1959).

53. *Shamrock Hilton Hotel v. Caranas, supra* note 47, and *Johnston v. B. & N., Inc., supra* note 52.

54. Except New York State, which allows foodservice operators to limit the ceiling for liability for lost or damaged property.

55. *Wentworth v. Riggs, supra* note 52.

56. *Black Beret Lounge & Restaurant v. Meisnere,* 336 A.2d 532 (D.C. App. 1975).

57. *Shamrock Hilton Hotel v. Caranas, supra* note 47; *Forte v. Westchester Hills Golf Club, Inc.,* 103 Misc. 621, 426 N.Y.S.2d 390 (1980) (unattended cloakroom).

58. *Shamrock Hilton Hotel v. Caranas, supra* note 47.

59. *Black Beret Lounge & Restaurant v. Meisnere, supra* note 56.

60. *Id.* See also *Forte v. Westchester Hills Golf Club, Inc., supra* note 57.

61. Cf. *Apfel v. Whyte's, Inc.,* 110 Misc. 670, 180 N.Y.S. 712 (1920). (No responsibility where restaurant employee took coat and hung it in close proximity to patron's table.)

62. *Ellerman v. Atlanta American Motor Hotel Corp.,* 126 Ga. App. 194, 191 S.E.2d 295 (1972) (bailment of guest vehicle) is authority for this principle of public policy preventing professional bailees from disclaiming responsibility for bailed property by contract.

63. However, New York has seen fit to give restaurant keepers a degree of protection by including them in its innkeeper's liability statute.

64. Sherry, *supra* note 10, sec. 17:8.

65. *Stark v. Grange Mutual Ins. Co. of Custer County,* 203 Neb. 154, 277 N.W.2d 679 (1979) (fire policy on business premises).

66. *SFI, Inc. v. United States Fire Ins. Co.,* 453 F. Supp. 502 (M.D. La. 1978), *aff'd,* 634 F.2d 879 (5th Cir. 1981) (burglary policy on business premises).

67. *Steigler v. Insurance Co. of North America,* 384 A.2d 398 (Del. 1977) (fire policy on residence); *Morrison Assurance Co. v. Armstrong,* 152 Ga. App. 885, 264 S.E.2d 320 (1980) (workers' compensation policy).

68. *Keddie v. Beneficial Ins., Inc.,* 94 Nev. 418, 580 P.2d 955 (1978) (fire policy on commercial fishing boat).

69. A theft of patron property by you as owner or occupier of the premises is a typical example. Your deliberate burning of your own building, the crime of arson, will prevent you from recovering under your policy of insurance. See *Steigler v. Insurance Co. of North America, supra* note 67.

70. *Citizens Ins. Co. of America v. Tuttle,* 96 Mich. App. 763, 294 N.W.2d 224 (1980), *rev'd,* 411 Mich. 536, 209 N.W.2d 174 (1981) (no-fault insurance).

71. *Youse v. Employers Fire Ins. Co.,* 172 Kan. 111, 238 P.2d 472 (1951) (no ambiguity in exception limiting coverage to hostile fires).

72. *Hawkeye-Security Ins. Co. v. Government Employees Ins. Co.,* 207 Va. 944, 154 S.E.2d 173 (1967).

73. *Id.*

74. *Pini v. Allstate Ins. Co.,* 499 F. Supp. 1003 (E.D. Pa. 1980), *aff'd,* 659 F.2d 1070 (3d Cir. 1981) (fire policy on residence).

6
The Law and Your Employees I
Selection and Supervision

Objectives

The purpose of this chapter is to:

1. Explain the legal rights and duties of employers and employees with regard to civil rights laws, wage and hour laws, employee screening and surveillance, safety requirements, and union-management relations.

2. Discuss the basic legal requirements for dealing with employees.

Case in Point

Nancy DeCarlo, owner and operator of Pizzas Plus, a full-service Italian restaurant in Chicago, leaves her restaurant in the capable hands of her assistant manager, Don Frederick, two nights a week.

One night when Don is in charge, one of the waitresses tells him that a patron "fondles" her everytime she goes over to the table to serve and even when she passes by. She reminds Don that this is the third time she has complained about this customer and would appreciate it if he did something about him. Don says he doesn't really know what he can do; the patron is neither drunk nor "disorderly." Don tells the waitress the patron is just having harmless fun and to ignore it.

Two questions for you to think about: Could Don have done anything? Could Nancy be liable for such an incident? The answer to both questions is yes. Don should have taken steps to stop the patron's unwelcome advances to the waitress. What he viewed as harmless fun, she obviously saw as sexual harassment, and Don had the authority and the obligation to stop it. Employers are liable for the actions of patrons and co-workers, including sexual taunts, sexual touching, and provocative comments and gestures by co-workers and patrons.

LEGAL FRAMEWORK

The law provides a *framework* for relations with employees. Beyond that it is up to the employer to clarify management policies and enforce them.

Keeping yourself on the right side of the law regarding employees is, of course, a good way to insulate yourself from liability. However, fairness and consistency when managing foodservice employees can earn a bonus: Your efforts as a manager can be immediately reflected through your employees and from them to your patrons.

EMPLOYMENT PRACTICES: FEDERAL CIVIL RIGHTS LAWS

Since 1963, a variety of federal and state equal employment opportunity laws have been passed. These laws regulate your foodservice employment practices.

The Equal Pay Act

Under the Equal Pay Act of 1963, you are required to provide employees of both sexes equal pay for equal work, as long as the work performed is equal in skills used, effort, and responsibility, and is performed under parallel working conditions.[1] The courts have interpreted the word "equal" to mean substantially equal.[2] You may not evade the law by simply making minor changes in the work done. For example, if you have two dishwashers, it would be very difficult to evade the law by saying that one worker does the breakfast dishes and the other the lunch dishes. If, however, one dishwasher buses tables in addition to washing dishes, that may justify a difference in pay.

This law is administered by the Equal Employment Opportunity Commission (EEOC). The Equal Pay Act only applies when both men and women are employed in substantially similar jobs. It does not apply where only one sex is employed in a job.

Remedies for Violations of the Equal Pay Act

The Equal Pay Act requires employers to pay employees discriminated against the same wage as other employees in similar jobs. You may not reduce the wage of any employee of the opposite sex to eliminate the inequality and to comply with the Act.[3] Neither do you comply by permitting the employees receiving unequal wages to obtain higher paying jobs as vacancies occur. Nor may the lower, unequal wages be frozen by a collective bargaining agreement adopted later.[4]

The Civil Rights Act

The Civil Rights Act of 1964, Title VII, prohibits all employer practices that discriminate on the basis of race, color, religion, sex, pregnancy, or national origin.[5] This law is far broader than the Equal Pay Act, since it regulates selection, referral, promotion, transfer, demotion, discipline, dismissal, separation, and pregnancy-related job benefits.

The following are foodservice examples of discrimination in violation of the Civil Rights Act:

Race: Preferential treatment, that is, better working conditions for white waiters than for black waiters, including better work stations and benefits.

Religion: A question on an employment application asking job prospects if they observe the Jewish holidays.

Sex: An abbreviated costume for female waitresses when male employees are completely dressed.

Pregnancy: Refusal to maintain job seniority for pregnant employees while other employees who take a disability leave maintain their seniority.

National origin: A steady history of refusal to promote southern Europeans in favor of western Europeans.

Such forms of discrimination occur in the foodservice industry *and are illegal.*

You must set up hiring and management policies to prevent illegal or even subtle forms of discrimination. In this way, you will lessen the chances of being held liable by an employee or group of employees who feel themselves treated unfairly in comparison to other employees. Once these policies are prepared, you must ask yourself: Are they fair? Will my employees be treated equally? Is there room for misunderstanding by my supervisors or managers?

The law is not asking you to hire people who do not have the proper skills or characteristics to perform your foodservice jobs, or to promote those who don't along with those who do. It does require that in selection and supervision you maintain non-discriminatory policies. If you don't, you may find yourself on the receiving end of a costly lawsuit.

All foodservice establishments are covered by the Civil Rights Act if they employ 15 or more employees and are engaged in or affect *interstate commerce.* Service to out-of-state patrons, as well as purchases of goods and services from out-of-state suppliers, is sufficient to affect interstate commerce. This act is also enforced by the EEOC.

Remedies for Violations of the Civil Rights Act

The Civil Rights Act of 1964 provides the following remedies for violations:

1. *Back pay.* The employee discriminated against is entitled to receive the difference between the actual pay earned and what should have been earned were it not for the discrimination. *Back pay* includes fringe benefits, regular and overtime pay, holiday pay, reasonable value of tips, and all other benefits, including uniform allowances.[6]

2. *Reinstatement.* This means not only getting the job back but also any seniority. Reinstatement is not required in every instance, but is decided on a case-by-case basis.[7]

3. *Court order stopping violation (injunctive relief).* The Civil Rights Act authorizes local courts to issue orders prohibiting employment discrimination. These orders are issued on a case-by-case basis.[8]

4. *Damages.* Normally employers are not required to pay compensatory or punitive damages under the Civil Rights Act, other than back pay. The employee must be able to prove financial loss to receive this.[9] This

means that if the employee is able to obtain another job at the same or better wage level, the employer is not required to pay back wages.

When an employee can prove that he or she suffered humiliation, embarrassment, or discomfort arising out of an employer's unlawful, discriminatory conduct, damages may be awarded under the Civil Rights Act of 1866.[10]

5. *Attorney's fees.*   The legal fees of an employee who wins a judgment against an employer for discrimination can be recovered by his or her attorney under the Civil Rights Act.[11] Because of the length of time and the costs of preparing legal papers, not to mention the trial and appeal time involved, such costs can be staggering. Sometimes legal fees can exceed the cost of back pay, restoration of seniority, and other benefits the court may award the employee.

Retaliation against an employee for filing charges with the EEOC or for opposing unlawful employment discrimination is prohibited.[12] If retaliation is proved, the employee may obtain a court order removing any adverse or negative comments from his or her employment records. For example, an employer who demotes an employee from waiter to dishwasher for no other reason than that he or she filed a discrimination charge may find himself or herself on the receiving end of a court order.

Defenses under Federal Law

The Civil Rights Law establishes two major defenses to any claim based on discrimination outlawed by the Act.

1. *Bona fide occupational qualification (BFOQ).*   A bona fide occupational qualification is any job-related requirement established in good faith that justifies a difference in treatment.[13] Suppose that you wish to establish an authentic Chinese restaurant, serving genuine Chinese specialties. You refuse to employ an American chef trained in Chinese cooking in preference to a Chinese chef who has had extensive culinary experience in those dishes you plan to promote. Is the refusal to hire the American a violation of the Civil Rights Act? No. You have established a BFOQ defense. The choice of a Chinese chef is both job-related and bona fide, meaning done in good faith for a legitimate reason.

The bona fide occupational qualification defense is a very narrow one, and you must be able to prove it should an issue arise.[14] It is not often used successfully by employers in employee civil rights cases.

2. *Business necessity.*   This defense is a broader one than the BFOQ defense, since it involves the claim that the business itself requires the discrimination. For example, the fact that customer preference in your restaurant dictates hiring waitresses rather than waiters, however true, will not, standing alone, justify a refusal to hire men.[15] However, requiring waiters to cut their hair short but allowing waitresses to wear their hair long may be justified by customer preference. Grooming standards, which reasonably differentiate between the sexes, are generally allowed, as long as they are not motivated by an intention to discriminate on the basis of sex.[16] Why the difference in the two hypothetical cases? In the first case, sex is immutable, meaning unalterable. You are either male or female, and you are normally not able to alter your sex. In the second case, sex is not an issue. What is at issue is hair length, a factor readily changeable by either or both sexes. Thus the courts have uniformly ruled that reasonable appearance and dress codes for employees that result in sex differentiation

The Law and Your Employees I: Selection and Supervision   87

may be dictated by the public and are legally justified.[17] *However, they must be related to the job.* (A requirement that women bank executives wear uniforms and men executives wear customary business suits was struck down when there was no business justification, and the difference in dress was found to be demeaning to the women.)[18] In a foodservice operation, an extremely abbreviated female outfit for cocktail waitresses when cocktail waiters are fully clothed might also be rejected as unjustified. The customer preference argument might not hold up, considering the demeaning nature of the women's outfits.

Age Discrimination Act

The *Age Discrimination in Employment Act of 1967* prohibits discrimination against job applicants and employees between the ages of 40 and 70.[19] This means that you may not create or increase burdens on persons in this group that are not imposed on younger employees. (However, you may differentiate between "younger employees" and minors in the types of jobs given.) Once again, the EEOC is the enforcement agency. You must employ 25 or more people to be covered by this law.

Vocational Rehabilitation Act

The federal *Vocational Rehabilitation Act of 1973* prohibits you from discriminating against job applicants or employees on account of mental or physical disabilities. However, you must be a federal government contractor or subcontractor to be covered by this law.

Employers with government contracts are required to engage in efforts to provide employment for all persons protected by this federal law. The Vocational Rehabilitation Act requires all government contractors with contracts worth $2500 or more to take affirmative action to employ handicapped workers. The Act covers both physical and mental handicaps.[20]

Federal Contractors

A presidential order, Executive Order 11246 (1965), prohibits *all forms* of employment discrimination by federal contractors and subcontractors that hold contracts or subcontracts worth $10,000 or more. This order is enforced by the *Office of Federal Contract Compliance Programs.*

These federal subcontract rules might affect you, for example, if a federally funded public university hires you to operate its student dining facilities. You would be barred from discriminating against job applicants and employees on any grounds covered by federal laws. You would also be required to take affirmative action to open up job opportunities for those persons protected by federal laws.

STATE EQUAL EMPLOYMENT LAWS

Only Mississippi has not passed a statute prohibiting employment discrimination. State laws follow the federal pattern and outlaw employment discrimination on the basis of race, creed, color, sex, national origin, age, or handicap. These laws are important for two reasons: (1) Under federal law the EEOC must first permit the state agency, if any, to attempt to resolve an employment discrimination suit before the EEOC steps in. (2) Some state laws provide other means by which the employee can sue and recover from employers. These laws may also provide stiffer penalties for employer violations.

New York and other states prohibit employment discrimination on the basis of marital status and arrest record, in addition to the areas covered by federal law.[21] San Francisco includes sexual orientation as a prohibited category of employment discrimination. This category is not included under federal law. Minneapolis includes status as a recipient of public assistance as well as affectional preference in its discrimination laws (affectional preference is the same as sexual orientation).

Federal, state, and local laws may act in concert or independently of each other in defining, regulating, and providing remedies for employment discrimination. Employers may be subject to three separate levels of law regarding employee rights.

Often the penalties for civil rights violations can multiply, such as in the case of a wrongful refusal to hire a black waitress. She is protected from discrimination based on her race and her sex.

This means you cannot afford to ignore your responsibilities in this area. The best course of action is not to violate the law in the first place. Even if you ultimately win your case, the loss of time and money, and the unwanted publicity, can be devastating (see Appendix G).

FEDERAL POLICY ON HIRING ALIENS

Employing aliens instead of U.S. citizens is an issue that is thick with controversy both pro and con. Employers must differentiate between aliens who are immigrants seeking permanent U.S. residence and citizenship, those who are here on a limited visa, and illegal aliens.

The hiring of illegal aliens is usually where most of the controversy arises. On the one hand, employers, including foodservice operators, often have jobs that do not interest U.S. citizens or legal aliens, but represent employment for people who would otherwise be unemployed. On the other hand, in a troubled economy, charges mount that illegal aliens take jobs for lower wages than U.S. citizens, thus preventing the latter group from obtaining employment. The following questions and answers should clarify your rights regarding aliens.

1. Is it illegal to hire aliens? No. Lawfully admitted or registered aliens may be hired. Those hiring illegal aliens may be subject to raids and legal sanctions. At least one federal Circuit Court of Appeals has ruled that all aliens are protected against employment discrimination under the Civil Rights Act of 1866 (42 U.S.C. sec. 1981), independently of Title VII.[22]

2. Are employers required to provide equal opportunity to employees solely on the ground that they are aliens? No. The United States Supreme Court said that Title VII of the Civil Rights Act, which bars employment discrimination on the basis of "national origin," does not include in that phrase "citizenship."[23] However, the high court stated that Title VII does prohibit discrimination against citizens and aliens on the grounds of race, color, religion, sex, or national origin. The high court defined "national origin" to mean "the country from which his or her ancestors came."

3. Are aliens who are hired entitled to the same protection as U.S. citizens? Yes. Once they are hired, labor relations with all *legal* aliens are governed by the National Labor Relations Act. In addition, legal aliens are entitled to all federal equal employment opportunity protections regarding benefits, wages, and promotions.

4. Is it a crime to harbor illegal aliens, meaning aliens not properly admitted to the United States? Yes, if employers do so knowingly or willfully.[24] Employers hire illegal aliens at risk. If found, illegal aliens may be deported and the operator will be out of some workers. In addition, the employer may be subject to a warning and civil legal action.[25]

   One federal Circuit Court of Appeals ruled that the reporting of illegal aliens to the federal Immigration Service that results in their deportation is an unfair labor practice subject to National Labor Relations Board sanctions if the purpose of the reporting is to discourage otherwise lawful attempts to unionize a business.[26]

5. What questions may you ask a prospective employee regarding citizenship?[27] You may ask if the applicant is a U.S. citizen, or if an applicant voluntarily discloses his or her lack of citizenship, you may ask: Do you have the right to remain permanently in the United States? Do you intend to remain permanently in the United States? You also have the right to tell the applicant that, if hired, he or she may be required to submit proof of citizenship or proof of current alien registration.

   As an employer, you *may not* ask the applicant: Are you or your parents or spouse naturalized or native-born citizens? When did you or your parents or your spouse acquire United States citizenship? You may not require an applicant to produce naturalization papers until hired. No question that is designed to determine national origin may be asked.

   Once hired, any proof of an employee's citizenship or alien registration may be checked for authenticity.

6. Can you be sued for damages by citizens or legally admitted alien employees who are displaced as a result of the hiring of illegal aliens? No. The law creates no private cause of action for displaced employees.[28]

Since the laws dealing with aliens fluctuate, you must consult with an attorney when involved in any dispute concerning the hiring or disciplining of alien workers.

The following case indicates the trouble foodservice employers can get into as a result of harboring illegal aliens.

United States v. Mount Fuji Japanese Steak House, Inc.
United States District Court, Eastern District of New York
435 F. Supp. 1194 (1977)

Facts. The defendants, the president and manager of a foodservice operation, were charged with inducing the entry of, bringing in, transporting, and harboring Japanese aliens not legally entitled to enter or reside in the United States, all in violation of Section 274(a) of the U.S. Immigration and Nationality Act. The defendants moved to dismiss the criminal indictments by the trial court, saying that there was no crime at issue. In particular, the defendants argued that the employer-employee relationship between the defendants and the aliens prevented the defendants' conviction for harboring illegal aliens. The motions to dismiss all indictments, including the criminal charge of harboring illegal aliens, were denied.

Reasoning. The employers' basic defense was that the harboring was related to the employment and therefore was legal and no crime had been committed. The court said:

> The statute makes illegal a person's "willfully or knowingly . . . harboring in any place" any illegal alien, "Provided, however, that for the purposes of this section, employment (including the usual and normal practices incident to employment) shall not be deemed to constitute harboring." 8 U.S.C. & 1324(a) . . .

Conclusion. This case shows the trouble employers can get into by harboring and hiring illegal aliens.

1. An employer may be subject to criminal penalties for harboring illegal aliens and may be out of a few employees as well.
2. When employer practices involve federal crimes, such as inducing the entry of, bringing in, housing, and transporting illegal aliens, employers may be prosecuted.
3. Harboring illegal aliens is considered more serious than hiring them as far as immigration officials are concerned. Penalties are stiff.

CHILD LABOR

Federal law prohibits hiring minors under 14 years of age. However, some states allow minors between 12 and 14 years old to work during the summers or school vacations. Minors can only be employed in nonhazardous food-service activities, such as cashiering, selling, assembling orders, light cleanup work, light kitchen work, and washing fruits and vegetables. Forbidden hazardous activities include the operation of heavy-duty power-driven machinery, such as food slicers, grinders, choppers, cutters, and bakery-type mixers.

Child labor laws are enforced by the Department of Labor. Penalties for violations of federal child labor laws include maximum civil penalties of $1000 per violation, and additional criminal penalties of $10,000 for first violations and $10,000 plus a six-month jail term for second offenses. The civil penalty can be imposed on unintentional violators by the Secretary of Labor without any court action. The criminal penalty is reserved for willful violators and requires court action.

State labor laws normally prohibit minors from working where alcoholic beverages are sold. State laws also may differ in the work a minor may do. Some states have more restrictions on hiring minors than the federal laws, and age requirements also vary. *When a state child labor law differs from the federal law, the law offering the greater protection to the minor will be applied.*

EMPLOYEE SCREENING

You may be limited in your employee screening practices by two major factors: (1) the Equal Employment Practices Acts at the federal, state, and local levels; and (2) the terms and conditions of your collective bargaining agreement—if you are under a union contract.

The test adopted by the EEOC and by various other state and local agencies in evaluating an inquiry is whether it is necessary to evaluate an applicant's ability to perform the job. For example, questions about a criminal record, if not barred by union agreement or by law, will be measured by how critical or sensitive the job is. For some jobs, such as dishwashing, it could be argued that this question is unnecessary. However, for a cashiering position, the question may be justified. The existence of a criminal conviction record, standing alone, should not always disqualify an otherwise capable applicant. The conviction record would have to be related in a substantial way to the job. For example, a conviction for speeding would not be grounds for a refusal to hire a cashier. (Figure 6.1 includes inquiries forbidden by law in California, a strict state.)

Testing

Foodservice operators may want to give job applicants various tests to determine whether they are fully qualified for a job. The EEOC has issued guidelines stating that tests should

Figure 6.1
Employee-Screening Inquiries Forbidden in California

Name. When name changed by court order, the former name.

Birthplace. Birthplace of applicant or parents, spouse, or relatives.
You may request a birth certificate or other proof of citizenship after employment.

Age. No questions which may identify applicants as over 40 years of age.

Religion. No questions as to religious denomination or affiliation, church, parish, synagogue, or observance of religious holidays.
No questions as to attendance at church services. No statement that your organization is Catholic, Protestant, Jewish, or agnostic.

Race or Color. No questions relating to racial makeup or skin color.

Photograph. No photograph may be required before hiring. You may require a photograph after hiring.

Citizenship. No questions relating to citizenship of applicant, parents, or spouse until after applicant is hired.

National Origin or Ancestry. No questions at all relating to applicant's nationality, lineage, ancestry, national origin, descent, or parentage; nationality of the applicant's parents or spouse; or language commonly used.
You may ask what languages applicant reads, writes, or speaks fluently; or level of fluency.

Education. Date last attended high school.
You may ask applicant's academic, vocational, or professional education, and schools attended.

Experience. Applicant's military experience. Type of military discharge.
You may ask about an applicant's work experience; military experience in U.S. armed forces, state militia, or particular branch of U.S. military service.

Character. Whether the applicant has ever been arrested. You may ask if the applicant has ever been *convicted* of a crime. If so, when, where, and the disposition of the case.

Relatives. Marital status or number of dependents; whether they reside with parents; or names and addresses of relatives, spouse, or children of adult applicant. You may ask for names and addresses of applicant's relatives already employed by employer; name and address of a parent or guardian if the applicant is a minor.

Notice in Case of Emergency. Name and address of *relative* to be notified.
You may ask for name and address of *person* to be notified.

Organizations. Names of all organizations, clubs, societies, and lodges to which the applicant belongs. You may ask an applicant about membership in organizations, clubs, professional societies, or other associations, *excluding* any names which disclose the race, religious creed, color, national origin, or ancestry of members.

References. Religious references.
You may ask by whom applicant was referred.

Physical Condition. Physical disabilities in general; general medical condition, whether the applicant is getting or has received Workmen's Compensation payments. You may ask if the applicant has any physical conditions that might limit his or her ability to perform the job applied for. You *may* tell the applicant that a job offer may be subject to passing a physical examination.

Miscellaneous. Any inquiry that is not job related or necessary for determining suitability.

be *job-related.* The U.S. Supreme Court has upheld the EEOC guidelines, pointing out that tests should be used only to evaluate job seekers for a specific job and not to discriminate on any other basis, such as race or religion.[29]

You may want to test potential employees, especially those seeking positions as supervisors, buyers, cashiers, and chefs. These tests can be written, or for a chef position you may want to give a cooking test. All job applicants may be tested as long as the tests can be proven to be job-related.

Employer Security

There is a judicial trend in some states to hold owners and occupiers of land open to the public to higher standards for the protection of patrons against assaults by employees.[30] This trend requires careful screening and supervision of employees, since lapses in your hiring and management policies can subject you to legal action, if someone is injured by your employees. However, you also have a corresponding responsibility to obey all equal employment opportunity laws when screening applicants. This apparent contradiction in responsibilities can be resolved by making use of whatever employment screening policies are *legally available to you.*

SUPERVISION OF EMPLOYEES

Union contracts and employee rights to privacy may also limit your right to monitor employee job conduct to protect your operation from criminal activity.[31]

The law, while it attempts to balance the rights of employers with those of employees with regard to hiring, is more uncertain when it comes to ongoing supervision and your rights to protect your operation from employee thefts and other employee-related security problems.

The foodservice industry is prone to employee pilfering of food and supplies. Pilfering can be hard to detect since it often involves small amounts over a period of time.

Stealing by employees is not a phenomenon unique to the foodservice industry, but it is often felt quickly in operations that must keep inventory costs down to maintain profitability. In Chapter 8 on security there are management tips on what you can do to prevent many security problems. The areas covered here, specifically regarding employees, tend to be gray areas as far as the law is concerned, however. You must use your best management judgment to determine if such steps are really warranted by the size of your problem.

In a food service, you are constantly involved with premises security, since your economic survival depends on protecting yourself, your employees, and your patrons from theft, violence, and other activities. The unwary manager is an easy mark for the criminally inclined employee.

Your dilemma is to increase security without violating employee rights of privacy or union collective bargaining agreements. You have the right to protect your property and your business from criminal misconduct, based on a history of crime on your premises or your location in a high-crime area.

Polygraphs

The lie detector has an uncertain legal standing. Eighteen states ban or limit the use of polygraphs, and other states require licensing of users (see Appendix H). Even where polygraph results are used, they have not met with great success. Moreover, their use may lower employee morale, thus making them counterproductive in verifying employee honesty.

Visual Surveillance of Employee Areas

When an operation has a history of burglaries, armed robberies, assaults, and vandalism, courts and union negotiators are more receptive to the installation of visual surveillance devices, such as closed-circuit TV monitors, to protect patrons, employees, and property. These devices may be used in work areas to prevent employee thefts or other illegal activities.

Generally, when the safety and security of the premises are threatened, the employee's right to privacy may yield to the right of the employer to protect both the business and its patrons.

If you feel that you need to take certain steps under the law to prevent employee crime, you should do so, particularly if your plan is cost effective as well as legal. You must insist on your right to take such steps at the bargaining table during labor negotiations. At minimum, you should have the right to use visual monitoring systems in work areas, including receiving rooms, locker rooms, kitchen areas, and employee parking areas, but not in employee washrooms, toilets, or lounges. However, employee assaults or sales of contraband in traditionally private areas might permit you to change your policies regarding these areas. Union contracts and the common law of your state are the sources for limitations here.

If your property has a history of crime, or is located in a high-crime area, you may make a strong case for installing a complete visual surveillance system for the entire operation, including your outdoor parking areas. Although this may be somewhat distasteful to management, patrons, and employees—because the system is expensive, intrudes on privacy, and is intimidating—the evidence to date supports its legality.

Metal Detectors

Manufacturers and distributors of metal products often use metal detectors in their plants or warehouses. Some large foodservice operations may use them to prevent the loss of silverware. There are presently no state laws prohibiting their use, but union contracts may prohibit them. Legality aside, they are often difficult to use and may prove more costly than replacing lost stainless utensils.

Inspection of Employee Work Areas

Constitutional protections prohibiting unreasonable searches of private areas, such as homes, without valid search warrants do not apply to private employers' inspections of work areas.[32] The work area is not a private place for your employees.

Periodic inspections of work areas may be your best form of "visual surveillance." A word of caution: It is important to remember that your objective in any type of inspection is to protect your business from theft and other crimes. Conducting inspections for any other reason, or using gestapo tactics in the process, is unnecessary and can result in low employee morale.

Sexual Harassment

Sexual harassment in the workplace is a major concern of women workers.[33] Because of the large proportion of women employed in the foodservice industry, and the fact that women employees usually work in close proximity to male supervisors, co-workers, and patrons, foodservice operators must develop effective policies to deal with a problem that could result in liability.

In 1980 the EEOC issued guidelines on this subject that broadly define both the forms of harassment and the scope of employer liability.[34] Briefly, the guidelines make employers liable for harassment activities by supervisors, co-workers, and patrons.

The guidelines are based on court decisions that found violations of Title VII of the Civil Rights Act existed whenever a woman agreed to her supervisor's demand for sexual favors as a condition of her employment.[35] Formerly, only if a woman were fired as a result of her refusal could she seek court relief. However, *direct employment consequences are no longer required to establish a violation of the guidelines.* The demand itself is enough. Moreover, the guidelines also hold employers responsible for sexual taunts, lewd or provocative comments and gestures, and sexually offensive touching by co-workers and patrons.[36] Employers may be liable if they were given notice of the harassment, and the harassment was *related* to the employment activities of the victim.[37]

Protection against harassment by patrons or non-employees is also contained in the guidelines. As an employer, you will be liable for harassment of your employees by patrons, if you knew *or should have known* of the conduct and failed to stop it. You are also responsible for the failure of your supervisors to stop harassment that they knew about.[38]

The guidelines specify the steps that you should take to prevent sexual harassment in your operation. You must (1) raise the subject of harassment with all employees, (2) express strong disapproval and develop appropriate penalties, (3) inform employees of their right to complain and how to do so, and (4) develop methods to make everyone fully aware of the problem and how to prevent it.[39]

The following case illustrates the consequences of management failure to deal with the problem of one harassed employee.

Norma L. Rogers v. Loew's L'Enfant Plaza Hotel
United States District Court, District of Columbia
526 F. Supp. 523 (D.C. 1981)

Facts.

In September 1979, plaintiff was hired by the defendant hotel as assistant manager of the Greenhouse Restaurant. Defendant James Deavers, manager of that restaurant, was plaintiff's immediate supervisor, with whom she was required to work closely in order to assure the smooth operation of the restaurant. Plaintiff alleged that after being employed a few weeks, Deavers began to make sexually oriented advances toward her, verbally and in writing, which extended over a period of two months. The defendant would write her notes and letters, pressing them into her hand when she was busy attending to her duties in the restaurant, or placing them inside menus that plaintiff distributed to patrons of the restaurant, or even slipping them into plaintiff's purse without her knowledge.

Plaintiff further claimed that defendant would also telephone her at home or while she was on duty at the restaurant, which conversations included sarcastic, leering comments about her personal and sexual life. Plaintiff was frightened and embarrassed by this defendant's actions . . . She contended that she continually rejected his suggestions and rebuffed his advances . . .

During this period, plaintiff received what she considered to be an abusive and violent telephone call from defendant Deavers' wife, who had apparently discovered a letter written by her husband to the plaintiff. Ms. Deavers warned Rogers not to become involved with her husband. Extremely disturbed by this call, plaintiff urged defendant to tell his wife that there was no relationship, other than a working one.

Plaintiff averred that for a short time after the telephone incident between herself and Ms. Deavers, the advances ceased, but soon they resumed again. This time, in addition to leaving more notes, Deavers would pull at plaintiff's hair, touch her, and try to convince her to spend a night or take a trip with him. The complaint stated that he offered her gifts and favors and at times used abusive crude language, stating that he found her attractive and would never leave her alone.

The explicit sexual advances ceased at the end of November, but then the employment atmosphere and working conditions at the Greenhouse became difficult . . . according to plaintiff. Defendant Deavers would sometimes exclude her from meetings of the Greenhouse staff; he suggested to the staff that plaintiff was unhappy with her job and might not stay; he used abusive language, belittling plaintiff in the presence of the staff; he refused to cooperate with her or share necessary information on occasion. Plaintiff claimed he generally made it difficult for her to perform her job.

During this period (1) Deavers tried to get her fired, (2) the hotel managers appeared unwilling to meet with her to discuss the problem, and (3) the hotel management did not offer to remove Deavers from his position even though it knew of other similar incidents.

Rogers brought suit against the employer and employer's parent corporation for both compensatory and punitive damages. The defendants moved to dismiss on the grounds that the cause of action did not relate to civil rights violation. They maintained there was no invasion of privacy, there was no proof of assault and battery, no damages were provided for emotional distress, and the parent corporation was not involved in the alleged activities.

The defendants' motion was granted in part and denied in part: (1) The court held that the plaintiff Rogers had sufficient cause of action to bring suit for invasion of privacy, assault, battery, and infliction of emotional distress. (2) The court held that neither civil rights statutes nor the Thirteenth Amendment related to the cause of action. (3) The parent corporations, which did not control the hotel management, were dismissed as defendants.

(4) The court found the plaintiff could be entitled to punitive damages if the allegation were proved.

Reasoning.   Pointing to the persistent phone calls, the court found that the plaintiff's invasion-of-privacy allegation could be upheld and was covered by the law.

As for the assault and battery claim, the court said that a defendant could be liable for assault and battery if that defendant acted with intent to cause harmful *or* offensive contact with another person and that person is put in apprehension of the act, and, finally, the conduct results. The hair-pulling incidents were noted by the court:

> To constitute the tort of battery: a defendant can be found liable for any physical contact with the plaintiff which is offensive or insulting, as well as physically harmful. Of primary importance in such a cause of action is the absence of consent to the contact on the part of the plaintiff, rather than the hostile intent of the defendant, although intent is required. The intent, however, is only the intent "to bring about such a contact."
>
> Here, clearly, an absence of consent has been asserted, since plaintiff specifically told Deavers that his advances were unwanted. Plaintiff also recites a touching, which included pulling her hair, and that Deavers intended to bring about this conduct . . . These allegations are sufficient to survive the motion to dismiss as to the battery claim.

As for emotional distress, the court said:

> In her complaint, the plaintiff has clearly alleged conditions and circumstances which are beyond mere insults, indignities, and petty oppressions and which, if proved, could be construed as outrageous. Emotional distress and physical harm could reasonably result from the conduct of Deavers, as stated, as well as from the conduct of the hotel management in response to plaintiff's plight. A cause of action for intentional infliction of emotional distress does, therefore, lie.

Conclusion.   This case may be an extreme example of sexual harassment resulting in litigation. However, it illustrates the need to keep the lines of communication open between women employees and management, especially regarding sexual harassment. Rather than encouraging discussion of the subject, the management here went to great lengths to avoid the issue. If management discourages such harassment and an employee still sues, the employer will be on better legal ground than if the behavior was never dealt with. Win or lose, such court cases are time-consuming, costly, and usually avoidable.

Minimizing Liability

You should take the following measures to minimize your potential liability for sexual harassment: (1) adopt a clear, written employment policy against such harassment; (2) appoint one person in your business to whom complaints of harassment can be reported; and (3) establish an action plan for dealing with a problem should one arise.

What you should remember is that you are not operating a restaurant for the fun and entertainment of your employees, nor are you operating it for the fun and entertainment of patrons at your employees' expense. What may seem like harmless fun to a patron might be harassment to a woman employee, and you might be liable—the patron's fun coming at your own expense.

Termination

At some point, a supervisor may have to face the fact that an employee is just not cut out for a certain job. Transferring the employee is one solution that could be considered. In some cases, the only solution is termination or firing. A number of states restrict employers' rights to fire employees under certain circumstances. If you do business in those states, you should check with your lawyer before terminating anyone.[40]

Firing an employee is distasteful to most managers, and need only be considered when all feasible attempts to rehabilitate the person have failed. The following guidelines not only should keep you on fairly solid legal ground, but provide the most humane methods for carrying out an unpleasant task.

1. *Give a warning.*   Employees do not generally have ESP, and may be quite in the dark about the fact that they're not doing a good job. If their work or relations with other people do not improve, you have at least opened the door to the next step.

2. *Give a reason.*   First, every employee deserves to know why he or she is being let go. Second, you are not helping an employee by not telling the truth. If you are honest this time, you give the employee a chance to improve in the next job. Give several reasons if possible. For example: "You've had too many accidents through carelessness"; "Your cooking is just not up to our standards, and it hasn't improved since the last time I talked to you"; or "You've had personality conflicts with everyone in the kitchen, and it is disruptive to production."

3. *Give the employee a chance to ask questions.*   Termination is a hard fact to face, and the employee is trying to sort it out in his or her mind. Give him or her time to do that. Fired persons who are encouraged to talk about it will be less likely to take legal action than if you handed them a pink slip and whisked them out the door. Among the questions they may have are: "How about my references?" "What do I do about unemployment?" Be prepared for such questions.

4. *Keep calm.*   Raising your voice above its normal tone is going to antagonize the employee and make the situation more unpleasant. Even if the employee raises his or her voice, be stoic. You have nothing to gain by doing otherwise, and everything to lose.

5. *Inform an employee of what you view as his or her good points.* Most people are not totally bad employees but have one or two points that make them unsuitable for a job. By describing their good *and* bad points, you tell them what they need to work on.

6. *Provide some sort of severance plan.* Unless an employee has stolen from you or committed some similar activity that prompted the firing, try to provide some severance pay. This will help lessen any bitterness, and you may avoid paying unemployment too soon.

7. *Keep a written record.* You should keep a written record of the events leading to the termination, the warning, the termination meeting, and any follow-up. You may need it if the employee takes legal action later. *Any major action taken with employees should be in writing.*

8. *Let go.* Finally, once the person has left, your task is over. Carrying on a personal vendetta or bad-mouthing an employee to a prospective employer invites legal action. When it comes to employee references, you need only give the dates of employment, the salary, and, in some cases, the attendance record. In addition, consider two common-sense tips: (1) Do not delegate the job of firing to someone else unless it is *directly* his or her responsibility, that is, that person is the employee's immediate supervisor. (2) Do not tell anyone except the supervisor beforehand. Word might get back to the employee sooner than it should.

In times of high unemployment, it appears people are more willing to take employers to court over the loss of work. In the following case the firing, coupled with the surrounding circumstances, resulted in a legal hassle for the foodservice employer when the alleged damages were "emotional distress." (Note the inconsistency in the employer's two "reasons" for the firing.)

Shirley Ann Counce v. M.B.M. Company, Inc.
Court of Appeals of Arkansas
597 S.W.2d 92 (1980)

Facts. The plaintiff, a waitress, was laid off from her job during the following sequence of events:

> The depositions reflect appellant was working with one other employee on the night shift on February 2, 1977, and had responsibility for the cash register, including inventory of funds in the register at the time of closing. The other employee had the key to the eating establishment and was responsible for locking up. The following day the manager called appellant and told her there was a shortage in monies in the register. Later in the day the manager called appellant and told her she was laid off because she had too much counter help. There was evidence there was no excess counter help. The appellee withheld $33.00 in excess of normal deductions from appellant's last pay. She took a polygraph test at the request of the appellee and it showed she had no connection with the money shortage. Notwithstanding this, appellee did not re-employ appellant or pay her the $33.00 withheld from her wages. The $33.00 was paid after an investigation by a federal or state agency.
>
> Appellant applied for unemployment benefits and appellee sent a report to the Employment Security Division showing appellant was terminated "because of numerous customer complaints and that she failed to follow company policy."
>
> Jerrell Moss, supervisor for the appellee owner of the food outlet, testified that he had telephone complaints from two customers about the service of a waitress meeting the description of appellant. The witness could not give the names of either of the parties making complaint. Appellant testified she called Mr. Moss, and asked why he had withheld her money and explained that she had passed the polygraph test and needed the money. He said, "I need mine, too."

The plaintiff brought suit against the employer. The employer filed for a summary judgment by the court, claiming there was no cause of action for the plaintiff's complaint.

The summary judgment was given in favor of the defendant. The plaintiff appealed. On her appeal, the plaintiff noted that a cause of action existed based on the breach of employment contract and the wrongful acts of the employer, which caused her "emotional distress." The appeals court reversed the summary judgment.

Reasoning.   The court found that a breach of contract did not exist because there was no infringement of a legal right owed the plaintiff.

However, on the allegation of a tort injury—that of mental distress—the court found differently, citing cases where damages were upheld for such distress. The court found that since there were factual issues in dispute (i.e., the reason for the firing, the problem with the missing money), a summary judgment was improper, and the plaintiff should have been allowed to argue her case fully.

Conclusion.   This case illustrates two points: (1) Termination for reasons that are nebulous, false, or simply unlikely to stand up in court can result in costly legal problems for the employer. (2) Follow-up "bad-mouthing" by an employer could precipitate a legal action that might not otherwise occur.

If you want to fire an employee for cause, be sure you have a legal leg to stand on.

UNIONIZATION: RESPECTIVE RIGHTS AND DUTIES OF EMPLOYER AND UNION

Employees have been unionizing to protect themselves since the beginning of the industrial revolution itself. Still, the foodservice industry is not as unionized as other industries, such as textile mills and car makers. This may be partly due to the high turnover in the industry. Or it may be attributable to the larger number of smaller commercial operations in the industry with fewer employees per unit than, say, automobile manufacturers or other businesses. Whatever the reason, the interest in unions in the industry is growing, and it is important that you know your own rights and the rights of your employees regarding unionization and collective bargaining.

Under the Labor Management Relations Act of 1947, as amended (popularly known as the Taft-Hartley Act), employees have five basic rights:[41]

1. To form or join a labor organization.
2. To select bargaining agents.
3. To bargain collectively with the employer.
4. To engage in acts of mutual support or protection.
5. To refrain from any union activity.

Basically, your employees have the right to hold union meetings, distribute literature, petition employers and the government, strike, picket, and engage in any legal activities to promote their common interests. But these rights are subject to restrictions. A court may stop any of these activities if carried out unlawfully. Plant or premises seizures, sit-down strikes, and violence are prohibited.

A union or pro-union group cannot force any employee to participate in union activities. However, employees may be required to listen to union solicitors, to pay union dues, and to join a union—if one is voted in—as a condition of continued employment. Under right-to-work laws in some states, the last requirement is prohibited, but even in these states non-union employees may still be required to pay union dues.

Prohibited Employer Labor Practices

Under the Act of 1947, the following labor practices by employers may be halted by a court order:

1. Interfering with employees' rights to unionize and take part in union activities.

You may express your anti-union viewpoint if your statements do not contain threats or unfair statements. You may *not* threaten to close the business if a union is formed, or to give a wage increase as a reward for voting against a union.

2. Either dominating or interfering with the formation or administration of any union. *Company-owned unions are forbidden.*

3. Encouraging or discouraging union membership by discriminating between union and non-union people in hiring, job tenure, and job conditions.

4. Discharging or discriminating against employees because they file unfair labor practice charges or testify against an employer. This provision of the Act prohibits the blacklisting of employees for exercising their legal rights. *It does not prevent an employer from disciplining employees who neglect their duties or are absent from work because of union activities.*

5. Discharging employees for legal strikes. A legal strike by lawful, nonviolent methods in protest of an unfair labor practice may not result in discharge of the strikers or their replacement. Through the federal *National Labor Relations Act,* the National Labor Relations Board (NLRB) has the power to order reinstatement of striking workers with reimbursement for wages lost because of an employer's illegal actions.[42]

Can the union and employer agree to a no-strike clause in their collective bargaining agreement and thereby eliminate the threat of strikes? Yes and no. The answer depends on the kind of strike being conducted by the union. A no-strike clause may prohibit an *economic strike,* one concerned with work hours, wages, and working conditions. A no-strike clause *may not* prohibit an *employee unfair labor practice strike*—a strike against an employer for denying workers the right to bargain collectively, for discriminating against union members, or for interfering with or restraining workers' attempts to bargain collectively.[43] The federal courts, which have the power to hear and determine controversies under the National Labor Relations Act, will not allow you to justify your violations of the Act by the use of a no-strike clause. Neither employer nor union unfair labor practices are made legal under the guise of a no-strike clause.[44]

What good is a no-strike clause? A no-strike clause gives you the right to hold the union financially responsible for business interruptions and other losses resulting from a strike. The no-strike clause is a means of making the union account in dollars for illegal strikes. The clause itself cannot stop the union from striking, but it can make any illegal strike very costly to employees, and hence less likely.

For example, a *wildcat strike* is a local strike, not sanctioned by the parent union, or voted on by a majority of the members. It is illegal. The NLRB can halt it and will uphold the firing of the striking employees. In case of a wildcat strike, a no-strike clause may permit you to recover monetary damages from the union. The no-strike clause serves to caution unions that illegal conduct that results in economic harm to the company will have to be paid out of the union treasury.

Prohibited Union Labor Practices

To prevent unions from abusing their powers over employers, the Act also contains the following prohibited *union* unfair labor practices. Union employees may not:

1. Restrain or coerce employees. This means that a union cannot use force, violence, or threats to compel an employee to join a union or to comply with union requirements. It cannot blacklist employees for

refusing to support a union or try to persuade employees to withdraw unfair labor practice charges.

2. Refuse to bargain with an employer's association. The union may not restrain the employer in the selection of the employer bargaining representative.

3. Cause an employer to discriminate against an employee because of refusal to join a union.

4. Refuse to bargain collectively with an employer. A union cannot bargain without the support of a majority of its members, or for an illegal purpose.

5. Encourage, threaten, or force any employee to strike or to refuse to handle work or products when the purpose is to compel an employer to join a labor union or employers' association; to bargain with a union not yet certified as such; to bargain with a union other than the one certified to represent the employees; or to prefer one union over another by assigning work on a preferential basis. Unions are forbidden to engage in a *secondary boycott* of a neutral employer to force that employer to harm another employer with whom the union has a dispute.[45]

   However, union members of the neutral employer may legally refuse to cross a picket line set up by the other union at the neutral employer's place of business. Likewise, the union can publicize its dispute at the neutral employer's place of business.

6. Require employees joining a union to pay excessive fees.

7. Cause an employer to pay or agree to pay for services that are not performed or not to be performed. This requirement is intended to eliminate *featherbedding,* the practice of paying employees for work that is not done. However, contracts for extra work not actually *needed,* but agreed to by the employer, are allowed.

8. Picket or threaten to picket any employer to force that employer to accept or to bargain with a union representative, unless the union is properly certified to do so. The purpose of this part of the Act is to prevent you, the employer, from getting caught in a dispute between two or more unions over which union will represent your employees.

   Informational picketing outside a restaurant by a union to advise the public that you do not employ their members is permitted. But if your employees refuse to cross such a picket line, then they violate the law.

9. Enter into any agreement with an employer where the employer agrees not to handle or deal in any of the products of another employer. Such a refusal to deal with other employers is called a *hot cargo clause.*

Filing a Complaint

How may an employee or employer proceed if he or she believes that the other party has committed an unfair labor practice? Anyone having a complaint can file a notice with the NLRB within six months after the activity occurs. If the charge has merit, the NLRB will issue a *complaint,* which will result in a hearing. If the NLRB finds that a violation of the Act has occurred, it may restore the parties to the conditions that existed before the start of the unfair practice. Either party may appeal an NLRB decision to the federal appeals court having jurisdiction and petition the Supreme Court of the United States to review the case.

The Act provides no penalties, either civil or criminal, for unfair labor practices. This means that no damages can be recovered by victims, nor any fines or jail terms imposed. However, a finding of a pattern or practice of violations will allow courts to impose heavier penalties when authorized by other provisions of the Act. A practice of violations creates a presumption of intentional misconduct.

Penalties are provided, however, for disobeying an *NLRB order* to correct a violation after one has been found. Like any other administrative order having the force and effect of law, your own or an employee's failure or refusal to comply with an NLRB order may result in punishment by a fine, or, in extreme cases, imprisonment. However, the National Labor Relations Board cannot alone make a refusal to obey their order a civil violation or crime. The NLRB must go to court to enforce the order if you or your employees refuse to comply with it. If on court review the order is reversed, it is unenforceable. If the reviewing court upholds the order, then you or the employees are in *contempt of court* if either of you still fail or refuse to obey the order. It is contempt of a court order that may cause criminal or civil penalties.

EMPLOYEE RELATIONS

You will want to maintain good relations with your employees. This responsibility is especially necessary in the foodservice industry, since many of your employees are in direct contact with patrons, who are your primary source of income. Any misjudgments on your part may result in poor employee morale, which will probably be reflected in indifferent employee attitudes toward your patrons. In the highly competitive foodservice industry your profit or loss statement cannot help but suffer if you fail to maintain constructive and consistent employee management policies.

The role of the law is to establish and enforce the rights and responsibilities of employers and employees to each other. These laws evolved from a common law, hands-off attitude, giving you sole discretion to hire, fire, promote, and determine working conditions,

to a series of federal and state regulations that restrict some management policies. You no longer can do as you please regarding employees. Where, however, the law does not intrude, you remain free to follow the dictates of the marketplace and your own conscience.

To enforce consistent management policies, you should consider preparing an employee manual, even if it's only a stapled photocopied handout. The importance is content and the content should reflect your own management policies, so that employees can see that you will be consistent and fair in management areas. You or a supervisor should go over the manual with a new employee so that any questions can be dealt with early. The manual should include the special policies and work rules of the restaurant as well as the typical personnel policies regarding attendance, sick days, and insurance.

In addition, any major incidents concerning employees should be described in writing, with a copy in the employee's file. This includes promotions, disciplinary actions, terminations, and work appraisals.

In any dealings with employees you should be able to answer yes to at least two questions: Is it fair? Is it businesslike? If you haven't answered yes, your relations with your employees may be strained—at the least.

SUMMARY

Your first responsibility as an employer is to comply with federal and state equal employment opportunity laws in screening and promoting employees. The federal laws, such as the Equal Pay Act of 1963 and Title VII of the Civil Rights Act of 1964, set the pattern, but may not be as inclusive as many state and city laws. State and local laws may cover other areas not regulated by federal acts. In some cities, employees may be protected from discrimination based on their sexual preference or on the fact that they may be recipients of welfare. Federal employment laws do not cover those areas. Once hired, aliens are covered by federal equal employment laws.

Your legal defenses for violations of the civil rights laws, normally based on your proving a *Bona Fide Occupational Qualification* (BFOQ) for the job or proving *business necessity,* are narrow and hard to establish under federal and comparable state laws. The costs and bad publicity involved in defending a discrimination case, regardless of the outcome, oblige you to *prevent* discriminatory practices.

Employer duties also carry over into supervision of foodservice workers. While it is important to maintain a secure operation, surveillance measures must respect employee rights and privacy.

Child labor laws come from both state and federal governments. The federal government usually sets conditions under which children may work. The state laws usually cover the number of hours an employee may work. Generally, the laws are concerned with the environmental conditions of jobs for minors and may prohibit their being given hazardous jobs handling foodservice equipment such as meat slicers and dishwashers.

Sexual harassment of female employees is of growing concern as more women enter the work force. This type of harassment by either employees or patrons should not be tolerated by foodservice employers.

QUESTIONS

1. A question on a job application asks, "Are your ancestors from Europe?" What is wrong with this question? Is it legal? If not, what law does it violate?
2. Marty of Marty's Marvelous Pies gives a baking test to applicants for baking positions. He also gives a grammar and math skills test to all applicants for every job, including dishwashers. Is there anything wrong with either of these tests? Why or why not?
3. When would a state child labor law be applied over a federal child labor law?
4. John Crown is the manager of a posh nightclub. He has a large number of women employees. What steps would you recommend John take to prevent sexual harassment of his employees and to minimize his liability?
5. Present an argument in favor of a no-strike clause in a union contract from the employer's viewpoint.

NOTES

1. 29 U.S.C. sec. 201 *et seq.* (1976 & Supp. IV 1980 & Supp. V 1981).
2. *Shultz v. Wheaton Glass Co.,* 421 F.2d 259 (3d Cir.), *cert. denied,* 398 U.S. 905 (1970).
3. 29 U.S.C. sec. 206(d)(1) (1976).
4. *Corning Glass Works v. Brennan,* 417 U.S. 188 (1974).
5. 42 U.S.C. sec. 701 *et seq.* (1976 & Supp. IV 1980 & Supp. V 1981). Discrimination on the basis of sex, religion, and national origin was prohibited by the Equal Employment Opportunity Act amendment to the Civil Rights Act in 1972. Congress amended the Civil Rights Act in 1978 to include pregnancy.
6. B. Schlei and P. Grossman, *Employment Discrimination Law* 249–50 (1976). "Interim earnings or amounts earnable with reasonable diligence by the person or persons discriminated against shall operate to reduce the back pay otherwise allowable." Civil Rights Act of 1964, *amended* 1972, sec. 706(g), 42 U.S.C. sec. 200e–5(g) (1976). The 1972 Amendments to the Civil Rights Act limit back-pay liability to a date not more than two years prior to filing of a charge with the Equal Employment Opportunity Commission. *Id.*
7. See *Kamberos v. GTE Automatic Elec., Inc.,* 603 F.2d 598 (7th Cir. 1979).
8. *Id.* Statutory authority is found at Civil Rights Act of 1964, *amended* 1972 sec. 706(g), 42 U.S.C. sec. 200e–5(g) (1976).

9. Schlei and Grossman, *supra* note 6, at 1258–59.

10. 42 U.S.C. sec. 1981 (1976). See *Johnson v. Railway Express Agency, Inc.*, 421 U.S. 454 (1975).

11. Civil Rights Act of 1964 sec. 706(k), 42 U.S.C. sec. 2000e–5(k) (1976). See *Newman v. Piggie Park Enterprises, Inc.*, 390 U.S. 400 (1968).

12. 42 U.S.C. sec. 2000e–3(a) (1976).

13. *Id.* sec. 703(e).

14. Schlei and Grossman, *supra* note 6, at 279. Employment of a French chef in a French restaurant was cited in the Senate Interpretive Memorandum on Title VII. Also see *Diaz v. Pan American World Airways*, 442 F.2d 385 (5th Cir.), *cert. denied*, 404 U.S. 950 (1971).

15. *Id.* (male airline stewards).

16. *Willingham v. Macon Telegraph Publishing Co.*, 507 F.2d 1084 (5th Cir. 1975).

17. Schlei and Grossman, *supra* note 6, at 99–100.

18. *Carroll v. Talman Federal Sav. and Loan Ass'n of Chicago*, 604 F.2d 1028 (7th Cir. 1979), *cert. denied*, 445 U.S. 929 (1980).

19. 29 U.S.C. secs. 621–34 (1976 & Supp. IV 1980 & Supp. V 1981).

20. 29 U.S.C. sec. 794a(A)(1) (Supp. IV 1980). See also *id.* secs. 701–94.

21. Human Rights Law, N.Y. Exec. Law sec. 296(2) (McKinney 1982).

22. *Guerra v. Manchester Terminal Corp.*, 498 F.2d 641 (5th Cir. 1974).

23. *Espinoza v. Farah Mfg. Co.*, 414 U.S. 86 (1973).

24. 8 U.S.C. secs. 1324, 1324(a) (1976).

25. *United States v. Mount Fuji Japanese Steak House, Inc.*, 435 F. Supp. 1194 (E.D.N.Y. 1977). The otherwise illegal harboring of unregistered aliens is a felony, and upon conviction subjects the guilty person to a maximum $2000 fine, or maximum five-year prison term, or both.

26. *NLRB v. Sure-Tan, Inc.*, 672 F.2d 592, 599 (7th Cir. 1982).

27. Where the purpose or effect of citizenship requirements is private discrimination on the basis of national origin, such a question is invalid. EEOC National Origin Guidelines, 29 C.F.R. sec. 1606.5 (1982). Otherwise each state is free to make citizenship a requirement for private employment.

28. *Lopez v. Arrowhead Ranches*, 523 F.2d 924 (9th Cir. 1975), citing *Chavez v. Freshpict Foods, Inc.*, 456 F.2d 890 (10th Cir.), *cert. denied*, 409 U.S. 1042 (1972) and *Flores v. George Braun Packing Co.*, 482 F.2d 279 (5th Cir. 1973). See also *Cort v. Ash*, 422 U.S. 66 (1975).

29. *Griggs v. Duke Power Co.*, 401 U.S. 424 (1971).

30. J. Sherry, *The Laws of Innkeepers*, sec. 11:1 (rev. ed. 1981).

31. See the following labor arbitration cases: *Electronic Instrument Co. (Eico)*, 44 Lab. Arb. 563 (1965); *EMC Corp.*, 46 Lab. Arb. 335 (1966); and *Colonial Baking Co.*, 62 Lab. Arb. 587 (1974) involving visual surveillance of employees by management. Only in *Eico* did the arbitrator rule in favor of halting management's visual surveillance practices (closed-circuit TV).

32. See *Rakas v. Illinois*, 439 U.S. 128, 140–48 (1978) (examination of privacy doctrine); *Thomas v. General Elec. Co.*, 207 F. Supp. 792 (W.D. Ky. 1962).

33. Waks and Starr, *Sexual Harassment in the Work Place: The Scope of Employer Liability*, 7 Employee Relations L.J. 369 (1981–82).

34. 45 Fed. Reg. 74676 (Nov. 10, 1980).

35. 42 U.S.C. sec. 2000e *et seq.* (1976); *Tomkins v. Public Serv. Elec. & Gas Co.*, 568 F.2d 1044 (3d Cir. 1977); *Barnes v. Costle*, 561 F.2d 983 (D.C. Cir. 1977); *Garber v. Saxon Business Prods., Inc.*, 552 F.2d 1032 (4th Cir. 1977) *(per curiam)*.

36. 29 C.F.R. sec. 1604.11(a) (1982).

37. *Ludington v. Sambo's Restaurants, Inc.*, 474 F. Supp. 480 (E.D. Wis. 1979).

38. 29 C.F.R. sec. 1604.11(3) (1982).

39. *Id.* sec. 1604.11(f).

40. The 14 states known to limit employers' rights are Arizona, California, Illinois, Indiana, Kentucky, Massachusetts, Michigan, New Hampshire, New Jersey, Ohio, Oregon, Pennsylvania, Washington, and West Virginia.

41. 29 U.S.C. sec. 141 *et seq.* (1976 & Supp. IV 1980 & Supp. V 1981).

42. *Id.* sec. 151 *et seq.*

43. *Id.* sec. 158 defines unfair labor practices. See also *Mastro Plastics Corp. v. NLRB*, 350 U.S. 270 (1956).

44. 29 U.S.C. sec. 158 (1976).

45. *Id.* sec. 158(b)(4)(A).

7

The Law and Your Employees II
Administration

Objectives

The purpose of this chapter is to:
1. Discuss insurance options and requirements.
2. Explain OSHA requirements.
3. Outline employer obligations regarding employee wages, taxation, and tax credits.

Case in Point

The Occupational Health and Safety Administration *inspector, or a person who says he is, is at Frank's High Street restaurant. It is high noon and the business crowd rush has begun. The inspector says he can find his way around the restaurant by himself. Two employees say they had to turn off the main oven so the inspector could check the interior safety features. The inspector tells Frank that he found three violations and that Frank will hear from the local agency "sometime." What legal options could Frank have used to protect his rights?*

For starters, Frank could have asked the man for credentials. For all he knew, the person could have been casing the operation to find the safe. Second, he should have arranged with the inspector to come at a more convenient time, when the restaurant was not quite so busy. That would have given Frank the opportunity to accompany him to point out safety compliance measures and answer questions. Finally, Frank could have asked the inspector to discuss the violations.

ADMINISTRATION AND THE LAW

There are administrative tasks involved in managing foodservice employees. Some of them are a matter of employer choice, such as whether to require certain employees to obtain bonding insurance. Others, such as minimum wages and taxation, may be regulated by both federal and state governments. This end of employee management may have legal implications for operators and requires them to be very astute when it comes to record keeping and supervision.

EMPLOYEE INSURANCE

There are various kinds of employee-related insurance plans. Some are designed to protect you, the employer, from liability for employee actions. Others compensate the employee for injuries suffered on the job.

Liability Insurance

Liability insurance provides protection (indemnification) against losses for damages resulting from injuries to a person or property by your employees. (See Chapter 5 on liability II.) This insurance is optional and employers must use their own judgment as to whether or not to use it, depending on the size of the operation, the turnover, and the type of job. Operators who serve alcohol, offer flaming dishes, or provide additional live entertainment may want to consider whether this insurance would be helpful. Others may want to rely only on good employee training to prevent liability.

Fidelity Insurance

This type of insurance protects you against dishonesty or embezzlement—taking property entrusted to one's care for personal use—by an employee. It is normally issued for key people who handle or transport cash receipts, such as a night supervisor in your restaurant. This form of insurance, called a *fidelity bond,* is issued by a bonding company.

As with liability insurance, the same exceptions and defenses are available to the bonding company, except that with bonding, criminal misconduct, as well as employee carelessness, is covered. *Your own* criminal misconduct, however, is the ground on which the carrier is exempted from responsibility in most policies.

As you might imagine, this is expensive coverage. Both the employer and the bonded employee are very carefully screened. It is solely within the discretion of the bonding company to accept or reject your application.

WORKERS' COMPENSATION

Before the development of major industrial growth, our society was rural, mostly agricultural, and economically self-contained. Work was simple and the family head was responsible for the few on-the-job accidents that occurred. In the eighteenth century the development of machines and the size and complexity of business enterprises created industrial hazards unknown to the pre-industrial period.

During the transition to an industrial economy, increased numbers of job-related injuries required remedial legislation. Two major types of laws were passed to cope with this problem: workers' compensation laws and Occupational Safety and Health Administration (OSHA) statutes.

At common law, the worker injured on the job had to sue the employer to recover compensation. To succeed, the worker had to prove that negligence or intentional misconduct by the employer caused the injuries. The employer could defend on the ground that the employee's own fault or inattention caused the injuries, or that the employee voluntarily assumed the risks of injury by accepting the job. The employer could also say that the injuries were caused by the carelessness or misconduct of *another* employee. Both defenses could defeat the injured employee's lawsuit.[1] Very few employees were able to recover under these rules of common law, and many lost their jobs as a result either of lawsuits or of the injuries.

The first effort to provide workers' compensation was the Federal Workmen's Compensation Act of 1908. Today every state has adopted some form of workers' compensation. However, federal law still covers federal employees. The state statutes are not uniform, but certain basic similarities do exist.

Each statute provides a plan to pay employees or their dependents for death, injuries, or physical disabilities caused directly by their employment. The carelessness of the employee is no longer a defense, nor need the employee establish any fault or misconduct on the employer's part. Further, an injured employee cannot sue the employer for injuries covered by workers' compensation.

Payable amounts for injuries are fixed by state or federal law, either at a definite sum for each type of injury or some percentage of the employee's weekly wage or salary. Compensation includes coverage of medical, doctor, hospital, and rehabilitation expenses, as well as payments for diminished earning capacity resulting from the injury. No payment is provided for injury-related pain and suffering, disfigurement, or loss of consortium (services) to a spouse.

For an employee to be covered under compensation, the injury must arise in the scope of the employee's duties to the employer. One test of the term "in the scope of" is whether the employee was acting for the benefit of his or her employer at the time of the injury. This time can include commuting time, mealtime, and washup time. It is an elastic term, depending on the facts of each case. The U.S. Supreme Court has rejected any narrow definition and held that it is sufficient if the condition of employment creates a *zone of special danger* out of which the injury arises. A worker injured while moving cases of wine in your storeroom is covered, as is the same employee mugged on the way to deliver your nightly totals to the bank.[2]

An injured employee is virtually compelled to claim workers' compensation benefits, since there is no legal alternative against the employer. But the employee *may sue a third party* who caused the injury and still recover workers' compensation. In such cases a lien or claim by the Workmen's Compensation Board is available to be applied against the third party, to reimburse the Board for any compensation payments made to the employee. Neither the employee nor the employer may initially have a court decide the merits of any claim. This is the function of the state workers' compensation hearing board. However, either side may appeal any adverse ruling to an appropriate reviewing court.

The courts recognize certain employer defenses to workers' compensation claims. An employee who deliberately causes an injury in order to collect benefits will be denied payment. Injuries caused by worker intoxication are also causes for denial of benefits.

Workers' compensation insurance *must* be carried by every employer. A failure to carry it, whether or not intentional, is a crime in many states, making violators subject to fines, and even imprisonment. If no insurance exists, the Workmen's Compensation Board may sue the employer for the value of any payments the Board makes to an employee.

As with any insurance, you are subject to an experience rating based on the number and frequency of claims filed and paid. To keep this necessary business cost reasonable, it is in your favor to make every effort to *prevent* employee accidents (Figure 7.1).

OCCUPATIONAL SAFETY AND HEALTH

Workers' compensation laws can only compensate for job-related deaths and injuries. They do not help *prevent* deaths or injuries caused by unsafe working conditions.

Confronted with the spiraling costs to industry of loss of production time, lost employee wages, and the increasing costs of workers' compensation insurance premiums, Congress enacted the federal *Occupational Safety and Health Act of 1970*.[3] This comprehensive statute encourages employers and employees to reduce job hazards by voluntary cooperation. To support this joint effort, Congress established responsibilities and rights for both employers and employees.

1. *General*   You are required to furnish your employees a workplace free from hazards that may cause death or serious injury. You must act on your own to remedy safety violations. *This duty is in addition to and not a substitute for state or local safety requirements.*

2. *Safety standards*   You must comply with any safety and health standards established by the Occupational Safety and Health Administration (OSHA), the regulatory agency that enforces the Act. The standards are often complex, not to mention costly to implement. Failure to comply, however, may be even more costly.

3. *Records*   It is a good idea to keep a record of every accident involving employees. A report of any accident causing death *or* resulting in injury to five or more persons must be filed immediately with the Department of Labor. You must post OSHA notices advising employees of their legal rights regarding safety.

4. *Safety programs*   You are encouraged to establish your own safety checklist to discover and correct job hazards. As a commonsense rule, you should create and implement your own training program in on-the-job safety. (Figure 7.2 is a good checklist and can serve as a self-inspection before the real one.) This program should include your current OSHA compliance

Figure 7.1
Ten Ways to Protect Yourself from Workers' Compensation Claims

1. *Know your state law.* This includes knowing the facts about the following areas:
   - Posting requirements—refers to mandatory notices that are posted for employees regarding benefits.
   - Time limits—refers to time permitted for filing and contesting workers' compensation claims.
   - Application—involves knowing the types of questions relating to claims that may be asked under state and federal laws.
   - Coverage—knowing whether you're responsible for criminal acts of customers against employees, and of employees against customers and employees, etc.
   - Insurance requirements—refers to the legality, costs, and advantages or disadvantages of being self-insured or commercially insured.
   - Related laws—involves knowing state and local laws regarding use of the polygraph, blood alcohol tests, and the like, in order to avoid liability.

2. *Have clear rules on the "scope of employees" and duties of employees.*
   - Let employees know that being off the time clock means being off duty.
   - Ensure that employees' driving of a company vehicle is the exception, not the rule.
   - Understand your obligation if your employees have more than one employer, such as in the case of banquet "extras."
   - Do not allow employees to engage in personal business in the workplace.
   - Do not permit horseplay in the workplace at any time.
   - Know your responsibility for any member of an "outside" staff, such as a sales staff. Many states have adopted the theory of "continuous employment" for the entire time an employee is required to be away from home as part of the job, including after-hours entertainment.
   - Check your liability for injuries during meal breaks. You may have no liability for injuries if there's a specific, scheduled break in which employees are free to do what they want.

3. *Develop a communications program.* It's important to maintain a consistent and effective communications program with employees on workers' compensation problems.

4. *Investigate accidents early.* It's important to investigate any accident promptly, to ensure getting all the relevant facts. Always obtain affidavits from witnesses. And contest the workers' compensation claim promptly if the employee is at fault.

5. *Pay valid claims without delay.* You have a legal and moral obligation to pay valid claims immediately. This also ensures good employee relations, and may be to your advantage when you contest a dubious claim.

6. *Keep accurate records.* Maintain a file on all claims, whether valid or not. Also, keep on file all witness affidavits that you obtain.

7. *Coordinate claims with your labor attorney.* Be sure to consider other labor cases that are pending with the same employee, such as wage and hour claims, unemployment insurance, and so on. Your labor attorney can advise you on whether admissions and testimony in one case can be useful in another.

8. *Do not reemploy the worker without a doctor's letter.* If any injury is serious enough for the employee to win workers' compensation payments, it's serious enough that you need a letter from the doctor to be sure the employee is able to be back at work.

9. *Do not change the employee's position on staff without a doctor's letter.* Protect yourself from future claims by requiring a doctor's letter stating that the employee is able to handle certain kinds of work before you reassign that employee. Take nothing for granted.

10. *Fight frivolous claims.* Perhaps the best way to discourage future frivolous claims is to fight each one as it comes along. Employees must know that you make a habit of investigating each claim and that you promptly pay valid claims, but must also be aware that questionable cases are going to be disputed.

Courtesy of Arch Stokes of Stokes, Lazarus and Watson law firm.

Figure 7.2
Safety Considerations for Owners/Managers Relative to OSHA Regulations

YES indicates satisfactory;
NO indicates immediate attention needed.

YES	NO	
____	____	1. Is an OSHA poster posted in a prominent place where employees report to work?
____	____	2. Are OSHA forms properly filled out and displayed if required?
____	____	3. Is a proper first-aid kit readily accessible to employees?
____	____	4. Is there an ongoing safety program?
____	____	5. Is a trained first-aid attendant on duty (required in 24-hour operations)?
____	____	6. Are safety feet on ladders?
____	____	7. Are portable metal ladders' connections of rungs or steps to side rails rigid and are they corrugated, knuckled, dimpled, or coated with skid-resistant materials?
____	____	8. Are floors dry and nonslippery from drippage, seepage, or splash?
____	____	9. Are duckboards or metal matting provided in wet floor areas?
____	____	10. Is the building free of protruding pipe ends, nails, and other obstructions?
____	____	11. Are floors clear of litter or other items that should not be on floors?
____	____	12. Are aisle ways clear of obstructions?
____	____	13. Is there sufficient clearance for carts or traffic?
____	____	14. Is a hand rail or railing on stairways?
____	____	15. Are floors, stairs, or aisles free of hazardous obstacles such as hoses, cords, etc.?
____	____	16. Are fire extinguishers tested (hydrostatic test every five years)?
____	____	17. Are fire extinguishers inspected (recorded on tag every year)?
____	____	18. Are empty extinguishers recharged?
____	____	19. For a hand extinguisher of gross weight not exceeding forty pounds, is the extinguisher top not more than five feet above the floor?
____	____	20. Are there sufficient exits for fire or emergency?
____	____	21. For a hand extinguisher of gross weight exceeding forty pounds, is the extinguisher top not more than three and one-half feet above the floor?
____	____	22. For extinguishers mounted in cabinets or wall recesses or set on shelves, are the locations conspicuously marked?
____	____	23. Are exits unlocked and unblocked?
____	____	24. Are emergency exits marked and illuminated?
____	____	25. Is the travel distance not more than seventy-five feet to reach the nearest exit?
____	____	26. Is the electrical wiring system grounded?
____	____	27. Are food mixers, grinders, slicers and other electrical equipment grounded?
____	____	28. Have all frayed or spliced electrical cords and broken plugs been repaired or replaced?
____	____	29. Are danger, caution or safety instruction signs or stickers posted?

Courtesy of Colorado–Wyoming Restaurant Association

Figure 7.2
Safety Considerations for Owners/Managers Relative to OSHA Regulations (*Continued*)

YES indicates satisfactory;
NO indicates immediate attention needed.

YES	NO	
___	___	30. Is cutting, chopping and grinding equipment guarded?
___	___	31. Is housekeeping good in general work areas, storage areas or utility rooms?
___	___	32. Are adequate toilet facilities provided for each sex?
___	___	33. Are adequate hand washing facilities with towels and cleansing agents provided?
___	___	34. Is receptacle covered in toilet room used by women?
___	___	35. Are toilets, lavatories and dressing rooms clean, illuminated and ventilated?
___	___	36. Is ventilation and illumination adequate in kitchen and storage area?
___	___	37. Are adequate exhaust vents on all cooking units?
___	___	38. Are vents equipped with proper filters and regularly cleaned?
___	___	39. Is there adequate food storage to prevent contamination?
___	___	40. Are all sweepings, solid and liquid wastes, refuse and garbage removed in such a manner as to avoid creating a nuisance or unsanitary condition?
___	___	41. Is instruction given on proper use of pressure cookers?
___	___	42. Is there a safety latch on freezer doors?
___	___	43. Is fire protection equipment and apparatus painted red?
___	___	44. Is green the color for designating "Safety," and your first aid equipment?
___	___	45. Are waterflow alarms provided on all sprinkler systems?
___	___	46. Is alarm apparatus readily available for inspection and repair on sprinkler systems?
___	___	47. Are sprinkler systems inspected annually and inspection reports filed by a competent inspector?
___	___	48. Are sprinkler head clearances above the top of stored materials at least thirty-six inches?
___	___	49. Is all fixed equipment (floor mixers, electric saws, etc.) securely anchored to prevent walking or moving?
___	___	50. Is all equipment protected against over-current?
___	___	51. Are transformers installed outdoors isolated from combustible materials?
___	___	52. Are no live parts of appliances (excepting toasters, grills, stoves, etc.) exposed to contact?
___	___	53. Are wall-mounted ovens and counter-mounted cooking units provided with a breaker or other approved disconnect?
___	___	54. Are infrared lamps and lamp holders of a type approved for infrared service?
___	___	55. Do you have a minimum ceiling height of 7'6" for means of egress and no projection from the ceiling less than 6'8" from the floor?
___	___	56. Are safety posters regularly posted?
___	___	57. Are monthly safety training sessions held with employees?
___	___	58. Is a Safety Committee appointed?

Courtesy of Colorado–Wyoming Restaurant Association

procedures and additional procedures recommended by OSHA. Your own safety rules should be posted and periodically reviewed with each employee. Continuous supervision and education for safety are your responsibility.

5. *Inspections*   An OSHA compliance officer is given broad authority to conduct an inspection of any work area at reasonable times and to interview employees. (However, a provision of the law giving OSHA inspectors the right to conduct an inspection over your objection—without a search warrant—has been held unconstitutional by the Supreme Court of the United States.)[4]

6. *Penalties*   Civil and criminal penalties are provided for violations of OSHA safety standards and failures to comply with OSHA violation notices (citations). The maximum penalty is $10,000 for each intentional or repeated violation of OSHA standards. If you fail to correct a violation or to prepare required reports, you can be fined up to $1000. Willful violations that result in death to an employee are punishable by a maximum $10,000 fine and/or imprisonment of up to six months. Fines and jail terms double for second offenders. Any person who informs an employer about a planned compliance inspection by an OSHA officer can be fined up to $1000 and/or imprisoned up to six months.

These penalties are independent of penalties prescribed by state or local safety laws.

The following factors are considered by OSHA in fixing any penalty: (a) the size of the business, (b) the seriousness of the violation, (c) the good faith of the employer (violation was not intentional), and (d) the history of violations by the employer.

Employer Rights

1. *Exemption from compliance*   If you determine that you cannot comply with a certain standard immediately, you may request a *variance,* or an exemption from the standard. To obtain the variance, you must show that you are unable to comply at present, that you are taking all possible steps to keep your employees safe from any hazards, and that you will have an effective safety program eventually. Variances are temporary and are limited to no more than one year in length, but can be renewed for good cause, especially for delays due to circumstances beyond your control.

2. *Establishment of standards*   You have the right to present your views on any existing or proposed OSHA standard to the National Advisory Committee on Occupational Safety and Health, which is made up of employer, employee, and professional safety representatives. You also have the right to comment on any proposed standards before they become law.[5] You are also entitled to request a public hearing on proposed standards.

Once any proposed safety standard is adopted by OSHA, it has the force of law, and the courts will enforce it as written, unless it is found to be arbitrary in enforcement or application. The normal rule of court review is whether there is substantial evidence to support the standard. If there is, the standard is binding on the courts. Courts will not typically second-guess OSHA's administrative expertise in safety.

3. *Compliance inspections*   You have certain rights regarding inspections that OSHA is required to respect:

   a. You have the right to review the credentials and identification of the inspector before allowing any inspection.

   b. You have the right to insist that the inspection be conducted at a reasonable hour.

c. You have the right to require the OSHA inspector to conduct the inspection in a reasonable manner, so as not to disrupt your food and beverage production.

d. You have the right to present evidence of your good faith in showing compliance, by pointing to existing safety programs and rules.

e. You have the right to accompany the inspector so you can answer questions and point out compliance steps you have taken.

f. You have the right to obtain copies of the inspector's findings.

g. In some states, you may also have the right to request a search warrant for any inspection of records.[6]

OSHA staffers are required to discuss any violations found and to fix a time period for you to correct the problem. OSHA should notify you within six months of the inspection if a citation or violation notice will be issued. Any OSHA citation must be in writing, stating the nature of the violation, the remedy required, and whether any penalty will be imposed.

Do you have the right to discipline an employee who refuses to comply with any OSHA standard or rule? Yes, although OSHA cannot penalize the employee.

Do you have the right to fire or discipline an employee for reporting a safety hazard covered by OSHA? *No. Retaliation of this kind is prohibited.* If you do so, you may be prosecuted and forced to reinstate the employee with all seniority rights, fringe benefits, and back pay.

A foodservice operation can be a hazardous place to work unless employers take steps to prevent accidents. Rather than relying on agencies such as OSHA to dictate safety steps, it is better to come up with your own workable safety program. Doing so not only will keep your own employees safe, but also will keep your insurance costs down.

Along with any safety program must go a training program for employees. Numerous safety signs all over your operation are not likely to have the same effect as a brief, practical safety training program. Skits and foodservice examples, as well as other training aids, might be useful methods. (The program might also involve a short first-aid training manual, including the use of stop-choking techniques, especially important in foodservice operations.)

ADMINISTERING WAGES AND BENEFITS

The federal Fair Labor Standards Act (FLSA) of 1938, enforced by the Wage and Hour Division of the Department of Labor, establishes requirements concerning minimum wages, work time, overtime pay, and equal pay for equal work (the Equal Pay Act of 1963), and regulates child labor.[7] The Age Discrimination Employment Act of 1967 prohibits age discrimination. (The EEOC administers the regulations on equal pay and age discrimination.)

Employment Terms Defined under the Act

An *employer* is any person who directly or indirectly manages, supervises, or acts in the interest of an employer in relation to an employee. Everyone from the president of a foodservice company down to a cafeteria manager is an employer, which means they can all be held responsible for wage and hour violations.

Employee means any individual employed by a covered establishment.

Employ means to permit to work, meaning an employer's knowledge of work done for him or her by another person. Proof that the employer supervises or manages the work of an employee *is not required.*

Trainees (or *students*) who work without any expressed or implied compensation agreement are *not* employees if *all* of the following criteria are met:

1. The training given on the premises is similar to that given at a vocational school.
2. The training is for the benefit of the trainees or students.
3. The trainees or students do not displace regular employees.
4. The employer providing the training derives no immediate benefit from the activities of the trainees.
5. The trainees are not guaranteed jobs at the end of the training period.
6. Both the employer and the trainees or students understand that no compensation is to be paid for the time spent in training.

Who Is Covered under the FLSA?

Coverage under the Fair Labor Standards Act is based on two tests: (1) individual employee status and (2) enterprise status.

Individual employees are covered if their jobs involve interstate commerce or they work in producing goods for transportation in interstate commerce. Working in interstate commerce means dealing with *patrons, goods,* or *services* that cross state lines; or the employee travels across state lines either to and from work or in the course of employment; or communicating across state lines is a major part of the job. Food production employees whose products cross state lines, as well as foodservice employees who deal with out-of-state patrons, are covered under the FLSA.

Enterprises are covered if they operate a business, individually or as a chain; engage in interstate commerce, or are in the production of goods for interstate commerce; and meet a *dollar volume of business test.*

The dollar volume of business test for retail or service establishments is met if the business makes yearly gross sales of $362,500, not counting retail excise taxes that are separately stated.

There is an important exception for *family operations.* The law does not cover these if the only employees are the owner and a spouse, children, and other members of the immediate family.

All *units* of a foodservice chain are covered even though an individual unit of a chain may not meet the dollar volume of business test, as long as the *total sales* of the chain equal or exceed the dollar volume amount.

Seasonal amusement or recreational establishments are also exempt from the Fair Labor Standards Act, if they do not operate for more than seven months in a calendar year *or* if the average receipts for any six months of the preceding calendar year were not more than 33.3 percent of the average receipts for the other six months of that year.

Work Time under FLSA

Work time includes not only all required hours the employee must be on duty or at a designated place to work, but also all times when the employee is permitted to work by the employer. Generally, employees must be paid *at least the federal minimum wage for all hours worked.*

In addition, every employee who works over the maximum number of hours in the *employer's workweek* must be paid at least one and one-half times his or her regular rate of pay for the overtime hours.

The Fair Labor Standards Act does *not fix the hours worked* in order to determine employee rights to overtime pay. There is no federal requirement for overtime pay for hours worked after, say, eight hours a day. However, your labor union contract or state labor laws may stipulate overtime pay rules.

According to the FLSA, permitting work includes voluntary overtime *you may not request but which you do not forbid.* Should you be challenged for overtime pay, the burden is on you to prove that you expressly prohibited overtime work. You must communicate and enforce overtime rules, or you may face very costly back-pay claims if you're challenged.

Absences caused by illness or disability and time off for holidays and vacations are not considered work time under the Act. It is up to you to decide how to pay for such times off the job, or to negotiate times off under any labor agreement with your employees.

When you require your employees to change clothes and wash up on *your premises,* time spent doing so is counted as *work time and must be compensated.*

Minimum Wage Requirements

The minimum wage fluctuates and is based on a *single workweek.* Each workweek is defined as a regularly recurring period of 168 hours in seven consecutive 24-hour periods. It need not be a calendar week, and it may begin on any day and any hour of the day.[8]

No state may require a minimum wage payment less than the federal scale. States may, however, require a higher minimum wage.

Tip Credit

Federal law provides for the fact that many foodservice employees receive tips from patrons. Employers may add a *tip credit* to the cash wage due tipped employees in order to meet the federal minimum wage scale.

A *tipped employee* is any employee engaged in an occupation in which he or she regularly receives more than $30 per month in tips.

A *tip* is a *voluntary* gratuity for services rendered by the employee, and is made by the patron in cash or by credit card. *A compulsory service charge, imposed by the employer, is not a tip, nor is a charge negotiated between employer and patron under a banquet or other standard function contract, nor is any tip-pooling agreement between employer and employee that requires employees to treat such tips as income to the employer. A tip is a tip when employees may keep most or all of it.* In no other case may you claim a tip credit. The tip credit permitted is 40 percent of the minimum wage. To qualify for the tip credit, the law requires you to:

1. Inform your employees about this allowance before you use the credit.
2. Permit your tipped employees to keep all tips, either on an individual basis or under a valid tip-pooling agreement among the employees. An employer cannot force the employees to agree to an arrangement.
3. Be able to prove that your tipped employees received the minimum wage after the credit was applied.
4. Pay every tipped employee at least half the prevailing minimum wage in the form of a direct cash wage for each hour worked.

If you do decide to forgo the tip credit and agree to a pooling arrangement between yourself and the employees, be aware that under such agreements, waiters and waitresses cannot be required to contribute a greater percentage of their tips than is customary and reasonable.

The following case is the tale of one foodservice employer who failed to fulfill the FLSA requirements regarding the tip credit.

Barcellona v. Tiffany English Pub, Inc.
Federal Court of Appeals, 5th Circuit
597 F.2d 464 (1979)

Facts.   Former waiters of TGI Friday's restaurant, which was doing business as Tiffany English Pub, sued Friday's for using their tips to satisfy the requirements of the Fair Labor Standards Act that every employer pay a minimum wage. The waiters also sued to recover back wages, damages, and attorney's fees, all of which are available remedies under the FLSA. The waiters said they were required to surrender their tips to the employer and had not agreed to the tip credit on that basis.

Friday's argued that the waiters had agreed to Friday's withholding of tips to satisfy the minimum wage law. The federal district trial court found no such agreement existed, and that Friday's had committed a serious violation of the FLSA. The court awarded back wages and attorney's fees, but refused, because of a failure to find that the employer intentionally violated the law, to award damages to the waiters. The district court findings of liability and award of attorney's fees were upheld. The district court finding of no justification for damages was reversed and remanded (sent back) for a further hearing on that question only.

Reasoning.   The appeals court found Friday's contention that it had a valid agreement with the waiters regarding the tip credit false, and if there was no agreement, the tips belonged to the employees. The court upheld the federal trial court's findings, saying:

> The restaurant contended that it had a valid agreement with the waiters that *all* tips belonged to the restaurant, to be surrendered to it to count towards satisfying its obligation to pay the waiters a minimum wage. In practice, however, the system in no way resembled that described by the restaurant. Although the restaurant introduced "acknowledgments" apparently signed by some of the waiters which attempted to create the impression that the waiters were employed by TGI Friday's on the condition and with the understanding that all of their tips belonged to the employer, there was substantial evidence that the waiters had never heard of such a policy or of any agreement that they were to relinquish ownership of their tips. The

> testimony of the restaurant's witnesses and the testimony presented by the waiters reveals such vast conflicts that only one version could have been accepted. The trial court, having the opportunity to observe the demeanor of the witnesses and exhaustively review the records of the restaurant, decided that "the evidence . . . has not shown or convinced the Court by a preponderance that the employer and these employees had any agreement or understanding as to such disposition of these tips . . ." Although there was evidence going both ways, the restaurant did not meet the formidable burden of upsetting the district court's findings . . .

In a curious maneuver, the employers used ignorance of the law as one of their defenses. This defense was used against the back pay award but not against the compensatory damages. However, the appeals court held that defense was insufficient and that the trial court's earlier finding of a flagrant violation by the employer contradicted its failure to require Friday's to pay damages:

> The only indication we can glean from the record concerning Friday's good faith and the reasonableness of its belief in the legalities of its actions is the restaurant's contention that the owners were merely a couple of farmers, acting for the first time as employers, with blind faith in their franchisor. Perhaps this argument was the basis for the district court's decision to deny liquidated damages due to nondefiant ignorance. This is curious because the court's conclusory justification for its denial of liquidated damages is so totally inconsistent with its earlier finding of a willful and flagrant violation of the FLSA.
>
> . . . In addition to our concern over the inconsistency between the finding of a flagrant violation and yet a later denial of liquidated damages based on nondefiant ignorance, we also doubt the validity of ignorance as a defense to liability for liquidated damages under [the law].
>
> We do not believe an employer may rely on ignorance alone as *reasonable* grounds for believing that its actions were not in violation of the [Act] . . .

Further, we feel that good faith requires some duty to investigate potential liability under the FLSA . . .

Even inexperienced businessmen cannot claim good faith when they blindly operate a business without making any investigation as to their responsibilities under the labor laws. Apathetic ignorance is never the basis of a reasonable belief.

Conclusion.   The foodservice operators were clearly in the wrong on two counts: They failed to set up a valid agreement with the waiters in order to qualify for the tip credit, and they failed to make themselves aware of the law regarding wages and tip credits. This reinforces the old maxim, "Ignorance is no excuse." We might add, "and can be very expensive."

Other Credits
You may also credit the minimum wage with the reasonable cost of board or lodging, or other benefits customarily furnished by you for your employees, *if* the costs of such arrangements are not excluded from wages they receive under a collective bargaining agreement. These benefits may include meals furnished by foodservice operators to employees and transportation between home and work when it is not part of the job. However, these benefits must be included as part of the regular wage in figuring overtime pay.

Uniforms and Uniform Maintenance
You are required to reimburse employees for the costs of purchasing uniforms necessary for their jobs. You are only required to reimburse them for maintenance of the uniforms if you require that they be washed daily, or if they require special treatment, such as dry cleaning. If the uniforms can be washed in the employee's regular laundry, you are not required to reimburse them for laundry costs. You may claim a uniform credit against each employee's wages, as long as each employee's pay is not reduced below the minimum wage.

If you require special maintenance, you must reimburse each employee an hour's pay per week at the minimum wage rate.

Federal Income Tax Laws
Payroll tax law is contained in the Federal Insurance Contributions Act (FICA), the Federal Unemployment Tax Act (FUTA), and the Internal Revenue Service Code.[9] FICA subjects you to liability for these taxes from the first day you employ any person and pay that employee wages.

Your spouse and your minor children (under 21) are exempt from FICA and FUTA taxes if they work for you in your own business. A corporation is not exempt. You are liable for FUTA taxes if you pay wages of $1500 or more in any calendar quarter, or if you have one or more employees at any time in each of 20 calendar weeks.

You are required to withhold federal income taxes from employee wages whenever you employ anyone. This requirement does not extend to certain religious, charitable, educational, or other organizations certified as exempt by the Internal Revenue Service.[10] Not every nonprofit organization qualifies for this exemption.

Under federal law, both withholding and FICA taxes are combined for purposes of payment. You must report all wages paid each calendar quarter. Bank deposits are the method of payment required by law, with the time of deposit determined by the total amount owed. Federal unemployment taxes are reported separately.

Meals
The value of meals you provide your employees is not subject to income tax withholding, *if* they are not paid as wages to your employees. Two requirements must be met: (1) You

must furnish the meals on your business premises. (2) You must be able to prove that the meals were furnished for your convenience, meaning a substantial business reason other than compensation for the employees; otherwise they are taxable as a benefit. A record must be kept of the value of meals provided employees. Free meals are classified as benefits and are taxable under both FICA and FUTA regulations.

Meal value for taxation varies with the circumstances. No fixed amount is used. Factors considered are the charges you enter on your accounting records, the type of meals you serve, where you serve them, and the nature of the meal service.

Taxation of Tipped Employees

Tips are considered wages subject to withholding by the employer. The Internal Revenue Code requires employees to report to you in writing tips of over $20 in any calendar month. You are not held responsible for the truth of such reports.

Income taxes on tips can be computed at a flat 20 percent rate, rather than the graduated withholding rates used for regular wages.

Tip Reporting

Under the 1982 amendments to the Internal Revenue Code, the tip reporting provision requires foodservice operators employing 10 or more employees in establishments in which tipping is customary to report to the IRS: (1) gross food and beverage sales (except carry-out sales and sales that have mandatory service charges of at least 10 percent); (2) total tip income reported by employees; (3) food and beverage credit sales; (4) total tips on credit sales; and (5) service charges of less than 10 percent.

All foodservice operators whose total reported tip income from all sources is less than a minimum percentage of total food and beverage sales must file information returns for the first quarter on Form 8027. Every employee will be told that his or her return will be subject to IRS audit if the minimum threshold is not met.

In case the minimum (called a safe harbor) is not met on the first quarter report, the following additional reporting requirements must be met for each calendar year (including the last three quarters of that year):

1. All foodservice operators must report each employee's share of tip income equal to the minimum percentage of total food and beverage sales.

   All large-scale foodservice operators will allocate tips annually among tipped employees to the extent of any actual amount of tips reported that is less than the minimum percentage of such sales.

2. The allocation of tips will be made either by good-faith agreement between employers and employees, or, where no agreement exists, by a mandatory formula, which the Secretary of the Treasury shall fix by regulation. In either case, the tip allocation will not affect FICA (Social Security), FUTA (Unemployment Insurance), or income tax withholding imposed on all employers by the Internal Revenue Code. Moreover, no employer will be held liable in any dispute with employees regarding allocation of tip income. Tip allocation is *not* the same thing as tip pooling.

3. Each tipped employee must receive a statement of the amount of tipped income allocated to that employee. The inclusion of the allocation of tipped income on the employee's W-2 Form will satisfy this requirement.

To exempt foodservice operators who do not meet the minimum, an appeal procedure will be established by the government in cooperation with the foodservice industry. Relief may be granted, on a case-by-case basis.[11]

Foodservice operators may avoid the tip reporting provision by instituting a mandatory service charge of at least 10 percent on all cash and credit food and beverage sales.

Federal Penalties

The *intentional* failure to pay federal employment taxes, including the *intentional* failure to file employment tax returns and to withhold income taxes, is a felony (serious crime), carrying severe fines and prison terms.

Tax authorities, like other government agencies, have powerful weapons to enforce compliance. A failure to withhold taxes from employee wages for income and disability purposes may give the Internal Revenue Service the right to seize and sell your business without a court order.

Unlike the normal rule of law in criminal cases that you are innocent until proved guilty, tax laws reverse the burden of proof. You are presumed liable until you demonstrate the contrary. The tax laws are complex and require your strictest attention.

State and Local Taxes

Many states and major cities tax employee wages and salaries as well as fringe benefits, and also make provisions for payment of unemployment and disability insurance taxes. The advice of your local attorney is needed to ensure that you are current and in compliance with all state and local requirements.

Record Keeping

Accurate, up-to-date wage and tax records are an essential management responsibility for all employers. There is a simple reason for this: The government is presumed right in tax cases, with the burden on you to prove otherwise.

Special Arrangements

Whenever you employ persons with special wage and salary arrangements, such as tipped employees, employees who receive pay in the form of board, lodging, or other facilities, and employees who are not covered by FLSA minimum wage and overtime requirements, you must maintain separate records verifying the arrangements.

FLSA requirements are detailed, complex, and interpreted strictly by the Wage and Hour Division. Always secure the latest publication of the Division to be sure that you are in complete compliance with the law.

The following FLSA record-keeping requirements will apply generally:

1. Name, employee identification number, home address, birth date for employees under 19, sex, and position (waiter, waitress).
2. Time of day and day of week on which employee begins the workweek.
3. Regular rate of pay per hour for every week of overtime worked and for which excess overtime pay is due; basis on which you pay wages; and amount and nature of each payment excluded from your regular wage rate under the FLSA.
4. Number of hours each employee worked each workday (consecutive 24 hours) and total hours worked each workweek (consecutive 168 hours or seven consecutive 24-hour periods).
5. Total daily or weekly regular wages, including overtime, but excluding excess overtime pay.
6. Total excess overtime compensation for each workweek.
7. Total additions to or deductions from wages paid during each pay period. Each employee must be provided a record of the dates, amounts, and nature of any additions or deductions.
8. Total wages paid for each pay period.
9. Date of payment and pay period covered by that payment.

The following special pay arrangements must be separately categorized, recorded, and maintained:

1. Restaurant employees exempt from the overtime pay required for a greater than 40-hour workweek.
2. Tipped employees.
3. Bona fide executive, administrative, professional and outside sales employees.
4. Commissioned employees of a foodservice establishment exempt from overtime pay.
5. Employees subject to collective bargaining agreements exempt from overtime pay, and employees who are permitted to be paid a constant weekly wage even when different amounts of weekly overtime are worked (these are called "Belo" wage contracts).
6. Learners, apprentices, messengers, students, or handicapped persons working under special certificates.
7. Board, lodging, and other facilities furnished employees for which wage deductions are made.

How long must records be kept? There are two broad categories of records that require different holding periods:

Two-Year Records
1. Basic employment and earnings records.
2. Order, shipping, and billing records.
3. Records of additions to or deductions from wages paid.
4. Explanations of any wage differentials based on sex for employees within the same establishment.

Three-Year Records
1. Payroll records.
2. All collective bargaining agreements, plans, trusts, and employment contracts affecting wages authorized under the FLSA.
3. Sales and purchase records.

All the preceding records must be kept in a secure place on the premises, preferably in a central office. Wage and Hour representatives are entitled to access to these records for inspection and copying at any time. Notify your attorney of every Wage and Hour inspection.

SUMMARY

Some form of workers' compensation is required by each state to cover worker job-related injuries. Workers' compensation protects both the employer and the employee.

Worker safety is enforced by OSHA under the federal act of the same name. You must comply with safety standards and record-keeping requirements, and may be inspected by OSHA.

You must comply with federal, state, and local income tax laws for employers. Such laws are broad in coverage and strictly enforced.

QUESTIONS

1. Under what circumstances would you wish to *bond* an employee? How does this type of insurance protect the employer?
2. How does workmen's compensation protect the employer if an employee is injured?
3. Why is a safety program for employees important? Be specific; include other issues from this book.
4. Bart runs a club. He wishes to add a tip credit to help meet the minimum wage in his state. He presently pools the employees' tips with them, as the employer. What must he do to use the tip credit?
5. Explain why you must keep good employee records, covering different topics in this chapter.

NOTES

1. H. Lusk, Hewitt, Donnell, and Barnes, *Business Law and the Regulatory Environment* 1108–10 (5th ed. 1982).

2. Thus the death of an employee who drowned while trying to rescue an endangered swimmer at a recreation area owned and operated by the employer for the employees was held to fall within the definition of the term. *O'Leary v. Brown-Pacific-Maxon, Inc.,* 340 U.S. 504 (1951).

3. 29 U.S.C. secs. 651–78 (1976 & Supp. IV 1980).

4. *Marshall v. Barlow's, Inc.,* 436 U.S. 307 (1978).

5. Standards must be published in the Federal Register before becoming effective.

6. 29 U.S.C. secs. 651–78 (1976 & Supp. IV 1980).

7. *Id.* sec. 201 *et seq.* and 26 U.S.C. sec. 3101 *et seq.* (Supp. V 1981).

8. Executive, administrative, and professional employees are exempt from both the minimum wage and overtime requirements of the FLSA if all of the following requirements are met:
   a. Primary duty involves management of the business or of a recognized subdivision or department.
   b. Directs the work of at least two other employees.
   c. Has authority to hire or fire or has clearly defined power to recommend hiring and firing of employees.
   d. Regularly exercises discretionary authority over assigned tasks.
   e. Nonmanagerial duties do not exceed 40 percent of his or her time (not applicable to an owner of at least 20 percent of the business or executive employee who is solely in charge of the business).
   f. Is paid at least $155 per week on a regular salary basis. All employees who earn a salary of over $250 per week, manage as a primary duty, and direct work of two or more employees qualify.

9. 26 U.S.C. sec. 3301 *et seq.* (Supp. V 1981).

10. *Id.* sec. 3121(b)(8)(B).

11. An IRS study of restaurant compliance with the new provision beginning with the 1983 tax returns is also required. Results of that study, to be conducted in at least eight major metropolitan areas and 16 smaller areas, must be reported to Congress by December 31, 1986.

8
Maintaining Security

Objectives

The purpose of this chapter is to:

1. Review crimes against foodservice operators committed by patrons, trespassers, and employees.
2. Outline procedures to prevent crimes and measures to deal with wrongdoers.

Case in Point

Tom Turner breaks into and enters the hotel room of Cannon Astor, a wealthy real estate tycoon. Upon going through Astor's personal effects, Tom finds an Amex gold credit card. Tom removes the card and proceeds to the Silver Room, a plush dining room situated atop the hotel, independently owned and managed by Jean Foster. Tom obtains a table and then runs up a three-figure bar, food, and entertainment bill for himself and a "friend" (actually a confederate). At the end of their dinner, Tom presents "his" gold card, expertly forges the name "Cannon Astor" on the bill as it appears on the card he lifted from Astor's room, and uses the card to charge the total bill to Astor's credit card account. The maître d'hôtel verifies the account by phone, is told that it is in order, and thanks Tom and his companion for their patronage and their generous tip, also charged to the Astor credit card.

What are Foster's rights in this situation? Is she simply out the money if Astor reports the missing card and refuses to pay? Can she bring criminal charges against Turner? The answer depends on which state the restaurant is in.

Under common law, Tom committed a theft of property when he stole Astor's card. He could be prosecuted and/or fined only for that crime against Astor. His "crime" against Foster —that is, theft of services—was not a crime under the common law, and Jean would be out the money. Her only recourse would be to try to persuade Turner's other victim, Astor, to pay the bill charged to his stolen credit card—an unlikely prospect.

Criminal prosecution for the theft of property at common law is insufficient to protect those who render services on the strength of the validity of a credit card.[1] In most states this legal loophole has been filled by the creation of "thefts of services" statutes protecting persons or parties who accept credit cards for payment in the normal course of their business operations.[2] In these states the foodservice owner can prosecute Tom for theft of services.

CRIME AND PROFITS

Keeping costs down is important to the profitability of a foodservice operation. Operators who practice poor security leave themselves open to a never-ending cycle of costly security problems, and, as a result, poor profitability.

If a restaurant has a reputation as a place where rowdies congregate and cause trouble, good customers will be driven away. Of if an owner gets a reputation as a soft touch or for running a loose operation, meaning a place that can be robbed easily, both amateur and professional criminals will mark him or her as an easy target for any type of flimflam, fraud, or outright robbery. Or if normally responsible employees and patrons can't resist stealing foodstuffs, or even silverware, simply because it is so easy, the owner will find the cash flow outgoing as he or she scrambles to replace the inventory. In any event, the bottom line will reflect carelessness.

Crime hurts. Mostly it hurts the pocketbook. However, patrons and employees alike have been victims of violence during robberies and other crimes. Tighter security may not prevent every type of crime against foodservice operators, but it will, in most instances, keep an operation from becoming a revolving door for a variety of criminals.

The effect of criminal misconduct is twofold. First, there is the economic loss. Whether the value of meals, lost property, and services is eventually recovered is of small comfort. Even if the owner will be reimbursed for the loss, he or she is immediately out the cash, and it takes time and effort to restore it.

Second, the harm to one's personal business reputation is also involved. Unless operators take immediate steps to prevent wrongdoing and to prosecute wrongdoers, they may become easy marks for professional rings of thieves who prey on the gullible without mercy, once given an opening wedge. No one can afford being known in criminal circles as a *soft touch,* since these artists can pick their targets clean and leave them empty-handed. Others must not be tempted to follow in their footsteps by, in effect, "giving away the store." Making it easy for the "pros" to commit crimes invites the amateurs to do likewise. This possibility multiplies the problem and can close an operator's restaurant doors at worst, or make operation unprofitable at best.

Security measures include the way you let your patrons pay for their meals, how you let them conduct themselves when they are in your operation, and what you may do legally if they become unruly. Security measures also include the supervision of your employees to protect your patrons and your property from worker mischief. Finally, they involve steps needed to protect the business from criminals who have no business there.

Maintaining security is a legal matter and a personal business decision. This chapter presents positive steps foodservice operators may *consider* to protect their business, patrons, and employees from crime. The decision as to whether or not to use them is one each operator must make on the basis of local laws, the seriousness of the problem, and the economic feasibility of the solution.

CRIMES AGAINST FOODSERVICE OPERATORS

Crimes against foodservice operators include crimes by patrons such as the passing of bad checks and thefts of services. Employee crimes usually revolve around theft, either of cash or of foods and supplies. Among third party crimes, or crimes by people who do not belong on the premises, are trespassing, burglary, and malicious mischief, as well as rioting and terrorism.

PATRON CRIMES

Patron crimes vary but most of them are related to either theft of services or patron conduct while in the operation. Liability as well as criminal charges may result from the latter.

Theft of Services

Most patron crimes against the foodservice operator occur when the time comes to go to the cashier and pay up; these are classified as thefts of services.

The law defines theft of services to mean either: (1) knowingly using a stolen, revoked, or canceled credit card to obtain services or inducing the supplier of services to accept payment on a credit basis; or (2) intentionally avoiding or attempting to avoid payment by failing to pay or by refusing to pay through misrepresentation of fact.[3] As a result of the increasing availability of credit as a method of payment, and its use in place of cash, the foodservice industry is being victimized by persons who wish to obtain service and products without paying.

A Word on Pricing
Unlike innkeepers, foodservice operators are not required to charge their patrons reasonable prices for food and services. No federal or state statutes regulate the prices you may charge patrons for your foods and beverages. This is not to suggest that the power to regulate prices is lacking. Price controls over a broad range of products were commonplace

during World War II. The government has merely decided not to exercise its power over meal prices, except in emergency wartime conditions.[4] Your competition and the costs of materials, labor, and production will be your guide to the prices you charge.

Credit Thefts

Thefts of services are mainly credit card thefts, that is, the use of a stolen, revoked, or canceled card for the purpose of obtaining food and beverages on credit.[5]

Extension of Credit.   Credit is defined as any method of payment other than in cash or in kind at the time goods are transferred or services are rendered by the seller. Credit means payment or performance made over a period of time agreed upon by the parties to the transaction.

As a foodservice operator you are entitled to receive cash in exchange for services and products provided to patrons in your establishment. This is a legal right, not a matter of discretion which your patrons may exercise as they see fit.[6] In the same vein, you have the right to reject or accept a credit card or check in place of cash. The patron cannot require you to extend credit as a condition of his or her business with you.[7]

Credit is a valuable, but not required, method of operating your foodservice business. Credit has the advantage of allowing you to market your services to patrons who may not have the cash with which to pay now, but who are reasonably sure to pay later. Credit enables you to market your services to more patrons by allowing them to borrow the cost of your food and beverages from you for a specified period of time that you establish in advance. Credit benefits the patron by enabling him or her to do business with you without the need to carry large amounts of cash, and, equally important to business customers, affords the ability to produce a written receipt for business and tax purposes.

The extending of credit also carries risks. Credit is granted on your assumption that the patron who uses it will pay the account on time and in the required amounts. Unfortunately, even in the best of circumstances, the patron may fail or refuse to pay. In that event you have two courses of action available: (1) to terminate future credit, or (2) to take steps to collect the amount owed to you, either with or without court action. The first remedy is the least expensive and least time-consuming. The second is more expensive and time-consuming, but also more likely to result in payment of your bill.

The choice of whether or not to extend credit remains your decision, not the patron's or the state's. Your refusal to do so at all is not a violation of the law.[8] Title II, the public accommodations section of the federal Civil Rights Act, does not make you liable for denying credit on these grounds.[9] The federal Equal Credit Opportunity Act, which does prohibit discrimination in credit transactions, does not, however, apply to foodservice operators. Only financial lenders, such as banks and savings and loan associations, may not discriminate in extending credit on the traditional civil rights grounds of race, creed, color, sex, national origin, and marital status.[10] The reason for the difference in treatment is based on Congressional recognition that a commercial foodservice operator's primary business is not that of extending credit, but of providing foods and beverages to patrons in return for compensation.

The nature of your operation will determine whether you should establish a credit policy. If you operate a fast-food establishment, with high turnover, a credit policy may not make sense. Why not? Because it is impossible to verify credit in advance under those conditions. However, if you have a heavy repeat patronage or established clientele, a credit policy could be considered. In any case, it is preferable to honor a national credit card rather than to set up your own credit system.

Why? (1) A system using a national credit card is easier to operate, and (2) the burden of collection is placed on the issuing company, not yourself, as long as you comply with the issuer's requirements.

No credit card company can compel you to do business with it. You in turn cannot require a credit card company to do business with you. In the same vein, you cannot compel a patron to use credit in every case. The patron must consent to do so. (Only private clubs can compel members to sign for all charges. These clubs usually send a monthly bill to patrons.)

The following guidelines should prove useful if you wish to use credit as a method of payment.

1. You must distinguish between individual credit and company or corporate credit transactions. Extending individual credit requires verification of that individual's credit standing *before* extending credit. This should be done independently of statements or claims made by the applicant.[11] You should require credit references.

2. When a company or corporation applies for credit, it must do so through an authorized officer or agent, since an institution has no human existence of its own.[12] No officer or other agent may legally establish his or her authority to act on behalf of a corporation or company through his or her own statements or claims.[13] This means that you must obtain a letter or corporate resolution establishing: (a) that the person representing himself or herself as an officer or agent is in fact authorized to act; (b) that the corporation has authorized that person to establish credit for the corporation; and (c) that the corporation has authorized the specific purposes for which the credit is to be used. Otherwise the company can legally refuse payment and, in some cases, recover payments already made.[14]

In addition, the officer or agent who signs as that corporation's officer or agent is not individually liable to pay, since the officer has revealed his or her position and the identity of the party who is to pay.[15] This means that both the corporate officer and the corporation are off the hook, unless the corporation has given you written authority to extend credit.

When dealing with a corporate or company officer or agent, always have the individual guarantee payment of the account in writing. If a guarantee of payment cannot be obtained, try in every case to obtain a written guarantee that you will be paid eventually; this is called a *guarantee of collectibility*.

3. Minors may disaffirm their credit transactions with you, which means that you extend credit to minors at your peril.[16] When dealing with a minor or person legally declared incompetent, always have a responsible adult guarantee payment.

The difference between the two forms of guarantee is important. A guarantee of payment makes the guarantor primarily responsible for payment, as if he or she alone had opened the account. A guarantee of collectibility makes the guarantor only secondarily responsible for payment, meaning that you must sue the party in whose name the account was opened first, *and then sue the guarantor* in the event the first party cannot pay.

4. When in doubt as to the credit-worthiness of an individual or institution, do not extend credit unless the applicant can provide a financially responsible guarantor of payment.

5. Always keep careful records of each credit account you open, including the application itself, credit reports from reporting agencies, any unusual credit activity, and the card or charge account holder's payment record.

6. Always review and terminate further credit to any holder who exceeds your established credit limits.

7. Vigorously pursue any seriously delinquent accounts and sue *if necessary*. A lawsuit should be reserved for cases where you have exhausted all other reasonable collection efforts without achieving results, and the amount justifies the legal expenses.

8. You should treat an *inability* to pay differently from a *refusal* to pay. Inability to pay can be resolved by a mutually satisfactory repayment schedule. Refusal to pay cannot, and requires sterner measures, especially when the refusal is unjustified. A refusal may be legally justified if you fail to provide the services agreed upon or on the date and time agreed upon.

One final reminder: Out-of-court methods of collection are preferable to litigation in court. Every overdue account that can be resolved by mutual agreement means continued patronage and repeat business. Litigation and criminal prosecution should be reserved for those who wrongfully refuse to pay or never had any intention of paying. Their presence on your premises is intended only to benefit themselves at your expense. You can ill afford to allow them to take advantage of you.

Handling Credit Cards to Protect Your Operation. Normally, when you contract with a credit card company to honor its card at your establishment, either the company or the cardholder will cover any losses you suffer from the theft or misuse of the card if, *but only if,* you follow the required credit card verification before accepting the card for charge purposes.[17]

Federal law limits the loss of any credit cardholder resulting from the unauthorized use of the card to $50, if the cardholder complies with the conditions set forth in the law (Truth in Lending Act).[18] This means that in most cases you may not recover over $50 from the cardholder, even if you follow the proper procedures at the time a card is submitted for payment.[19] The act defines "unauthorized use" to mean no "actual, implied, or apparent authority for such use" by the person obtaining credit with the card, and from which use "the cardholder receives no benefit."[20] Fraud, duress, or other wrongdoing caused by a third person constitutes unauthorized use of a credit card.

What procedures should you follow to make sure you recover from the card company or issuer for losses you suffer? These steps are required of you and any of your employees who handle credit payments:

Check the card against a list of canceled cards furnished to you by the card issuer. This is essential, since you will be held responsible for the entire loss if you fail to verify that the card is current.

Check the signature on the card against the signature on the credit card receipt. If it looks suspicious, or they do not seem to match, don't accept the card, and instead request payment in cash or by other acceptable credit, such as a traveler's check drawn on a U.S. or international bank with which you are familiar.

Make a telephone call to the number provided by the card issuer to determine whether the charge is within credit limits or will be treated as an overcharge. If the charge exceeds the credit limits established for that card, you may accept the card for charges up to that limit and require the card user to make up any difference due you in cash or by other authorized credit.

Don't under any circumstances allow cashiers or other personnel to short-circuit these procedures when they become preoccupied with impatient customers or heavy patron traffic. Such excuses are not legal justifications for failing to check with the card issuer. The result is inevitable: You lose. The card issuer is not responsible to guarantee payment because you failed to fulfill the contract requirements you agreed to perform. Your failure to perform a material requirement of a contract excuses performance by the other party.[21] Proper and timely verification of a credit card presented to obtain credit is a requirement that is a prerequisite to the card issuer being legally bound to reimburse you. If you play instead of paying attention, you pay. The fact that you may dismiss or discipline the employee responsible can only act as a deterrent to future carelessness by other employees. It cannot make good your loss.

What about patron charge accounts? Whether to extend charge accounts to patrons is a business judgment solely within your discretion. If you run a large operation, you may wish to issue your own credit card for identification and billing purposes. In either case, the following commonsense rules will help you avoid "getting stuck with the check":

1. Before establishing any credit, be sure the patron has an acceptable credit rating. Always verify the patron's name, address, occupation, and bank account.
2. Place a dollar ceiling on the amount of credit you will authorize at any given time.
3. If you issue a card, make it as tamper- or counterfeit-proof as possible.
4. Make the patron sign an agreement that he/she will remain fully responsible for payment regardless of who is authorized to use the card *and* regardless of whether the card is lost, stolen, or otherwise wrongly used. As a private creditor you are not required to use credit practices enforced by the federal government, since you are not a credit card company or lending institution.[22] To remove any doubt on this question, you must put this and any other terms and conditions in writing and have the agreement signed by the cardholder.

5. Police all accounts. Be especially watchful for sudden increases in any individual's spending habits.
6. Always require payment in full within 30 days of billing, unless you wish to approve other special credit arrangements in writing.
7. Always post up-to-date lists of delinquent or closed accounts for your cashiers. Adapt for your own operation the procedures you are required to follow by a national credit card company. The best rule of thumb for your employees is: When in doubt as to identity, signature, or credit limit, always check with management.

Another aspect of credit card use deserves mention. When you check on a credit card, whether your own or that of a national credit card issuer, you are protecting two parties: yourself and the cardholder. Your self-interest bears an additional dividend in terms of patron goodwill. You are protecting patrons from unauthorized use of their cards, saving them the anxiety and frustration involved with having to inform you or the company of misuse. Honest, diligent people will appreciate the fact that you protected their interests by performing your responsibilities in a professional manner.

Do not extend long-term credit unless you are properly financed to do so. Otherwise you risk draining your cash flow. Accept national credit cards rather than institute your own credit system. If you opt to use your own credit cards, always review them and cut off credit on overdue accounts. Many credit card users are businesspersons who know the value of prompt payment of their own invoices. A tactful but firm reminder should be enough to restore the account. Above all, remember that you are not a money lender or your operation a refuge for delinquent accounts.

Passing Bad Checks

Foodservice operators are especially prone to receiving bad checks and bogus money. The foodservice business usually depends on high turnover for profit, and it is easier for criminals to run a check or counterfeit money scam during peak business periods. Unlike with the credit card game, the check or money is totally worthless, and recovery from either the wrongdoer or third party is either difficult or impossible.[23]

First, we must define what we mean by a "bad" check. A bad check may be a *totally fabricated check,* a *forged* or *raised* genuine check, or a *genuine check that cannot be cashed.*[24]

The *totally fabricated* check is an imaginary check, meaning that the name of the account, the person or party to whom the check is payable, and the name of the drawer, the person who wrote the check, are nonexistent. Even the name of the bank on which the check is drawn may be imaginary, especially if the bad check artist has a printer to make up a check blank.

A *forged check* is genuine except for the signature of the drawer or check writer. Here the name of a real person who has a real checking account at a real bank is imitated with a signature that the forger attempts to deceive you into believing is that of the real drawer.

The *uncollectible* or *uncashable genuine check* is one drawn on a real account opened by the check passer, but deliberately written even though there are insufficient funds to cover it or the account has been closed.

Figure 8.1 lists procedures that will protect operators from bad checks.

Prosecution for the crime of passing bad checks requires proof beyond a reasonable doubt that the writer intended to obtain credit knowing the check was uncollectible. Failure of a bank to cash a check, standing alone, is

Figure 8.1
Check-Cashing Guidelines

1. Accept no postdated, out-of-state checks.
2. Accept no checks made payable to other than the person who will cash them.
3. Accept no checks over your stated credit limit.
4. Never cash any check that looks at all suspicious.
5. Never cash a prewritten check. Always require the check writer to make out the check in your presence to avoid any possibility of an altered or raised check: one in which the amount, date, or signature has been changed.
6. Always require proper identification from the person cashing the check. This will enable you to compare the signature on the check with the signature on the identification item. An excellent form of identification is a driver's license, especially in states where the license contains the photograph of the license holder.
7. Avoid cashing checks of minors, even those carrying a valid driver's license, unless you know that the minor is creditworthy or an adult agrees to guarantee payment. A minor may disaffirm his or her contract to pay for certain services, except necessaries or where a statute prohibits the minor to do so.
8. Above all, have a check-cashing policy and train your employees to adhere to it.

not proof of intent knowingly to issue an uncollectible check.[25] The fact that the account on which the check was drawn has insufficient funds may create a presumption of knowledge, but that presumption is not conclusive, and may be denied by the accused.[26] In some states no crime is committed if the check is re-deposited and clears within 10 days after the bank's first refusal to honor the check.[27]

Counterfeit Money and Foreign Currency
Bogus bills and coins will continue to be passed by professional counterfeiters, by amateurs as a joke, or by patrons who substitute genuine foreign money (French francs or Spanish pesetas) for U.S. money.

The counterfeit article may be a high-quality item, depending on the resources of the counterfeiter. However, even the best counterfeit bill can be detected if carefully examined. The special paper, steel engraving plates, and other techniques used in producing real money are virtually impossible to duplicate. Both the bogus paper and the printing ultimately reveal less sharpness of detail in portraits and background, as well as broken lines not found in genuine bills.

Bogus coins, as compared with the real thing, are examined for the preciseness of the indentations along their outer edges. Counterfeit coins are not as precisely or evenly "reeded" as genuine coins. Their indentations are broken or uneven, a sure warning to your cashier, waiter, or waitress that something is wrong. Another sign is the tensile strength of the coin. The counterfeit coin often can be cut or will bend with little effort.

Foreign currency, genuine where issued, but not readily convertible in the United States, is generally distinguishable in most characteristics from U.S. money, and so should present no serious problem to anyone except the most indifferent employee.

In some countries currency controls forbid currency exports outside the country of origin, in which case the currency cannot be converted. Iron curtain countries, such as Poland and East Germany, are examples. The practical problem of fluctuating conversion rates and time consumed in conversion are good reasons to be on the lookout for foreign currency, and to instruct your employees not to accept it.

Shortchange Artists
Shortchanging can take several forms. Mostly cashiers will find themselves victimized during rush periods when they are in a hurry and become easily distracted. If you institute the cashier procedures mentioned under *Employee Crimes* in this chapter, you should have fewer problems. The important preventive tool here is concentration. Your cashier should not be easily distracted by other patrons or employees. When a bill is handed over, simply saying "change for a twenty" is a big deterrent to would-be shortchange artists. The cashier's identification of the bill up front will be hard for the patron to contradict. Also, the time-honored practice of putting the bill right outside the cash register drawer while making change rather than putting it in with other money will help prevent shortchanging.

Walkouts
A restaurant owner or manager has a right to detain a patron for a reasonable time, and for a reasonable investigation, when the owner/manager has grounds to believe that the patron has not paid for what he or she received, or is attempting to take merchandise without payment.[28]

A number of states have enacted shoplifting statutes, which make it easier for operators to defend themselves against a patron claim of false imprisonment.[29] The shoplifting statutes basically say that when you have reasonable grounds to suspect a patron of shoplifting, you can escape liability for false imprisonment.

The following case, decided in a state that does not have a shoplifting statute, illustrates the available defenses.

Keys v. Sambo's Restaurant, Inc.
Supreme Court of Louisiana
398 So. 2d 1083 (1981)

Facts.   Keys, a patron, became heavily intoxicated one night while celebrating the birthday of a friend. Keys and the friend, Wells, then stopped at Sambo's for a late-night supper. Wells agreed to pay for the meal. After the two had ordered chicken dinners and eaten, Wells became indisposed and left Sambo's to sleep off his drinking bout in his own car parked in Sambo's parking area. A waitress informed Keys of Wells' departure. Keys told the manager that he would pay for Wells' meal and his own if Wells did not return. Later Keys attempted to leave Sambo's without paying for either meal. The manager caught up with Keys, before he had gone through the door, refused to accept part payment, and when Keys became belligerent, locked Keys in the men's rest room and called the police. When Keys became unruly after the police arrived, an officer struck Keys, removed him from the premises, and took him to the police station. Keys was charged with disturbing the peace, failure to pay for a meal, and resisting arrest.

Later the criminal charges were dropped. Keys then sued Sambo's for injuries suffered because of his arrest, false imprisonment, and his broken ankle. The trial court found in favor of Sambo's and dismissed Keys' lawsuit. The intermediate reviewing court upheld the judgment of the trial court. Keys then petitioned the Supreme Court of Louisiana for final review, which was granted. That court upheld the decisions of both lower courts in Sambo's favor.

Reasoning.   The Supreme Court found that (1) the plaintiff committed a felony by refusing to pay; (2) the plaintiff attempted to defraud Sambo's according to state law; (3) the plaintiff did not dispute the attempts to defraud or refuse to pay; and (4) the plaintiff's injuries were a result of his attempt to resist arrest; and that these factors combined justified affirming the lower courts' decision in favor of Sambo's.

Conclusion.   This case is important for a number of reasons. First, the case notes the existence of criminal statutes in many states that make getting food from a restaurant without intending to pay for it a serious crime (felony). Second, the case establishes a food-service operator's legal right to make a citizen's arrest when a patron attempts to leave under such circumstances. Third, the case establishes the operator's legal right to detain a person until the police arrive.

A word of caution is in order. A citizen's arrest is usually authorized only if (1) the person arrested is a felon (a major criminal); (2) a felony has been committed, and there are reasonable grounds to believe the person arrested committed it; or (3) a misdemeanor amounting to breach of the peace is committed in the presence of the person making the arrest. A public disturbance, such as being drunk and yelling on a public street so as to disturb the good order and tranquillity of the neighborhood, would be a breach of the peace. Some states have extended the right to make a citizen's arrest to a criminal trespass on private property.

Police should be called when a crime has been committed or a threat or use of deadly force or bodily harm exists. Otherwise calling the police may be unjustified and wasteful of police time and resources.

Once a customer walks out without paying, there is little you can do except call the police and let them take care of it. Don't go beyond the restaurant to pursue a walkout. It is too dangerous. The best advice is for you to prevent it in the first place by having employees watch customers who are about to leave.

The wisest policy is to try and settle with the customer peacefully on the premises. Most patrons don't want to risk embarrassment, so unless they have, or feel they have, a legitimate reason for not paying (for example, the steak was cold), they will usually pay, once given a friendly reminder.

Malicious Mischief

Most statutes define malicious mischief as the malicious injury or destruction of the real or personal property of another.[30] Malice is not limited to situations where the person committing the crime intended to injure the owner of the property. Rather, malice has been extended to include situations in which the injury or destruction is committed wantonly and without justification against any property other than the property of the accused person.[31]

In the foodservice industry, any wanton, unjustified act resulting in damage or destruction of property, caused by anyone, including patrons, intruders, employees, and the general public, is malicious mischief. A *wanton act* is one committed in total disregard of the consequences. An *unjustified act* means one that is not provoked or caused by your own conduct and in response to that conduct, or not otherwise justified by law or public policy.

A patron, while seated at a table in your restaurant, takes out a pair of jewelry shears and cuts all of your crystal stemware into tiny pieces, without warning or any provocation on your part. The patron is guilty of malicious mischief, since all of the elements necessary to establish the crime are present. The fact that he or she did not threaten or injure any person on the premises is immaterial, since the crime is against your property, not a person. It must be differentiated initially from a criminal trespass because the patron was legally admitted by you. However, once the patron committed the unjustified destruction of

property, an act you clearly did not authorize, the patron's status changed. Now you have the right to evict the patron as a trespasser, since the unjustified destruction of your property was itself a crime. But to do so, you would normally be required to request the patron to leave, and upon a refusal have him or her removed with all reasonable force. But because of the seriousness of the patron's conduct, you would also be authorized to make a citizen's arrest or request a police arrest, with either or both followed by a criminal complaint covering both the trespass and malicious mischief.

More typically, malicious mischief results when a group of rowdies enter your premises, reasonably attired and behaved, but then, without warning, start to "trash" your tables, chairs, and furnishings, just "for kicks." This wanton misconduct all too frequently occurs where a bar or cocktail lounge adjoins your restaurant. These individuals, of all ages, backgrounds, and nationalities, are hard to detect and, for that reason, extremely dangerous. They are often not content to damage your property, but instinctively provoke fights and brutally assault anyone in sight. Since many of these lowlifes carry concealed weapons, you must seek police assistance at the first sign of trouble.[32]

THIRD PARTY CRIMES

If you operate a foodservice business, whether your own or someone else's, you occupy the land the establishment is on. You also run a foodservice business on that land. According to the law you have the legal right to protect your premises and business from any unauthorized entry or unauthorized stay of any person resulting from misconduct or other wrongdoing.[33] The fact that you operate a public place of business does not mean that any member of the public has the right of access or the right to remain under any and all circumstances.[34] Third party crimes are crimes committed by people who have no business on your premises.

Trespass

The legal term for an unauthorized entry is a *trespass to land.* Such a trespass can take two forms: a civil trespass and a criminal trespass. A civil trespass, such as entering a private club without permission, is a tort, a civil wrong, and the owner can recover compensatory damages for any loss suffered. If the trespass was malicious or made with intent to harm the owner or the premises, the operator may also recover *punitive* damages.[35]

A criminal trespass such as a burglary differs only in that, to commit the crime, the trespass must be committed knowingly and consist of an unlawful entry or unlawful stay on the premises.[36] The trespass need not result in injury to the premises in order for the owner to receive a legal remedy. Knowing the difference between a civil trespass and a criminal trespass is important.

A foodservice operator, like an innkeeper, has the legal right to make a citizen's arrest without liability *if* a criminal trespass can be established. This holds true even in those states that have no statutes authorizing an eviction for failure to obey a valid house rule, or for disorderly conduct or intoxication. Almost all states have criminal trespass statutes. However, the better procedure to follow is not to make a citizen's arrest, *but to call the police and have them arrest the trespasser.*

Burglary

Every foodservice operator needs to maintain a safe or strongbox on the premises for the safekeeping of cash receipts until these monies can be deposited in the bank. However,

professional thieves may try to burglarize such safes, and you need to take measures to prevent that. Burglary refers to the breaking into and entering of a building, at night, with the intent to commit a felony, or serious crime.[37] Most modern state statutes have eliminated both the "breaking" and "night" requirements.[38] In practice, thieves can break into your safe most successfully at a time when your premises are not occupied or when few employees are in the area of the safe.

There are steps you should take to minimize the successful accomplishment of this crime:

1. Install a time lock device on the safe, set to release the lock only at those times when security personnel are present. Why? Because the time lock will make it impossible for any unauthorized person to force the safe open. This holds true even where an employee with the combination is ordered to open the safe at gunpoint. The time lock, by helping to minimize the risk of loss, will also reduce your property insurance premium rate and the likelihood of insurance claims. Remember, lower costs help to generate increased profits.
2. Whenever possible, install a safe or strongbox that meets your insurance carrier's standards for burglar resistance. Why? It will help reduce your insurance premium rates, and will prevent burglary by creating enough delay to cause the burglars to leave empty-handed and to better the police officers' chances to apprehend them in flight.
3. Install an additional protective device, such as a silent alarm system, to alert the police to the presence of burglars before they have time to make off with your cash. Why? For the same reasons previously noted—to keep insurance costs down and to intercept the burglar in the act.

4. Train and supervise your employees to prevent anyone from leaving the safe open and unguarded or failing to set the alarm system. Police the safe deposit area, and maintain a log of all persons who withdraw or deposit funds from the safe, including the date, time, name of person, what was removed or deposited, and the signature or initials of a responsible witness.

5. Every suspicious incident, including finding the safe unattended or open at unauthorized times, should be described in writing and kept on file for review and, if a loss occurs, reported promptly to your insurance carrier. Carelessness not reported to employees will go uncorrected. Carelessness that is not corrected is an open invitation to crime. Finally, carelessness may cause your insurance to be inoperative at the very time you need it.

6. Keep your safe deposits to a minimum and transfer those deposits to the bank as soon as possible. The longer the deposits remain on the premises, the greater is the temptation to would-be burglars.

Robbery

The crime of robbery is treated as a felony in all states, whereas larceny may be less serious (petit) or more serious (grand), depending on the value of the property. Robbery is a felony regardless of the value of the property taken. Why? Because robbery adds two new elements to the crime of larceny: (1) that the property must be taken from the person of the victim or in the victim's presence; and (2) that the taking be accomplished by force or violence or by putting the victim in fear of force or violence.[39]

The typical scenario involves entry by armed intruders who force the manager or employee to open the safe or the cash register and then lock the manager in a small room.[40]

The cardinal rule for you and your employees to remember during an armed robbery is: If it's your money or your life, there's no question about which is more valuable. The procedures in Figure 8.2 will give you good general guidelines to follow during a robbery. Procedures for employees to follow in case of a robbery should be posted on bulletin boards and included in an employee manual.

There is no real protection against the threat of armed robbery by professional criminal rings. You are not expected to risk your life to protect the lives and property of your employees and patrons. By the same token, your employees and patrons are not expected to risk their lives to protect your life and property. Use of good security measures to protect your premises should protect your patrons and employees, as well as your property, against reasonably foreseeable risks.

Civil Unrest

The threat of extraordinary, organized criminal activities confronts all public service businesses, including foodservice operations. Although, by their very nature, such civil disturbances cannot always be anticipated, operators must exercise reasonable care, and be prepared to implement and supervise procedures to cope with unusual problems. The absence of emergency procedures, as well as the failure to carry them out in a reasonable manner, may be evidence of negligence to a judge or jury should injury to patrons result.[41]

Your vulnerability to civil disturbances will affect your need to anticipate and deal with such situations. If you operate in a large city, and are close to areas used to hold demonstrations, the need for adequate disaster planning is obviously greater than would be the case if you were located in a remote, rural village.

Figure 8.2
Protective Measures During Robberies

There is a possibility that a criminal may some day select this business as the target for a holdup. For this reason, we are providing guidelines for the behavior of employees who might be present.

First You are expected to cooperate in every way with an armed robber. Any person committing an armed robbery is bound to be under great tension. No crew member should do or say anything that will increase this tension.

Second You are expected to give up any cash or supplies that the criminal demands. There should be no resistance, no attempt to deceive the criminal concerning the amount or location of what he asks for. At the same time, no information should be volunteered.

Third You are expected to carefully observe all physical characteristics of the criminal, so they can later be relayed to the police.

Fourth After the criminal has departed, each witness should write down all the facts that can be remembered. Each person should write without consulting others who are present. When questioned by the police, full and complete cooperation should be given.

Descriptions and the written summary of the incident should be based on the following outline, which may be used as a guide:

What was the criminal's height?
Look straight into his eyes. If his eyes are above yours, he is taller; if his eyes are below yours, he is shorter. Estimate how many inches taller or shorter.

What were the color of his eyes?
When looking into his eyes to gauge his height, look at the color.

What was the color of his skin?
Even a masked criminal will have exposed skin around the eyes, or his hands, or around the collar.

What was his weight or body-type?
You may have trouble estimating what a person weighs, but, in describing the criminal to the police, you can compare him to another employee, or a member of the police. You would say, "The criminal was built like that person, but slightly heavier."

How would you describe the criminal's voice?
A voice would, first of all, be male or female. Then, it would be high-pitched, or low. The criminal would speak slowly or rapidly. Did he speak with an accent?

Was he right- or left-handed?
He will probably carry his weapon in the hand he favors. Remember which hand it was, and did he switch hands to perform some other act.

How was he dressed?
Look at each item of clothing from top to bottom.

How did he leave?
Don't follow the criminal outside when he leaves. Look through the window. Try to get the make, model and color of his car. Get the license number if possible. Notice which way he turned. □

Courtesy of Leon Gottlieb, Leon Gottlieb & Associates, International Food Service, Operations, Training and Management Consultants, Box 1767, Encino, CA 91316. (Mr. Gottlieb is the publisher of Gottlieb's Bottom Line, a monthly newsletter for the foodservice owner, supervisor, and manager.)

Riots

A demonstration, harmless when contained, may be transformed into a riot when the activity gets out of control and tempers run high. Often this situation is deliberately provoked by skilled agitators who co-opt the peaceful demonstration, break through police lines, and overwhelm law enforcement personnel. Unless riot police are assembled, the normal police force may be forced to resort to violence, which merely fuels the rioters.

The greatest threat to everyone within the path of a riot is fire. Fire bombing is a typical ploy since it creates panic while destroying property, thus frustrating rescue and fire-fighting efforts. If time permits, all flammable material outside your premises should be removed; employees should be assigned fire extinguishers to cover fire-prone points; gas jets and other exposed fuel outlets should be rendered inoperative; and employees not involved in fire fighting should be assigned to give first aid and comfort to injured persons.

Communication with the outside world is essential. The telephone should be used to maintain contact with police and fire departments until an "all clear" is given or evacuation is ordered. The premises should not be completely abandoned, as a fire-resistant building occupied by patrons and employees will provide a less inviting target for looters.

Terrorism

Terrorist activities may assume the form of bomb threats, hostage taking, and the holding of hostages on your premises. Although more likely to occur in hotels and convention centers, terrorism is not confined to any type of public property and can take place anywhere without warning.

Bomb threats require attention, since the question will arise as to whether the threat is serious enough to disrupt business and evacuate patrons. In every case a plan of action is required, whether you decide to evacuate or not.

The following suggestions will enable you to plan intelligently:

1. Train your staff to get as much information from the caller as possible. The identity of the caller may be extracted from such clues as accent, background noises, and tone of voice. This information should be recorded and turned over to the responsible authorities. With luck, the caller may identify the size, type, and location of the bomb.

2. A reasonable test of whether the caller is a crank or is serious is the calmness and detail with which the caller describes the threat. An irrational, uncertain, or slurred speech pattern may mean that the call is a hoax.

3. Report all threatening calls to the police as soon as possible, first by phone and, when time permits, in writing. Let them advise you as to whether or not to evacuate the premises.

4. Cooperate fully with the authorities when they arrive on the scene. Try to keep a floor plan available for examination, and have a responsible member of your staff work with the search team.

5. Anticipate potential threats when political leaders, celebrities, and other public figures reserve space on your premises. Be ready to work with the FBI, Secret Service, and state and local authorities who may send an advance security party to canvass your operation and instruct your staff. The fact that such figures may only dine with you and so be on your premises a relatively short time in no way excuses you from responsibility to plan safeguards.

If the federal and other security authorities place armed personnel inside your restaurant, you should require them to give you a hold-harmless written agreement, meaning that if any patron, employee, or other party is injured as a result of a shootout, your risk of legal liability is cushioned because of the agreement.

Hostage Taking

The likelihood of a terrorist group attempting to take a political figure or other celebrity hostage is a possibility, particularly if your establishment is located within easy access to escape routes. Obviously there is no master preventive plan that will fit all situations. If you hear of a planned attempt, you must notify the police immediately. If you have adequate warning of a possible incident and fail to warn of it or to evacuate the intended victim when you had sufficient time to do so, you *may* be held responsible if he or she is injured. Although it is unlikely that the President or a foreign visitor of equal rank would sue you, a private citizen of similar stature might very well do so. Even a regular patron would have the right to sue, irrespective of the class or quality of your establishment. All that the law would require is that the reasonableness of your security measures be tested against the class and quality of your establishment, to determine whether your conduct met a reasonable-care standard.

EMPLOYEE CRIMES

Employee thefts of cash, food, beverages, and other foodservice property, as well as thefts of patron property, either alone or in the company of professional thieves, can occur in your operation unless proper precautions are taken.

The temptation to steal is always present. However, proper screening of job applicants and thorough supervision of their activities will drastically reduce incidents of stealing.[42] In large measure your employees will be honest and law-abiding, and should be treated as such. However, there are always a few employees who would take advantage of you. What follow are measures directed at preventing, detecting, and eliminating employee misconduct.

Thefts of Cash

Cashiers and other cash-handling employees are obviously in the best position to steal your cash. The traditional method is to avoid ringing up or recording all cash sales on the cash register and then pocketing the difference between actual and recorded sales.

How can this practice be prevented? The following basic rules should be adopted:

1. Require each cashier to keep the cash register closed until a transaction is started and completed.
2. Require each cashier to ring up all transactions as received.
3. Require each cashier to announce each transaction as it is rung up, so that patrons can self-audit their transactions.
4. Require each cashier to note any voids, errors, or overrings. You should initial these tapes and enter the amounts on a control sheet.
5. Require each cashier to keep all employee wraps, packages, containers, and briefcases away from the register.

In addition, the register must be audited by you regularly. Look for the following discrepancies in your cashier's tapes:

1. Totals over or under over a long time period.
2. Any break in the consecutive numbering of patron invoices.
3. Numerous "no sale" entries.
4. Numerous voids or overrings inconsistent with your standard operating procedures.

Finally, in the event you continue to have problems, you may wish to employ undercover agents to watch your cashiers.

Inventory and Property Thefts

There are a number of techniques available to you to control inventory and property thefts by employees. *Physical control* of inventory or stock is one commonsense method. This involves making someone responsible for the item at all times, from when it arrives and is stored to when it is released from storage for use. At each stage a receipt should be prepared, with all receipts tallied against control forms. Control must be followed by unannounced personal audits of the inventory on hand. Physical paper controls must be checked by your storeroom personnel and rechecked by you.

Inventory control also includes strict security: locking all entrances or doors when rooms are not in use; allowing only authorized persons access to storage areas; allowing removal of inventory or stock only by written authorization; and daily record keeping.

Control of Employees to Prevent Thefts

Unless you have collective bargaining restrictions or local laws to the contrary, you should require employees to use one entrance and exit that is guarded during all hours of operation, possibly with a metal-detecting device and/or scale to check *all* packages before entry or exit is permitted. Each employee should be required to sign a release allowing management to search his or her locker and to use visual monitors in designated work areas. No off-duty employees or unauthorized outsiders should be permitted in work areas. Passes, which identify shifts and hours off and include a photograph, should be issued and checked.

Employee theft or other illegal conduct occurring during work should be made grounds for dismissal and for criminal prosecution. An employee contract may also contain the right to fire any employee disobeying security rules, such as drinking or taking nonprescription drugs on the job. You should insist on this right at the bargaining table if your operation is unionized.

Failure to take effective and prompt steps to rid your workforce of dishonest employees will not only make your operation less profitable, but may also undermine your reliable, honest employees, injure your overall reputation, and, finally, cause your business to suffer permanent harm. If allowed to continue unchecked, ultimately it may even cause you to go out of business.

Crimes by Employees against Patrons

Crimes against patrons by employees can be doubly serious. First, there is the potential harm to your business if word gets out that employees steal from or even verbally or physically abuse patrons in your foodservice premises. However, you may also be held accountable for the actions of your employees that result in injuries to patrons.[43] (Chapter 5 on liability explains how this may occur.)

Thefts of Property

Theft of patron property by employees is not the problem in foodservice operations that it is in hotels. Still, it happens. Usually the only time you must be on guard against theft of patron property is when you check coats or other wraps in your operation. Keeping a trusted employee on duty in the checkroom is the simplest way to avoid thefts. You should also set a limit on the estimated value of the items you check. In other words, you may want to ask patrons to keep their full-length mink coats with them. If your operation is strictly first class, however, that may not be feasible. At the least, keep an employee watching checked items and only you or another supervisor should provide relief.

Thefts of Cash

An employee will not usually slip into a patron's purse or coat pocket while the patron is eating. They don't need to—there are easier ways to accomplish the same thing. They might shortchange your patrons, especially during rush periods. This is harder to detect, but by periodically "observing" the cashier you may be able to do so. However, if you institute some of the cash control procedures suggested previously, you should expect fewer problems. Too many patron complaints about being shortchanged should be cause for action on your part.

In another method of stealing cash, one usually used in bars, an employee, after providing change for patron purchases, may "sweep" the counter with a rag, thereby sweeping the change into a stash area. If the bar is busy enough, patrons may not notice. Again, this is only possible to detect if you are regularly observing your employees.

Verbal and Physical Abuse of Patrons
Waiters and waitresses especially are often victims of verbal abuse by rude patrons, but sometimes the tables are turned. Verbal abuse is not illegal unless a threat is involved, and then the patron may bring an assault charge against the employee. Of course, rudeness on the part of your employees should not be tolerated, legality notwithstanding. It's simply bad business. The best way to control verbal abuse is to keep your ears open. Any employee who verbally assaults a patron without provocation should be terminated.

Physical abuse is much more serious. If one of your employees injures a patron, you may be held liable along with the employee. (See Chapter 5.)

LEGAL RESPONSIBILITY

You are ultimately responsible for foodservice security and the prevention of crime. The success or failure of your operation may depend in large measure upon the skill and diligence with which you plan, train, and supervise your staff in preventing antisocial or criminal behavior and policing and controlling the persons involved.

You are not legally responsible for anticipating every conceivable occurrence that results in injury to your property, your patrons, or your employees. You are required to exercise reasonable care to protect yourself and others against unreasonable risks. If you fail or refuse to take reasonable precautions to prevent, deter, and halt criminal activity or to

warn patrons and employees of its presence, you may foot the bill for any resulting injuries. (Insurance coverage for property losses or liability claims due to criminal misconduct is often conditioned on your compliance with security requirements fixed by the insurance carrier or independently by law.)

The types of security measures you use to protect your business and patrons must depend largely on the seriousness of the problem. If your business is in a high-crime area, you may want to consider alarm systems, visual surveillance, and other security devices. Remember, though, that costly security measures not justified by security problems, the area, or other factors will just cost more than they help. Do what you need to do to make your business secure, but as with any other decision, make it a sound business judgment.

SUMMARY

Patron crimes in the foodservice industry often take the form of credit thefts of services and the passing of bad checks. You are susceptible to such crimes if your business policy is to accept credit in any form. You are not required by law to extend *any* credit. If you do, use an established credit card, rather than your own system. *Always* follow the card-verification procedures established by the credit card company. Your failure to do so makes you alone liable for any loss, since reimbursement of credit extended on canceled, stolen, or expired accounts is possible only if you verify the card's existence, validity, and credit limit before extending credit.

Patrons may also try to use counterfeit money. Shortchange artists may turn up during peak periods and attempt to confuse the cashier. Simply walking out without paying is another common method patrons may use.

Malicious mischief is serious in that it can include violence as well as damage to property. While operators could make a citizen's arrest, it is advisable to call the police once a crime has been committed.

Third party crimes are committed by people who have no business on the premises in the first place and are there solely to steal property, hurt people, or both. There are a number of preventive measures operators can take, but they should be justified by the cost and size of the problem.

Theft leads the list of employee crimes and may be hard to detect. Employees may steal cash or inventory. Preventive measures require continuous supervision by employers.

QUESTIONS

1. Massimo Ciotto does a lot of credit business at his first-class restaurant, the Italian Aroma. He rarely has any trouble, since he uses only national credit cards and trains the cashiers. One Saturday night, however, patrons were backed up in the cashier line, blocking those trying to enter the restaurant. The cashier took a credit card from a patron for a dinner bill totaling $150, checked the signature, and ran it through the machine. What did the cashier do wrong, and what is the possible result?
2. What steps should you take to remove a trespasser from your premises?
3. You are training your cashiers. List some tips to help them avoid being short-changed.
4. Describe the difference between robbery and larceny.
5. Chuck keeps shaking his head as he looks over the cash register tapes. He knows he had a heavy turnover tonight because of the baseball game, but the cash just does not coincide with the volume. He has also noticed a number of "no sale" entries on the tapes. What do you think has happened? How could this have been prevented? What should Chuck do now?

NOTES

1. See J. Sherry, *The Laws of Innkeepers,* sec. 22:1 (rev. ed. 1981).
2. Cal. Penal Code, sec. 537 (West. Supp. 1982); N.Y. Penal Law, secs. 165:15–17 (McKinney 1975 & Supp. 1982) are representative statutes.
3. See N.Y. Penal Law, secs. 165:15–17 (McKinney 1975 & Supp. 1982).
4. J. Sherry, *The Laws of Innkeepers,* sec. 27:2 (1972).
5. See N.Y. Penal Law, sec. 155.00 (McKinney Supp. 1978).
6. Unless you demand cash payment for goods and services rendered, the buyer may pay for them by personal check or by any other reasonable means, such as a traveler's check drawn on a United States bank. If you demand cash when the buyer offers a check, you must give the buyer a reasonable time to obtain cash. This opportunity to obtain cash need not be given if you previously advised the buyer that the transaction would be all cash. See U.C.C. sec. 2–511.
7. *Id.*
8. Only when you choose to extend credit does section 296(a)(2) of the New York Executive Law require you to do so on a non-discriminatory basis.
9. The federal Civil Rights Act does not cover credit transactions.
10. H. Lusk, C. Hewitt, J. Donnell, A. J. Barnes, *Business Law and the Regulatory Environment* 1075–76 (1982).
11. *Dudley v. Dumont,* 526 S.W.2d 839 (Mo. App. 1975). (The existence and scope of agency cannot be established by the declarations of the person or party claiming to act as agent.)
12. Lusk *et al., supra* note 10, at 391–92. *Wild v. Brewer,* 329 F.2d 924 (9th Cir.), *cert. denied,* 379 U.S. 914 (1964). (A corporation does not enjoy the Fifth Amendment privilege against self-incrimination, even when it is claimed for the benefit of the sole stockholder. In most other respects, a corporation is considered to be a person apart from its stockholders. Corporate management is defined as business conduct by its officers and directors.) See also *First Nat. Bank of Boston v. Belloti,* 435 U.S. 765 (1978). (First Amendment rights of freedom of speech cannot be restricted by the legislature to corporate activities that materially affect its business, property, or assets.)

However, the separate corporate identity of a fast-food franchise holder as a parent corporation to its 10 subsidiary corporations will be disregarded for inclusion of all subsidiary income as taxable to parent company. *Wisconsin Big Boy Corp. v. Commissioner,* 452 F.2d 137 (7th Cir. 1971).

13. *Goldenberg v. Bartell Broadcasting Corp.,* 47 Misc. 2d 105, 262 N.Y.S.2d 274 (1965).

14. *Bentall v. Koenig Bros., Inc.,* 140 Mont. 339, 372 P.2d 91 (1962). (In the absence of special authority, a corporate president has no power, merely by reason of his or her office, to execute negotiable paper in the name of the corporation.)

15. *Id.*

16. Lusk *et al., supra* note 10, at 157.

17. The credit card contract you execute mandates compliance with stated verification procedures, and is standard operating procedure for all national credit card companies.

18. Truth in Lending Act, 15 U.S.C. sec. 1643(a) (Supp. IV 1980).

19. *Martin v. American Express, Inc.,* 361 A.2d 597 (Ala. Civ. App. 1979).

20. 15 U.S.C. sec. 1606 (1978 & Supp. IV 1980 & Supp. V 1981).

21. *Id.*

22. 15 U.S.C. sec. 1602(f) (Supp. V 1981).

23. Sherry, *supra* note 1, sec. 22:9.

24. State laws must be consulted for the statutory definition of "bad check."

25. See W. LaFave and A. Scott, *Criminal Law* 678–81 (1972).

26. *Id.*

27. N.Y. Penal Law sec. 190:15 (McKinney 1975) is a representative example.

28. See 32 Am. Jur. 2d, *False Imprisonment* sec. 74 (1982).

29. The South Carolina shoplifting statute is set forth in S.C. Code Ann. secs. 16–13–110, –111,–120,–140 (Law. Co-op. 1977 & Supp. 1982). See *Faulkenberry v. Springs Mills, Inc.,* 271 S.C. 377, 247 S.E.2d 445 (1978).

30. R. Perkins, *Criminal Law* 333 (2d ed. 1969).

31. *Id.*

32. Your negligent failure to do so may inflict liability upon you to patrons injured by such misconduct. See Sherry, *supra* note 1, sec. 11:13.

33. See Chapter 5.

34. See Chapter 3 *supra.*

35. Lusk, *et al., supra* note 10, at 60. See generally *Dial v. City of O'Fallon,* 81 Ill. 2d 548, 411 N.E.2d 217 (1980).

36. See, for example, N.Y. Penal Law secs. 140:05, :10, :15 (McKinney 1975 & Supp. 1982).

37. LaFave and Scott, *supra* note 25, at 708–17.

38. *Id.*

39. *Id.* at 692–704.

40. *Commonwealth v. Homer,* 235 Mass. 526, 533, 127 N.E. 517, 520 (1920).

41. *Edwards v. Great American Ins. Co.,* 146 So. 2d 260 (La. App. 1962) (innkeeper).

42. See generally Sherry, *supra* note 1, secs. 11:4–11:8. Also see Chapter 6 for pre-employment screening procedures.

43. See Chapter 5, *supra.*

9
Foodservice Contracts

Objectives

The purpose of this chapter is to:

1. Define the elements of a contract.
2. Discuss various foodservice contracts within the framework of the contract requirements.
3. Outline tests for the legality, validity, and enforceability of contracts and the remedies available when one party fails to perform.

Case in Point

Martin and Muriel Glick owned and operated the Chef's Delight Restaurant, a popular, well-established operation located in a new suburban development. They had water-seepage problems in their basement. Martin hired Shepard, a plumber, to install a sewer line into the restaurant to correct the problem. There was no written contract. After Shepard performed, but before payment of the agreed-upon price, Martin died. Muriel refused to pay, claiming that the oral agreement to install the sewer was only between her late husband and Shepard. Muriel did not dispute the quality of the work performed or the contract price. Shepard sued for payment for his services, arguing that he had performed according to a valid contract entered into by both *Martin and Muriel.*

Was Shepard right? Was Muriel a contracting party? Yes, on the basis of the following rule of law: A contract exists if implied from the conduct, situation or mutual relations of parties, and enforced by the law on the grounds of reason and justice. An oral contract is presumed valid when there is a meeting of the minds of the parties and the contract meets the legal requirements for contracts. *There was no dispute that a definite oral contract was entered into by Martin.*

In this case unjust enrichment of the party (Muriel) trying to avoid the contract would have resulted in Shepard being the loser, even though he had entered into the contract in good faith. Why was Muriel a contracting party according to the law? She was a co-owner of the restaurant, including the land and the building; she knew the work was necessary and wanted it done; and she co-signed an advance deposit to Shepard. Moreover, Muriel did not object to the terms and conditions when Martin negotiated with Shepard in her presence and guaranteed him payment.[1]

TYPICAL FOODSERVICE CONTRACTS

Foodservice managers must negotiate and deal with a variety of agreements in order to operate their businesses. The life of any foodservice business requires that agreements with manufacturers and suppliers; with professionals such as lawyers, florists, entertainers, architects, and engineers; and with government bodies at all levels be enforceable.

These agreements, called by their legal name *contracts,* provide the foundation for business relations. This foundation enables foodservice operators, suppliers, and patrons to structure day-to-day dealings.

A *contract* is any legally enforceable agreement, whereby each person *agrees to perform or not to perform some act.* The law gives each party to a contract reciprocal rights and responsibilities. In any contract each party has the *right* to receive the performance agreed to by the other party and the *responsibility* to perform any duty agreed to under the terms of the contract.[2] If one party fails to receive the performance agreed to by the other, he or she may seek a legal remedy, usually money damages or the performance of the act.

There are three forms of foodservice contracts: (1) contracts used to negotiate purchases of goods and services from foodservice manufacturers, growers, suppliers, and professionals; (2) contracts used to negotiate sales of finished products and services—foods, beverages, or the use of space or function rooms—to patrons; and (3) *management contracts* between establishments such as hotels and hospitals with foodservice firms for management of their foodservice operations.

In the first form, most foodservice operators use a *purchase order* to buy goods, such as meats, poultry, and vegetables, from a seller (vendor) on a printed form provided by either the seller or buyer. Terms and conditions of the order are contained on the form. This purchase order is actually a simple contract form.

Foodservice operators will also negotiate *service contracts,* with professionals who furnish entertainment, decorations, and special lighting, as well as legal or accounting services. In the first category are repetitive service contracts for which a standard form may be used. In the second category, the uniqueness of the services (law or accounting) usually requires that the buyer negotiate from a contract provided by the professional.

Almost every commercial foodservice operator will negotiate *reservation* and *function contracts* with patrons. A reservation contract involves the use of tables, generally available for walk-in patrons, *except* that a specific table or tables or space is reserved *in advance* for the patron for a specific date and time. A standard menu is used and no charge or deposit is required to hold the reservation.

A *function* contract is a form of reservation contract. The operator agrees to reserve *private* space in the establishment for a patron in the future, rather than merely regular table space for future patron use. A function is a special event, such as a wedding, banquet, or an awards dinner, for which the patron wishes to buy the exclusive use of space. Usually a function involves preplanned food and beverage service, at an agreed-upon price per portion, rather than the regular menu selection. An advance deposit is usually paid by the patron to assure performance by the operator.

Management contracts are common among institutions, especially those whose primary purpose is not to serve food but to offer other services, such as education, mental health care, and shelter. Hotels, schools, prisons, and recreational parks may contract with foodservice firms to manage all or most of their foodservice operations. The firm either may be paid outright or may split the profits. The foodservice firm is usually in charge of staffing, as well as the purchasing, preparing, and serving of food.

Each of those foodservice agreements has *elements* that make it an enforceable, legal contract. When an element is missing or the terms of the agreement are misunderstood by one or both parties, a court may have to step in and untangle the mess. An understanding of the elements of a contract should prevent foodservice operators from having legal problems in this area.

CONTRACT LAW

Before discussing contracts further, the purpose of *contract law* needs explanation. Contract law assures the enforcement of agreements without resort to physical violence or economic warfare.

Most people voluntarily live up to business agreements as a moral duty. However, when adverse economic conditions make it costly or disadvantageous to do so, moral duty may not be enough to compel compliance from everyone. Here contract law steps in to provide an impartial method of contract enforcement. In this way the wronged party to a contract is given relief and the party who broke the contract is held responsible.

Contract law is the foundation on which business relationships are created and enforced. Without contract law business transactions would constantly suffer from uncertainty. Some understanding of contract law will help foodservice operators avoid unnecessary and costly mistakes.

TYPES OF CONTRACTS

Contracts are classified in various ways: how they are stated, which of the parties must perform, how they are formed, stage of performance, and to what extent they are legally binding. By analyzing the service contract example in the Case in Point, we can easily see into which categories it falls.

How Contracts Are Stated

An *express contract* is one in which all of the terms and conditions are fully stated, either orally (by spoken words) or in writing. An oral express contract was made between Shepard and Martin to install a sewer line. An *implied contract* is one in which the terms and conditions are implied from the conduct of the parties, rather than their words.[3] Muriel's conduct as a co-signer of the deposit check created an implied contract between her and Shepard to pay him for the sewer line.

Who Must Perform

In a *bilateral contract* a promise is exchanged for a *promise,* and both parties are bound to perform. In a *unilateral contract* one party promises to perform only in exchange for an *act* of the other party.[4] In this case only the party promising to perform the act is bound. A unilateral contract existed between Shepard and the Glicks, but once Shepard performed, the Glicks were bound to pay for his work. Until the agreed-upon act is completed, the other party need do nothing, and

may in fact withdraw the promise without liability. For example, if Smitty, the owner of a carry-out operation, agrees to obtain a 15 percent discount from Carol for 500 paper bags in exchange for his agreement to buy 600 bags next month, they exchange promises to perform, and have a bilateral contract. Carol will give Smitty a 15 percent discount for the bags, and he will buy 600 bags next month. If Carol tells Smitty she'll deliver 500 bags to him next Tuesday, only a unilateral contract exists. Only Carol has agreed to perform. Smitty has agreed to nothing until Tuesday, and he may change his mind. However, in such cases the courts normally prevent injustice to the party performing the act by holding the other party liable for the reasonable value of the benefits received.[5] Thus Smitty might have to pay Carol the reasonable value of the bags.

How Contracts Are Formed

A *formal contract* is actually a *negotiable instrument,* a promise to pay for goods or services. Checks, notes, drafts, and certificates of deposit are examples of negotiable instruments. The source for the law of formal contracts is the Uniform Commercial Code. All other contracts are *informal contracts.* A purchase contract is an example. No special form is required, except in the case of real estate transactions.[6] The service contract between Shepard and the Glicks was an informal contract.

Quasi-contracts are a legal classification. They are not really contracts at all, since they are created by the courts to avoid injustice. No agreement or consent between the parties exists. Rather, the courts *impose* duties on one party to prevent unjust enrichment, or one party getting something for nothing without legal justification.[7] Under this doctrine, Muriel might have been required to pay Shepard for the fair value of his services even in the absence of any written contract.

Stage of Performance

A contract fully performed by both parties is an *executed contract*. A contract not yet completed by one is an *executory contract*.[8] Shepard had executed his responsibilities under the sewer installation contract. Muriel had not yet paid for the services Shepard rendered. Her part of the contract remained executory.

Extent Contracts Are Legally Binding

Contracts are either *valid, void, voidable,* or *unenforceable.* This classification determines which, if any, legal remedies are available in the event one of the parties violates the contract.

A valid contract is one that contains all the essential elements of a contract and is fully enforceable. The service contract contains all the essential elements.

A void contract is not a contract at all, meaning that it will not be recognized as one that is legally enforceable. Neither party is required to perform and no legal obligations exist. A contract to hire someone to murder a business competitor is an example.

A voidable contract gives one of the parties the option to avoid performance without liability or to perform at his or her option.[9] Performance of a voidable contract is called a *ratification*.[10] If one party chooses not to perform, then both parties are released from performance. If one party performs, the other party is obliged to perform. Until the contract is avoided by the party choosing to do so, it is fully enforceable. Contracts made by a minor are voidable by the minor, *but not by the adult with whom the minor contracts*. Other examples are contracts induced by fraud, duress, or undue influence, which may be avoided by the innocent party.[11]

An unenforceable contract is a contract in all respects except one, which makes it legally unenforceable. For example, if a party to a contract fails to sue to enforce it within a time period (the statute of limitations) required by law, that person is prevented from enforcing any claim based on that contract, even though all other necessary elements of a contract exist.[12] A statute of limitations is the maximum amount of time after something happens for a remedy to be sought in court. If Shepard had failed to sue within the proper time period, and Muriel had raised that as a defense, the court would have dismissed Shepard's claim even though it was otherwise valid.

PURCHASE ORDERS

Purchase orders are actually informal express contracts to buy foods and nonperishable items such as silverware, tables, and chairs.

Purchase orders must contain all essential contract elements to be enforceable. In these contracts a promise to deliver goods is made by the seller and the buyer promises to pay for them when received. These are typically unilateral contracts with the buyer promising to pay only if the seller delivers the goods. Figure 9.1 is a typical purchase order between a foodservice operator and a supplier.

By seeing how this simple contract meets the legal elements, the law of contracts should be clearer. There is nothing hidden or mysterious about a contract that only a lawyer should know. Foodservice operators should know their legal rights and responsibilities for all the different contracts they must use to perform their jobs and maintain their operations.

ESSENTIAL ELEMENTS OF A CONTRACT[13]

The law requires every contract to contain certain elements without which the courts are unable to grant or deny appropriate relief.

Agreement, consideration, capacity of the parties to contract, legality, and *genuineness of assent* are the major elements.

Agreement

Contract law requires that one party make an *offer* and the other party *accept* the offer on the terms contained in the offer. This is *agreement.* Each of these elements includes other factors that are essential to enforcing an agreement. The offer must identify the parties, the subject matter of the contract, the time for performance, and the price. If all of these terms are expressed in the contract, the contract is enforceable.

A purchase order is really nothing more than an *offer* to purchase goods or services from a seller, and does not become a contract until *accepted* by the seller. The purchase order in Figure 9.1 is enforceable. It contains the essential contract terms. (Sometimes the courts will imply reasonable terms as long as the intentions of the parties are not violated.[14] If the purchase order did not state an exact price, but rather "cost plus 15 percent" for the items, the court might imply a reasonable cost figure.)

The Offer

The offer itself must also contain three elements: (1) an *intention* that the court can ascertain objectively from the conduct of the parties if it is not otherwise expressed; (2) definiteness; and (3) communication.

Intention by the seller to make an offer is illustrated by the seller leaving the blank purchase order form with a potential buyer, or by notifying buyers by a circular or other means that the seller wishes to obtain business. This means that courts will ignore the secret, unspoken intentions of the parties.

At common law the offer must be *definite* on all essential terms, meaning identification of the parties, the subject matter, the time for performance, and the price. The Uniform Commercial Code covers otherwise indefinite terms. The purchase order may be enforced by the establishment of a reasonable price, place of delivery, time for shipment or delivery, and time for payment. The common law test adopted to determine whether an offer is definite is as follows: Are its terms *specific* and *firm enough* for the court to measure the damages directly related to the violation or breach of that contract? The purchase terms in the Dover Inn order are specific. Let's take a less obvious example, so you can determine the difference.

Let's suppose that the Glicks wish to hire you to manage their restaurant. The written employment contract provides a fixed monthly salary, but the Glicks orally promised you "a reasonable share of the profits" as an additional inducement. After 10 years you voluntarily end your employment. Then you request an accounting of the profits. The Glicks refuse.

You sue to recover your share of the profits; the total profits on which the share would be based add up to $2,000,000 over the 10-year period. You would probably lose your case.[15] A *reasonable share* of the profits is too indefinite a term on which to base any damage award. Had the Glicks agreed to pay you a fixed salary plus 10 percent of the annual profits, this promise would meet the test of definiteness and permit you to recover your share.

For the foodservice industry, the Uniform Commercial Code also permits omitted or indefinite terms to be supplied by "custom and usage" in trade and by prior dealings. This means that if practices such as a blank purchase order or special delivery terms are widely accepted in the foodservice industry, and are legal, then they may be enforced as long as both parties understand the terms. If terms customarily have one meaning in the foodservice industry, they are acceptable, even if they have other meanings in other types of business. It is up to the party claiming custom

Figure 9.1
Typical Purchase Order

PURCHASE ■ **■ORDER**	ORIGINAL · W ACCOUNTING · Y RECEIVING · P DEPARTMENT · G

TO

Maxi-Fish & Suppliers, Inc.
255 Pier Street
Boston, Mass.

DATE ___April 2, 1985___

PURCHASE ORDER NO. ___732___

hereby orders from you the goods or services specified below. The Purchase Order Number must appear on all packages, papers and invoices pertaining to this order. Invoices must be submitted in duplicate and a packing slip must accompany each shipment.

Company Telephone No.

QUANTITY	DESCRIPTION	PRICE EA.	AMOUNT
50	Fresh Grade A filleted codfish	$ 1.00	$ 50.00
2 cases	cocktail sauce	20.00	40.00
1 case	cream of tartar sauce	15.00	15.00
25	lemons	.25	6.25
			$161.25
			+ 6 percent
	Delivery needed by April 10.		

SHIP TO

Dover Seafood Shoppe
10 Massachusetts Street
Boston, Mass.

CHARGE ACCT. NO.	AMOUNT
Kitchen 12	

AUTHORIZED BY ___Billy Dover, Jr.___

ORDERED BY ___cb___

RECEIVED BY _____

DATE RECEIVED _____

and usage to prove such existence and application to any issue in dispute. Suppose you ordered frozen chickens from a poultry seller for resale to restaurant patrons as a weekly chicken feature. When the chickens were delivered, you discovered that they were "stewing chickens" rather than "young chickens" suitable for broiling and frying. The sales contract did not define the word "chicken," and you failed to prove that the generic word "chicken" in the foodservice business always means "young chickens." There was no clear definition of what you wanted in the contract.[16] To the courts the word "chicken" means any chicken suitable for human consumption. You got more than you bargained for, and would have been forced to pay for chickens you did not want. There was no breach or violation of any warranty of fitness by the seller.

The offer must be *communicated* by the person making the offer, the *offeror*, to the person intended to receive the offer, called the *offeree*.[17] Every person who offers goods or services to another has the right to limit the offer to certain specified persons.[18] In the purchase order, Dover Inn is the offeree and Maxi-Fish is the offeror. Once the offeree accepts an effective, valid offer, the offer and acceptance together make up a legally binding agreement or contract.[19] Assuming that all other elements of a contract exist, only those persons may accept the offer and thereby create a contract.[20] This means that a total stranger cannot accept an offer intended for another person, even though the stranger is willing and able to accept the offer. In other words, Seafoods, Inc., could not accept the special offer intended for Dover.

Termination of Offers
Offers can be terminated in a number of ways.

1. Just as a person can limit the offer to meet his or her requirements, the offeror can *revoke* the offer before it is accepted. Maxi-Fish could state that a fish special is no longer a special and the Dovers have to pay full price. A withdrawal of the offer must be specific and communicated to the offeree before he or she accepts.[21] Otherwise the acceptance will create a valid contract. The rule of revocation permits offerors to revoke any time *before* acceptance, even though they may have promised to hold the offer open for a specified time period.[22]

The only exception to the right of revocation is if the offeree enters into an *option contract* by paying the offeror for the promise to hold the offer open for a specific time period. Payment for the promise to keep the offer open makes the option right binding upon the offeror.[23] Although contained in the offer, it is a separate, enforceable agreement. This is why it is called an option contract. The offeror remains free to refuse to provide an option, but once such a bargain is made, is bound to honor it for the time specified.

The Uniform Commercial Code does away with payment or other consideration in the case of a *firm offer*. The firm offer rule applies as follows: If a merchant dealing in goods sold in the regular course of business signs a written offer stating that it is open for a specified period, it is firm for that time period, not to exceed three months.[24]

Sometimes courts prevent a legal revocation when the offeree changes position in *reasonable reliance on* the offer.[25] If Dover had turned down a lucrative deal with Just Fishin' to buy the special from Maxi-Fish, and suffered losses because of Maxi-Fish's withdrawal of the offer, Dover could sue.

2. Another method of termination of an offer is *rejection by the offeree*, the person or party to whom the offer is made. Mr. Dover can simply decide he could get a better deal elsewhere. As in the case of revocation, a rejection of the offer must be received by the offeror to be effective.

3. Offers are also terminated by *operation of law,* meaning by circumstances beyond the control of the parties but recognized as legal grounds for termination.[26] Four general situations fall into this category of termination:

- The *lapse of the time period specified* to accept an outstanding offer. Failure to accept within a reasonable time period constitutes a rejection of the offer, unless unusual circumstances justify late acceptance. For example, a reservation contract for a business luncheon for the local athletic club may contain a provision requiring a deposit before the contract is accepted. Failure to make the required deposit within a certain time period will automatically terminate the offer. This frees the restaurant from any duty to perform for the club and allows the manager to negotiate a new reservation, either with the club or with another group.

   When no time period for acceptance is specified, the courts will create a reasonable time period for termination. This concept of "reasonableness" will vary with circumstances, price fluctuations, and market conditions, among other factors.[27] Sales of perishable commodities such as fresh meats and vegetables used in your restaurant will require a shorter time period for acceptance than would the sale of tables and chairs. Fuel oil to heat your operation might also require a shorter time for termination, not because the commodity is perishable, but because a short supply may cause sharp changes in the market price.

- *Destruction of the subject matter* is another ground for termination by operation of the law. In this case the circumstances causing the destruction must occur before acceptance of the offer.[28] If a supplier offers to sell dressed poultry for delivery to your restaurant, and you show interest but do not commit yourself by signing or accepting a purchase order, the destruction of the supplier's poultry warehouse automatically prevents you from accepting the offer.

- *Death or incompetency of either the offeror or the offeree* will also terminate any offer.[29] If the Maxi-Fish supplier died after making the offer, and he had no business partner, the offer would have terminated.

- *An offer legal when made but later declared illegal* by a court or legislation before acceptance also terminates the offer.[30] Suppose that under existing laws you are able to buy imported alcoholic beverages at wholesale from private warehouses for resale to your customers. You receive an offer from the wholesaler for imported Polish vodka. Before you are able to accept the offer, the federal government places an embargo on all shipments from Poland and prohibits sales of Polish products already on hand. Such government intervention makes the vodka sale to you illegal, preventing you from accepting the offer.

Any of these situations could short-circuit the formation of a legal contract based on a purchase order. However, the Uniform Commercial Code does permit merchants to vary the terms of an acceptance or add new terms that automatically become part of the contract unless (1) the buyer requires acceptance of the original terms of your offer, (2) the new terms materially alter the contract, or (3) the buyer rejects the new terms.

Non-offers

Not all statements made by one party to another are offers. To know what an offer is, you should also know what it is not. The following non-offers should help clarify this point.

1. When a party expresses an *opinion about a future happening,* that expression is not

an offer that, if accepted, makes the opinion legally binding.[31] If the Maxi-Fish salesman said the cod would probably increase dinner sales, any drop in those sales would not be a breach of contract by Maxi-Fish. The supplier was not guaranteeing anything, but merely expressing an opinion.

2. *Preliminary negotiations,* or an expressed willingness to negotiate, are not offers.[32] If Mr. Dover merely asked Maxi-Fish to submit a bid for the items, the invitation to bid is not an offer, nor does Maxi-Fish bind Dover by submitting the requested bid. Once the bid is submitted, it is an offer Dover is free to accept or reject.

3. *Statements of intention,* such as promises to make a future contract, are also non-offers.[33]

4. *Advertisements, circulars,* and *catalogue promotions,* made to the general public, are non-offers because the seller (offeror) does not have an unlimited supply of merchandise, and everyone who "accepted" could sue the seller for breach of contract. However, if the advertisement contains all the essential elements, it can create contract liability, if accepted.[34] Thus sellers may protect themselves by including the phrase "subject to prior sale" in their promotion material.

5. *Non-contracts.*   A contract is an agreement, but not all agreements are contracts.
   The law excludes *social transactions* from the field of offers.[35] If the Dovers invited the Maxi-Fish supplier to a free meal at the restaurant as a friendly gesture, and not as an occasion to discuss future business, a social obligation would be created, involving a *moral duty* on the Dovers to provide the promised meal.[36] If they refused to do so when the supplier arrived at the appointed date and time, he could not sue for breach of contract, even though he

may have spent money to get there. A social obligation is not a legal obligation. Had the invitation been business-related, the supplier would have a better chance of creating a contract by accepting the invitation.

Acceptance must normally meet buyer requirements. This means that the seller may not attach new or different conditions. The UCC creates some leeway on the terms of acceptance between merchants.

Acceptance of the purchase order must be *communicated* by the seller to be effective. The normal rule is that an offer by mail is accepted when the signed purchase order is mailed, not when it is received. *The acceptance of a valid purchase order is the point in time at which a purchase contract is created.*

Acceptance

How does one accept an offer? *Communication* is the key to acceptance of an offer.[37] This means by words or conduct *communicated* to the offeror that shows the offeree's agreement to the terms of the offer. Under common law the acceptance must normally be made in the manner stated in the offer, and must be without conditions that change the offer.[38] Any changes will create a *counteroffer,* meaning a rejection of the original offer.[39] A counteroffer, if accepted, creates a new contract.

One party may express dissatisfaction with the offer without creating a counteroffer. The Dovers, in responding to Maxi-Fish's offer, could agree to the terms, but add, "We accept, but want credit rather than a cash deal." That condition is a counteroffer, and not acceptance of the original contract.

The Uniform Commercial Code changes this common law acceptance rule. An acceptance of an offer to sell goods that changes the terms of the offer *slightly* is enforceable because the changes are treated as *additions* to the contract. The requirements of the UCC to meet this criterion are as follows: (1) both parties must be merchants, and (2) the proposed changes are enforced unless the offer specifically states that the offer must be accepted without any changes, or the changes significantly alter the contract, or the offeror objects to the changes within a reasonable time. If neither party is a merchant, then the offeror must agree to any changes.[40]

Silence (neither verbally accepting nor rejecting the offer) does not usually mean acceptance of an offer. There are three exceptions to this rule, however: when the offeree accepts the benefits of the offer with an opportunity to reject goods or services and understands that the goods or services are not intended as gifts; where the recipient must notify the offeror only if rejecting the goods or services; and when the recipient exercises possession and control over the goods. If the Dovers cooked the codfish, it is a safe bet that the court would find they had accepted the fish. This use establishes an intention to pay for the reasonable value of the goods.[41]

Generally any reasonable and appropriate acceptance is effective unless the offer requires a specific kind of acceptance. Normally the acceptance must be transmitted by the same method used in transmitting the original offer. Where an offer is mailed, mailing the acceptance would be reasonable.[42] Any improperly posted and mailed acceptance will not be effective until actually received.

Consideration

A second major element of every contract is consideration.[43] This term means something, usually money, given by one party to the contract in exchange for something given or to be given by the other party. In the purchase order Dover exchanged the promise of money for the food he would receive. The giving may take the form of an act, or a promise to act.

It may also consist of a promise to refrain from acting.[44]

Consideration does not have to be economically valuable to be legal.[45] *Detriment* is necessary to prove that the consideration for the bargain made is legally sufficient.[46] Both parties to a contract suffer detriments and gain benefits at the same time in any legal bargain.[47] Dover has to give up his money and Maxi-Fish has to give Dover the goods—on time. Negotiation can help minimize the detriments and maximize the benefits.

Certain promises can be enforced without consideration. For example, if you are persuaded by a fast-foods owner to give up your restaurant to run a franchise and rely on assurances that the franchise will be granted, and the franchise owner does not grant it, you can recover damages for the losses suffered when you gave up the restaurant. The franchisor is prevented from raising the issue of lack of consideration for the promised franchise. The courts can only avoid an injustice by requiring the franchisor to make good your losses.[48]

The Uniform Commercial Code eliminates the question of consideration when a *firm offer* is made.[49]

Capacity of Contracting Parties

The third major element of an enforceable contract is that both parties must have the *capacity* to enter into a contract. Capacity means the emotional maturity to understand the consequences of a contract.[50]

Non compos mentis, the legal phrase used to describe the state of mind of the person trying to avoid a contract, means that person is unable to understand the legal consequences of his or her conduct. The legal test of *non compos mentis* is objective, meaning that a person's conduct under the circumstances is examined to determine his or her ability to understand legal duties.[51]

In this area, transactions with *minors* represent the most difficulty. Minors are given special treatment not accorded adults. (In most states a minor is any person who has not attained *majority,* usually the age of 18.)[52]

In general, contracts entered into by a minor are voidable if the minor chooses to avoid them, but only by the minor. The adult who contracts with the minor cannot avoid the contract. Unless the minor chooses to avoid a contract, it is presumed valid and enforceable. The adult party is bound unless the minor exercises the legal right to avoid the contract.[53]

The exercise of a minor's right to avoid a contract obligation is called a right to *disaffirm,* that is, to set aside the contract. Such disaffirmance may be expressed by words or conduct.[54] A minor may disaffirm at any time during minority or for a reasonable time after reaching the age of majority.[55]

Let's assume that Billy Dover, Jr., was only 16 years old. Might the purchase order still be enforceable? Probably, since it was on the regular form used by Dover. However, if Billy went to Maxi-Fish, said he wanted the cod for "his foodservice," and then changed his mind, the supplier has a problem.

Operators or suppliers dealing with minors should know exactly whose signature is valid when it comes to purchase orders. Operators in the catering business especially have to be on the lookout for minors who want to contract for a party. Find an adult to sign agreements.

When a contract has been fully performed by the seller, the minor must *restore* the goods or services received to the seller, as long as they are in his or her control. Such property may be returned "as is," without compensating the seller for any damage caused, in the majority of states.[56] A few states compel the minor to provide *restitution,* meaning returning the seller to his original position.[57] A minor cannot disaffirm a part and retain the benefits of the rest of the contract. The disaffirmance *must be total, not partial.*[58] Given the perishability of items in the foodservice industry, this is small comfort.

What happens when a minor misrepresents his or her age to a seller? Statutes in some states prohibit disaffirmance by a minor who lies about his or her age. Other state courts require the minor to repay the full value of the consideration received in such cases.[59] A third group of state courts allow the minor to disaffirm, but permit the seller to recover damages on the basis of fraud.[60]

Parents are *not usually liable* for contracts made by their children. Therefore, to protect yourself, it is wise to obtain the co-signature of a parent or other responsible adult for any contracts involving a substantial value, for example, the sale of a foodservice van. That signature will make the parent a guarantor of payment, meaning that the parent is personally responsible for payment, even if the minor disaffirms.

Minors present a serious dilemma to all businesspersons. Foodservice managers are not as vulnerable as some sellers of high-cost durable goods (business vehicles, restaurant equipment), since foods and beverages are usually paid for at the time of sale. The contract, completely performed by both the minor and operator, is over or *discharged.* There is nothing for the minor to disaffirm. However, the minor may disaffirm foods and beverages bought on credit with the restaurant's own charge system. To reiterate, caterers should be wary of minors contracting for a party. Find a parent to sign the actual agreement. Since this can run into large sums of money, credit transactions with minors should be reviewed carefully.

Intoxicated persons are another class of individuals who can avoid their contracts. To do so, the intoxicated person must prove that he or she was so drunk as not to know what he or she was doing. If the salesman was drunk when he said he had 50 codfish and actually had 50 halibut steaks, Billy may have to change his menu—and his supplier. Intoxication does not *automatically* void a contract. The contract is enforceable until the intoxicated person chooses to avoid it.

Incompetent persons are also able to avoid otherwise binding contracts. Incompetence is defined as lack of *mental capacity* to understand the legal consequences of one's actions. *Physical incapacity* is *not* a ground on which someone may disaffirm or avoid contracts, unless physical incapacity impairs one's mental capacity to make contracts.

Insanity recognized by a judicial body makes all contracts of the declared incompetent *void*. If insanity is not judicially declared, that person's contracts cannot automatically be avoided. Rather, the issue is whether the person was incompetent at the time the particular contract was executed. If the contract of an otherwise incompetent person was executed by that person in a "lucid interval" (a period of mental competence), it will not be voided by the courts.

Legal *aliens* who are legally residing in the United States have the same power to contract, sue, and be sued as United States citizens. *Illegal aliens are denied the right to assert contract claims in the courts.* Some states deny all aliens the right to own real property. Enemy aliens from a country with whom the United States is at war will be denied the right to enforce contract claims, if such claims would afford aid to the enemy country.

The *death* of one of the contracting parties automatically terminates an agreement. In our Case in Point, however, it was determined that Muriel, as a co-owner of the business, was obligated as a full contracting party to pay Shepard.

Legality

Let's assume that neither Billy nor the supplier was underage, drunk, incompetent, or an illegal alien, and that the purchase order meets these requirements. The contract must also be *legal*. The purchase order also meets the contract requirements for legality.[61] A contract that is not legal will not be enforced by the courts. Nor can either party hold the other to performance or consideration. Illegal contracts include business loans at interest rates higher than permitted by law and contracts that illegally restrain trade if they tend to create a monopoly or restrict competition.[62] (Chapter 11 deals with franchising and antitrust pitfalls.)

Unconscionable contract clauses are also illegal since they violate public policy, additional grounds for legality.[63] Unconscionable clauses are clauses that are so unfair that no court could enforce them. A foodservice operator persuaded to contract with the local police for "extra protection" would be an example. Both at common law and under the Uniform Commercial Code, courts are empowered to strike out unconscionable clauses.[64]

Another type of illegal, unenforceable contract clause is an *exculpatory* clause. Here one party conditions the offer on a waiver by the other party of all legal rights arising out of the first person's negligence or willful misconduct in the performance of the promises.[65] If Maxi-Fish had conditioned the purchase order on Dover's promise not to take legal action if the supplier failed to deliver, such a clause would not hold up in court. This is to prevent the law from being used as an instrument of injustice by permitting people to benefit by wrongdoing.[66]

Using illegality as an excuse to get out of or terminate a contract is not always a sure solution. Courts are quick to terminate contracts that are obviously illegal but not those that tend to involve hazy areas where even the law is not clear, and especially when the contract does not address an illegal issue or require illegal action as performance. Courts tend to view with distaste attempts to escape contracts by various ploys. Such attempts may backfire, as a case in this chapter will illustrate.

Genuineness of Assent

A final requirement necessary to create a contract is *genuineness of assent,* a legal phrase meaning that a contract must be *voluntarily* negotiated by both parties. A contract by definition is an agreement. When either party induces the other to contract by *mistake, fraud,* or any other conduct other than normal business risks, the innocent party may cancel the contract and avoid the duties the contract creates.[67] The purchase order meets this final requirement. If Maxi-Fish had misrepresented the quality of the items, Mr. Dover might have a legal right to bow out of the contract.

Mistake

There are two kinds of mistakes. The first involves a *mutual mistake,* a mistake made by both parties, for which neither party is responsible.[68] Suppose the Dovers wish to employ a new chef. They contact a reputable foodservice recruiter, and the recruiter gives them the name John Snyder. The Dovers believe the identity of the person to be the famous chef John Snyder, Sr., whereas the recruiter believes they want to hire John Snyder, Jr. John Snyder, Jr., is sent to work, and when the Dovers do not hire him, the recruiter sues to recover the agreed-upon finder's fee. The lawsuit will be dismissed. No contract existed between the parties, because both were *innocently mistaken* as to the identity of the

subject matter of the contract. This rule requires that the mistake be serious or *material;* that is, neither party would have made the contract had they known the true facts.

When only one of the contracting parties makes a mistake, the law defines it as a *unilateral mistake,* one not wrongfully caused by the other party, and that party cannot normally cancel the contract.[69] This means that if only the Dovers were mistaken as to the identity of the Snyder they wished to employ, the recruiter could win his lawsuit and recover the finder's fee.

Fraud

Fraud requires the innocent party to show: (1) a *misrepresentation* of a material fact, meaning a false statement or conduct, which leads the person to believe something that is not true; (2) that the false statement or conduct is known to be false by the party making the statement or performing the act, as a dealer concealing a dangerous defect in a van being sold to the Dovers for business purposes; (3) that the deception or false statement is intentional; (4) that the innocent party is justified in relying on the false statement or deception; and (5) that the innocent party suffered some damage or injury as a result of the false statement or deception.[70]

When all of these requirements are met, the innocent party has two choices. One is to cancel the contract and be restored to one's original position, such as getting back a down payment or deposit given to the seller at the time the contract was signed.[71] The other is to enforce the contract and sue to recover for any injury suffered as a result of the fraud.[72]

Previously we noted that silence does not normally mean an acceptance of a contract. *Likewise, silence does not normally mean fraud.* The fact that not all pertinent information is volunteered by one party is not a legal reason for the other to cancel a contract. However, when the other party is under a duty to speak, his or her silence is not legally justified, thus permitting the innocent party to cancel. For example, if a condition is dangerous and cannot be discovered by reasonable inspection, the seller must inform the buyer of it.[73] When the Dovers buy equipment that contains a concealed defect (called in law a *latent* defect as against a *patent* or obvious defect) or a potential risk that a reasonable person could not detect, such as pressure-cooking equipment that may explode without warning unless precautions are taken, *the seller has a duty to warn them.* This is a requirement imposed by the Uniform Commercial Code, which requires a product to have an implied warranty of fitness for its intended purpose. Fraud is also a *common law concept applicable to situations where the UCC does not apply, such as in real estate sales, employment contracts, and contracts for personal services.*

When a misrepresentation is *innocent,* meaning there was no intention to deceive, the innocent party can cancel but cannot recover damages for any losses suffered.[74]

All five elements must be present to form a contract. In any major agreement, operators should keep these elements in mind as a sort of checklist. If any of the elements "seem to be missing," it may be wise to contact a lawyer either to fill in the gaps or to help renegotiate the agreement.

SALES CONTRACTS

Purchase orders are used in day-to-day business purchases. They are informal contracts—once accepted—that are used to buy food and supplies to run a restaurant. Negotiation is usually kept to a minimum between orders, as many of these supplies are used up and must be replaced weekly, or even daily. Sales contracts are used less often, are more formal, usually involve more money, and may involve a title transfer of the right to the property.

The foodservice operator is likely to encounter sales contracts when buying a building for a restaurant, a vehicle for restaurant business, or foodservice equipment, or placing very large food orders.

Transfer of Ownership to Buyer in Sales Contracts

Various requirements must be met under the Uniform Commercial Code before a buyer may take title to or ownership rights in goods purchased with sales contracts. *First,* the goods must exist at the time of sale.[75] Ownership cannot be transferred, or title cannot pass from seller to buyer, *on goods yet to be grown or produced. Second,* the goods must be identified in the contract of sale.[76] Identification is a technical term meaning that the goods must be set aside or distinguished from other similar seller goods.

The buyer should obtain insurance on goods for protection against the loss or damage of goods while in the hands of a common carrier and, equally important, to ensure the right to recover if someone damages or steals the property during shipment.

Once goods are in existence and are identified, title passes; that is, ownership is transferred from seller to buyer under the Uniform Commercial Code in the following ways.

Agreement between the Parties
This is the most normal means of transferring ownership rights. Both parties to a contract agree on when ownership rights will be transferred. Ownership rights should be explicit—not left to guesswork—and be in writing so that a court interpreting the contract can rely on the provisions to determine each party's rights and responsibilities.[77]

When the Seller Completes Delivery

Unless the contract specifies otherwise, the title is transferred when *physical* delivery of goods is made by the seller at the time and place agreed upon.

The nature of the contract determines when in the delivery process title passes. A *shipment contract* requires the seller only to deliver the goods to a carrier (railroad, air, marine, or motor carrier). Then title passes to the buyer on delivery of the goods to the carrier. A *destination contract* requires the seller to deliver the goods to the destination specified, either to the buyer's business or to the buyer's agent (a refrigerated warehouse in the case of meats and poultry). Title passes to the buyer when the goods are delivered to that destination, or are *tendered. Tender* means to do all those things required of the seller under the contract.

When the contract involves *documents of title,* title passes when and where those documents are delivered to the buyer. A *bill of lading* or *warehouse receipt* is a document of title. To illustrate, you wish to buy vegetable oil for your kitchen. The seller has the oil you want in a warehouse near your restaurant. You agree to buy a specific quantity of the oil at a certain price. When the seller delivers a warehouse receipt to the restaurant, title to the oil passes to you, even though the oil itself remains in the seller's warehouse.

When the contract *does not involve documents of title,* and the goods are not physically shipped to you, title passes the moment the contract of sale is drawn up, so long as the goods are identified (segregated and marked as belonging to you) by the seller.

Ownership rights are not transferred until goods are accepted by the buyer. Goods may be *rejected* if they are not the type ordered, are damaged, or the shipment is incomplete. *However,* contracts should contain clauses that cover who takes the responsibility for lost or damaged goods.

Risk of Loss or Damage under Contract of Sale

When There is No Breach of Contract

Normally the parties will agree in the contract as to who is to bear the risk of loss or damage when neither party is the cause. Otherwise, in *shipment contracts* risks transfer to the buyer when the goods are delivered to a carrier by the seller. In *destination contracts* risk of loss or damage passes to the buyer when goods are presented to the buyer at a buyer-specified destination. In destination contracts the goods may also be available for pickup by the buyer.

When the Contract Is Breached by the Seller[78]

If the goods delivered by the seller are defective or not in conformity with the contract, the buyer may reject them. The risk of loss does not pass to the buyer until the seller corrects the defects. However, if the buyer accepts the goods, defects and all, he or she waives the right to reject. Sometimes a buyer does not discover that the goods are defective until after acceptance. In that case acceptance may be revoked by the buyer.

When the Contract Is Breached by the Buyer[79]

A buyer who breaches a sales contract automatically assumes any risk of loss or damage. This general rule applies when (1) the goods have been identified in the contract by the seller, (2) the duration of the risk does not exceed a reasonable time after the seller learns of the buyer's breach, and (3) the buyer's liability is not more than the difference between the seller's insurance coverage and the amount of the seller's loss caused by the breach.

The following example illustrates the consequences of a buyer's breach.

> John Smith, owner of a fast-food chain, ordered 40,000 pounds of frozen hamburger from Jones Meatpackers. The order was filled on schedule and Jones repeatedly requested release orders from Smith, since the order was perishable and taking up space in Jones' refrigerated warehouse. Smith did nothing, claiming labor problems and vacation schedules. Jones' warehouse was destroyed by a tornado. Jones sued Smith to recover the contract price. Smith defended on the grounds that there was no valid delivery, and that he was not liable since the risk of loss had not passed at the time of the destruction of the goods.
>
> The court disagreed, ruling that the *offer to deliver* was commercially reasonable, that the failure of the seller to pass title to the buyer was immaterial under the Uniform Commercial Code, and that the buyer had clearly breached the contract by refusing to authorize release of the goods for shipment. That the goods were perishable made the buyer responsible for the consequences of his own misconduct, regardless of whether he could have anticipated the actual cause (the tornado) of the loss.

APPROVAL AND RETURN SALES UNDER CONTRACT OF SALE

Two special types of sales occur frequently and special rules regarding them deserve mention. *Sales on approval* and *sales or return* enable a prospective buyer to obtain goods on a trial basis, with specific risks remaining with the seller. These sales obviously do not include foods, but are used to sell durable goods.

In a sale on approval, when the goods are delivered for use, not resale, neither title nor risk of loss is assumed by the buyer until "approval" or acceptance of the goods by the buyer. The terms and duration of the approval are negotiated by the parties.

In a sale or return transaction, when the goods are delivered for resale, the risk of loss is with the buyer, who retains title unless the goods are returned. Return expenses and all risks of loss or damage during return remain with the buyer.

Figure 9.2 is a checklist of factors that may be covered in contracts of sale or purchase orders. However, not all the factors apply to every contract. Buyers should check over what factors are critical and negotiate to see that they are covered in the contract.

SERVICE CONTRACTS

Service contracts are another important contract used in the foodservice industry. Service contracts are used to buy live or recorded entertainment, interior decorating, and renovation or repair of the premises, and for the hiring of extra staff for special occasions from an independent employment service. Service contracts also are used for purchasing accounting, consulting, computing, and legal services.

Service contracts are treated differently in law from purchase orders. Here the strict, and sometimes uncertain, rules of the common law apply and the more consistent and flexible provisions of the UCC do not. Why not? Because the UCC governs sales of goods, not services. A court decides whether a sale of goods or services is involved, before determining which law to apply.

At common law, an acceptance of a service contract requires compliance with the conditions or terms determined by the buyer or seller. In other words, both the buyer and the provider of services are free to negotiate the contract. Normally the service provider will fix the method of acceptance of the offer. Contracts for services such as legal and accounting consultations are usually standard, although there may be some room for negotiation.

Figure 9.2
Checklist of Terms and Conditions

_____	1. Purchase order is exclusive agreement.
_____	2. Conditions of acceptance.
_____	3. Packaging and crating charges.
_____	4. Payment of invoices.
_____	5. Guarantees and warranties.
_____	6. Time is of the essence in performance.
_____	7. Buyer to be held harmless in the event of patent and copyright infringement.
_____	8. Compliance with purchase order specifications.
_____	9. Right of change of order by buyer.
_____	10. Right of inspection by buyer and customer.
_____	11. Disposition of rejected material and rights of buyer.
_____	12. Disclosure of information.
_____	13. Conditions of use, protection, and liability for buyer's material and equipment.
_____	14. Rights of buyer to discoveries and developments arising from research and development work.
_____	15. Default.
_____	16. Termination.
_____	17. Conformance by seller with legislation.
_____	18. Order of precedence of documents and terms and conditions.
_____	19. Listing of specific applicable federal regulations.
_____	20. Assignments.
_____	21. Limitation on subcontracting.
_____	22. Limitations on liability of buyer.
_____	23. Quantity tolerance on overshipments and undershipments.

The common law rules must be applied to guide a court in deciding whether or not a contract exists.

1. The offer must be communicated to the person or organization providing the service. The buyer has the right to limit the offer to as few or as many persons or parties as he or she sees fit. The only restriction is the legal capacity of any person to accept, and any laws prohibiting businesspersons from refusing to deal with certain individuals, such as civil rights laws.

2. The method chosen to communicate the offer determines the method of communicating acceptance, unless a contract clause says otherwise. If the buyer telephones an offer, the provider must normally telephone the acceptance.

3. An acceptance is effective to form a contract when sent to the provider. This means that a mailed acceptance, in response to an offer by mail, is effective *when mailed, not when received.*

4. The offer must be accepted without any new conditions or terms that change the original offer. Any such changes will operate as a counteroffer, which legally is a rejection of the original offer.

All of the preceding rules apply in the absence of specific contrary provisions in the contract. Negotiation is usually possible in contracts involving entertainment or interior decorating, or even repair services. Contracts with attorneys and accountants may be more rigid and less open to negotiation. Operators seeking any of these services, however, must explore what areas are open to negotiation. Fees, modifications in services, dates and times, and additional services may all be negotiable.

FUNCTION CONTRACTS

Another type of foodservice contract is the function contract that operators negotiate with patrons, individually or in groups, for special parties.

Unlike the purchase order contract, usually prepared by the supplier, the foodservice operator has control over the terms and conditions of the function contract. The operator has a choice of standard clauses for function contracts, which must be chosen carefully to suit business needs. Some terms may develop into standard clauses used for each function contract. Others may be used by the operator as negotiable terms to attract business. Figure 9.3 is a typical function contract.

The terms and conditions in Figure 9.3 are similar in purpose to those contained in the purchase order. The menu is usually filled in before the contract is legal. The following explanations are keyed into the numbered clauses in Figure 9.3.

1. *Definitions.* All parties to the agreement are defined, as is the event, to include any private function forming the subject of the agreement.
2. *Taxes.* All taxes applicable to the event are a separate charge payable by the patron in addition to all other charges.

3. *Guarantee.* The minimum number attending the event must be communicated in writing by the patron to the restaurant 48 hours beforehand. This figure represents the number of *covers* for which the patron must pay, regardless of how many actually attend. *Cover* is a catering term meaning the unit used to compute the final bill.
4. *Deposit.* This assures that the patron will perform or the party will show up. It is similar to a security deposit. Such a deposit should be large enough to cover operation expenses (i.e., ordering of extra food ingredients, beverages, and dining staff salaries) over and above the fixed costs, yet remain competitive with other establishments.
5. *Cancellation.* The patron's cancellation or breach of the agreement gives the operator the right to recover a minimum cancellation fee of $100 when the date can be rebooked, and, in the case of a refusal to perform, recover actual losses together with compensation for attorney's fees to collect those damages.

   When the date cannot be rebooked, the cancellation fee should be the difference between the contract price (which includes the profit) and normal function expenses, plus any other reasonable expenses, such as flowers and special foods and beverages, that cannot be used on another date.

   Notice of cancellation by the patron via registered or certified mail is essential to enable the operator to rebook the date. This protects the operator and the patron against unreasonable losses. The operator minimizes his or her losses. The patron, by giving the restaurant the chance to rebook, reduces his or her potential liability to the operator.

Figure 9.3
Typical Function Contract

ST. JAMES on-the-Park, Inc.
70 Park North • New York, N.Y. • 10017 • (212)555-9999

NAME   DATE

ADDRESS   TELEPHONE   TIME

ORGANIZATION   ROOM

FUNCTION   GUARANTEE

This AGREEMENT includes the Menu and Arrangement Proposals set forth below together with the CONDITIONS on the reverse side which are made part of this Agreement.

MENU	ARRANGEMENT PROPOSALS

This contract must be returned within ten days of receipt.

The acceptance of this agreement will consititue a contract between the signatories hereto.

St. James on-the-Park, Inc.
By ....
....
Accepted

This contract is subject to the terms and conditions printed on the reverse side and made a part hereof.

Figure 9.3
Typical Function Contract

All details of the food and beverages to be served shall be set forth on a separate menu and arrangements proposal which is made a part thereof.

1. DEFINITIONS: As used herein, the following terms shall have the following meanings:
   "Event"—the banquet, reception, or other private function forming the subject of this Agreement;
   "Restaurant"—
   "Patron"—the person, corporation, entity, organization, or association contracting with the Restaurant for the Event.

2. TAXES: All federal, state, municipal, and other taxes imposed on or applicable to the Event or this Agreement, shall be paid for separately in addition to the prices set forth elsewhere in this Agreement.

3. GUARANTEE: Patron agrees to specify in writing to the Restaurant at least 48 hours prior to the date of the Event the exact number to be in attendance. This number shall constitute a guaranteed minimum and the Patron will be charged accordingly.

4. DEPOSIT: A deposit in the amount of $ shall be paid by Patron to Restaurant at the time of signing of this Agreement.

5. CANCELLATION: If Patron cancels the Event or otherwise terminates this Agreement, or if this Agreement is terminated by Restaurant for breach thereof by Patron, and Restaurant is able to rebook the date, Patron shall remain liable for a cancellation fee not to exceed five percent (5%) of the contract price, or $100.00, whichever is less, plus actual damages sustained by reason of Patron's breach, including attorney's fees.
   If Restaurant is unable to rebook the date, Restaurant's cancellation fee shall represent the difference between the total contract price and the cost of performance, plus actual expenses reasonably incurred.
   Patron shall provide evidence of his intent to cancel the Agreement, by registered or certified mail, return receipt requested.

6. PAYMENT IN ADVANCE: Unless credit for this Event has been established in advance by Patron to the satisfaction of Restaurant, payment in full of the entire contract price must be made, in cash or by certified or bank check, at least three (3) days prior to the date of the Event and, if such payment is not made, Restaurant may terminate this Agreement and retain all or part of Patron's deposit, in accordance with the provisions of Section 5 above. If credit has been established, payment will be due in accordance with the terms therefor agreed upon between the parties hereto.

7. FOR BANQUET PERSONNEL: An amount equal to seventeen percent (17%) of the charge to Patron hereunder for food and beverages will be added to the account, of which twelve percent (12%) will be distributed to waiters, waitresses, and, where applicable, bus help and/or bartenders engaged in the function, and five percent (5%) to supervisory, sales, and other banquet personnel, and Patron agrees to pay such amount.

8. PRICE INCREASES: Prices quoted herein are subject to proportionate increases to meet increased costs of supplies or operation at the time of the Event due to increases in costs of commodities, labor, taxes, or currency values subsequent to the signing of this Agreement and Patron agrees to pay such increased prices. Alternatively, Restaurant, at its option, may in the event of such increased costs make reasonable substitutions in menu items and Patron agrees to accept such substitutions.

9. EXTRAS: In the event Restaurant at Patron's request furnishes any food, beverages, or any other services not specifically provided for in this Agreement, Patron agrees to pay Restaurant the charges therefor.

Figure 9.3
Typical Function Contract (*Continued*)

10. EXCUSED NONPERFORMANCE: If for any reasons beyond its control, but not limited to strikes, labor disputes, accidents, government requisitions, restrictions or regulations on travel, restaurant operation, commodities or supplies, acts of war or acts of God, Restaurant is unable to perform its obligations under this Agreement, such nonperformance is excused and Restaurant may terminate this Agreement without further liability of any nature, upon return of Patron's deposit. In no event shall Restaurant be liable for consequential damages of any nature for any reason whatsoever. If for any reason the space reserved hereunder is not available for the Event, Restaurant may substitute therefor other space in the Restaurant at least comparable in quality thereto and Patron agrees to accept such substitutions.

11. DISPLAYS AND DECORATIONS; PATRON'S PROPERTY: All displays and/or decorations proposed by Patron shall be subject to the prior written approval of Restaurant in each instance. Any personal property of Patron or Patron's guests or invitees brought onto the premises of the Restaurant and left therein, either prior to or following the Event, shall be at the sole risk of Patron and Restaurant shall not be liable for any loss of or damage to any such property for any reason.

All flameproofing regulations of the City of New York shall be complied with and before any decorations of a combustible nature shall be installed, notarized affidavits of flameproofing must be furnished.

PATRON AGREES NOT TO ENTER INTO ANY CONTRACTS FOR MUSIC OR OTHER FORMS OF ENTERTAINMENT, FLORAL DECORATIONS, OR OTHER SERVICE OR ACCOMMODATION IN CONNECTION WITH THIS FUNCTION, WITHOUT PRIOR WRITTEN CONSENT OF THE RESTAURANT.

12. PROVISIONS OF BEVERAGES: No beverages of any kind will be permitted to be brought into the Restaurant by the Patron or any of the Patron's guests or invitees from the outside without the written permission of the Restaurant, and the Restaurant reserves the right to make a charge for the service of such beverages.

13. CONDUCT OF EVENT: Patron agrees to begin its function promptly on the scheduled time and agrees to have its guests, invitees, and other persons vacate the designated function space at the closing hour indicated. The Patron further agrees to reimburse the Restaurant for any overtime wage payments or other expenses incurred by the Restaurant because of Patron's failure to comply with these regulations.

Patron undertakes the conduct the Event in an orderly manner, in full compliance with applicable laws, regulations, and restaurant rules. Patron assumes full responsibility for the conduct of all persons in attendance and for any damage done to any part of the Restaurant's premises during any time such premises are under the control of Patron, or Patron's guests, invitees, employees, or independent contractors employed by Patron.

Restaurant reserves the right to exclude or eject any and all objectionable persons from the function, or the Restaurant premises, without liability.

Patron hereby indemnifies and holds harmless Restaurant against any and all claims, liabilities, or costs, including reasonable attorneys' fees and whether by reason or personal injury or death or property damage or otherwise, arising out of or connected with the Event or this Agreement, caused or contributed to by the negligence of Patron, or any guest, invitee, or agent of Patron or any independent contractor hired by Patron. Upon the request

Figure 9.3
Typical Function Contract (*Continued*)

---

of Restaurant, Patron shall procure and maintain, at its expense, policies of insurance, in such amounts, upon such terms and with such responsible insurance companies as shall be satisfactory to Restaurant, including comprehensive general liability coverage (with a specific endorsement acknowledging the insuring of the contractual liabilities assumed by Patron under this Section) and such workmen's compensation, employer's liability, and automobile liability coverages as may be required by Restaurant. Certificates of the issuance of each such policy shall be delivered to Restaurant at least three (3) days prior to the Event. Each such policy shall name the Restaurant as additional insured. Such insurance shall be considered primary of any similar insurance carried by any of the parties.

14. SECURITY: If required, in the sole judgment of Restaurant, in order to maintain adequate security measures in light of the size and nature of the Event, Patron shall provide, at its expense, a minimum of uniformed guards (not to carry weapons), supervisors, and ushers (the "Security Personnel"). All Security Personnel shall be supplied by a reputable licensed guard or security agency doing business in the City of New York. The Security Personnel are to coordinate with Operator's regular security force and shall concern themselves only with access to the space reserved hereunder, or substituted therefor, restricting their presence to these areas of the premises of the Restaurant.

15. In the event that this Agreement is signed in the name of a corporation, partnership, association, club, or society, the person signing represents to the Restaurant that he has full authority to sign such contract, and in the event he is not so authorized, he will be personally liable for the faithful performance of this contract.

16. Patron hereby waives trial by jury in any litigation arising out of or in any way connected with this Agreement or any breach hereof.

---

6. *Payment in advance.* This clause assures full payment by the patron who has not established credit in advance. The operator is protected against any failure or refusal to pay after the event. A certified or bank check prevents the patron from stopping payment and makes the bank that certifies the check or issues its own bank check a guarantor of payment. This guarantee does not affect the operator's right to recover for breach of contract against the patron.

7. *For banquet personnel.* This clause covers tips for service workers.

8. *Price increases.* This clause protects operators against supplier price increases that must be recovered. It does not give the operator the right to increase prices arbitrarily, without justification. In case

of any dispute, the operator bears the burden of proving that any price increases added were justified: supplies, operation due to higher costs of commodities, labor, taxes, or currency values *after* the agreement was signed. In case of dispute, the operator would also bear the burden of proving that any menu substitutions, which the patron agreed to accept, were reasonable.

9. *Extras.* Since the patron requests the extras, the patron is expected to pay for them.

10. *Excused nonperformance.* The operator's only responsibility is to terminate the agreement and return the patron's deposit. No *consequential damages*—that is, the loss of profits—are recoverable by the patron.

11. *Displays and decorations; patron's property.* This clause gives operators the right to permit or refuse to allow patrons to use certain displays or decorations. Further, operators assume *no* responsibility for property brought onto the premises by the guests. The specific language concerning combustible material is to place liability for any claims arising out of fires caused by such material on the patron. Fire codes prohibit the use of some combustible materials; they must be obeyed regardless of patrons' special desires.

12. *Provisions of beverages.* Operations that provide alcoholic beverages usually want to prevent other liquor coming into the establishment. This allows the operator to control the types and amounts of liquor served, to prevent liability and to enhance the profits of the operation.

13. *Conduct of event.* This clause places the responsibility for the control of the event on the patron; makes him or her liable for any overtime labor costs caused by the patron's failure to vacate the function space on time; and makes the patron liable to make good any claims or lawsuits against the operator arising out of the negligence of guests, agents, or independent contractors during the event.

14. *Security.* This clause requires the patron to provide suitable security personnel if in the operator's judgment such personnel are necessary to protect property, other patrons, and employees. These security guards, supervisors, and ushers should limit their activities to the space assigned to that function, for the main purpose of keeping out uninvited guests.

The uncaptioned clause concerns the responsibility of the person signing the agreement when he or she signs in a representative capacity, that is, as an agent for a partnership, corporation, association, club, or society. The signer becomes *personally liable* for payment in the event he or she lacked legal authority to bind the organization.

The waiver of trial by jury is to eliminate delays in the trial of any claim or lawsuit brought against the patron, by allowing a judge to hear and determine all questions of fact and law. Usually the jury must decide questions of fact, and it is more likely that a jury would decide those questions in favor of the patron. Juries are often more sympathetic to an individual being sued in a commercial case, where the other side represents "big" business. No matter how faulty that view is, juries unconsciously favor the underdog, whereas a judge may not be so swayed.

Letters of Intent

Letters of intent may be used by both buyers and sellers of function space. These are letters that announce either the function or available space for a specific function. The question often arises as to the legal effect of a letter of function issued by the function host or foodservice manager concerning a forthcoming event such as a wedding or business luncheon. Is such a letter a function contract, or merely a promise to make a contract in the future? The difference is critical. If the letter is merely a promise to make a contract in the future, it is not enforceable as a contract, meaning that the function host is free to walk away, find a better deal, and leave the manager empty-handed. Of course, the operator also has that option, but takes the risk that he or she may be unable to reschedule a new function in time to avoid an economic loss.

The common law of contracts covers this problem. Generally oral or written statements of intent to do something *are not offers and may not be accepted to form a contract.*

For example, a printed form letter sent to the business community reads: "I have function rooms available for business luncheons. I am asking $10.00 per cover for a fixed menu, which I have enclosed. Beverages are extra, as set forth on the menu. Minimum number of covers: 15 per room. I look forward to serving you. The Metropolitan Restaurant, by *signature,* Bill Morgan, Proprietor."

Does such a letter of intent create a contract if the function host receives it and replies in writing: "I accept your offer. Reserve 15 covers for September 15, 1982, at $10.00. List of attendees to follow. The Utopia Chamber of Commerce, by *signature,* Harry Hargraves, President."?

The answer is no. Why not? Because the intent to contract must be demonstrated by the language used by Mr. Morgan. The courts must find intent in the oral statements or the writing. The test of intention to contract is an objective one, not what was in the mind of Bill Morgan. The fact that he said he wanted function business is not enough, since wanting to do business at some future time and contracting to do business at a specific date are not the same. Courts will also support this conclusion, pointing out that a form letter is usually understood by businesspersons to be sent indiscriminately (not intended for any particular person or party), and that the seller can only sell to a limited number of function buyers.

Nonetheless, any spoken or written communication that contains all the essential terms of a contract is a contract, and will be enforced. Assume that the letter had been addressed to Mr. Hargraves personally, and said: "I offer the Utopia Chamber of Commerce the Red Room, seating 25 persons, at $10.00 per cover, on September 15, 1982, at 1:00 p.m., plus 15 percent gratuities to be added to the bill. Closed bar. Menu items to be as follows: fruit cocktail, roast ham, candied yams, green beans, rum raisin ice cream, coffee or tea. Signed The Metropolitan Restaurant, by Bill Morgan, Proprietor." This is an offer, meaning a promise to perform.

The practical difference is this: In the first case Morgan merely made a statement of future intention. The intention to perform is not a promise to perform. In the second case he made a definite promise to perform in the future.

Because each spoken or written communication stands on its own, there is no magic formula that will yield the right answer in every case. Each communication must be examined to determine what the parties intended by their exchange of words.

RESERVATION CONTRACTS

When a patron calls up and wants to reserve a table for a party of four at a certain time, and you agree to hold the table at that time, you and the patron have just created a reservation contract. A reservation contract need not be in writing, and usually isn't, but it is enforceable, especially by the patron.

A reservation contract is another form of service contract, but differs in that the service is rendered *by* you, the foodservice operator, directly to a patron, rather than by a provider of a service *to* you.

MANAGEMENT CONTRACTS

Management contracts between institutions and foodservice management firms usually call for considerable negotiation. Often institutions are legally bound to accept some liability and some functions cannot be delegated. However, courts tend to frown on the use of illegality as a contract out, especially in vague areas.

Thacher Hotel, Inc. v. Economos
Supreme Judicial Court of Maine
197 A.2d 59 (1964)

Facts. Thacher, a corporate hotel owner, entered into a foodservice management contract with Economos relating to the operation of dining rooms previously licensed to serve liquor in Thacher's hotel. Thacher sued Economos to recover minimum payments due under the contract for sales, social security, and state and federal unemployment and withholding taxes, which Economos admitted were due. Economos did not dispute Thacher's lawsuit for payment. Rather, Economos argued that Thacher's management contract was illegal, and therefore unenforceable.

The defense of illegality raised by Economos rested on the claim that the Maine liquor control statute prohibited Thacher from operating his dining rooms other than under the hotel management. Under the management contract Economos argued that she was an independent operator, and that the statute had been violated. This being so, her contract with Thacher was illegal and not enforceable.

The Maine Superior Court, which heard the case, entered judgment in full for Thacher. Economos appealed to the Supreme Judicial Court to reverse the judgment for Thacher and to dismiss the lawsuit. The judgment for Thacher was upheld, and Economos' appeal denied.

Reasoning. The following sections of the management contract are relevant to the case:

1. The Owner shall employ the Food Manager for the term of five (5) years from [January 3, 1955] until the close of business on the Saturday following [January 3, 1960], as manager of the Coffee Shoppe and Dining-Cocktail Room located in the premises of the Owner known as Thacher Hotel.

(a) The Food Manager will have exclusive direction and responsibility of purchasing, storage, preparation and service of all food within the Thacher Hotel, specifically set forth as the kitchen, Coffee Shoppe, Dining-Cocktail Room, and in the rooms of the Hotel whenever such is required by guests of the Hotel.

(c) The service of beer, wines and liquors will be made by the waiters or waitresses, and such sales of beer, wines and liquors shall be accurately recorded on a separate check from the food check, and such separate checks shall be identified as Cocktail Bar checks, and payment of such Cocktail Bar checks shall be made after each serving in a manner prescribed by the Owner, and shall not constitute in any manner a part of food income.

(e) The Food Manager will have the exclusive responsibility for the food operation without undue interference by the Owner, except in such cases specifically referred to herein. However, at times mutually agreeable, the Food Manager and the Owner or the Owner's representatives shall discuss and consider matters which may be of mutual interest in maintaining efficient and profitable operation . . .

7. The Food Manager shall have the authority and responsibility to operate the food business without interference from the Owner. It is understood, however, that the Food Manager will conduct the operation in a high grade and orderly manner, and will not permit questionable conduct or entertainment on the premises; that the Food Manager will pay all food and other expenditures of said operation from the income thereof and within a time consistent with good business practices, and not through negligence impair the good credit of the Owner . . .

12. It is understood by the Owner and the Food Manager, that wherever the word 'food' or 'food operation' is used herein, beer, wines and liquor are specifically excluded therefrom and that the Food Manager has no connection therewith or responsibility therefor.

1. The court found nothing to indicate that the hotel had given up management of the dining room; in fact, the hotel retained

management due to licensing laws. The court said:

> The "management contract" was unquestionably entered into with the operation of dining rooms to meet the requirement of the liquor laws in the minds of the parties. In short, the contract was in furtherance of the operation of the hotel with a liquor license.
>
> The Thacher Hotel, that is the plaintiff corporation, met without challenge on this record the strict requirement that it is a "reputable place operated by responsible persons of good reputation." It chose to give broad authority to a "food manager." It did not, however, give up or transfer, or lose its "management" of the dining rooms and thereby fail to qualify for the license so obviously a vital part of the business enterprise . . .

2. To the defendant's claim that "public policy" denies recovery to the hotel because the contract was illegal, the court decided public policy did not protect the defendant from escaping a contractual obligation. The court found no wrong on the part of the hotel to cause them to terminate the contract.

Conclusion. This case illustrates the point that courts are not likely to upset contracts on the grounds of illegality unless no other reasonable conclusion is possible. Here there was no proof of evil motive or intent of the hotel owner to operate outside the scope of the Maine liquor control law. The purpose of the Maine law, requiring that a hotel liquor license for public dining facilities be under the same management, is to prevent control over the service of alcohol from being transferred by the license holder, the hotel owner in this case, to an unlicensed foodservice manager. This is a universal requirement under virtually all liquor control laws. The usual way for a hotel owner to transfer *complete* control of the foodservice operation to an independent operator is to lease the restaurant facilities and require the operator to obtain his or her own liquor license.

PERFORMANCE OF CONTRACTS

Every party to a contract is obligated to perform the duties promised. Not to do so is a breach of contract. Standards of contractual performance are either (1) complete or satisfactory, (2) substantial, or (3) unsubstantial enough to constitute a material breach of the contract.[80]

The common law of contracts speaks of performance in terms of *discharge*. To the degree that the promised performance measures up to the standards of the contract, the party performing is relieved or discharged of any further duties to perform.[81]

Some contracts, such as those requiring the transfer of a deed for title to real property, can be performed completely or satisfactorily without any need to determine how completely the promise was performed. Building and construction contracts, however, do not require complete performance. *Substantial performance* is enough to permit the builder to recover payment, with an allowance to the owner for remedying minor defects.[82] A substantial performance may occur when the operator performs all the requirements for a banquet contract, except that blue tablecloths are used instead of blue and white as specified in the contract.

Most businesses will fulfill the terms of contracts. People are generally honest and want repeat business enough to comply with their legal obligations. There are situations where complete fulfillment might have to be delayed, as when a number of items on a purchase order are back-ordered or equipment in a certain color has to brought from out of town. Foodservice operators should recognize whether the other person is making an honest effort to fulfill the contract or is simply trying to get out of it by cheating.

A material breach of contract means that the party in question has failed to meet the standards of performance required by the contract. If workmanship on kitchen plumbing is shoddy enough that the operator has to have someone else do it over, this is a material breach. In such a case, the other contracting party is relieved of any responsibility to pay or perform.[83]

Partial performance is not to be confused with *substantial performance.* Partial or unsubstantial performance is incomplete performance. An example would be if a painter painted only half of your dining room when the contract included the entire room. If one party accepts partial performance, then that person is obligated to pay the fair market value of the services provided, but not the contract price.[84] If partial performance is not accepted, then the job must be completed.

Contracts to Personal Satisfaction

A contract to the *personal satisfaction* of one or the other of the parties means that the party's performance must be to the personal satisfaction of the other party. Performance is tested by the *subjective* reactions of the party, and not by an *objective* standard of a reasonable person.[85] For this reason, such promises should be avoided. No one can please all of the people all of the time.

WRITTEN AND ORAL CONTRACTS

Some contracts must be in *writing* to be enforceable. In case of doubt, a written contract is preferable to an oral contract. This is true not only to satisfy the *form of contract,* but to avoid possible memory lapses and fraud where the contract must be proved by oral testimony. The most obvious example of a contract that must be in writing is one dealing with real estate.[86]

Oral contracts are enforceable, but disputes more readily lead to trouble. As the following case illustrates, whether a contract is or is not a contract, it is going to be harder to prove the facts.

Jones v. Hartmann
Court of Appeals of Colorado
514 P.2d 123 (1975)

Facts. Jones, an architect, was hired by Hartmann and his business associate to build a lodge and restaurant building. Hartmann was to perform according to a letter of agreement containing fees for various aspects of work proposed by Jones and sent to Hartmann. This letter was to include a clause giving Jones the right to charge extra fees for work beyond making the schematic drawings. The agreement was never signed by Hartmann nor returned to Jones. Jones began work on the drawings. He then sent a standard architect's contract to Hartmann, which Hartmann never signed. This contract included a 9 percent fee for additional work. Jones then sent two bills, one of which was paid by Hartmann's wife. Jones sent Hartmann a series of letters on the work progress, and advised him to obtain a building permit. Finally, Jones appeared at a hearing for a liquor permit.

A dispute over the fees charged by Jones and billed to Hartmann arose. Jones, not being entirely paid, filed a mechanic's lien on the lodge and restaurant building, a legal claim ultimately authorizing him to seize and sell the building to liquidate his bill. Jones then sued both Hartmann and his associate for the reasonable value of the services (called a suit in *quantum meruit*). The trial court found for Jones against both Hartmann and his associate individually and awarded damages. The trial court also said that Jones could recover 75 percent of the original contract price even though the work was unfinished. Hartmann appealed. The appeals court upheld the trial court's decision for Jones.

Reasoning. The appeals court upheld the trial court's ruling that there was an oral agreement. The court said the agreement was in keeping with Hartmann's schedule to obtain a building permit and a liquor license.

The appeals court also upheld the trial court's finding that a contract existed, saying that this was a question of fact for the lower court to decide.

On the 75 percent contract price finding, the appeals court said that this partial payment was justified by the work done under the legal theory of *quantum meruit,* or compensation for work done.

Conclusion. This decision makes it clear that an oral contract for services is enforceable, when there is sufficient proof to establish the contract. When this is so, the nature of the services found is a question of fact for the court. Obviously, written contracts are best for both buyers and sellers.

BREACH OF CONTRACT: PURCHASE ORDERS, CONTRACTS OF SALE, AND SERVICE CONTRACTS

A *breach of contract* exists whenever a party to a contract fails to perform those duties he or she promised. A breach, unlike a discharge of contractual duty, requires the party violating the duty to respond in damages or perform the duty. A discharge ends a contractual duty without imposing liability on either party. A breach, if serious or material, ends the contractual duty of the innocent party but imposes liability on the guilty party.

Contract law, including the common law and sales of goods under the UCC, provides a variety of remedies to the innocent party. These remedies include damages, rescission and restitution, specific performance, reformation, and creation of a quasi-contract.

Damages

This is usually an award of monetary compensation, known as *compensatory damages.* Damages enable the innocent party to recover the loss of the bargain. This means that he or she is to be placed in the same position he or she would have been in had the contract been fully performed. Damages to compensate the innocent party must rest on some form of economic loss. If that party suffers no loss, then the court can only award *nominal damages,* a trivial amount for the technical breach of the contract.

In sales of goods the measure of damages is an amount equal to the difference between the contract price and the market price of the goods at the time and place of performance, usually delivery of the goods to destination.

In a typical case of a purchase contract for food, the buyer would obtain the difference between the contract price of a refrigerated carload of dressed beef, costing $15,000, and any rise in price, say to $20,000, caused by the supplier's failure to deliver on time; the damages would be $5000.

The innocent party may also recover *consequential* or special damages that arise only from the results of the original breach of contract. In our example let's say that the buyer had contracted to resell the carload of dressed beef as individual portions to a patron for an office party. Consequential damages would consist of the operator's *loss of profits* from the party contract. Consequential damages are available in addition to compensatory damages. To recover these special damages, the buyer would have to prove that the meat supplier knew of the resale of the dressed beef for the party.

Liquidated damages are usually included in a contract by agreement of the parties. This provision specifies a certain amount to be paid in the event of a failure to perform or breach of contract. A foodservice operator might negotiate with a supplier to receive $100 for every day beyond the delivery date the shipper fails to deliver the meat under the purchase contract. Since such a provision is negotiable, the buyer needs sufficient economic clout to include such a provision in a contract.

In contrast, a *penalty clause* requires a payment designed to penalize the party who violates the contract.

Liquidated damage clauses are enforced by the courts; penalty clauses are not. The courts use the following two tests to determine whether or not a provision is a penalty clause: (1) the difficulty of estimating damages under the contract when executed; and (2) whether the amount set is reasonable. If the damages are difficult to estimate, and the amount set reasonable, the provision is enforceable.

Rescission and Restitution

Rescission is a legal term meaning the right to cancel the contract. *Restitution* is the right of each party to be returned to the position each occupied prior to the contract. Fraud, duress, mistake, or failure of consideration will trigger rescission. Restitution may be required by each party as a condition of canceling the contract.

Specific Performance

In certain cases courts will require one party to perform the duties that person agreed to perform in the contract, rather than award money damages to the innocent party. This remedy may be applied in service contracts. In sale contracts this remedy is normally not available, because the law requires proof by the innocent party that there were no adequate money damages available. In the dressed beef example, money damages would be considered adequate, since identical goods can be purchased in the open market, albeit at a higher price, from either the original supplier or someone else. However, if the goods

or services are unique and unobtainable from other suppliers, then a court might order specific performance.

Reformation

The common law permits revision of a contract by a court to express the real intentions of the parties. Fraud and mutual mistake are the grounds most often used to reform a written contract, but both grounds must be established by clear and convincing evidence. For example, if both the buyer and the meat supplier in the example were mistaken as to the kind of meat to be delivered, then the court could correct the error and allow the parties to perform the contract they truly intended to perform.

Quasi-contracts

A court may create a *quasi-contract* when no contract exists, to avoid unjust enrichment of one party. Let's assume that the now famous meat contract is unenforceable. Let's further assume that the buyer partially performed by making an advance payment on the contract price. Here the supplier received a benefit. In such a case the court would probably permit the buyer to recover the fair market value of the meat.

BREACH OF A FUNCTION CONTRACT

A function contract might be violated by either the foodservice operator or the patron or host organization.

A breach by the operator would occur when he or she failed completely to perform, by not holding the promised function at all.

Another example of an operator breach would be a *partial breach,* such as holding the function but not providing the foods and beverages agreed to, using substitutes without the consent of the patron.

Another partial breach would be to furnish less than the standard of table service agreed upon by not providing enough waiters or waitresses, or providing stainless steel instead of silver flatware or water goblets instead of wine stemware.

Another breach would be to cancel the scheduled function without notice and without justification.

An unjustified breach would consist of any delay, cancellation, or failure to perform a material or important contractual promise.

A justified breach would excuse performance without any liability to the patron. One example is a contract clause allowing the operator to cancel if the patron fails to make required payments under the contract. This is called a *discharge by agreement of the parties.*

A *discharge by operation of law* would occur in the event of the total destruction of the restaurant premises by a flood or earthquake. Although it is always desirable to cover this type of occurrence in the contract, it is likely that a court would excuse performance even if the contract were silent on this point.

The obvious example of a patron's breach would be a failure to perform by not showing up at the appointed date and time.

A partial breach would consist of a failure or refusal to pay the full price agreed to without any legal justification. Such a lack of justification is illustrated by unproven claims that the soup was "cold," the meat entree was "raw," the bread was "stale," and the like. On the other hand, serving non-kosher food instead of a promised kosher dinner would justify a total or partial patron refusal to pay the promised price.

Another patron breach of contract is a failure to disclose an illegal purpose of the function or the identity of the host, which might change the operator's mind about holding the function. Reputable operators might not wish to provide function space for a terrorist organization, fugitives from justice, or an illegal gambling syndicate.

Yet another example of a patron breach or contract violation is when the patron submits false credit information, which would otherwise put the operator on notice not to deal with that person.

If either the breach or the justification for a breach is legally insufficient, the contract will be enforced, and will be applied to aid the innocent party.

BREACH OF A RESERVATION CONTRACT

The normal remedy for a breach by the operator is money damages to compensate the patron for the cost of substituted services (another meal at your establishment or elsewhere). For an individual patron, this is often too small an amount to justify a lawsuit, and is settled on the spot or at a future time and date. However, when the failure to honor a group reservation is established, then the individual loss of the benefit of the bargain is multiplied by the number of disappointed patrons, and can be much more expensive.

In case of a partial breach of contract by the operator, the measure of damages is the difference between the value of the reservation contracted for and the market value of the reservation, determined by comparing other local establishments. This is usually a token amount. *But* if you were told by the patron that the reservation was made to conclude a business deal, and the patron would lose money on that deal if the reservation was not honored, *and* you in turn guaranteed to honor the reservation on that basis, then *consequential damages* for lost profits could be recovered by the patron.

Additionally, damages for *emotional harm* and *mental distress* are recoverable in cases where there is a total failure to honor the reservation or where the broken reservation was deliberate, rather than merely careless.

Specific performance is not generally authorized for your breach of contract. Why not? Because the compensatory money damage remedy is adequate, since a reasonable substitute for the reservation is generally available elsewhere, from you or from some other foodservice operator.

Rescission and restitution, or cancellation and return of any sums paid to hold the reservation, are generally available in those rare cases where a deposit is paid. Since a typical phone reservation contract is not made with a deposit, this is not generally used.

Inasmuch as your restaurant reputation as well as legal standing are at stake, it is best not to overbook. Regular customers will appreciate your meeting your end of the bargain, and are more likely to call if they must cancel.

NEGOTIATION

Negotiation is the key to obtaining good deals in business contracts. Negotiation is the process of discussing contract arrangements to come up with the most workable contract for both parties. Negotiation may involve compromise—trading desires for critical concessions. More often it involves a step-by-step discussion of the key factors of a contract. Many sales contracts are standard, but usually there are flexible clauses and it is up to the buyer to find out what they are, since the seller may not volunteer that information.

The law is not set up to enforce wishful thinking, and both parties to any contract must know going in what they want. Negotiate from this point and in this order: What do I want? What can I get? What does the other person want? What can I give up?

In any real estate deal you should have a lawyer. Knowing what you want and knowing your own rights will help the lawyer negotiate a good deal for you. Take advantage of the opportunity to negotiate. It's a good business practice.

CONTRACT GUIDELINES

As a manager you will be making business decisions involving contracts with vendors, suppliers, employees, and patrons on a daily basis. Most of these transactions, it is hoped, will be carried out without the need for lawyers or court action. However, there is the chance that either you or the other party may sue. To ensure the successful defense or prosecution of a lawsuit, as well as to minimize the likelihood of litigation, you must know what the contract says, what contract rights you have, and what you need to do to enforce them.

Make your contracts in writing. It is easier for the law to enforce written than oral contracts.

The following is a reference for the contract steps explained in this chapter. Use it as a checklist for contracting in any part of your business.

1. Every contract must contain an *offer* and an *acceptance.* One party must offer to make a contract, and the other party must agree to the terms and conditions by communicating an acceptance of the offer in the manner required.
2. The promises or acts agreed upon by the parties must be supported by legally sufficient *consideration,* an exchange of something that the law recognizes as sufficient to bind the parties. A *binding* agreement is one in which each party has legal rights and duties that can be enforced by a court of law.

3. Every contracting party must have the *capacity* to contract. This means competence to understand not only the terms and conditions, but also the consequences of any contract made by the parties. An adult is presumed to have both types of competence. A minor is presumed to lack understanding of consequences, and because of this may elect to avoid contracts.
4. Every contract must have a *legal objective*. No illegal contract will be enforced.
5. Both of the parties must legally *consent* to the contract.
6. To be truly enforceable, the contract must be in proper legal form. *Form* means *in writing,* not necessarily the style of writing.

As a manager you must know *the effect* of a failure of a contract to contain any of the above requirements.

SUMMARY

Foodservice operators will find themselves dealing with a variety of contracts to buy and sell goods and services. Contracts are the foundation of business relations with suppliers, patrons, and others. Contracts with suppliers include purchase orders, contracts of sale, and service contracts. Contracts with patrons include reservation and function contracts.

Contracts are classified according to how they are stated (express or implied), who must perform, how they are formed, the stage of performance, and the extent to which they are legally binding.

All the elements of a contract must be present in order for a contract to be enforceable. The elements are agreement, consideration, capacity of the parties to contract, legality, and genuineness of consent. These elements themselves contain requirements which may help a court determine whether the agreement is enforceable.

All contracts require some sort of performance by one or both parties. Standards of performance are the guides the law uses to determine whether a party has performed or not. These standards are complete or satisfactory, substantial or unsubstantial.

In sales contracts legal rights to goods may be transferred from one owner to another by one of two methods—agreement between the parties or delivery. If goods are damaged or lost, either the buyer or seller may bear the risk. This is one area that should be covered in sales contract during negotiation.

Sales on approval and sales or return are special sales that enable buyers to receive durable goods on a trial basis.

A breach of contract occurs whenever one party fails to perform according to the terms of the contract. The remedies for breach of contract are usually imposed by the court in a dispute and include damages, rescission and restitution, specific performance, reformation, and creation of a quasi-contract.

Most contracts contain negotiable elements and it is up to each party to use negotiating skills to obtain the best deal.

QUESTIONS

1. A purchase order and a contract of sale are both legal contracts. How are they the same? How are they different? Give an example of each.
2. Harry and Mike Alvin are brothers. Mike owns a restaurant with a bar. They draw up a contract to transfer Mike's liquor license to Harry when Harry takes over the restaurant. The contract is written and appears to contain the essential elements of a contract. What is wrong with it?
3. You receive an offer from a wholesaler to accept a special price on two convection ovens. The federal government orders manufacturers to stop the production and

distribution of the ovens and to recall any held by distributors. Can you accept the wholesaler's offer? Explain.

4. Some junior high schoolers want to give a birthday party for a friend and to use Ethel's Catering for the food. What should Ethel do to protect herself legally? Why is such protection necessary?

5. Under what circumstances might *specific performance* be required to compensate for breach of contract?

NOTES

1. *Shepard v. Glick,* 404 S.W.2d 441 (Mo. App. 1966) (sale of home).

2. Simpson, *Contracts,* Second Edition—1 (1965) n.1.

3. *Id.* at 5.

4. *Id.* at 5–6. *Cook v. Johnson,* 37 Wash. 2d 19, 221 P.2d 525 (1950).

5. *Dyer Constr. Co. v. Ellas Constr. Co.,* 153 Ind. App. 304, 287 N.E.2d 262 (1972).

6. Simpson, *supra* note 2, at 4–5.

7. *Puttkamer v. Minth,* 83 Wis. 2d 686, 266 N.W.2d 361 (1978).

8. Lusk, Hewitt, Donnell, Barnes, *Business Law and the Regulatory Environment* (5th ed. 1982).

9. *Id.* at 89.

10. A *ratification* is the right of a party to create an enforceable agreement even though the agreement is otherwise avoidable at his or her election. You may ratify such an agreement by your conduct as well as by your words. The concept of ratification most often deals with agency law.

11. Lusk *et al., supra* note 8, at 156.

12. Under Uniform Commercial Code, U.C.C. sec. 2–725(1), contracts for the sale of goods are governed by a four-year limitations period in which the party suing must commence his or her lawsuit. Both parties to such a contract may reduce the limitations period to not less than one year but may not extend it beyond the four-year statutory period. The period begins from the date the breach of contract occurs, regardless of the lack of knowledge of the breach by the party suing.

13. Simpson, *supra* note 2, at 7–8.

14. *Savoca Masonry Co. v. Homes & Son Constr. Co.,* 112 Ariz. 391, 542 P.2d 817 (1975).

15. *Petersen v. Pilgrim Village,* 256 Wis. 621, 42 N.W.2d 273 (1950).

16. *Frigaliment Importing Co. v. B.N.S. International Sales Corp.,* 190 F. Supp. 116 (S.D.N.Y. 1960).

17. *Barnes v. Treece,* 15 Wash. App. 437, 549 P.2d 1152 (1976); *Lucy v. Zehmer,* 196 Va. 493, 84 S.W.2d 516 (1954); *McAfee v. Brewer,* 214 Va. 579, 203 S.E.2d 129 (1974); and *Glover v. Jewish War Veterans of the United States, Post No. 58,* 68 A.2d 233 (D.C. App. 1949).

18. See generally *Belger Cartage Service, Inc. v. Holland Const. Co.,* 224 Kan. 320, 582 P.2d 1111 (1978); *Goldstein v. Rhode Island Hospital Trust National Bank,* 110 R.I. 580, 296 A.2d 112 (1972).

19. *Savoca Masonry Co., supra* note 14.

20. *Glover v. Jewish War Veterans, supra* note 17.

21. *Cushing v. Thomson,* 118 N.H. 292, 386 A.2d 895 (1978).

22. Lusk *et al., supra* note 8, at 102–3.

23. Clarkson, Miller, Blaire, *West's Business Law* (1980) at 96–97.

24. Lusk *et al., supra* note 8, at 105–6.

25. *Hoffman v. Red Owl Stores, Inc.,* 26 Wis. 2d 683, 133 N.W.2d 267 (1964).

26. Lusk *et al., supra* note 8, at 103–4.

27. *Id.*

28. *Id.*

29. Simpson, *supra* note 2, at 40.

30. *Id.*

31. *Hawkins v. McGee,* 84 N.H. 114, 146 A. 641 (1929).

32. *Mellen v. Johnson,* 322 Mass. 236, 76 N.E.2d 658 (1948).

33. *Id.*

34. *O'Keefe v. Lee Calan Imports, Inc.,* 128 Ill. App. 2d 410, 262 N.E.2d 758 (1970).

35. Simpson, *supra* note 2, at 1.

36. *Osborn v. Old National Bank of Wash.,* 10 Wash. App. 169, 516 P.2d 795 (1973).

37. *Rothenbuecher v. Tockstein,* 88 Ill. App. 3d 968, 411 N.E.2d 92 (1980).

38. *David J. Tierney, Jr., Inc. v. T. Wellington Carpets, Inc.,* 8 Mass. App. Ct. 237, 392 N.E.2d 1066 (1979).

39. *Zeller v. First National Bank and Trust of Evanston,* 79 Ill. App. 3d 170, 398 N.E.2d 148 (1979); *City of Roslyn v. Paul E. Hughes Const. Co.,* 19 Wash. App. 59, 573 P.2d 385 (1978).

40. U.C.C. sec. 2–207.

41. Simpson, *supra* note 2, at 57–59; *Corbin-Dykes Electric Co. v. Burr,* 18 Ariz. App. 101, 500 P.2d 632 (1972); *Hobbs v. Massasoit Whip Co.,* 158 Mass. 194, 33 N.E. 495 (1893). However, the Postal Reorganization Act of 1970 permits any receiver of unordered merchandise to keep and use it without being required to pay for it. Under common law, a mailed acceptance is effective when mailed, not when received by the offeror, unless the offeror makes receipt of the acceptance a condition of the offer. The *mailbox rule,* as this form of acceptance is called, requires proper posting and mailing.

42. *Morrison v. Thoelke,* 155 So. 2d 889 (Fla. App. 1963), *hearing denied,* 172 So. 2d 604 (1965).

43. Simpson, *supra* note 2, at 80–106.

44. For example, if an uncle promises to give you his restaurant business if you in turn refrain from smoking and drinking until your 25th birthday, this exchange of promises for your performance is sufficient consideration to create a contract.

45. *Dedeaux v. Young,* 251 Miss. 604, 170 So. 2d 561 (1965).

46. The giving up of your right to smoke may have little monetary value, but it is nonetheless a *detriment,* or a loss to you. You were induced by your uncle to surrender your legal right to indulge yourself.

47. Simpson, *supra* note 2, at 80–84.

48. *Hoffman v. Red Owl Stores, Inc., supra* note 2.

49. U.C.C. sec. 2–205. The firm offer rule applies as follows: If a merchant dealing in goods sold in the regular course of business signs a written offer and states that the offer is not revocable for a specified period, the offer is firm for that period of time, not to exceed three months.

50. *G.A.S. v. S.I.S.,* 407 A.2d 253 (Del. Fam. Ct. 1978) (mental incompetence).

51. *Williamson v. Matthews,* 379 So. 2d 1245 (Ala. 1980); *Lucy v. Zehmer, supra* note 17.

52. *Gastonia Personnel Corp. v. Rogers,* 276 N.C. 279, 172 S.E.2d 19 (1970).

53. Simpson, *supra* note 2, at 215–18.

54. *Id.* at 288.

55. Lusk *et al., supra* note 8, at 156–58.

56. *Quality Motors, Inc. v. Hays,* 216 Ark. 264, 225 S.W.2d 326 (1949).

57. *Terrace Co. v. Calhoun,* 37 Ill. App. 3d 757, 347 N.E.2d 315 (1976) (restitution not applicable to an intangible service).

58. *Langstraat v. Midwest Mutual Ins. Co.,* 217 N.W.2d 570 Iowa (1974). *Gastonia Personnel Corp. v. Rogers, supra* note 52. An *exception* to the rule allowing minors to disaffirm or avoid contracts exists in the case of purchases of "necessaries." Here the minor may disaffirm the contract, but must pay the reasonable value of the goods or services. Necessaries include such basic needs as food, clothing, shelter, medicines, hospital costs, and the costs of an education. A minor's station in life and social status are used by the courts to determine whether a particular item meets this definition.

59. *Mechanics Finance Co. v. Paolino,* 29 N.J. Super. 449, 102 A.2d 784 (1954).

60. *Rice v. Boyer,* 108 Ind. 472, 9 N.E. 420 (1886). Certain contracts cannot be avoided by a minor. Statutes in some states compel minors to honor loans for education or medical care. However, loans of money are often avoidable. This means that you extend credit to minors at your own risk.

61. Lusk *et al., supra* note 8, at 170–71; *Abramowitz v. Barnett Bank of West Orlando,* 394 So. 2d 1033 (Fla. App. 1981).

62. *Id.* at 175.

63. *Id.* at 175–76.

64. U.C.C. sec. 2–302; *Brokers Title Co. v. St. Paul Fire and Marine Ins. Co.,* 610 F.2d 1174 (3d Cir. 1979).

65. *Hy-Grade Oil Co. v. New Jersey Bank,* 138 N.J. Super. 112, 350 A.2d 297 (1975); *Henrioulle v. Marin Ventures, Inc.,* 20 Cal. 3d 512, 573 P.2d 465, 143 Cal. Rptr. 247 (1978).

66. *Williams v. Walker-Thomas Furniture Co.,* 350 F.2d 445 (D.C. Cir. 1965).

67. *Boyd v. Aetna Life Ins. Co.,* 310 Ill. App. 547, 35 N.E.2d 99 (1941).

68. *Ohio Co. v. Rosemeier,* 32 Ohio App. 116, 288 N.E.2d 326 (1972).

69. *Clover Park School Dist. No. 400 v. Consolidated Dairy Products Co.,* 15 Wash. App. 492, 550 P.2d 47 (1976).

70. Lusk *et al., supra* note 8, at 125–26.

71. *Roberts v. Sears, Roebuck & Co.,* 573 F.2d 976 (7th Cir.) *cert. denied,* 439 U.S. 860 (1978); *Gardner v. Meiling,* 280 Or. 665, 572 P.2d 1012 (1977).

72. *Griffith v. Byers Constr. Co. of Kansas,* 212 Kan. 65, 510 P.2d 198 (1973).

73. *Janinda v. Lanning,* 87 Idaho 91, 390 P.2d 826 (1967); *Walsh v. Edwards,* 233 Md. 552, 197 A.2d 424 (1964).

74. *Yorke v. Taylor,* 332 Mass. 368, 124 N.E.2d 912 (1955).

75. U.C.C. sec. 2–105.

76. U.C.C. sec. 2–401 *et seq.*

77. U.C.C. sec. 2–302. Courts usually assume that the buyer and seller have equality of bargaining power; that is, parties to a contract can protect their own interests adequately. Only in those rare cases where one party can convince a court that he or she was forced to sign a contract, and that its terms and conditions were shocking or oppressive because of that inequity of bargaining power, does a court have the power to declare the oppressive provision unenforceable. For example, if the contract itself or a provision were put on a "take it or leave it" basis, and the buyer had no choice but to comply since there was no other source for the product, the buyer might have recourse *if* the courts found he or she was "coerced" into buying. Still, a court is not automatically required to strike down such a contract. The fact that the bargain struck is hard or ill-conceived is not, standing alone, sufficient reason for the court to act.

78. Absent any breach of contract, risk of loss is governed by the contract you make with the seller. Where the contract is silent, and the goods are to be moved by the seller, then the Code remedy depends on the type of contract. In a *shipment* contract risk of loss passes upon delivery to the carrier by the seller. In a *destination* contract risk of loss passes when the goods are tendered to you by the seller at that destination. See U.C.C. sec. 2–509(1) and (1)(b).

In nonshipment or destination cases (no movement of goods), if the seller is a *merchant,* risk of loss passes to you when you take physical possession of the goods. If the seller is a non-merchant, risk of loss passes to you when delivery is tendered to you by the seller, that is, when the goods are offered to you. See U.C.C. sec. 2–509(2) and 509(3).

79. U.C.C. sec. 2–510(3).

80. *Id.* at 204–5.

81. Leete, *Business Law,* 191–92, 2d ed. (1982).

82. *Hunter v. Andrews,* 570 S.W.2d 590 (Tex. App. 1978).

83. *New Era Homes Corp. v. Forster,* 299 N.Y. 303, 86 N.E.2d 757 (1949).

84. Leete, *supra* note 81, at 1197.

85. *Kichler's Inc. v. Persinger,* 24 Ohio App. 2d 124, 265 N.E.2d 319 (1970); *Columbia Christian College, Inc. v. Commonwealth Properties, Inc.,* 286 Or. 321, 594 P.2d 401 (1979).

86. Lusk *et al., supra* note 8, at 190–93.

10
Property Rights

Objectives

The purpose of this chapter is to:

1. Define various kinds of property and the legal rights and responsibilities created by each.
2. Explain how property is acquired and transferred.
3. Outline types of zoning restrictions that may be imposed by local governments.
4. Discuss contracting and working with real estate agents to buy property.
5. Discuss various ways of financing a purchase of property.

Case in Point

Yancy, a landlord, leased first-floor restaurant premises to Gill, who later sold the restaurant business to Roberts and his son. A five-year lease was drawn up between Yancy and Roberts. Several months before that lease was to expire, Roberts and his son moved their restaurant business to a new building.

When they left, they removed restaurant stools, sinks, dishwashers, refrigerators, and other items of restaurant equipment used by them in their restaurant business. They also removed the restaurant lighting fixtures, paneling, sheetrock nailed to the walls, and false ceilings above the dining booths and above the bar. Unused portions of the lighting fixtures and paneling were thrown away.

The removal of the stools, sinks, dishwashers, refrigerators, and other restaurant equipment was not disputed by Yancy. These were conceded to be trade fixtures properly removable by Roberts.

Yancy sued to recover damages for the removal of the lighting fixtures, paneling, sheetrock, and false ceilings; and the damage done to the remaining premises by Roberts' methods of removal of these items.

The trial court awarded Yancy $2500 for all damages suffered by Yancy. Roberts and

son appealed, arguing that they were legally entitled to remove all of these trade fixtures as tenants occupying the premises for the conduct of their restaurant business. The judgment for Yancy was upheld by a higher court.[1]

What was the difference between the two types of property? The movable equipment such as stools, dishwashers, and refrigerators were trade fixtures, and Roberts was entitled to take them. However, equipment such as lighting, paneling, and sheetrock are considered immovable if fixed to real estate, especially if their removal could damage existing property. Both landlords and renters have legal rights under the law.

PROPERTY: LEGAL RIGHTS AND RESPONSIBILITIES

Foodservice operators at some point may own, rent, buy, or sell property. *Property* consists of legally protected rights in and ownership of anything having recognized value. Legal rights refer to the right to use, sell, and protect property against trespass or theft.

Property includes real estate and equipment used for business as well as personal property. A refrigerator in a foodservice operation and a refrigerator in a private home both provide the owners with legal rights. A buyer of a restaurant and a buyer of a home both have legal rights in the property and responsibilities to local government and their neighbors for maintenance of the property and payment of taxes.

Foodservice operators have the same rights to own, maintain, and sell property as other businesspersons, but their *responsibilities* may differ. Responsibility for maintaining proper conditions on foodservice property is enforced strictly because members of the public are invited on that property, and in most cases operators will be subject to tight regulation.

Property is safeguarded by our Bill of Rights and by the Fourteenth Amendment to the Constitution, which prohibit persons and states from depriving individuals of private property without due process of law.[2] The Bill of Rights also prohibits any person or government from depriving another of private property for public use without just compensation.[3]

Kinds of Property

Personal property is movable, such as a regular-size refrigerator. *Real property* or *real estate* is immovable, such as a restaurant building.

Tangible personal property has physical substance. A delivery truck is tangible personal property, as is a refrigerator. *Intangible* personal property has no physical existence, but consists of rights represented by tangible property. For example, a stock certificate is tangible paper, but the rights it represents are intangible. That is, the certificate represents ownership rights in the assets of the corporation whose name appears on the certificate. The owner of the certificate who sells the stock does not sell the assets, but only intangible rights in these assets.

Services such as telephone, gas, and electricity, and rights represented by credit cards are also treated as intangible property. When a person intentionally uses such services in an unauthorized manner, for example, by using a phony credit card to obtain meals at your restaurant, that person commits a theft of services—a crime in most states.[4]

Obtaining Ownership of Property

Ownership and title, the legal right to own, use, and transfer personal property, may be established in a variety of ways. Property may be acquired by the following methods.

Possession

Simple ownership or possession is the most obvious way to control property. The right of possession means the right to control property, and to keep others from controlling it. This includes the right to recover the property from another who wrongfully takes it or attempts to take control of it. Unless the right to the property is challenged by the true owner, the possessor has the right to retain and control the property against the claims of others. You have a clock in your restaurant that has been in your family for years. You own it. Only you can dispose of it. This is possession.

Purchase

Foodservice operators, like other businesspersons, usually obtain property by buying it from a seller. Personal property transactions are governed by the Uniform Commercial Code, which regulates the transfer of tangible goods by sales contracts. The Code governs the rights of buyers and sellers. It creates separate rules for merchants and for consumers. (A *merchant* is a person who deals in the kinds of goods involved in the transaction and who represents himself or herself as having expert knowledge of the goods.) Purchases of food supplies, paper napkins, and heavy equipment such as dishwashers are all covered by the Uniform Commercial Code. (See Chapter 8 on contracts for a thorough discussion of purchasing contracts.)

Gifts

A gift is another way of acquiring real and personal property. A gift is a voluntary act whereby property is transferred by the giver, the *donor,* to the receiver, the *donee,* free of any requirement that the receiver give something of value in return. However, a gift must be *completed* to have this effect. A promise merely to make a gift in the future requires some exchange of value by the receiver.

The requirements to make a gift legally effective or binding are (1) delivery, (2) the intention to make a gift, and (3) acceptance by the receiver.[5]

Delivery usually means physical delivery. However, a constructive delivery is sufficient, that is, delivery of a tangible representation of the gift itself. Moreover, a delivery requires the giver to give up complete control over the gift.

Intent is determined from the language and actions of the gift giver and the surrounding circumstances. Courts look with suspicion at large gifts to a competitor or personal enemy. Likewise, courts closely examine a very large gift to one outside the family or business circle to ascertain if fraud or duress (physical or mental compulsion) were used to obtain it. If so, the gift will be returned to the donor or donor's estate, since the essential requirement that the gift be voluntary does not exist.

Acceptance by the donee or receiver usually presents no problem, since most individuals, businesses, charities, schools, and the like are more than happy to accept gifts.

Accession

Accession means *adding on* to some form of property. When you employ a painter to paint the interior of your restaurant with paint you provide or pay for, you own the *improvements* but must pay the *contract price* of the job. Problems in this area come up when large sums are spent by someone renovating or making repairs without the owner's permission. Normally the owner is entitled to recover *damages* to a business caused by "improvements" that the owner did not request or approve. However, if the operator had the opportunity to stop the accession, but failed to do so, then he or she may be liable to the accessor for the fair market value of the improvements made.

Inheritance

Property may be inherited on an owner's death by a last will and testament, or by the laws covering the estate of a person who dies without a will.

Under a transfer by will, the owner may name the person or party (corporation, partnership, government body, charity) to whom ownership of property will pass on his or her death. Unlike a gift, title and ownership do not pass to the person or party named *until death*. Only death makes the will effective.

Under a transfer by *intestate succession,* that is, in a case where the owner dies without leaving a will, state laws determine how and to whom the property will be transferred. In these types of cases, property is transferred to the living heirs (those persons in the direct line of descent, such as a surviving spouse or surviving children) of the deceased person. No provision is made for transfers of property to other than living persons. Transfers of property to charity, a government body, a corporation, or partnership must be made by a will, and are not imposed by state laws.

Confusion

Confusion means a mixing or commingling of the property of two persons, so that the individual property of each person can no longer be distinguished. For example, if another restaurateur deliberately and without your consent mixes his potatoes in a bin shipment with yours so as to cause confusion, you as the innocent party may be entitled to the entire shipment.

This principle of law does not apply where the mixing occurs by (1) agreement, (2) an honest mistake, or (3) the act of a third party. In such a case, the owners own the total potato shipment equally. If you as one owner claim a greater share of the potatoes, you must be ready to prove that greater ownership if a dispute arises. Otherwise the courts will presume that you and your competitor share the whole shipment equally. If you bought a shipment of potatoes with a nearby restaurateur at a good price, and did not specify the amounts you each would receive, a court would probably divide the shipment equally. This is also true if the whole shipment is accidentally damaged or destroyed. All losses are spread equally unless you can prove that your share of the lost shipment was less than that of the other buyer.

Lost and Found Property: Finders

The common law recognizes three types of property rights for finders of property, depending on how and where the property was found.

1. When the property is *mislaid* property, meaning the owner or rightful possessor voluntarily put it aside and then accidentally forgot where he or she put it, the finder holds the property for the true owner as a caretaker, until that person returns to claim it. For example, if a patron of your restaurant accidentally left her purse, coat, or parcel in the booth where she ate, and it is turned in to you by another patron, you must take reasonable care of the article until the patron returns to claim it. If you or an employee negligently delivers the article to an imposter, you may be liable to the owner for its value. If the true owner does not reclaim the article within a reasonable time, then you as the restaurant owner have the right to keep it. Why? Because if the article were misplaced, most states give the owner of the premises and not the "finder" first claim if the property owner is not located.[6]

   What if an employee finds the article? Your rights as owner and employer prevail over the employee's rights as finder. Why? Because the article was discovered by the employee in the course of his or her employment.[7] A practical solution is to require all employees to give up any rights to found patron property if the owner does not claim it.

2. *Lost* property is property that is not voluntarily put aside and forgotten. As a general rule, every finder of lost property is entitled to keep it from everyone but the true owner.[8] However, the finder is required by law in some states to make a reasonably diligent search to locate the true owner and return the property to that person. A deliberate, intentional retention of property that does not belong to the finder is larceny in many states.[9]

   Some states determine a finder's rights to lost property on the basis of *where* the lost property is found.[10] On the other hand, a finder of property in a public space, such as a hotel or restaurant dining area, foyer, lobby, or any other area to which the public is given access, prevails over the owner of the premises.[11]

   However, an exception exists in the case of an employee who finds lost property in the course of his or her employment. In that case, the employer or owner of the premises has a superior right to possession, unless he or she agrees to turn the property over to the employee as a reward for honesty.[12]

   Some states have passed statutes intended to promote the return of found property and, in the event the owner does not claim an article within a certain time period, to reward the finder by giving him or her full ownership rights. These statutes change the common law rule that always permitted the true owner the right to recover lost property at any time.

3. *Abandoned* property is property deliberately discarded by the true owner, who has no intention of ever reclaiming it. Abandoned property becomes the property of the finder in most states. Your finding a painting in the garbage outside a gallery next

door would be an example—as long as you do not trespass to get it. There is no duty to hold, protect, or return abandoned property, or to turn it over to the police, as is true of mislaid and lost property.

Protection of Intangible Property

Foodservice operators should know the various ways in which property rights may be protected. In case of real property the deed and contract of sale are the owner's protection, and in a dispute the courts will look to those items to help resolve ownership rights. Ownership in property such as tables and silverware transfers to the buyer. Other types of property include continual-use items that are disposed of in the course of use. These items may be tangible and disposable and physically the buyer may do what he or she wants with the actual physical property, but intangible rights to the owner are protected such as the process of invention and artistic work. It is important that operators know what these rights are either to use them or to prevent infringement on others' rights, which could result in liability.

The law protects property rights in a variety of ways.

1. A *trademark* is an identifiable mark, symbol, or device that is fixed, stamped, or printed on tangible goods. The Federal Lanham Act of 1946 permits a trademark to be registered by the owner or user.[13] Coca-Cola, for instance, has a registered trademark for its soft-drink products.

    Protection depends on the use to which the goods carrying the mark are put. If use is continuous, no other person may use the mark without prior consent. Such unauthorized use is called *infringement,* and the original owner may sue to stop the infringement and recover for damages suffered as a result of the unauthorized use.[14]

Use by consent takes the form of a licensing or franchise agreement where the owner transfers the use of a trademark to another for a fee—often called a royalty. A franchise agreement to sell Kentucky Fried Chicken, with its 11 different herbs and spices, is an example of use by consent.

2. A *service mark* performs a function similar to a trademark. Such a mark identifies and distinguishes the services of one owner or user from another. A service mark need not be attached to goods, but may be registered and will provide the protection given property under trademarks.

3. A *patent* is a government grant that provides an inventor the exclusive right to make, use, and sell his or her discovery for a period of 17 years. Subjects that are unpatentable are laws of nature, physical phenomena, and abstract ideas.

    The term "patent" includes not only tangible items, but a *process* separate from the article created by that process. The process, to be eligible for a patent award, must consist of *new and useful* acts or a series of acts performed on a particular subject whereby the subject is made into a different thing. Arthur Treacher's has a special patent for its fish recipe.

    Patent law is intended to create a reasonable balance between two competing economic interests: (1) the right to promote free enterprise or competition in property transactions and (2) the right to encourage invention by rewarding inventors with temporary exclusive rights over the fruits of their inventive efforts.[15]

4. A *copyright* is a means of protecting the *form* of original literary, musical, dramatic, pictorial, audio, and audiovisual works. Some foodservice operators and members of chain restaurants copyright especially creative menus or advertising

materials. The ideas, concepts, or methods of operation themselves are not subject to copyright. To obtain protection, registration is required by application to the Register of Copyrights, together with payment of a nominal fee and with one or two copies of the work. No public distribution of the work must be made by the applicant prior to the effective registration date, since prior public distribution makes the copyright unavailable. The period of life of the copyright is 50 years beyond the death of the last surviving author. No right to renew the copyright exists.[16]

Once granted, the copyright gives the holder an exclusive right to reproduce, perform, or display the work. An exemption is granted for "fair use" by the public. Fair use means a use without the consent of the copyright holder. In broad terms, fair use means very limited noncommercial use of copyrighted work for teaching, research, criticism, comment, or news reporting.

An unauthorized use is called an *infringement* of the copyrighted work. *Innocent infringement,* if proven, makes the infringer liable for any actual damages the copyright owner can establish. Independently, a court may award not less than $250 and not more than $10,000 in punitive damages if no actual damages are suffered. *Willful or deliberate infringement* permits heavier fines to be imposed together with a one-year prison term.

"Fair use" requires a case-by-case analysis of the facts by the courts. Four factors are usually examined: (1) the purpose and character of the use; (2) the nature of the work; (3) the amount of the material used in relation to the copyrighted work as a whole; and (4) the effect of the use on the copyright holder's potential market for the work.[17]

Where foodservice operators are most likely to encounter copyright law is in the use of music in their restaurants. A concern in the industry is the controversy over whether foodservice operators must pay royalties on recorded copyrighted music played on the premises by means of home-type radios and loudspeakers. The issue has not been fully resolved.[18] Music played by means of coin-operated jukeboxes or radios that are rented is currently exempt from the copyright laws, unless the restaurant operator owns the machine or refuses, on request, to identify its owner.

Music performed live is another matter. The general rule is that songs played by a group or individual performer on a song-by-song basis are not a problem. Songwriters, however, may sue for royalties if their songs or arrangements are played exclusively in your restaurant; for example, if you play country music in your western-type bar and grill, chances are you may be playing a few favorites by specific songwriters, and you may be required to pay them royalties for use of their songs.

Two songwriting societies own most of the music rights to recorded songs and represent performers and songwriters. You may have to pay one or both of these societies royalties for rights to use songs. They are the American Society of Composers, Authors, and Publishers (ASCAP) and Broadcast Music, Inc. (BMI). The best method is to choose songs from one society and you may only be required to pay royalties to it, thereby limiting this business cost.

Another way to sidestep conflicting claims and contracts when playing recorded music is to contract directly with those companies offering "piped-in" music, such as Muzak. They handle payments of royalties to performers, and the music is generally of the same quality and type.

Purchases of Property from Non-owners[19]

You want two vans for your catering operation, and are looking for a deal when you spot a sign advertising just the models you want at a low price. You call the number listed, meet the owner in a parking lot, inspect the vans, and proceed to buy both of them. Several days later two police officers are outside checking your new vans. They tell you that the vans are "hot" and you will have to surrender them.

What happens when you purchase property from someone who does not own it or have a legitimate interest in it—for example, if you unknowingly purchase goods from a thief?

The Uniform Commercial Code makes a distinction between a *void* and a *voidable* title. A *void* title to property means that the seller has nothing to sell. A thief does not obtain title to property through a criminal act. Since the thief does not have a title to transfer, you as the buyer cannot receive title. Even if you act in good faith without knowledge that the goods were stolen and pay value for the goods, their transfer to you does not affect the rights of the true owner to recover them. An innocent buyer's only right to recover losses is through the thief—and good luck.

Title is *voidable* when a seller obtains goods by fraud or trickery and resells them for value without giving the buyer knowledge of the fraud. Here the buyer can rightfully keep the property free of any claims by the true owner. However, the law does not permit a wrongdoer to benefit entirely from wrongdoing. It permits the true owner to recover from the fraudulent party. But since the seller had some title, the seller may transfer the property to a buyer without notice to the owner. If the purchaser knows about the fraud, then he or she either must return the property or pay the true owner the money value of the goods.

You should exercise care when buying goods that seem too good a bargain to be true. The goods may be stolen and without title, and you may be forced to return them or make payment to the true owner.

Financing Purchases of Equipment, Fixtures, and Inventory

Foodservice operators may wish to finance the purchase of foodservice equipment, food and beverage inventory, and fixtures rather than use cash.

To protect their interests, creditors or lenders will want to obtain a *security interest* in the property, and will want to make sure that their interests have priority over the claims of other creditors. A security interest is the right of the lender or seller to take property back if the debtor defaults on the payment for the item. Article 9 of the Uniform Commercial Code applies to these transactions.

Article 9 defines *equipment* as "goods used or bought for use primarily in business"; defines *inventory* as "goods held for sale or lease or for use under contracts of service as well as raw materials, work in process, and materials used or consumed in a business"; and defines *fixtures* as "goods so affixed to real property as to be considered a part of it." Equipment, in this sense, would include refrigerators, dishwashers, and smaller items such as knives and plates. Inventory would include the foods and beverages you prepare for resale. One typical foodservice fixture is a walk-in refrigerator, which could be sold along with the building, since the original owner is unlikely to want to remove it.

Every creditor wants his or her security interest to be good against three parties: (1) the debtor; (2) other creditors; and (3) a person purchasing the property from the debtor. How is this accomplished? The creditor *attaches* the property and by doing so *perfects* his or her security interest.

By *attachment* we do not mean physical attachment. Rather, this term is a legal word that requires (1) a security interest in the property given by the debtor to the creditor, and (2) the creditor to give something of value in return to the debtor. For example, the creditor will give you the dishwasher you want in return for the collateral you put up as security if you don't pay for the dishwasher. A written security agreement is required unless the goods to be financed, the collateral, are already in the hands of the creditor. This agreement may cover *future advances* to be made by the creditor to the debtor. This means that you may obtain additional credit on the strength of the collateral already in existence, and need not provide additional collateral to do so. This agreement may also create a security interest in proceeds of the collateral (cash received from your use of the collateral) and in *after-acquired property* you purchase (new equipment, inventory, or fixtures).

The security agreement, to be effective, must be signed by you and must contain an accurate description of the property for which the interest is created. A failure to provide an adequate description may cause the security interest to be insufficient, meaning that the creditor's rights will be jeopardized.[20]

The second requirement, *perfection,* is the legal claim that a creditor or seller needs to take action if the bill goes unpaid. Perfection requires use of one of the following methods: (1) public filing of a *financing statement;* (2) taking possession of the property (collateral); and, in more limited cases, (3) attaching the security interest itself.

A *financing statement* is filed at either the secretary of state's office (state capital) or at the local recorder of deeds office (county seat), depending on the type of collateral involved. The filing is good for five years in the absence of a maturity date. This initial period can be extended for an additional five-year period by filing a continuation statement. When you have paid off the loan, you are entitled to receive a termination statement that clears your financing statement from the records.

As for *priority of payment,* the first security interest to be perfected has priority over any interests perfected later or any that are not perfected. If none of the security interests are perfected, then the first security interest to attach has priority.

Where *fixtures* are collateral, it is important to note that special care is required of a creditor who wishes to maintain priority over other creditors who obtain security on the land and building. Otherwise, once the fixtures are permanently attached to the real estate, they will lose their identity as personal property, and the creditor will find his or her claim inferior to that of a real estate creditor.

What happens to the property if you default? Unless you agree otherwise, the creditor (secured party) has the right to take physical possession of the property (collateral). If the property is bulky or hard to move, the creditor may sell it at a public or private auction. However, the creditor must act in good faith and the sale must be commercially reasonable. The proceeds of the sale are usually distributed as follows: attorney's fees, satisfaction of indebtedness, junior creditors, and the balance to you as the debtor. In most cases (unless otherwise agreed), the creditor may obtain a deficiency judgment against you personally if the sale proceeds are insufficient to cover the loan balance. Where you have paid 60 percent of the debt, and the property secured is consumer goods, the creditor must sell the property, and the debt is canceled if the sale makes up for the debt. If you have paid less than 60 percent of the debt, the creditor, after notifying you, may keep the property and cancel the debt.

REAL ESTATE

Real estate is all immovable property, consisting of land, buildings, trees, crops, and other natural or artificial improvements permanently attached to the land. Land includes mineral and water rights under or on its subsurface and air rights above it.

Real estate is treated differently in law from other forms of property. More rights and responsibilities go with ownership of real estate than with other property. Foodservice operators will encounter more restrictions on ownership of restaurant real estate than on personal real estate or property used in other business ventures.

Personal property attached to real estate and associated with the land is known as a *fixture.* Fixtures are treated as real estate and are transferred to a new owner with the land unless otherwise provided in the sales contract. The *intention* of the person affixing it to make it a fixture and the actual *affixation* or attachment determine whether personal property will be treated as a fixture by the law. For example, the lighting and paneling installed by Roberts and his son in the Case in Point were permanent fixtures. Floors, ceiling, plumbing, central air-conditioning equipment, walk-in refrigerators, custom-built cabinets, and storm windows all qualify as fixtures. The test of intention is *objective,* meaning that the court will examine the *words* and *actions* of the owner and not attempt to determine unexpressed thoughts.[21]

Trade fixtures are items of personal property installed by an occupier of land under a lease contract permitting the use of land owned by another for a specific purpose. Trade fixtures also apply to commercial leases. If fixtures, such as window air conditioners, shelves, and partitions, are removable without materially altering or changing the premises, and the lease does not treat them as part of the real property, then they are removable at the end of the lease by the tenant. The tables, chairs, tablecloths, and flatware purchased by the tenant are movable, and are removable.[22]

Land Ownership

Land ownership is classified according to its type, duration, and the amount of interest a person holds in the property. *Freehold* estates are held indefinitely; *non-freehold* estates are restricted and may only be held for a specified time.

Types of Ownership

If you obtain land for a restaurant, you should be aware of the type of ownership conveyed to you. Some types are restrictive of owner rights.

1. The most complete land ownership is ownership in *fee simple absolute,* or in *fee simple.* A fee simple estate is an estate without restriction on its disposal or use. This estate gives the owner the largest bundle of rights and powers the law can provide. As long as the owner does not interfere with the rights of others, he or she may use the land unconditionally. The owner may sell it or convey it by inheritance to heirs through a will. The owner is free to give the property away. The owner may *commit waste,* meaning deplete the land of value without any requirement that trees, crops, herds, and other renewable items be replaced or restored. Nor need the owner account for natural resources such as minerals, or set up any replenishment reserve.[23] Short of any local zoning and fire restrictions, the land is the owner's to use or misuse.

2. A *life estate* is non-freehold and is a less absolute form of ownership. Ownership rights are conveyed for life only by the owner to a *life tenant.*

   A life tenant is a non-owner, an occupier of land, and has fewer rights than an owner in fee simple. This tenant may not commit waste without the owner's express permission, since doing so would adversely affect the value of the land to the future owner, who obtains the land when the life tenant dies. The rights of the future owner are called *future interests*.[24]

A life tenant *can* mortgage or *encumber* the land, meaning it can be put up as security to finance improvements.

The following example illustrates the rights and restrictions of a life estate.

Jerry Jameson, wealthy restaurant executive, conveys valuable real estate to his daughter Emily for life, and after her death to his nephew George Boomer. The land has potential value for development of a restaurant. In the conveyance to Emily there are no restrictions against development. Lacking the money needed for development and not wishing to commit her own money, Emily mortgages the land and obtains construction financing from a group of local banks. The banks require a 99-year mortgage commitment from Emily as a condition of the financing. Emily is now 35 years old and in all likelihood will die prior to the end of the stated period.

Can she mortgage the land? Yes, but only with the consent of her cousin George. Her authority to mortgage the land ends with her death, and the mortgage cannot extend beyond her lifetime. Why? Because George's rights are affected as the holder in the future interest in the land. By consenting to the long-term mortgage, George has voluntarily given up his right to object to the mortgage. In this way the interests of Emily, George, and the banks are protected.

3. Landholding by *possession* is another right in land. Only non-freehold rights are created. No interest in ownership exists, but merely the right to *possess* and use the land for a specified period of time. This form of land rights is most commonly known by its paper contract, the *lease*. The owner is normally called a *landlord* and the occupier a *tenant*. A lease gives the tenant the right to occupy and use land for a specific period of time. Those starting a restaurant may want to consider this form of land use.

Leasing Real Estate

Non-freehold estates include *tenancy for years, tenancy from period to period, tenancy at will,* and *tenancy at sufferance.* In each case the owner (the landlord) leases use and possession to an occupier (the tenant) but *qualifies* the tenant's right to possession by reserving the right to evict the tenant for failure to comply with the lease. Nonpayment of rent, holding the property over the date specified for surrender, committing waste, and improper use are examples of situations that permit landlords to remove tenants.

Tenancy for years is the most common form of tenancy, and its duration is specifically stated in the lease. When the lease term or duration is over, possession returns to the landlord, unless the lease contains a renewal clause or extension provision.

A *tenancy from period to period* is created when the lease does not specify any duration, but requires that rent be paid at certain times, for example, on the first day of each month. Such language creates a tenancy from month to month. Since the duration of the occupancy is not specified, the landlord must notify the tenant of termination of the lease. This notice provision is fixed by state statutes, with 30 days the normal requirement when a month-to-month tenancy is created.

A *tenancy at will* is one created by the landlord for as long as he or she desires. Either the landlord or the tenant can terminate a tenancy at will without notice. It usually comes into being when a tenant remains in possession of the premises after a tenancy-for-years lease ends—the legal term is *holds over*—with the consent of the landlord. The death of either party terminates this form of tenancy.

A *tenancy by sufferance* or "squatting" or mere occupation of the land is not recognized by the law.[25] The tenant is a trespasser who has no right to possession. The landlord may create a lawful tenancy by accepting rent from such a squatter, but is not required to do so.

Non-freehold estates create tenancies and possessory rights that limit the use, with the owner always retaining the right to recover possession should the tenant fail to comply with requirements for use. We will examine the rights and responsibilities of the landlord and tenant.

Landlord's Responsibilities
In each lease of premises, whether for residential or for business purposes, the law requires a warranty or guarantee by the landlord that the tenant will have the sole right to possession and a covenant or promise that the tenant will have *quiet enjoyment* of the premises. Quiet enjoyment means that the landlord will not evict the tenant except for misconduct.

However, a tenant may *want* to leave under certain circumstances. For example, Roberts, a landlord, leases a restaurant to Bailey. Bailey takes possession, not knowing that part of the premises was not available for occupancy because of Roberts' failure to exterminate vermin and rodents after he promised to do so. The infestation is a *constructive eviction,* giving Bailey the right to terminate his tenancy without liability for rent. A constructive eviction refers to conditions brought about by the landlord, through either negligence or activity, that make the property untenable. Under such conditions the tenant may be "forced to leave" and may not be held liable for rent.

At common law, a landlord was not under any obligation to repair premises rented to a tenant or to guarantee that they were suitable for the particular purposes for which rented. Only if the landlord voluntarily agreed to do so under the lease was he or she responsible for repairs or liability. Under most state statutes today, residential tenants are protected by an *implied promise,* one imposed by the law, that premises are fit to live in. A landlord cannot renounce this guarantee unless both parties agree to do so. Most recent decisions also place duty upon the landlord to repair and maintain the structure and all its *common areas* and *permanent fixtures,* such as corridors, public sidewalks, and stairways.

These legal duties are generally limited to protecting residential tenants. They have not yet been widely extended to commercial tenants. This means that if you are seeking to rent space for your foodservice operation, you cannot rely on the protection given apartment dwellers. Your only protection rests in your making a *careful inspection* of the premises before signing any lease and by insisting that the lease contain promises by the landlord to keep the premises in repair.

An exception in the law exists, however. When a landlord rents premises for purposes that involve admission of the public—such as patrons of a bar, tavern, or restaurant—and at the time the lease is signed or renewed, the premises are in a dangerous condition, *the landlord may be held responsible for patrons' injuries caused by the dangerous conditions.*[26]

Tenant's Responsibilities
The most basic responsibility of a tenant is to pay rent to the landlord, in either money, labor, or services. A lease not only transfers possession, but is a contract requiring the parties to exchange something of value to make their agreement legally enforceable. Usually the rent amount and when it is due are spelled out in the contract. When the rent amount is not contained in the lease, the duty to pay is limited to reasonable rent, due only at the end of the lease period.[27]

Lease Terms
The lease is a contract, and must be negotiated in the same way as any contract. Some states will enforce an oral lease of residential

premises if the lease does not exceed one year—but not for commercial property.[28] A written record is always desirable, in either case, to avoid disputes. In a dispute oral leases must be proved in court by oral testimony, and the credibility of your testimony is usually left for a judge or jury to decide. A clever liar may make a better witness than a person who is truthful but nervous.

A lease creates far more restrictive rights for the tenant than in the case of outright sale. This is so because with a lease ownership of the property remains with the landlord. A lease may include an option to purchase, but that is not usually exercisable until the lease period is over.

A landlord is always free to sell the real estate to anyone else. Does the sale terminate the tenant's rights under a preexisting lease? No. The buyer takes the real estate with existing leases in effect.[29] Can a landlord shift liability for his or her negligence to the tenant? The answer is also no.[30]

A word about unconscionable lease terms is appropriate. Oppressive commercial lease terms imposed due to unequal economic bargaining power can be eliminated by a court. This doctrine is not limited to residential leases. One example of unconscionable conduct is a landlord's unjustifiable refusal to renew a restaurant's lease after the tenant has spent large sums of money to improve the premises and build up the business. Generally courts look with disfavor on such refusals.[31]

When leased premises are destroyed by fire before the tenant takes possession, the tenant may terminate the lease without liability to the landlord.[32]

What happens if the destruction of the premises—by, say, a restaurant fire—occurs *after* the tenant moves in? Leases usually provide that the landlord must rebuild or restore the premises within a reasonable time, with a further provision that the lease automatically terminates in the event the landlord fails to do so.[33]

In most leases the landlord reserves the right to cancel the lease in the event of sale of the property by giving notice to the tenant. Since such a right can drastically affect the use and occupancy of the premises, the courts construe the exercise of that right strictly. Only the landlord may exercise this right, not the prospective purchaser. Unless the lease provides otherwise, notice of cancellation must be served personally or by registered mail.[34]

The duty to repair the premises usually rests with the landlord if the repairs are structural, or out of the ordinary, such as the replacement of built-in refrigeration units or other immovable fixtures. The tenant is responsible for repairing the interior of the premises, trade fixtures, windows, and items that are nonstructural. The parties should define their respective duties in the lease.[35]

What about substantial structural improvements made by the tenants? Unless specifically permitted, or to be undertaken at the landlord's cost and expense, such improvements become part of the real estate and belong to the landlord when the lease expires. This means that the tenant has no claim for reimbursement against the landlord, even though such improvements may enhance the value of the real estate.[36] *Don't make substantial improvements without a clear understanding of who is to pay for them, because you may find yourself donating the improvements to your landlord.*

The Case in Point at the beginning of the chapter illustrated this issue. The difference is between trade fixtures and property permanently attached to the building. Unless the lease provides otherwise, you may remove trade fixtures when you leave. However, fixtures that cannot be removed without damaging the building are not treated as fixtures according to law *and belong to the landlord.*

Trade fixtures are usually items of property installed by a tenant at his or her expense to operate a foodservice business, with the understanding that they are to be removed by the tenant when the lease ends, unless landlord and tenant agree otherwise. A tenant who removes items of property that are not legally trade fixtures may be liable not only for the difference between the value of the premises with the items left intact and the value with them removed, but also for the damages caused by the improper manner in which the items were removed.

When a landlord is to construct a new building for you, there may or may not be an implied warranty that the property is habitable. Some courts imply such a guarantee for property constructed for commercial purposes, but it is up to you to insert a clause assuring habitability where state laws do not automatically require it.[37]

Previous mention was made regarding a landlord's liability to patrons of a tenant's business, when the landlord knowingly rents premises to a tenant for a restaurant business open to the public.[38] In what situation is the *tenant* liable? A tenant is liable to *business patrons,* those persons accommodated or served, for negligence or willful misconduct occurring on that portion of the premises exclusively occupied and controlled by the tenant.[39] A landlord is responsible for common areas such as elevators, stairwells, and other areas used by other people and not exclusively by your patrons and employees.

Can a landlord grant, through a lease provision, a tenant's exclusive right to operate a foodservice business within a specified locality? This matter is of critical importance, since the value of the tenancy may be diminished if the landlord is free to lease to a competing business later on. Generally such a provision is legal as long as it is not inserted for the sole purpose of enhancing revenue for the landlord, and is necessary to protect the legitimate economc interests of the tenant as well

as the landlord.[40] Care must be taken to determine if such exclusive arrangements violate state or federal antitrust laws. Usually such a provision will be upheld if the duration of the lease is reasonable.[41]

You must know whether you have a *gross lease* or a *net lease.* In a gross lease the tenant's sole responsibility is to pay rent. All other expenses, such as real estate taxes, insurance, and special assessments, are paid by the landlord. In a net lease the tenant assumes all of these costs. This means that any increases in these costs during the lease become liabilities that the tenant must bear.

Lease Assignment

An *assignment* is a transfer of the entire interest in the leased premises, in which the tenant/assignor gives up any right to the property. When a tenant under a lease assigns the lease to a third person, does the tenant terminate the obligation to pay rent to the landlord? No. An assignment merely transfers the obligation to pay to another, but does not terminate or extinguish the original tenant's obligation to the landlord. If the *assignee,* the person to whom the tenant assigned the lease, fails or refuses to pay the rent, the landlord may sue the *assignor,* the original tenant, for the rent due.

Generally leases contain a clause requiring the landlord's written consent to any assignment, with a further requirement that such consent will not be unreasonably withheld or refused. However, the law does not imply any duty on the landlord's part to assign a lease. This is a matter of negotiation between landlord and tenant.

Subletting

A *sublease* differs from an *assignment* in that a sublease gives the original tenant the right to reenter if the rent is not paid and thus involves a transfer of less than the tenant's total interest in the lease. The act of subletting, even when consented to by the landlord, does not relieve the tenant of the obligation to pay rent under the original lease. Leases often prohibit subletting without the landlord's consent.

Destruction of the Premises
Under the common law, destruction of the premises through no fault of a tenant did not relieve the tenant of the obligation to pay rent. Nor did it permit the tenant to terminate the lease. Today residential statutes qualify this rule by suspending rent payments until the premises are restored by the landlord. Commercial tenants are not afforded relief as an implied legal right and *must protect themselves by inserting such a provision in the lease.* To obtain suspension of rent, the destruction must make the premises totally unsuitable for use.[42]

Abandonment
A common leasing problem arises when the tenant unjustifiably, without the landlord's consent, abandons the premises. Does this release the tenant from liability for rent for the balance of the lease term? No. The tenant remains fully liable for any rent due. The landlord must minimize or mitigate damages and make a good faith effort to relet the premises and thus lessen the original tenant's liability—at least in residential tenancies.[43] There is a split of authority, or a dispute among the courts, as to whether the landlord's duty to attempt to lessen damages for tenant liability applies to commercial tenancies in the absence of language in the lease. It is best for a foodservice tenant to insert a provision regarding abandonment in the lease.

Acquiring or Transferring Ownership of Real Estate

Transfers of title to real estate may be accomplished in a number of ways.

1. As with personal property, an owner may transfer real property by *will* or *inheritance.*
2. The most common way of obtaining real property is through *purchase.* Buying real estate for a foodservice operation requires a lawyer and knowledge of the local zoning regulations.
3. *Eminent domain* is another method by which real estate may pass from one owner to another, and usually involves the federal, state, or even local government. Eminent domain (condemnation) is the power of the government to acquire land for a public use. For example, your state may wish to put a highway across your fast-food parking lot. The state has the legal right to do so in some cases by merely filing a map showing the land needed in the county in which the land is situated. In other cases, the state may begin a condemnation proceeding in court at which you, as landowner, may object and try to obtain a court order preventing the taking of your land. Under either method, you as the owner have the legal right to receive just compensation for any such public taking of your property. Fair market value is determined by a court hearing when you and the state cannot agree on that value.
4. *Adverse possession* is a means of acquiring title to real property without any voluntary transfer by the owner by either gift or will and testament. Essentially, adverse possession is a right to own real property acquired by the person remaining in possession of that property for a number of years fixed by state statutes, usually 20 years or longer. At the end of the statutory period, the occupant acquires title by operation of law, that is, without any voluntary transfer being made by the true owner. The law steps in, making the consent of the true owner unnecessary.

Four elements must be satisfied to apply the law of adverse possession: (1) Possession of the real estate must be *actual* and *exclusive*. This means that only the possessor physically occupies the land. (2) Possession must be *open, visible,* and *notorious,* meaning that the occupancy must be for everyone to see. (3) Possession must be *continuous* and *peaceable* for the required statutory time period. This means that neither the true owner nor any other person steps in to occupy the property. Service of an eviction notice or an actual eviction will stop the adverse possession and interrupt the statutory period required by law. (4) Possession must be *hostile* or *adverse*. This means that the person must remain on the property without the consent of the true owner.

If you are the owner of real estate, you cannot afford to allow someone to occupy your land illegally for too long a time period. If you do so, you may find that your ownership rights in the property have vanished—according to law. For example, if you own a large unused area and allow a street vendor to use à corner of the lot to sell hot dogs, and he occupies it for a certain number of years, he may have the right to ownership.

Deeds

Typically, legal transfers of real estate, including restaurant property, are accomplished through either sale, inheritance, or gift. In all cases of transfer, a *deed* must pass between the previous owner and the new owner. A deed is a written instrument by which legal rights to own as well as use property are established. Unlike a lease, which is a contract and requires an exchange of value between the parties to make it enforceable, a deed does not require *consideration* or exchange of value. This is so because a deed is not a contract but merely a *document of title,* a piece of paper legally accepted as proof of a right to own and use property.

A valid deed requires the names of the buyer and seller, words showing the intent to transfer the property, an adequate legal description of the property, the signature of the seller, and date of delivery to the buyer.

Deeds are divided into various types, depending on the extent of the rights conveyed.

1. A *general warranty* deed conveys the largest number of rights, including:

    The right to exclusive title (warranty of *seisin*) and the right to convey whatever estate the deed covers.

    The right to hold the property free of any limitations or encumbrances that will diminish the value of the land, such as mortgages to others, or rights given to others to drive vehicles on or use a portion of the property for a specific purpose. If such a limitation is not spelled out in the deed, the buyer can hold the seller responsible for any damage suffered because of an undisclosed encumbrance.

    The right to quiet enjoyment. This right protects the buyer against unauthorized use or occupancy of the premises by the seller or others that may disturb the buyer's use. An example would be the seller giving parties periodically in your restaurant. Specifically, this guarantee gives the buyer the right to recover damages if such disturbances take place.

2. *A special warranty* deed provides less protection, because the seller promises only that the seller or, in the case of a gift, the grantor has not and will not act in any way to diminish the value of the land transferred to the buyer. This means that acts of a third person will not result in seller liability. However, if the acts are connected to the seller, then the seller may be held liable.

3. A *quitclaim* deed provides the buyer the least protection. In effect, such a deed says: You (the buyer) take the land as is, and assume all the risks of defective title, undisclosed encumbrances, and lack of quiet enjoyment.[44]

Contract of Sale

The *contract of sale* for land is also critical to the buyer of land for commercial purposes. Most real estate transactions must be in writing to be valid.[45] This document defines the kind of title the buyer will receive; how, when, and where the seller will prove that the title is good; and what will be done and by whom if the title is found to be defective. Other important matters that should be resolved in the contract are:

1. If the land on which a restaurant business is to be operated is vacant, do any zoning or environmental ordinances hamper, limit, or prohibit the use of the property? For example, an area zoned for residential use only is a serious limitation if you wish to operate a restaurant. If an existing building is to be renovated, are there any special restrictions, such as off-street parking requirements?
2. Will the structure comply with height, depth from the street, and other requirements of the local building code? If an existing building is to be renovated, will the building meet current electrical, water, and fire requirements? A building built prior to the enactment of new codes is often exempt from the newer requirements. This is called a *grandfather clause*. However, when an existing building is renovated or a new form of business is established, then the building must be brought up to the newer standards.

3. Does the intended business require the issuance of a permit or license? For example, many restaurants wish to sell alcoholic beverages. This usually requires a license issued at the discretion of a state licensing body. The licensing law restricts the distance of the business from churches, schools, and banks. The personal character of the applicant and freedom from conviction for felonies or crimes involving moral turpitude are also of interest when licenses to sell liquor are reviewed. Without the license, sales of alcoholic beverages included in profit projections would be forbidden.
4. Is there any likelihood that the property will be subject to a government takeover for a highway or for other public purposes?
5. If the purchase requires outside financing, what happens in case the financing does not materialize, or the cost of financing becomes too high?
6. Is the restaurant business planned on the property insurable? If so, are the rates affordable? Who is responsible for fire or other catastrophes that destroy the premises before title passes?

These and other questions may be handled by inserting language in the contract of sale that would terminate the contract automatically if any problems arose that could not be corrected, removed, or modified.

The contract, once signed, is binding on the parties regardless of what happens later. The fact that the property is destroyed before the buyer obtains title and possession does not terminate the contract unless the seller has agreed in the contract to do so.

Foodservice operators must anticipate what may be required in terms of zoning, building and environmental ordinances, licenses, permits, insurance, and cost and availability of financing, and negotiate the contract accordingly. The old Latin phrase *caveat emptor,* let the buyer beware, has even more meaning for sales of real property than of personal property. A mistake in real estate is usually very costly.

In residential sales there is a trend to protect buyers through specific rules of law.[46] *Potential buyers of property for commercial use, however, must protect themselves in the contract.*[47]

Subsurface and Air Rights

Subsurface and air rights that go with land may be extremely valuable, and may be transferred or sold to third persons for development and use separate from the land itself. Any unjustified entry on privately owned subsurface or air space is a trespass or intrusion that may be halted by a court order and for which damages may be recovered.[48]

To Purchase or Lease

Whether to buy or rent is as much an issue for foodservice operators seeking space for a foodservice operation as it is for people seeking a place to live. There are advantages and disadvantages to each. Figure 10.1 gives the factors restaurateurs should be concerned with when making a decision.

In times of high interest rates and a tight real estate market, buying property may not be the wisest business choice. On the other hand, leases generally do not allow the tenant to build up any equity in the property, even though an operator may have to spruce up or make additions to a building to make it into a restaurant or to make it attractive to potential patrons.

The best guide is to use long- and short-term business plans when making a decision. For those starting out in the business, leasing with an option to buy may be the best choice.

Long-term plans should allow for some expansion, not just in the restaurant building itself, but in the parking facilities and the surrounding area. For example, if you are in a high-density area, and the zoning laws require off-street parking, you should choose an "expandable" chunk of land for your restaurant. Parking is one of the biggest sources of headaches when it comes time for restaurateurs to expand. Plan early.

Financing the Purchase of Real Property

In most cases a buyer of real estate does not have enough money to buy vacant land or land with a building. The buyer must seek a loan from a bank or other financial institution. To persuade the bank to approve a loan, the purchaser usually gives the bank a *mortgage.* This is a form of *security interest* or *lien* on the property, giving the bank the right to *foreclose* or take possession of and sell the property if the borrower does not repay the loan. A security interest is interest in personal property, which secures payment or performance of an obligation.

When the cost of the loan is too high, the seller may agree to lend the buyer the purchase price in exchange for a mortgage. This is a *purchase money mortgage.* Sometimes a bank will agree to make a first mortgage loan for part of the total purchase price, and the seller will lend the balance, using a second purchase money mortgage. A first mortgage means that the bank's security interest—its right to sell the land and liquidate its loan—is superior to that of the seller. Only after the bank's loan is repaid does the seller have the right to claim any remaining proceeds under the second mortgage.[49]

A mortgage is also a *conveyance of land,* but its main use is to provide security for payment of a debt. Typically the lender, the *mortgagee,* seeks a regular return on a safe

Figure 10.1
Purchase Versus Lease

	Purchase	Lease
Interest Transferred	Title; ownership complete	Use and occupation (possession)
Method of Transfer	Sale, gift, inheritance	Contract of lease. No gift or inheritance without landlord's consent
Rights	Unlimited	Limited by contract
Financing	More likely	Less likely
Warranties	a. *Title*—full or partial b. *Premises* if building new. Otherwise none implied in commercial sales c. Quiet enjoyment	a. *Title*—none b. *Premises* if residential; otherwise none implied
Taxation	Cost of premises depreciable for federal and state income tax purposes	Rent payments deductible as business expenses for federal and state income tax purposes
Assessments	Payable by buyer	Payable by landlord unless net lease negotiated
Liability	Buyer primarily liable for third party injuries	Landlord primarily liable for structural defects—both landlord and tenant liable for injuries to third parties
Fixtures	Buyer entitled if attached to real estate and seller intended to transfer	Landlord retains all fixtures except trade fixtures
Termination	Fixed by nature of estate or interest conveyed	Fixed by contract—never to exceed owner/landlord's estate or interest
Remedies—Default	*Seller's default* a. Rescission or cancellation of contract b. Lien as security for repayment of downpayment c. Compel seller to perform d. Damages *Buyer's default* a. Retention of buyer's downpayment b. Forfeiture of installment contract c. Foreclosure d. Rescission or cancellation e. Damages f. Compel buyer to perform	*Landlord's default* a. Surrender premises without liability for rent b. Damages c. Compel repair and restoration d. Compel performance e. Enjoin or halt violations *Tenant's default* a. Evict b. Accelerate lease and recover total rent due c. Compel performance d. Enjoin or halt violations

investment and does not wish to assume any management responsibilities. The lender does not want to have to take possession in the event of a default in mortgage payments by the buyer/mortgagor. The lender may require the borrower to execute a mortgage note making the latter personally liable if the mortgaged land and building do not yield sufficient funds from foreclosure to satisfy the mortgage debt.

Existing Mortgage

Often a buyer will want to take over an existing mortgage to obtain property, since the interest rate on such a mortgage may be lower than the current rate.

The bank or other lender must agree to the take-over. In such cases it is important to understand the difference between a buyer who *assumes* an existing mortgage and one who *takes subject to* a mortgage.[50] The buyer who assumes a mortgage obligates not only the mortgaged land and improvements, but also personal assets, to possible foreclosure. The personal assets may make up the difference between what the land and improvements yield and the balance due on the mortgage. The buyer who takes subject to a mortgage is usually not personally liable for payment of any deficiency. The difference is critical to a buyer who does not wish to risk tying up personal assets for a mortgage loan on a restaurant operation. If you have a choice between assuming and taking subject to an existing mortgage, your natural choice would be to take subject to the mortgage.

Foreclosure

If a mortgagor defaults on a mortgage loan, the lender has the right to take the property through foreclosure.

The normal method of foreclosure is the *foreclosure lawsuit*. In such cases the court will order a public auction of the property. Up to the time of sale, the borrower, the borrower's spouse, or even a tenant of the mortgagor, may step in, pay off the mortgage, and halt the sale. This right to prevent foreclosure is called the mortgagor's *equity of redemption.* The period in which these parties have the right to redeem the property is usually fixed by state statute. Notice of default must usually be recorded and a stated period of time must elapse before the sale is held, in order to enable the mortgagor to pay up.[51]

The *doctrine of unconscionable conduct* is applied to foreclosure sales to protect the mortgagor. *This means that foreclosure will be denied unless the borrower is three or four payments behind and a reasonable effort has been made to settle without foreclosure.*[52]

If you buy property through an auction, you may get a real bargain for the money, but you must be cautious. If you become an owner of property through foreclosure, you must see to it that all current insurance policies are endorsed over to you—or that new policies are issued. Such coverage includes workers' compensation, public liability, dramshop, fire, and other insurance. This is especially important if a restaurant is to be operated on the property. If there are existing leases, they should be examined to see if they have been voided after foreclosure. If so, new leases should be prepared. You may want to prepare new leases just to add new provisions to protect yourself. The real estate, federal, and state tax ledger should be reviewed. The building itself should be checked for compliance with all federal, state, and local laws governing protection of tenants, patrons, and employees; and for any condition that could reduce the marketability of the property.

In the case of a purchase money mortgage, the seller and the lender are *one and the same.* Any default in payment of the mortgage should trigger recovery of the property through normal foreclosure proceedings.[53]

Financing a Lease

Lease Mortgage

A tenant with a lease may mortgage his or her leasehold interest unless the lease *specifically prohibits it.*[54] Why? Because the leasehold may be of enough value to cause a bank to make a loan to the tenant with the leasehold as collateral. However, a lender may not approve a loan without assurance of the continued existence of the tenancy. For example, you may want to use your lease as collateral to finance improvements on your restaurant. If you have a five-year lease, the bank might approve a loan. With only a two-year lease, it is doubtful. If you violate the terms of the lease by defaulting on one or more rent payments, the landlord may declare the lease *forfeited,* or given up. If default and forfeiture occur, the mortgage interest of the lender is ended.

Sale and Leaseback

Sale and leaseback is a real estate transaction where the seller sells land for its full value and the buyer simultaneously grants the seller an option to repurchase the land. A new restaurant operator might not want the full *obligations* of ownership, and may want to consider this. However, he or she will not have *equity* either, but is only building up equity for the seller/landlord.

Often the buyer/tenant leases back the land to the seller/landlord for a period of years. Here the seller gets full value instead of the smaller amount he or she might obtain from a mortgage loan, and is not required to repay this amount as long as he or she does not exercise the repurchase option. Under this arrangement the landlord benefits by not having to foreclose if the seller/tenant defaults in rent payments since no mortgage is created, but merely a sale and lease.

For the tenant there are two major disadvantages to this arrangement. First, he or she will not benefit from any increase in the value of the land or improvements. Only the landlord who leases back the premises gains in such a case. Second, the tenant has all the burdens of ownership without the usual ownership benefits. The tenant must pay all taxes, assessments, and insurance charges as an owner would, but must get the buyer's consent to sell, demolish, or remodel the building. In other words, the tenant's hands are tied. The buyer/landlord regains possession if the tenant defaults or otherwise violates the lease.[55]

When the landowner leases land and space for a restaurant, the landlord and the lending institution are especially concerned with a prospective tenant's credit standing, since good standing is their basic assurance that the rent will be paid.

Because the tenant selected is critical to the lender, as well as the landlord, the lease usually will not permit any assignment or sublease without the landlord's consent. The situation is different with a *ground lease* where the landlord rents vacant land and the tenant agrees to erect a building. Then the landlord looks to the building for security and to the tenant to protect the investment by timely rent payments and by tenant financing for construction of the building. This requires the landlord to permit the tenant to mortgage the leasehold interest, and the lease should so provide. Finally, the lease should say that special notice be given to the lender of a tenant's default so that the lender can cure the default and prevent cancellation of the mortgage.

The right of unlimited assignment of leases is basically intended to protect the landowner and the lender. However, it is also of importance to tenants. Why? Because a tenant's ability to obtain institutional financing for a restaurant may depend on whether he or she can assign a lease to a lender. Assignment gives those tenants the right to transfer the lease to another operator in the event of illness or disability.

Real Estate Agents

It is customary for the sellers and buyers of restaurant property to use the services of a real estate broker or agent, although the law does not require it.

Many states require that a real estate broker's agreement be in writing to be enforceable.[56] Such a contract is called a *listing contract,* and usually permits the broker to recover a commission or a percentage of the selling price by producing a buyer who is ready, willing, and able to purchase real property on the terms and conditions agreed to with the seller. The refusal of the seller to complete the sale, or the destruction of the premises prior to the sale, will not deprive the broker of his or her commission, unless the listing contract provides otherwise.[57] In a few states this basic rule of agency law has been modified by the courts to require that the sale be concluded and title transferred from the seller to the buyer before the broker's commission must be paid. The only exception is where the failure to conclude the sale is caused by the seller.[58]

Buyers of property must be sure that the seller is either the actual owner or an authorized party for the owner. Otherwise the buyer may not have any legal rights in the property and may have to surrender it to the real owner.

In any purchase of real property, you will very likely deal with a seller through a real estate or sales agent, the latter often used in negotiating restaurant franchises. To avoid grief, you must thoroughly understand the *authority* of the agent to negotiate, *who* is responsible for the agent's commission or fee, *when* the agent's commission becomes due and payable, and *when* and *under what circumstances* you may hold the seller liable for the agent's false statements or other wrongdoing.

What legal responsibilities do you have to your real estate agent once a valid contract is drawn up? You must not do anything to prevent the agent from performing the objectives of the contract. You may not terminate the agency contract without just cause.[59] Both the seller and the agent must perform the contract in good faith. As a seller you are liable for any substantial damages you cause which result in wrongful interference in or termination of the contract.[60]

Your agent owes you a *fiduciary duty* (a duty of trust) not to create any conflict of interest in representing you by disclosing any potential conflict to you beforehand and receiving your consent to continue.[61] This duty is called a duty of absolute loyalty. The violation of this duty is illustrated by an agent who, instead of representing your interests in selling property, tries to make a secret profit for his or her own benefit. Another example is that of an agent who represents *both* a buyer *and* seller in a real estate sale without informing either of the parties of this dual agency. This conduct is so frowned upon by the law that the agent must return any sales commission obtained from either the buyer or seller, even though the agreement may have resulted in an otherwise proper and profitable deal.[62]

The following case is not a common occurrence, but is an extreme example of agent dishonesty.

Henderson v. Hassur
Supreme Court of Kansas
594 P.2d 650 (1979)

Facts. Henderson, a real estate developer, was hired by Hassur to locate possible sites for Pizza Hut restaurants in Mexico. Hassur told Henderson that he owned the Mexican franchises. Along with his partner Perry, Henderson agreed to locate both the sites and landlords for the Mexican properties. Hassur agreed to pay Henderson and Perry $4000 per site location plus 1 percent of the gross revenue derived from each location for the lease period.

While in Mexico, Henderson met a building contractor named Vorhauer, who worked with Henderson in buying one site, required by Mexican law to lease other sites, for Hassur. The cost to Henderson and Vorhauer of that site, called the Satellite City site, was $56,000 but it was turned over to Hassur for $88,000. The profit of $32,000 was kept by Henderson and Vorhauer, who split the amount 50–50 and drew up an agreement to split future profits from the Hassur deal. This profit was not disclosed to Hassur.

Ultimately Henderson was additionally paid $16,000 by Hassur for locating four Pizza Hut sites, including the Satellite City site.

Later Henderson sued to recover the 1 percent of the gross revenues for each site he secured, for which Hassur never paid him. Hassur counterclaimed for breach or violation of the fiduciary duty owed him by Henderson. The trial court found for Hassur on his counterclaim, and entered a judgment in his favor for actual damages of $48,000 and punitive damages of $215,000, based on a court verdict for actual damages and a jury verdict for punitive damages. The judgments entered by the trial court for actual and punitive damages were upheld.

Reasoning. The Supreme Court pointed to the facts of the case and current law in upholding the lower court's finding that Henderson had breached his duty. The court then went on to examine the damages paid. The amount in dispute was the actual damages. In applying the damage award, the trial court had not only awarded to Hassur the profit amount which Henderson and Vorhauser had pocketed, but the entire commission paid for the sites. In upholding this award, the court said:

> An unfaithful servant forfeits the compensation he would otherwise have earned but for his unfaithfulness. This court considered this legal principle in *Bessman v. Bessman,* 214 Kan. 510, 520

P. 2d 1210 (1974), where it is held: "As a general rule an agent who realizes a secret profit through his dealings on behalf of his principal not only must disgorge the profit but also forfeits the compensation he would otherwise have earned."

The Supreme Court agreed with the trial court that the second agreement to share profits permeated the entire transaction, whether profits were actually shared or not.

Conclusion. This Kansas Supreme Court decision is a clear warning of how strictly the common law views the duty of loyalty and good faith required of a real estate agent or broker to a client. Actual damages may be recovered from an agent or broker for any secret profit the broker obtained at the expense of the client. This was a prime example of breach of contract by a real estate agent.

Business Tax Incentives for Property

The Economic Recovery Tax Act of 1981, among other things, provides *recovery deductions* replacing previous depreciation deductions. Under this Accelerated Cost Recovery System (ACRS), purchases of buildings may be written off in 15 years; purchases of machinery and heavy equipment may be written off in 5 years; and purchases of automobiles, light-duty trucks, machinery, and equipment used for research and development may be written off in 3 years.

In addition, leasing transactions qualify for ACRS treatment, meaning that lessees who rent buildings and equipment can shift these benefits to their lessors, should these landlords or building and equipment owners be in a better position to use them. This may be used to obtain a lower rent or better lease terms from a landlord.

Investment tax credits for building rehabilitation and renovation have been liberalized. The tax credit for structures at least 30 years old is 15 percent; the credit for structures at least 40 years old is 20 percent; and the credit for certified historic structures is 25 percent.

BULK PURCHASE OF BUSINESS ASSETS

At some point you may wish to acquire the major portion of the assets of another business to add on to your own operation or to establish a new business in another location. A *bulk transfer* is any large transfer of a major part of the material, supplies, merchandise, or inventory not made in the ordinary course of the transferor's business, such as food and beverages sold to patrons. For example, a bulk transfer would consist of the food and beverage inventory, tables, chairs, china, silverware, and other items you agree to buy from a restaurant that is closing. Article 6 of the Uniform Commercial Code is the law for this type of transaction.

You must be cautious. The seller of the business may have numerous creditors whose claims have not been paid. An honest seller would pay off these obligations with the proceeds of the sale. But sometimes a dishonest debtor would take the purchase money and depart, leaving the creditors empty-handed, and leaving the buyer with the creditors. To prevent this abuse of creditors, Article 6 of the UCC, entitled Bulk Transfers, was enacted.

Under the Uniform Commercial Code, a potential buyer of a *business* must exercise care to see to it that the seller provides a list of existing creditors, that both parties prepare a list of property to be sold, and that the purchaser notify the seller's creditors of the proposed sale of all or a majority of the assets no later than 10 days before the physical transfer of the assets or the payment for such assets, whichever occurs first.

Failure to comply with the UCC on bulk transfers means that the assets purchased may be subject to the claims of the seller's creditors. In short, the buyer purchases the seller's *obligations* as well as the assets. Only third parties who buy the assets without receiving any notice of existing creditor claims take the assets free and clear. This requirement is critically important to you if you purchase a business. You do not wish to assume someone else's obligations in the process.

Bulk transfers involve major *physical* assets that are included as part of the sale of a business. They do not involve transfers of intangible items, such as health and liquor licenses. You must apply for those on your own.

ZONING LAWS REGULATING LAND USE

Once you buy or lease property for a restaurant, the law will continue to affect your business. No owner or user of real property has such absolute control as to keep the government from regulating some aspect of the ownership—least of all businesses—and of those, least of all foodservice businesses.

Unless you immediately adjoin or lease property from the federal government, most land-use regulations come from state and local authorities. Usually the only time you will encounter problems with the federal government is if you own land in which Uncle Sam is interested. Then you may find yourself in a heated battle over just compensation for your property.

There are two methods of regulating land use. One is by *private controls*, meaning that a seller of land has the right to sell on terms satisfactory to the seller, including the right to restrict the use of the land as the seller sees fit. The other method is by *public controls* to protect the public interest. This form of control is exercised for the most part by state and local governments.[63]

Zoning

Land-use regulation by public control usually takes the form of *zoning*. Zoning means allocating land into areas reserved for a specific purpose. Industrial, commercial, and residential uses are the most common purposes.

As a foodservice operator you will be dealing with *commercial zoning,* or *mixed commercial and residential zoning*. Zoning involves the exercise of a state's or community's police power. This requires that a reasonable balance be struck between private ownership and public benefit. In a dispute the courts will examine the character of the community, and the strain of your proposed use on utilities, transportation, and public services, as well as traffic congestion, off-street parking, noise, and other factors.[64] When the regulatory agency seeks to limit or prohibit a particular use, such as pornographic bookstores, and that prohibition is challenged, the general test is whether the prohibited use bears a reasonable relation to public health, safety, and welfare.[65]

State and local land-use regulations are subject to review by the courts as a check against possible violations of state and federal constitutional protections. A state may not regulate land use arbitrarily or unreasonably, since this conduct would be a denial of due process under the Fourteenth Amendment of the United States Constitution.[66] Likewise, local or urban land-use regulations may not violate similar protective provisions in state constitutions. A state or locality may not discriminate against classes or individuals in buying or leasing land on the basis of race, religion, or nationality.[67] Discrimination on other grounds, such as prohibiting entry of low-income groups, may be justified if there is a rational or reasonable basis for doing so.[68] This means that if the zoning regulation is not intended to keep out minorities, it will not violate constitutional requirements.

Usually zoning land regulation takes two forms. One form is by eminent domain, taking private property for a governmental purpose, such as for public school, highway, or hospital construction.[69] Regulation which totally deprives the landowner of any beneficial use of his or her property is a *confiscation* of property, meaning a taking for public use for which the landowner must be paid the fair market value of the land.[70] The other form is by the use of *police power;*[71] for example, forbidding a food and liquor operation in a family residential zone. The preferred method is by police power, because eminent domain requires the payment of reasonable compensation to the private landowner, whereas the exercise of police power does not.[72]

Nonconforming Use

If the area around your business becomes residential and is zoned for that purpose, you can usually apply for your land to be designated for *nonconforming use*. This will allow you to continue operating your restaurant in the area until you sell the property, at which time its use must comply with current zoning requirements.[73] Thus a cafeteria might be operated in a residential area for a reasonable time to give the owner/operator a chance to wind up the business without undue hardship.

Accessory Use

Accessory use occurs when another type of business is incidental to the main type of business for which an area is zoned. Accessory use is usually upheld if it is *commonly* incidental to the main business. For example, if you were to build a bowling alley under existing zoning regulations, you would probably be able to provide refreshment facilities.[74]

Variance

What if you wish to change the use of your land? Suppose you wish to convert some existing property, a small office building, into a restaurant. Your present-use terms do not include a foodservice operation. Are you "locked in" without any alternative except to sell and build a restaurant in another area? No. A *variance* issued by the city will authorize you to convert your property. The following tests are used by the courts to determine whether you are legally entitled to a variance, a special use authorized on an individual basis:

1. The landowner must prove it would be impossible to obtain a reasonable return on the land under the existing regulation.
2. The negative effect on the use must be peculiar to the individual landowner, and not also apply to others in the area.
3. The approval of the variance must not cause the remaining area to change substantially. This is the most important consideration.[75]

Landmark Designation

Zoning regulations protecting *historic areas* and *landmarks* have been generally approved as well within the concept of public welfare or benefit. This court-developed doctrine is especially favored where the economy of the area depends on tourism attracted by the area's historical qualities.[76] This means that if you and other restaurant operators in the area show a positive correlation between the historic area and your tourism business, the restaurants may be designated for *preservation zoning*. However, an individual landmark not located within a historic district may not be "frozen" in the midst of high-density economic development.[77]

A number of restaurants and hotels throughout the United States have been designated landmarks and zoned accordingly.

Landmark status may result in problems. Usually you may not make any structural changes in the premises without obtaining the prior approval of the local landmark preservation commission. Approved changes must meet strict aesthetic and historical requirements as to materials and designs used. Compliance with these requirements may be expensive as well as time-consuming. If you wish to purchase a landmark building, you should understand what is involved *before, not after,* you purchase.

You can appeal a landmark designation, if you can prove it would bring hardship to you and your business. The fact that landmark status might diminish the cash value of the property and that a "higher" or "more beneficial use" of the property might exist has been held insufficient proof of hardship, however.[78]

Sometimes a landowner will seek a change in the zoning law to apply only to a single property, to increase its value. Such zoning, called *spot zoning,* is illegal when the change in zoning does not benefit the public and injures the surrounding zoning.[79] For example, a firehouse in a residential area and a shopping center in a residential area at a main traffic artery may be permitted, since they are justified by the benefit to the surrounding area.[80] A tavern, however, may not fall into this category.

Incentive Zoning

Incentive zoning is a relatively new concept of particular importance to commercial land users. In this type of zoning, a city or village will provide additional floor space to a high-density commercial developer to induce the landowner to allocate certain space for "desirable" uses. This innovative land-use plan has the advantage of stimulating voluntary inclusion of public improvements by using a financial incentive, rather than by compelled use. *Compelled* use means that the developer or landowner may be discouraged from investing, since it may be unprofitable to include the required improvements. Compelled use may be adverse to the city because a new use could mean a corresponding loss of tax revenue. As a result, some cities now see incentive zoning as the preferred method of regulating land use, with the traditional compelled land-use regulation held out as a last resort.[81]

Problems

In some cases private landowner controls may conflict with public ones. Suppose you wish to purchase a lot on which to build a foodservice operation in a shopping center. At the time the lease or sales contract is prepared, the seller restricts the use of the premises to a restaurant, and the location is zoned for this form of use. Later the area is zoned for professional office use. You decide to subdivide your premises and lease a portion for use as a dental or law office. Can you do so? Probably. More recent cases allow such use, on the theory that where a change in the character of the neighborhood is involved, the zoning ordinance overrides the former owner's sale restrictions. Normally, however, the courts take a hands-off attitude, allowing the lease or sale restrictions to be enforced notwithstanding the rezoning of the area.[82]

The following examples illustrate typical problems that may confront you in dealing with zoning boards in your local communities. They are provided to give you insight into court controversies affecting foodservice operators throughout the United States.

You wish to build two restaurants in a shopping center. The zoning board rejects your application on the grounds that a moratorium exists on new restaurant construction. You sue to test the legality of the board's decision. The board then argues that your intention to build two restaurants on one lot violates the one-building/one-lot ordinance. In court you argue that the ambiguous ordinance does not apply to shopping centers. The trial court agrees with you. On the board's appeal, the reviewing court upholds the trial court's decision, saying that the court was right in accepting your argument that the ordinance is ambiguous, and having created the ambiguity, the zoning board must accept the consequences.[83] You can build your restaurants.

You own a delicatessen exempt from city off-street parking requirements for establishments in that zone. You decide to convert the premises to a restaurant and cocktail lounge and apply for a variance to permit increased seating capacity *without* providing off-street parking facilities. The planning commission denies your application. You sue to reverse the board decision. Are you entitled to the variance? No. The variance you sought is a *use variance,* and genuine hardship must be demonstrated before the courts can overturn the board's decision. No real hardship on your part is shown to exist.[84]

Suppose you own and operate a restaurant under a nonconforming use status. You apply to the zoning board for permission to convert a lot near your premises into a parking area. You submit proof that the highest and best use of the land would be for parking. Residential owners across the street object that such a change would reduce their property values. Permission is denied by the board. You seek to overturn the decision in court. Will you succeed? No. The adverse impact on residential properties outweighs the economic gain to you in this situation.[85]

Suppose that under existing ordinances construction of a high-rise residential hotel is permitted. No specific provision is made in the ordinance for the installation of a full-service restaurant, or of food and beverage vending machines. Are such uses authorized? Yes. The courts uniformly treat these functions as *accessory uses* which are incidental to, even though different from, the main or permitted use.[86]

You are the owner of a small restaurant in an up-state New York community. From reliable sources you learn that a large shopping mall is to be constructed on land near your restaurant. After a year's notice, you do not bring legal action to stop construction of the mall until three months after the commencement of construction. You go to court to stop the construction of the mall, arguing that the large size of the mall would have an adverse impact on the downtown area, causing economic blight and deterioration of that section in which your restaurant is located. Will the court grant your request?

No. You waited too long to seek court review of the construction of the mall. Although the court had the power to stop construction, doing so was not justified by the facts.[87]

Building and Safety Codes

Most states and cities have adopted building codes that contain detailed requirements on structural safety, fire prevention, the size and number of rooms, exits, lights, heating, ventilation and refrigeration, and sanitary equipment.[88] These include general requirements that apply to all commercial buildings. In addition, you as a foodservice owner or operator must comply with specific health and sanitary rules regarding food handling, equipment, and cooking temperatures, to mention only a few. These rules extend the scope of regulation to operation of the business itself, not merely to the structure in which you operate.

Because you deal with members of the public by inviting them to use your restaurant, and there is a greater likelihood of harm to more than one person as a result of a failure to comply with local building requirements, your risk of liability may be greater.

When it comes to safety codes, you don't have much room for compromise in most areas. Nor would you want to. The safety of yourself, your patrons, and your employees should outweigh the cost and inconvenience of complying with local codes. A failure to do so not only can cost you your business as a result of a fire or other accident, but can leave you open to lawsuits if it is proved that your negligence was the cause of the incident.

As a manager you are just as responsible for adherence to safety codes as the owner, if you are on the premises and acting in that capacity.

Whether you are opening a new restaurant, purchasing an existing one, or running the business for an absent owner, one of your first tasks should be to study the local building regulations for businesses. In addition, you may want to institute further safety improvements or procedures. While you will still want to insure the premises, the best insurance is *prevention*.

When new construction of your premises, major repairs, or alterations to an existing building take place, most building regulations require the building to be inspected by the local inspector. Until the inspection is complete and the inspector is satisfied, you may not occupy or use the building. Satisfaction usually means the issuance of a *certificate of occupancy*. If you are going to buy or lease an existing building, don't close the sale or lease until you have that certificate. Without the certificate or other form of approval, you will not be allowed to operate.[89]

Suppose that at the time you purchased or leased your foodservice premises, the building code requirements were relatively light in terms of cost and time allowed for compliance. Later the state or local authorities enacted a much tougher code, which may make it unprofitable for you to stay in business. Are you protected from the new code rules because they were not in existence when you bought or leased your restaurant premises? The answer is generally no, *unless the new code contains a "grandfather clause"* permitting existing businesses to operate under the previous rules.[90] Even in cases where the state or local (city) code contains such a clause, *any* alterations or substantial repairs made usually require the building owner to comply with new code requirements, or to "bring the building up to new code standards." When building codes do not include a grandfather clause, you are compelled to comply with new code rules as a condition of staying in business, as long as the rules are reasonable.

When you lease a building for your restaurant, you must insert a clause in the lease protecting you in case the owner fails or refuses to bring the building in which you operate up to new code standards. Additionally, your landlord (owner) may try to shift this burden onto you under a lease. This means that if the owner must comply, he or she may try to obtain reimbursement from you for the costs of compliance.

How can you find out whether the owner or operator of an existing building is in violation of local codes before you buy? Violations are recorded by the department involved in the county or city clerk's office. Those records must be searched (checked) before you buy or lease the building, since most laws require the seller or landlord to eliminate the violation before a sale. This requirement is extremely important to you. It means that the cost of eliminating the violation is placed on the seller, not on you. *However,* once you take title to a building with existing violations on record, you become responsible for the costs of removing them. Since *you* may not wish to delay closing the deal, you may wish to retain a portion of the purchase price as security until the seller removes the violation.[91]

Code requirements are checked periodically by the department (fire, health, electricity) involved. If any violations are found, the owner or operator—the person or party occupying the premises—must bring the premises into compliance by making the changes or repairs required. Failure to do so could result in a fine if the violation is minor,

or loss of the certificate of occupancy if it is serious. Failure to comply is also a crime in most states and localities, and a serious, intentional violation can mean a jail sentence.[92]

When a building is structurally unsafe, the state or city may demolish it without being required to compensate the owner. This is so because the owner created a public nuisance, justifying the use of the police power to remove a danger to the public.[93] In some states the appropriate regulatory body may file a *lien* or legal claim on the remaining land to reimburse itself for the costs of demolishing the building. This *demolition lien* often must be paid before other claims against the owner, including mortgages.[94]

Code violations can give rise to lawsuits by patrons or customers injured by a landlord's failure or refusal to comply. Originally such claims were only upheld for violations of state codes, but the present trend is to extend liability to city codes where the city is given *home rule* powers to regulate building construction and maintenance.[95] (Home rule is a grant by the state to certain cities to enact their own legislation over certain matters. When the city enacts its own code, it may be tougher than the state code.)

You are responsible for structural code violations if you are the owner of a business. As a tenant you are typically not liable for structural code violations, unless you voluntarily assume such liability by agreeing to keep the building in repair under the lease with your landlord.[96]

PROPERTY MANAGEMENT

Property rights are best enforced in writing. Whatever you buy—food items, silverware, or real estate—should be bought on the basis of a written agreement. The agreement need be no more than a purchase order or it may be as complex as a real estate contract. Not every property deal must be in writing. But if the law is to enforce your rights, it is easier when you have those rights in some tangible form that can be reviewed. Otherwise it is your good word against your opponent's in a dispute, and the court can go either way.

Before you negotiate any property deal, especially in real estate, you must know what is critical to you. If you're leasing, is it more important to you to have the right to remove trade fixtures or to have a lower rent? If you buy, you will want to make sure the previous owner takes his or her creditors instead of leaving them for you to settle with. None of this is automatic and must be negotiated.

Regulatory bodies of all kinds can affect your decision to buy, sell, or lease real estate. You must carefully review local zoning, building, and fire regulations to be sure that the kind of building you seek to build or lease will permit a foodservice business. Also, you may need a license or permit to conduct business, and the cost of the license should be included in your financial planning.

You must familiarize yourself with the business tax incentives you may receive under the current Internal Revenue Code for buyers of real and personal property. Increased and accelerated depreciation allowances can make it more financially attractive to buy real estate, inventory, equipment, and fixtures. These allowances reduce your taxable income, thereby providing additional working capital to finance additions and improvements to your business. By doing so you are afforded the opportunity to generate higher revenues, and greater profits.

SUMMARY

Property is defined as ownership of and legally protected rights in anything of recognized value, and is safeguarded by federal and state laws.

Property includes *real property,* such as land and buildings or fixtures attached to real property, and personal property. Property may be tangible, having physical substance, or intangible, having no physical substance.

Property may be acquired through possession, purchase, gift, accession, inheritance, confusion, or by finding it.

Protection of ownership rights depends on the type of property and the rights desired. Acquiring trademarks, service marks, patents, or copyrights on formulas, fixtures, or printed material will protect the substance of the property.

To obtain complete rights in property, it must be obtained from the real owner or an authorized agent of the owner. Otherwise the buyer may not have any legal rights over the property.

There are various ways to finance property. Usually creditors will want to have a security interest in the property or collateral to assure that if the loan is not paid or the borrower goes bankrupt, their claims are legally sound.

Land ownership is classified according to type, duration, and the amount of interest held.

Leasing property involves no ownership rights but the right to possess property for a specific period of time. Various types of tenancies, along with varying time periods, are negotiated between the landlord and tenant. Both have rights and responsibilities according to the law.

Transfer of ownership to real estate must be in writing in many states, and even if it is not required, it is advisable to prevent disputes. A deed or title is one written form that passes between the buyer and the seller. There are three types of deeds: general warranty, special warranty, and quitclaim.

The contract of sale is the other real estate document that is necessary and should be in writing. It is the negotiable part of any real estate transaction.

Whether to purchase or lease property is a business decision that must be considered with factors such as potential expansion, zoning, interest rates, and whether the restaurant business itself is new or well established.

There are several ways to finance the purchase of real estate. Most often the lender will want the option to foreclose or take over the property if the debtor defaults. In some circumstances, a tenant may mortgage a leasehold interest to obtain a loan.

Sale and leaseback is another way of obtaining land. However, the would-be tenant must look carefully at the advantages and disadvantages before entering into this arrangement.

For those seeking a business site, real estate agents may be used to search for and handle real estate negotiations. Buyer, seller, and agent each has various rights and responsibilities.

There are various business tax incentives to buying and using property. The Economic Recovery Tax Act of 1981 provides for recovery deductions for purchases of building and leasing equipment.

Operators may want to purchase business assets in bulk. Such buyers must ensure that any seller creditors do not become the buyer's creditors.

Zoning laws are local laws used to regulate land use. Private controls, such as sales contracts between sellers and buyers, also may control land use. Mostly, zoning is used as a public control of land use by either local, state, or federal governments. Zoning regulation may include eminent domain or use of police power.

In case of new zoning regulations, a foodservice operator may be able to apply for nonconforming-use designation or for variance. If a use is incidental to the designated use, then that use may be legal as an accessory use.

Landmark designation is also called preservation zoning, and has advantages and disadvantages for foodservice operators. Landowners can appeal this type of zoning before the building is designated.

Incentive zoning is a way of regulating land use by making it attractive to landowners to improve buildings and public areas.

Building codes are used to regulate foodservice operations. These local laws may require a certain number of fire exits, regulate the size and capacity of dining rooms, and mandate other safety features.

QUESTIONS

1. What is the difference between real and personal property? Give an example of each.
2. What is the duty of landlords to patrons of the tenant?
3. Detail a policy, consistent with the law, for yourself and your employees regarding lost property.
4. You have rented a building for your restaurant business for five years and are moving out. Among the items that you've used or have installed are tables, chairs, a built-in bar, paintings, and a heavy crystal chandelier built into the wall. What can you take, and what must you leave? Why?
5. Name some of the advantages and disadvantages of landmark designation.

NOTES

1. See *Sears, Roebuck and Co. v. Seven Palms Motor Inn,* 530 S.W.2d 695 (Mo. 1975); *Roberts v. Yancy,* 165 S.E.2d 399 (Va. 1969) (restaurant lease dispute over what items tenant could remove at end of lease term).

2. Fifth Amendment to the United States Constitution.

3. *Id.*

4. N.Y. Penal Law sec. 165.15 (McKinney Supp. 1978), sec. 165.17 (McKinney 1969), is a representative statute.

5. See *Hebrew Univ. Assn. v. Nye,* 26 Conn. Supp. 342, 223 A.2d 397 (1966).

6. Smith, Roberson, Menn, and Roberts, *Business Law,* Fifth Edition (1982), Chapter 44, p. 901, *Paset v. Old Orchard Bank and Trust Co.,* 62 Ill. App. 3d 534, 378 N.E.2d 1264 (1978) (safety deposit examining booth).

7. Sherry, *The Laws of Innkeepers* (rev. ed. 1981), Chapter 16, see 16:22. *Jackson v. Steinberg,* 186 Or. 129, 200 P.2d 376 (1948), *reh'g denied* 186 Or. 140, 205 P.2d 562 (1949) (hotel employee).

8. Smith, Roberson, *et al., supra* note 6.

9. Sherry, *supra* note 7, see 16:23. *Erickson v. Sinkin,* 223 Minn. 232, 26 N.W.2d 172 (1974), citing Minn. Stat. Ann. 622.11 (1945) (hotel guest room).

10. Sherry, *supra* note 7.

11. *Id.*

12. Aigler, *Rights of Finders,* 21 Mich. L. Rev. 664, 681 (1923) (footnote), cited with approval in *Jackson v. Steinberg, supra* note 7.

13. 15 U.S.C. secs. 1050–1127 (1946).

14. *Steak and Brew Inc. v. Beef and Brew Restaurant, Inc.,* 370 F. Supp. 1030 (N.D. Ill. 1974); *Howard Johnson Co. v. Henry Johnson's Restaurant,* Civ. Case No. 1258 (D.N.C. 1964). Also see *Tisch Hotels, Inc. v. Americana Inn, Inc.,* 350 F.2d 609 (7th Cir. 1965); *Holiday Inns, Inc. v. Holiday Inn,* 364 F. Supp. 775 (D.S.C. 1973).

15. Lusk, Hewitt, Donnell, Barnes, *Business Law and the Regulatory Environment,* Fifth Edition (1982), at 990.

16. Lusk *et al., supra* note 15, at 987–88.

17. *Iowa State University v. American Broadcasting System,* 621 F.2d 57 (7th Cir. 1980).

18. The holding of the Supreme Court in *Twentieth Century Music Corporation v. Aiken,* 422 U.S. 151 (1975), exempting small foodservice operators from liability for such royalty payments has been rendered uncertain by passage of the 1976 Copyright Act (17 U.S.C. sec. 101 *et seq.*). Therefore, we must await further review of the problem by the High Court.

19. U.C.C. sec. 2–403.

20. *American Restaurant Supply Co. v. Wilson,* 25 U.C.C. Rep. 1159 (Fla. App. 1979).

21. Lusk *et al., supra* note 15, at 610.

22. *Id.*

23. Lusk *et al., supra* note 15, at 614–16.

24. *Id.*

25. Lusk *et al., supra* note 15, at 641.

26. *Tortwick v. Lisle,* 268 Minn. 197, 128 N.W.2d 330 (1964).

27. Lusk *et al., supra* note 15, at 649.

28. Kratovil and Werner, *Real Estate Law,* Seventh Edition (1979), secs. 1054–55.

29. Kratovil and Werner, *supra* note 28, at sec. 1091.

30. *T. Weaver v. American Oil Co.,* 276 N.E.2d 144 (Ind. 1976).

31. See *Shell Oil Co. v. Marinello,* 307 A.2d 598 (N.J. 1973).

32. The landlord may insert a clause to the contrary, and then a court must decide whether such a clause is fair. If the clause is upheld, it is binding on the tenant. You must read a proposed lease carefully and negotiate to have such a clause removed. See Kratovil and Werner, *supra* note 28, at sec. 1085.

33. *Id.* at sec. 1084.

34. *Id.* at sec. 1088.

35. Kratovil and Werner, *supra* note 28, at secs. 1075–76, 1083.

36. *Id.* Chapter 3, secs. 29–36, 1083.

37. Kratovil and Werner, *supra* note 28, at sec. 1003 reviews the authorities pro and con.

38. See *Tortwick v. Lisle, supra* note 26.

39. Kratovil and Werner, *supra* note 28, at sec. 1081. Also see *Horn & Hardhart Co. v. Junior Building, Inc.,* 40 N.Y.2d 927, 358 N.E.2d 514 (1976).

40. *Peoples Trust Co. v. Schultz Novelty and Sporting Goods Co., Inc.,* 244 N.Y. 14, 154 N.E. 649; *Davis v. Wickline,* 135 S.E.2d 812 (Va. 1964).

41. See Bergfield, *Principles of Real Estate Law* (1979), at pp. 371–72. Sherry, *The Laws of Innkeepers,* (rev. ed. 1981), sec. 12:19 (New York law).

42. Lusk *et al., supra* note 15, at 649.

43. See *Sommer v. Kreidel,* 378 A.2d 767 (N.J. 1977); *Markoe v. Naiditch and Sons,* 225 N.W.2d 289 (Minn. 1975).

44. Lusk *et al., supra* note 15, at pp. 625–30.

45. See *Gene Hancock Construction Co. v. Kempton & Sneliger Dairy,* 510 P.2d 752 (Ariz. App. 1973). A contract to give a mortgage for the sale of real estate must also be in writing. *Fremming Construction Co. v. Security Savings & Loan,* 566 P.2d 315 (Ariz. App. 1977).

46. See *Old Town Development Co. v. Langford,* 349 N.E.2d 744 (Ind. App. 1976); *Pines v. Perssion,* 111 N.W.2d 409 (Wis. 1961).

47. *Service Oil Co., Inc. v. White,* 542 P.2d 652 (Kan. 1976); *Van Ness Indust., Inc. v. Claremont Paint Co.,* 324 A.2d 102 (N.J. 1976); *Yuan Kane, Inc. v. Wm. Levy,* 26 Ill. App. 3d 889, 326 N.E.2d 51 (1975).

48. *United States v. Causby,* 328 U.S. 256 (1946).

49. Lusk *et al., supra* note 15, at pp. 918–21.

50. *Id.* at p. 919.

51. Kratovil and Werner, *supra* note 28, at sec. 633 *et seq.*

52. See *FNMA v. Ricks,* 372 N.Y.S.2d 485 (N.Y. 1975).

53. See *Morris v. Weigle,* 383 N.E.2d 341 (Ind. 1978).

54. Kratovil and Werner, *supra* note 28, at sec. 1090.

55. *Id.* sec. 572.

56. See 9 A.L.R. 2d 747 for review of legal authorities.

57. *Bonanza Real Estate, Inc. v. Crouch,* 517 P.2d 1371 (Wash. 1974); *Russell v. Ramm,* 200 Cal. 348, 254 P. 532 (1927); *Hecht v. Mellor,* 23 N.Y.2d 301, 244 N.E.2d 77 (1968); and also 74 A.L.R. 2d 437 for review of legal authorities.

58. *Ellesworth Dobbs Inc. v. Johnson,* 50 N.J. 528, 236 A.2d 843 (1967), cited and followed in *Tristram's Landing Inc. v. Wait,* 327 N.E.2d 727 (Mass. 1975), and in *Shumaker v. Lear,* 345 A.2d 249 (Pa. 1975).

59. See generally *Pailet v. Guillory,* 315 So. 2d 893 (La. App. 1975) (authority of husband of owner of real estate under lease to cancel lease); *Gunn v. Schaeffer,* 567 S.W.2d 30 (Ct. Civ. App. Tex. 1978) (authority of apartment house manager to borrow money from tenants).

60. *Hilgendorf v. Hague,* 293 N.W.2d 272 (Iowa 1980).

61. *Id.* Also see *Montgomery Ward Inc. v. Tackett,* 323 N.E.2d 242 (Ind. App. 1975) (franchise sales agency).

62. *Henderson v. Hassur,* 594 P.2d 650 (Kan. 1979) (Pizza Hut restaurant site location agency); *Taborsky v. Matthews,* 121 So. 2d 61 (Fla. App. 1960); *Sierra Pac. Industries v. Carter,* 104 Cal. App. 3d 579, 163 Cal. Rptr. 764 (1980).

63. Clarkson, Miller, Blaire, *West's Business Law* (1980), Chapter 53, Zoning, pp. 878–80.

64. Kratovil and Werner, *supra* note 28, at sec. 689, pp. 305–7.

65. See *Young v. American Mini-Theaters,* 96 S. Ct. 2440 (1976), where a municipal ordinance confining pornographic movies, bookstores, and nude-dancing establishments to a single "combat zone" was upheld.

66. *United States v. 564.54 Acres of Land,* 506 F.2d 796 (3d Cir. 1974).

67. *Southern Burlington County NAACP v. Township of Mount Laurel,* 336 A.2d 713 (N.J. 1975) (racial discrimination); *Dailey v. City of Lawton,* 296 F. Supp. 266 (W.D. Okla. 1969), aff'd, 425 F.2d 1037 (10th Cir. 1970) (same).

68. *Village of Euclid v. Ambler Realty Co.,* 272 U.S. 365 (1926); *Village of Belle Terre v. Boraas,* 416 U.S. 1 (1974).

69. Lusk *et al., supra* note 1, at Chapter 32, pp. 632–33.

70. However, when the zoning ordinance (law) is found to be totally unreasonable as applied to particular land, the courts will invalidate it as confiscatory (a taking of land without just compensation). *Fred F. French Inv. Co. v. City of N.Y.,* 30 N.Y.2d 587, 350 N.E.2d 381 (1976).

71. Police power in this context means the exercise of the appropriate government's power to regulate land use in the public interest. See Lusk *et al., supra* note 15, at pp. 631–32.

72. *Urban Renewal Agency v. Gospel Mission Church,* 4 Kan. App. 2d 101, 603 P.2d 209 (1979); also see note 68, *supra.*

73. But you may not substantially alter the structure, meaning a physical change or a conversion of the building into a new or substantially different structure. Such a change will jeopardize the nonconforming use. *Selligman v. Van Allmen Bros., Inc.,* 297 Ky. 121, 179 S.W.2d 207 (1944). An abandonment of such a use also causes the nonconforming use to be lost. *Beyer v. Mayor of Baltimore,* 182 Md. 444, 34 A.2d 765 (1943).

74. See *Newark v. Daly,* 85 N.J.S. 55, 205 A.2d 459 (1964).

75. Kratovil and Werner, *supra* note 28, at sec. 716, pp. 321–23.

76. See Symposium of Historic Preservation, 36 Law and Contemp. Prob. 309–444 (1971); *Rebman v. City of Springfield,* 111 Ill. App. 2d 430, 250 N.E.2d 282 (1969); see also 63 Col. L. Rev. 708, 720.

77. An exception to this general rule has been made in New York, *Lutheran Church in America v. City of New York,* 34 N.Y.2d 121, 304 N.W.2d 371 (1974); and *Penn Central Transp. Co. v. City of New York,* 438 U.S. 104, 98 S. Ct. 2646 (1978), *reh'g denied* 439 U.S. 883, 99 S. Ct. 226.

78. *900 G Street Assocs. v. Dep't of Hous. and Community Dev.,* 430 A.2d 1387 (D.C. App. 1981).

79. Kratovil and Werner, *supra* note 28, at sec. 710, pp. 318–19.

80. *Temmick v. Baltimore County,* 205 Md. 489, 109 A.2d 85 (1954) (shopping center); *Conner v. Herd,* 452 S.W.2d 272 (Mo. App. 1970) (firehouse).

81. Kratovil and Werner, *supra* note 28, at sec. 706, pp. 314–15.

82. *1.77 Acres of Land v. State,* 241 A.2d 513 (1968); *Blakely v. Gorin,* 313 N.E.2d 903 (Mass. 1974); *Chuba v. Glasgow,* 61 N.M. 302, 299 P.2d 774 (1956); *Schwarzchild v. Wolborne,* 186 Va. 1052, 45 S.E.2d 152 (1947).

83. *People ex rel. J.C.Penney v. Village of Oak Lawn,* 349 N.E.2d 637 (Ill. App. 1976).

84. *In re Off-Shore Restaurant Corp. v. Linden,* 331 N.Y.S.2d 397 (1972).

85. *Vasilopoulos v. Zoning Bd. of Appeals,* 340 N.E.2d 19 (Ill. App. 1975).

86. See *Newark v. Daly, supra* note 57.

87. *Dalsis v. Hills,* 424 F. Supp. 784 (W.D.N.Y. 1976).

88. Kratovil and Werner, *supra* note 28, at sec. 739, pp. 335–37.

89. *Id. supra* note 23, at Chapter 28, sec. 739, p. 336; Chapter 34, sec. 1008, pp. 437–38.

90. *City of Chicago v. National Management,* 22 Ill. App. 2d 445, 161 N.E.2d 358 (1959) (transient hotel automatic sprinkler ordinance upheld).

91. If you have paid the full purchase price before discovering the violations, you as buyer may sue the seller for damages. *Gutowski v. Crystal Homes Inc.,* 26 Ill. App. 2d 269, 167 N.E.2d 422 (1960); *Brunke v. Pharo,* 3 Wis. 2d 628, 89 N.W. 221 (1958); *Schiro v. W. E. Gould & Co.,* 18 Ill. 2d 538, 165 N.E.2d 286 (1960).

92. See note 28, *supra* at Chapter 34, sec. 1008.

93. *Spur Industries, Inc. v. Del E. Webb. Development Co.,* 494 P.2d 700 (Ariz. 1972). Where the nuisance is found to exist, the municipality may demolish the structure without paying compensation to the owner. *City of Honolulu v. Cavness,* 45 Hawaii 232, 364 P.2d 646 (1961).

94. Kratovil and Werner, *supra* note 28, at sec. 739, p. 336.

95. See *Whetzel v. Jess Fisher Management Co.,* 282 F.2d 943 (D.C. Cir. 1960).

96. Liability to your landlord to repair the building must be distinguished from liability to third persons, such as your patrons, who are injured as a result of structural defects. This topic is covered in Chapter 5.

11
Franchising

Objectives

The purpose of this chapter is to:
1. Define a franchise and explain its legal
   significance.
2. Examine the rights and duties of
   franchisors and franchisees to each other
   and to third parties.
3. Discuss the advantages and
   disadvantages of foodservice franchising.
4. Examine antitrust laws relevant to
   franchising.

Case in Point

Mr. and Mrs. Frick invested their life savings in a franchise business with Buffalo Bill. They drew up a written agreement to sell Buffalo Bill's barbecue burgers and other fast foods, using Buffalo Bill's promotional materials, architectural style, food ingredients, and methods of operation in return for paying a franchise fee. The duration of the agreement was to be five years. The franchisor, Buffalo Bill, reserved the right to terminate the agreement prior to the end of that period for specific reasons, such as the franchisees' failure to make fee payments on time or to live up to Buffalo Bill's operating standards. No provision existed giving Buffalo Bill the right to terminate at will, that is, at any time, without reason.

After two years of operation, Buffalo Bill suddenly terminated the franchise. When Mr. and Mrs. Frick refused to give up the franchise, Buffalo Bill sued to force its termination, claiming that as a franchisor he had an implied right *to terminate at will independent of any* express right *contained in the agreement. Who won this legal battle?*

The court found in favor of Mr. and Mrs. Frick. Without any proof of violation of the franchise, the court said that Mr. and Mrs. Frick could justifiably expect not to lose their substantial investments of time, effort, and money as a result of Buffalo Bill's arbitrary decision to end the franchise. The reasonable expectations of Mr. and Mrs. Frick, as shown by their total commitment to carrying out the franchise, and Buffalo Bill's legal duty to deal with the franchisees in good faith and in a reasonable manner, required a ruling in favor of Mr. and Mrs. Frick.

FRANCHISE DEFINED

Reduced to its essentials, a *franchise* is a license from the owner of a trademark or trade or service name which permits another to sell a product or service under that name or mark. In a franchise agreement the *franchisee,* the party to whom the license is granted, agrees to conduct a business or sell a product or service according to operating procedures specified by the *franchisor,* the party granting the license to sell. The franchisor agrees to assist the franchisee in the management of the product, service, or business through advertising, promotion, and advisory services.

In effect, the franchisor offers such intangibles as goodwill and reputation, as well as products and services, in exchange for franchisee investment and management. The investment is usually a fee, normally a standard amount plus a percentage of the franchisee's annual sales.

The foundation of any franchise is the trademark or trade name of the product or service licensed.[1] The *uniformity* of the product or service and the *control* of its quality motivate the buying public to patronize a franchised outlet rather than a nonfranchised outlet. The franchisor furnishes a publicly recognizable product or service. A businessperson with limited capital can take advantage of the quality the public identifies with the product.

This public recognition does not, however, guarantee the successful or profitable operation of the franchise. It *may do so,* depending on other factors such as location, adequate market, or existing or future competition.

A foodservice franchisee is an independent businessperson who furnishes money, time, and management skills and operates his or her own establishment. A franchisee is *not* an employee of the franchisor. The day-to-day operation of the business is the franchisee's sole responsibility. The success *or* failure of the franchised product or service rests on the business skill and ability of the franchisee. (The franchisee may be a sole proprietor, a partnership, or a corporate form of business organization, although one or two individuals will usually run the operation. Chapter 12 on forms of business organization covers these types.)

The chain operation is typical of the type of franchise in the foodservice industry. This type requires the franchisee, Mr. and Mrs. Frick in our case, to follow the franchisor's prescribed methods of operation. The franchisor keeps the right to check up on the franchise operation through frequent inspections to ensure compliance with company procedures. The agreement permits the termination of the franchise for *stated reasons;* requires the adoption of a specific architectural style, layout, and use of signs; and prescribes the purchase, preparation, and service of the food.

Advantages of Franchising

The basic advantage of the franchise is that for a relatively modest investment you may obtain the franchisor's trade names, trademarks, goodwill, customer acceptance, and national advertising. Other pluses may be the expertise of the franchisor in operational know-how, training, and bookkeeping methods.

For the franchisor the major advantage lies in the development of rapid market expansion and exposure with a minimum capital outlay.

Disadvantages of Franchising

Because most franchisors are large, well-financed, and well-managed concerns in comparison with most potential franchisees, economic leverage in negotiating the terms and conditions of the franchise rests with the franchisor.

Until recently the franchisor was at liberty to disclose very little about financing, method of operation, ownership, and other data to the franchisee. The franchisee did not have all the facts necessary to make an informed business judgment on how to compare franchisors or whether to accept a franchise at all. Inexperience and lack of equality in bargaining power could result in the franchisee's acceptance of unreasonable terms and conditions. Such problems eventually led to the 1979 FTC Franchise Disclosure Rule.[2]

In some cases the franchisee must deal exclusively with the franchisor to obtain raw materials and supplies, when the produce the franchisor markets is unique or cannot readily be duplicated by others.[3] This can be an advantage, because quality standards are usually consistent and prices are often the same for all franchise buyers. However, when prices are inconsistent with local markets, the franchisee is at a disadvantage compared with competitors, who are free to compare and accept bids from local suppliers.

The FTC Franchise Disclosure Rule

Inadequate information furnished by a franchisor to a potential franchisee can spell disaster to an inexperienced person who must finance and operate the franchise independently. The lack of a legal duty of franchisors in the past to disclose pertinent information created a climate that invited fraud and misrepresentation. Further, the common law required that franchisees who felt they had been taken prove franchisor fraud. It was extremely difficult to prove fraud, and the common law was inadequate to provide relief to franchisees. Meanwhile a franchisee might have suffered substantial losses in the initial operating phases of the business.

In 1979 the Federal Trade Commission (FTC), through its authority to regulate business practices found to be unfair or deceptive, issued a trade regulation designed to curb some of the problems encountered by franchisees and franchisors.[4]

Under the FTC regulation, a franchisor is required to give every prospective franchisee a *disclosure statement* 10 days before the franchisee signs a contract *or* makes any payment for a franchise, whichever occurs first.

Detailed information must be furnished concerning the franchisor's finances, experience, size of operation, and involvement in litigation. Among other required data are total costs of the franchise to the franchisee, including whether any portions are refundable, and the recurring expenses of the franchise. Specific limitations on the franchisee's operations regarding goods and services that may be offered, customers to whom the franchisee may sell, geographic limitations, and territorial protection (if any) from competing company franchises must be explained. Finally, conditions of termination, renewal, and transfer of the franchise, as well as detailed verification of franchisor claims as to sales, income, and gross or net profits, must be provided.

False statements as to sales, income, or profits are prohibited—punishable by a $10,000 fine for each violation. The FTC indicated that franchisees may sue for damages resulting from false statements made in the disclosure statement.

Franchisor Rights and Duties

The franchisor has the right to enforce all terms and conditions included in the agreement with a franchisee, as long as the requirements are not illegal, or illegally obtained through fraud, duress, or undue influence. Every franchise contract is presumed valid and enforceable until declared otherwise, in whole or in part, by a court or government regulatory agency. The burden rests on the party claiming wrongdoing to prove it in order to be relieved of any duty to perform that contract.[5]

A franchisor has a legal duty to fulfill the terms and conditions agreed to with the franchisee and to do nothing that interferes with the proper performance of the franchisee's duties. If the franchisor agrees to limit the entry of new franchise operations that might adversely affect the franchisee's business, the franchisor must act in good faith in keeping such promises.[6] The creation of new competition in violation of such a contract would enable the franchisee to recover losses suffered as a result. Further, the franchisor cannot use resulting losses in sales, on which its franchise fee may be calculated, as a means of terminating the franchise. However, the franchisee must prove that the losses were caused by the actions of the franchisor.[7]

Every franchisor has a lawful interest in requiring franchisees to maintain quality standards.[8] This provision is the means by which a franchisor can protect the name, goodwill, and reputation of the company. Any lessening of quality through the fault of the franchisee usually reflects more on the franchisor product than on the franchisee.

However, a franchisor may not, without very good reasons, force a franchisee to purchase *all* supplies exclusively from the franchisor or dealers specified by the franchisor. This exclusive dealing arrangement may run afoul of the antitrust laws.[9] As long as franchisees can maintain quality standards while purchasing in the open market, then they must be given this opportunity to reduce costs, and the franchisor must allow other suppliers to sell to its franchisees.

The franchisor has the right to terminate a franchise. However, the law does not favor sudden and arbitrary terminations, unless specifically covered in the franchise agreement.[10] Even so, such clauses are strictly interpreted in favor of the franchisee—in some cases on the grounds that the franchisee lacked equality of bargaining power; and in other cases on the grounds that reasonable notice of the termination was not given.[11] Still other cases examine the length of the franchise and require that a reasonable time elapse before termination so that the franchisee may recoup any investments.[12]

However, these cases do not deprive the franchisor of the right to terminate when proper provision for termination exists in the agreement.[13] The mere fact that the termination rights of the franchisor may be hard on the franchisee is not grounds for a court to declare them unenforceable.[14]

Franchisee Rights and Duties

A franchise agreement is usually a standard type of agreement designed to benefit the franchisor. In some cases there is little the franchisee can do to negotiate a better deal—aside from forgoing the franchise entirely. The FTC disclosure regulation helped to correct one major problem, namely, lack of accurate and complete information on which to base a decision as to whether to invest in a franchise.

The franchisee is under a *continuing* obligation to carry out the agreement with the franchisor. A hard bargain creating a franchise does not, standing alone, prove that the bargain was illegal. Lack of profitability or diminished expectation of profit does not excuse performance by the franchisee. These are business risks voluntarily assumed in order to obtain profits.

The franchisee has the right to expect the franchisor to provide support in advertising, marketing, and management as outlined in the agreement. Each franchisee has the right to the same fair treatment others receive, although fair treatment is harder for the courts

to determine. A franchisee should closely monitor the situation to ensure that what he or she is getting from the franchisor is what the agreement promised.

A franchisee has the right to buy some supplies from local dealers, as long as this does not compromise the quality standards of the franchise agreement.

As a foodservice operator, the franchisee is directly responsible to patrons and the public for negligent or insufficient security, and is liable for breaches of implied warranties of food and beverage fitness.[15] The franchisee is responsible for meeting local building, health, and sanitary codes; for correcting faulty or defective premises; and for enforcing alcoholic beverage control laws and other legal requirements. The franchise agreement *does not* insulate the franchisee from liability to the buyer of foods and beverages, or from government regulations. Nor does the franchisor assume such responsibilities unless specifically stated in the agreement.

Franchisor Responsibility for Franchisee's Misconduct

Standard franchise contracts may contain a clause specifying that the franchisor will not be responsible for any liability arising out of the operation of the business by the franchisee. Additional language may require the franchisee to *indemnify,* or hold the franchisor harmless against any losses suffered by the franchisor in connection with the management of the franchise by the franchisee. Often the contract uses the term *independent contractor* to define the status of the franchisee.[16] Such clauses are aimed at, among other things, preventing the franchisor from being held responsible for injuries to others due to franchisee negligence or intentional misconduct.

However, two legal theories have been applied to impose liability on franchisors in spite of such language. One theory rests on the exercise of an ample degree of operational control by the franchisor over the activities of the franchisee.[17]

Control by the franchisor usually exists when the agreement (1) requires the franchisee to build the facility as specified by the franchisor; (2) imposes strict adherence to specific operating methods and gives the franchisor the right to enforce compliance with frequent inspections; and (3) permits the franchisor to cancel the agreement for any substantial violation of the contract. Collectively such agreement rights can establish enough franchisor control possibly to justify franchisor liability for the misconduct of the franchisee.

The second theory of franchisor liability is that of the degree of authority or control *represented* to patrons through advertising or other representations.[18] The use of the trademark or name, and the fact that the franchisee is part of a national system of franchises with elements of identical interior and exterior decor, are examples of such control. Once these representations, sometimes called *manifestations of authority,* are communicated to third persons, the franchisor is unable to deny control or authority over the franchisee.

However, the law recognizes that the franchisor is not liable for the acts of an independent contractor (franchisee) that cause harm to a third party (patron) arising out of the negligence or intentional misconduct of an *employee* of the franchisee. Only the independent contractor is liable under the theory of *respondeat superior,* which means let the employer respond for the legal wrongs of his or her employees, even though the employer may be blameless. However, to allow the franchisor to escape liability, the courts must decide whether the franchisee was indeed an independent contractor.

Antitrust Rules and Franchises

Encouraging competition is an overall objective of economic policy in the United States. Prior to the development of antitrust laws, the business community was guided by the doctrine of *laissez-faire,* meaning that survival in the marketplace was achieved by the accumulation of market power rather than by government regulation. Market power was acquired at the expense of competition, through creation of a monopoly over production or service, by (1) establishing *pooling arrangements* to divide up the market for a product; (2) price discrimination in favor of designated customers; (3) customer discrimination as to quality, quantity, packaging and so forth; and (4) price fixing with other producers.[19]

The first legislation aimed at attacking anticompetitive marketing activities was the *Sherman Act of 1890.* This federal law prohibits contracts, combinations, or conspiracies in restraint of trade or commerce among the several states or with foreign nations, and "monopolies or attempts to monopolize."

Later the *Clayton Act of 1914* and the *Robinson-Patman Act of 1936* were adopted to curb price discrimination, exclusive agreements, and mergers, but only where the effect of these practices may be to lessen competition substantially or to create a monopoly in any line of commerce.

The most recent federal enactment is the *Hart-Scott-Rodino Antitrust Improvement Act of 1976,* which, among other things, empowers a state's attorney general to sue, on behalf of citizens of that state, businesses that violate the Sherman Act.[20]

Regulated Practices

There are several practices, interpreted by the courts, which are violations of these antitrust acts.

"Per Se" Violations

The first may be grouped under the heading "*per se* violations," or violations that cannot be justified by good motive, lack of intent to injure competitors, or economic necessity.

1. *Price fixing* is the most serious *per se* violation.[21] A franchisor may not fix the price at which the product or service must be sold by the franchisee. The franchisor may *suggest* retail prices but cannot make the franchisee sell at those prices.

    Likewise, a group of franchisees within the same franchise may not agree orally or in writing to fix the prices of products sold to the public.

2. A second *per se* violation involves *division or allocation of a given market* by groups of competitors. Competing franchisees cannot agree to divide up the market geographically or territorially among themselves. Only the franchisor may establish and enforce geographic or territorial restrictions with relation to each of its franchisees.[22]

    For example, for the life of the franchisee agreement with Mr. and Mrs. Frick, Buffalo Bill could agree not to allow establishment of another franchise outlet within a designated area. *But* Mr. and Mrs. Frick could not agree with other Buffalo Bill franchisees in the area to deny the entry of a new franchise operator.

3. A *group boycott* by competing franchisees is another *per se* type of violation.[23] Franchisees may not agree to compel a supplier of goods or services to fund a local promotion of the franchised product. Compulsion means *blacklisting* the supplier from further dealings with the group members for refusing to pay the required promotion fee.

Rule-of-Reason Violations

The second category of antitrust violations is called the *rule of reason*. Rule-of-reason violations include marketing activities that create monopolies or threats to monopolize specific markets. Since in most cases these activities will involve franchisors rather than franchisees, it is enough to point out that such conduct *may* be justified by proof of economic necessity. For example, if Buffalo Bill required Mr. and Mrs. Frick to agree not to acquire a Bigger Burger franchise within Buffalo Bill's market, such an agreement could be considered an unreasonable restraint of trade—although if Buffalo Bill could prove that the clause was justified on reasonable economic grounds, he might be allowed to hold the Fricks to the agreement.[24] However, a *combination* of clauses imposed by Buffalo Bill, such as a clause prohibiting Mr. and Mrs. Frick from obtaining a franchise in any area where a company-owned outlet was established, together with one giving the Fricks veto power over the entry of new franchisees, would be a *per se* violation—without economic justification—of the antitrust laws.[25]

Tying contracts to the exclusive purchase of a franchisor's products in exchange for obtaining the franchise is a rule-of-reason violation.[26] The franchisor agrees to license the main tying product, the trademark or name, on condition that the franchisee agrees to buy the franchisor's other products, such as ice cream, hamburger patties, napkins, and silver, called the *tied products,* either directly from the franchisor or from franchisor-designated sources. These violations may not be considered violations at all, *if* the franchisor can justify the arrangements.

Such contracts are not *automatically* illegal, but become so when the following conditions exist:

1. There are separate products, one the tying product and the other the tied product.

2. There is enough economic power for the tying market (trademark or formula) to force the purchase of the tied product (furniture and fixtures).
3. There is plenty of competition in that market.
4. The arrangement would affect competitors in the tied market.[27]

In the event of a court action, the franchisor may try to prove that any or all of the conditions do not exist, and thus be excused from liability. The franchisor may also try to prove that the arrangement was reasonable on economic grounds. It is then left to a jury to decide these issues.

The following case gives an example of a tying arrangement that the court found to be (1) unjustified and (2) in violation of the Sherman Act.

Siegel v. Chicken Delight, Inc.
448 F.2d 43 (9th Cir. 1971)
cert. denied 405 U.S. 955 (1972)

Facts.   Siegel, a Chicken Delight fast-food franchisee, brought a *class action* suit (an action on behalf of himself and other Chicken Delight franchisees) to have a federal court declare illegal certain requirements contained in the franchise agreement.

The requirements were that the franchisees buy all of their cooking equipment, dry-mix food items, and Chicken Delight's products exclusively from Chicken Delight as a condition of getting a Chicken Delight trademark franchise. Siegel argued that Chicken Delight violated federal antitrust laws by tying the purchase of essential operating items to obtaining a franchise. Chicken Delight argued at trial that the tying arrangements were economically justified and therefore legal.

The federal district court found that the arrangements were tying contracts; that the Chicken Delight trademarks used to tie these purchases by Siegel and other franchisees were monopolistic; and that Siegel had been injured. A jury found separately that there was no economic justification for these tying arrangements. The district court's findings of tying arrangements and of Chicken Delight's economic clout to create a monopoly were upheld. The jury's finding of no economic justification for Chicken Delight's contractual requirements with Siegel was also upheld. The damage judgment in favor of Siegel was *reversed* and sent back for a new trial on that question only.

Reasoning.   Chicken Delight maintained that the requirement that franchisees buy their products exclusively from Chicken Delight was economically justified. Chicken Delight argued that the requirement was reasonable because it helped to measure and collect revenue, and that it preserved the distinct flavor, uniformity, and quality of the food product.

Regarding whether or not a tying arrangement existed, the court said:

In order to establish that there exists an unlawful tying arrangement plaintiffs must demonstrate: *First,* that the scheme in question involves two distinct items and provides that one (the tying product) may not be obtained unless the other (the tied product) is also purchased . . . *Second,* that the tying product possesses sufficient economic power appreciably to restrain competition in the tied product market . . . *Third,* that a "not insubstantial" amount of commerce is affected by the arrangement . . . Chicken Delight concedes that the third requirement has been satisfied. It disputes the existence of the first two. Further it asserts that . . . there is a *fourth* issue: whether there exists a special justification for the particular tying arrangement in question . . .

A. *Two Products*
   The District Court ruled that the license to use the Chicken Delight name, trademark, and method of operations was "a tying item in the traditional sense . . . the tied items being the cookers and fryers, packaging products, and mixes . . .

The hallmark of a tie-in is that it denies competitors free access to the tied product market, not because the party imposing the arrangement has a superior product in that market, but because of the power or leverage exerted by the tying product. [S]ale of a franchise license, with the attendant rights to operate a business in the prescribed manner and to benefit from the goodwill of the trade name, in no way requires the forced sale by the franchisor of some or all of the component articles . . .

. . . The relevant question is not whether the items are essential to the franchise, but whether it is essential to the franchise that the items be purchased from Chicken Delight. This raises not the issue of whether there is a tie-in but rather the issue of whether the tie-in is justifiable . . .

We conclude that the District Court was not in error . . .

Conclusion. In this case no justification for a tying arrangement could be established by Chicken Delight. The issues relevant to such tying arrangements are whether they can be justified by the franchisor or whether they are an unreasonable restraint of free trade and violate antitrust laws.

A franchisor may require a seller of a product available to franchisees to meet the franchisor's required quality standard, or require the franchisee to request approval of another product.

State Antitrust Laws

Some states, such as California, New York, Texas, and Wisconsin, have enacted their own antitrust statutes. These states have made efforts to supplement and reinforce the federal laws. This is important because these states are able to deal with activities within their own borders, whereas much of the federal efforts are limited to activities *among* the states.

Foodservice operators who do business within a single state and serve mostly intrastate patrons must comply with the state antitrust regulations. However, if a significant number of patrons are from out of state, or a significant portion of basic food ingredients is purchased from out-of-state sources, then *both* federal and state antitrust laws apply.

Infringement

Franchisors are interested in protecting their trademark and products from infringement by those who would like to "cash in" on a recognized name. Infringement may take the form of using recognized marketing strategies, capitalizing on the franchised name, if only by changing it slightly or copying other aspects of the franchised company's products and services.

The following case is one illustration of how the courts may view claims of trademark infringement by taking into account the widespread use of the name as well as the geographic location.

T.G.I. Friday's, Inc. v. International Restaurant Group, Inc.
International Restaurant Group, Inc. v. T.G.I. Friday's, Inc.
United States Court of Appeals, Fifth Circuit, Mississippi 569 F.2d 895 (1978)

Facts. According to the court:

Friday's is a New York corporation formed . . . for the purpose of organizing and promoting restaurant franchises outside of New York City where the original T.G.I. Friday's restaurant is located. The name "T.G.I. Friday's" was registered as a service mark with the United States patent office. Under licensing agreements with Friday's, various third parties have opened Friday's restaurants in Shreveport, Houston, Dallas, Memphis, Nashville, Atlanta, Little Rock, Jackson, Indianapolis, and Columbus. The motif of the restaurants is "turn of the century," an effect created through the placement of various period pieces such as Tiffany lamps, back-lit stained glass, beadboard paneling, tin ceilings, wooden floors, old pictures, and outdoor awnings. Placemats, napkins, menus, and matches displaying the names of all the days of the week are an additional decorative peculiarity characterizing Friday's restaurants.

On December 15, 1971, Friday's entered into a restaurant licensing agreement with Tiffany granting Tiffany an exclusive license to operate a Friday's restaurant in Jackson, Mississippi. The agreement was negotiated and signed on behalf of the corporation by appellees Pittman and Trainor, the sole shareholders and chief operating officers of Tiffany. The contract contained the following provision:

"A. Licensee acknowledges (1) that Licensor has a vital interest in the names and marks, 'Tuesday's,' 'Wednesday's,' 'Thursday's,' and 'Sunday's' (the 'other marks') and expects to develop interest in businesses operated under the other marks; (2) that Licensor's present use of the other marks has materially assisted in the creation of the national image and goodwill associated with 'T.G.I. Friday's'; and (3) that no rights to the use of the marks is granted hereby.

"B. Licensee covenants and warrants that during the term of this agreement and subsequent to its termination Licensee, its successors or assigns, shall not utilize the names of the days of the week singly or in combination with other words in connection with the operation of a business."

In connection with the opening of the Tiffany's Friday's restaurant in Jackson, Friday's furnished general assistance to Tiffany by providing an "opening team," recipes, an "operations Manual," and suppliers of items needed to furnish the restaurant in order to ensure that the restaurant conformed to the specifications of the licensing agreement.

In December of 1972 Pittman and Trainor discussed with Friday's the possibility of purchasing an additional franchise for the Baton Rouge area, but their request was turned down. Pittman and Trainor then formed International in February 1973 and in December of that year opened a restaurant in Baton Rouge which they called "Ever Lovin' Saturday's." Both International and Tiffany initially operated out of the same office space

and had some of the same personnel. In fact, certain expenses incurred by International were mistakenly billed to Tiffany's Friday's in Jackson by restaurant suppliers who were furnishing items to International. However, the financial structures and assets of the two corporations have been kept scrupulously separate.

"Ever Lovin' Saturday's" in Baton Rouge is strikingly similar to a Friday's restaurant from its turn of the century motif to its menus. It is this similarity which is at the heart of the dispute presented on appeal.

Suit was brought against franchisor of "Friday's" restaurant chain by franchisees who sought a judgment declaring that their opening of an "Ever Lovin' Saturday's" restaurant in Baton Rouge, Louisiana, did not violate the terms of franchise agreement pertaining to a Friday's restaurant in Jackson, Mississippi. The franchisor thereafter filed a suit seeking an injunction against further operation of the Baton Rouge restaurant and damages for breach of contract, service mark infringement, and unfair competition. The United States District Court . . . entered judgment in favor of the franchisees, and franchisor appealed. The Court of Appeals . . . held that: (1) the franchise agreement was ambiguous and, when construed against the franchisor-drafter, did not prohibit use of the word "Saturday's" by anyone bound by the agreement; (2) use of the name "E. L. Saturday's" on the Baton Rouge restaurant that was markedly similar to the "Friday's" restaurant in Jackson did not constitute trademark infringement; and (3) consumers in Baton Rouge would not identify the restaurant there with the Friday's organization, and there was thus no unfair competition.

Reasoning. The appeals court addressed the issues of breach of contract, trademark infringement, and unfair competition.

1. *Breach of contract*:

". . . the names of the days of the week singly or in combination with other words in connection with the operation of a business" was ambiguous as to whether it meant the names of the seven days of the week, or only referred to the four days of the week specified in the agreement's preceding provision, viz., Tuesday, Wednesday, Thursday, and

Sunday, and since an ambiguous agreement must be construed against the drafter, the agreement did not prohibit use of the word "Saturday's" by anyone who was bound by the agreement.

2. *Trademark infringement:*

Franchisees' use of the name "E. L. Saturday's" on a Baton Rouge, Louisiana, restaurant that was markedly similar to the franchised "Friday's" restaurant in Jackson, Mississippi, did not constitute trademark infringement, since the mark "T.G.I. Friday's" and the designations "E.L. Saturday's" or "Ever Lovin' Saturday's" were dissimilar visually and phonetically, and since, the "Friday's" chain having no reputation in the Baton Rouge area, the physical similarities between the restaurants were irrelevant to the issue of infringement.

. . . Proper legal test of trademark infringement is whether the use of the allegedly infringing mark is likely to confuse consumers as to the source of the product.

Likelihood of confusion is a question of fact, and the trial court's findings will not be set aside unless clearly erroneous.

3. *Unfair competition:*

Since the "Friday's" restaurant chain was not known in the Baton Rouge, Louisiana, area and since, while the decor of the franchisees' "E.L. Saturday's" restaurant in Baton Rouge was an obvious copy of the trade dress of "Friday's," that "turn of the century" theme was not exclusive to "Friday's" and in fact is used in hundreds of different restaurants throughout the United States, consumers in Baton Rouge would not identify the restaurant there with the "Friday's" organization, and there was thus no unfair competition.

Law of unfair competition extends only to practices which induce confusion and deception of the public and does not apply when the possibility of deception and confusion is absent.

Franchisees of a "Friday's" restaurant in Jackson, Mississippi, did not appropriate any confidential information when, in respect to their opening of a restaurant in Baton Rouge, Louisiana, they made use of the "know-how" gained during their experience with "Friday's," and they therefore committed no fraud in that regard.

Conclusion. Franchises tend to be very protective of their trademarks since they are the center of their licensing agreements and the basis of their profitability. Operators must be aware of the difference between trademark infringement, which is very serious, and using knowledge of common marketing strategies and services to appeal to customers. Geographic location must also be taken into account. Had the franchisees established "Ever Lovin' Saturday's" in Jackson or Nashville where other Friday franchises were located, the court might have taken a different view.

FRANCHISE GUIDELINES

You may decide to enter the foodservice business by obtaining a franchise from an established company willing to use this means of expanding its market for its product or service.

A franchise gives you the right to use the trademark of a product or service in return for an investment. Such an arrangement gives you a leg up on your nonfranchised competitor, since you have the advantage of a known product plus the advisory services of your franchisor.

However, you remain an independent owner or operator of your own foodservice business. You are primarily responsible to state and local authorities for complying with all building, health, and sanitary codes; to your patrons for personal injuries and property damage or losses arising out of your negligence or intentional misconduct or that of your employees; and to federal and state regulatory agencies that enforce antitrust activities.

Essentially, buck-passing stops at your door. You may not shift your responsibilities without the consent of the franchisor, who is under no obligation to take on your burdens.

Rather, most franchise agreements strongly favor the franchisor, making you responsible for any losses suffered by the franchisor due to your own failure to carry out your legal responsibilities.

You must weigh the pros and cons of franchise against the lease or purchase of food-service premises. You are aided by the FTC Franchise Disclosure Rule, which requires the franchisor to give you the raw data on which to decide. Nonetheless, disclosure does not guarantee success. The FTC will not make good your losses in the event the franchise does not meet your economic expectations.

Court judgments notwithstanding, it is up to you to read the franchise agreement carefully to see whether it contains tying arrangements, and to decide whether you would be placed in a less competitive position because of them. Know before you sign. A court case is costly—and you may lose.

You must exercise extreme care in choosing to operate a franchise, and in choosing the franchise itself, especially if you are inexperienced in this field. The marketing and operational edge you may acquire may not offset the risks you take under the franchise contract.

The only sure guide to your rights and responsibilities is the agreement. Independent of antitrust laws, courts are not likely to impose any more responsibilities on the franchisor than are contained in this contract. Although most franchise agreements are standard, it would still be a good idea to have a lawyer go over the agreement. If you are in doubt about what it says, an attorney can clarify it for you. In the final analysis, you must decide whether the franchise agreement meets your management standards, is flexible enough, and offers the best arrangement for your investment. Failing these criteria, and in the event that the franchise proposal is not negotiable, your best bet is to look elsewhere.

Take your time before you sign. Don't be too eager to invest your life savings in a franchise until you've looked around. Investigate. Talk to different franchisors. Study the potential markets for your franchise. Look at different locations. Call up your local restaurant association and see what information it has on franchises. Operating a franchise can be a profitable and enjoyable business experience—for the right person—with the right franchise agreement.

SUMMARY

A franchise is a license from the owner, the *franchisor,* of a trademark or a service mark that permits another, a *franchisee,* to use the name and conduct the business according to specific procedures.

A franchise usually offers standardized products and goodwill as well as management help to its licensees. Still, the day-to-day management is up to the franchisee. The success of the operation rests as much on the skills of the franchisee as on the name and product identity of the franchisor.

There are advantages and disadvantages to franchising. Often contracts may be standardized in favor of the franchisor. It is up to the franchisee to negotiate the best deal. The FTC Franchise Disclosure Rule offers some protection in that it requires franchisors to disclose information on company finances, size, and involvement in litigation.

Franchisors and franchisees have rights and duties, usually spelled out in the contract. Franchisors may not be liable to the franchisees' patrons unless the law provides for liability. Usually the franchisee is directly responsible to patrons for injuries or illness caused on the premises.

A number of federal antitrust laws affect both franchisors and franchisees and are designed to prevent monopolies and to protect free trade and competition. Violations of these laws can result in heavy fines, or even jail terms, for violators. In addition, several states have antitrust laws.

QUESTIONS

1. What tangible and intangible advantages can a franchise offer a potential franchisee?
2. An agreement for a hamburger franchise requires you to purchase all supplies from the franchisor. Should you sign? Why or why not?
3. What type of information should a potential franchisee expect to obtain from the franchisor? How will this information help the would-be franchisee decide?
4. Give an example of a franchisee violation of an antitrust law. Categorize the type of violation.
5. How does the law make a franchisor liable for franchisee conduct to patrons or third parties? How is the franchisee liable?

NOTES

1. H. Brown, *Franchising, Realities and Remedies* 1–15 (rev. ed. 1981). But see *McDonald's Corp. v. Markim,* Inc., 209 Neb. 49, 306 N.W.2d 158 (1981), holding that a franchisee's contractual right to be given first consideration for a renewal of the franchise did not require the franchisor to give its franchisees thoughtful or sympathetic regard in preference to everyone else.
2. Disclosure Requirements and Prohibitions Concerning Franchising and Business Opportunities, 16 C.F.R. sec. 436 (1982).
3. But such exclusive dealing arrangements have been held to violate the Sherman Antitrust Act. See *Siegel v. Chicken Delight, Inc.,* 448 F.2d 43 (9th Cir. 1971), *cert. denied,* 405 U.S. 955 (1972). Contra see *Principe v. McDonald's Corp.,* 631 F.2d 303 (4th Cir. 1980), *cert. denied,* 451 U.S. 970 (1981).
4. The FTC was established to provide expert and ongoing enforcement of antitrust policies lacking

under the Sherman Act. The Commission is an administrative regulatory agency, not a court of law. Its purpose is to investigate unfair methods of competition, which include any of the anticompetitive activities found to violate the Sherman Act, to issue cease and desist orders in appropriate cases, and to issue trade regulation rules. Its orders and trade regulation rules are subject to judicial review. Congress recently set limits upon the FTC's authority to issue trade regulation rules.

Unlike a private cause of action or lawsuit for an antitrust violation, which enables the person or party injured to recover treble damages, the FTC does not create any treble-damage remedy. The FTC is established to protect the public interest; the injured person or party must find his or her treble-damage remedy within the Sherman Act. A court of law, not the FTC, decides this and related issues.

5. Brown, *supra* note 1, at 8–23.
6. But no such right exists in the absence of a contract clause precluding the franchisor from operating a company-owned unit nearby. *Snyder v. Howard Johnson's Motor Lodges, Inc.,* 412 F. Supp. 724 (S.D. Ill. 1976). See *T.G.I. Friday's, Inc. v. International Restaurant Group, Inc.,* 569 F.2d 895 (5th Cir. 1978). See also *Druker v. Roland Wm. Jutras Assoc., Inc.,* 370 Mass. 383, 348 N.E.2d 763 (1976), where the Supreme Judicial Court of Massachusetts adopted the following language: "[I]n every contract there is an implied covenant [promise] that neither party shall do anything which will have the effect of destroying or injuring the right of the other party to receive the fruits of the contract which means that in every contract there exists an implied covenant of good faith and fair dealing."

   Uproar Co. v. National Broadcasting Co., 81 F.2d 373, 377 (1st Cir.), *cert. denied,* 298 U.S. 670 (1936), quoting from *Kirk LaShille Co. v. Paul Armstrong Co.,* 263 N.Y. 79, 87, 188 N.E. 163 (1933).
7. *Id.* at 385, 348 N.E.2d at 765. Where intentional fraud is established as the cause of the breach of contract, both compensatory and punitive or exemplary damages may be recovered. See *Slater v. KFC Corp.,* 621 F.2d 932 (8th Cir. 1980) (case sent back for new trial to determine whether jury verdict based on actual fraud or only on concealment) (seafood franchise); *Clinco v. Carvel Corp.* (N.Y. Sup. 1977) found in 7 IFA Franchising World (April 1977) (ice cream franchise).

8. Brown, *supra* note 1, at 3–21, –22, –23, *Kentucky Fried Chicken Corp. v. Diversified Packaging Corp.,* 549 F.2d 368 (5th Cir. 1977).

9. See note 3, *supra.*

10. Decisions to terminate or not to renew a franchise, provided for by the franchise agreement, must be made in entirely good faith and not capriciously or arbitrarily. *McDonald's Corp. v. Markim, supra* note 1.

11. See generally *Arnott v. American Oil Co.,* 609 F.2d 873 (8th Cir. 1979), *cert. denied,* 446 U.S. 918 (1980). Contra *Zapatha v. Dairy Mart, Inc.,* 1980 Mass. Adv. Sh. 1837, 408 N.E.2d 1370 (1980). Also see *Milsen Co. v. Southland Corp.,* 454 F.2d 363 (7th Cir. 1971).

12. See Brown, *supra* note 1, at 1–15.

13. *McDonald's Corp. v. Markim, Inc., supra* note 1.

14. *Ungar v. Dunkin' Donuts of America, Inc.,* 68 F.R.D. 65 (E.D. Pa. 1975), *rev'd,* 531 F.2d 1211 (3d Cir.), *cert. denied,* 429 U.S. 823 (1976).

15. *Eastep v. Jack-in-the-Box, Inc.,* 546 S.W.2d 116 (Tex. Civ. App. 1977); *Zabner v. Howard Johnson's, Inc.,* 201 So. 2d 824 (Fla. Dist. Ct. App. 1967).

16. A typical indemnity clause would read as follows: "Under no circumstances shall FRANCHISOR be liable for any act, omission, debt or any other obligation of FRANCHISEE. FRANCHISEE shall indemnify and save FRANCHISOR harmless against any such claim and the cost of defending against such claims arising directly or indirectly from, or as a result of, or in connection with, FRANCHISEE'S operation of the franchised business." Brown, *supra* note 1, at A–26.

An independent contractor is a party over whose activities the other party has no control or supervision concerning the performance of the contract existing between them. A typical franchise contract provides that: "This Agreement does not constitute FRANCHISEE as an agent, legal representative, joint venturer, partner, employee, or servant of FRANCHISOR for any purpose whatsoever; and it is understood between the parties hereto that FRANCHISEE is an independent contractor and is in no way authorized to make any contract, agreement, warranty or representation on behalf of FRANCHISOR, or to create any obligation, express or implied, on behalf of FRANCHISOR . . ." *Id.* at A–25.

The fact that the contract establishes an independent contractor status between franchisor and franchisee is not binding on a third party patron who wishes to pursue legal remedies against both parties for injuries suffered as a result of an act or omission on the part of the franchisee itself or its employees. The question as to whether the franchisee is or is not an independent contractor is for the court and jury to decide. The contract language is evidence that the parties intended to establish that relationship, but the patron was not a party to that contract and therefore did not agree to be bound by the contractual status of independent contractor. See *Peters v. Sheraton Hotel and Inns,* N.Y.C.J., July 6, 1979, at 7 (N.Y. Civ. Ct. 1979).

17. *Billops v. Magness Constr. Co.,* 391 A.2d 196 (Del. 1978) (motel franchisor liable for intentional torts of its franchisee's banquet director in disrupting a party). See also *Wood v. Holiday Inns, Inc.,* 508 F.2d 167, 175–77 (5th Cir. 1975) (franchisor liable for its franchisee's night clerk who negligently revoked motel guest's credit card and breached motel franchisee's common law duty to provide its guest with courteous and considerate treatment). *Peters v. Sheraton Hotel and Inns, supra* note 16 (franchisor must defend negligence action based on defective bed involving infant guest of franchisee).

18. *Sapp v. City of Tallahassee,* 348 So. 2d 363 (Fla. Dist. Ct. App. 1977), citing *Wood v. Holiday Inns, Inc., supra* note 17, on the law of apparent authority conveyed by representations the franchisor makes to the public. (Either theory states good cause of action against franchisor where motel guest alleges inadequate security precautions.)

19. A pooling arrangement is an unofficial collective agreement among suppliers of facilities or services to combine their facilities, goods, or services so as to exclude nonmember competitors from participation in the subject matter of the pool. See *Associated Press v. United States,* 326 U.S. 1 (1945). To illustrate, the pooling of a unique computer hotel reservation service, not readily duplicated, by a group of hotels for the purpose of shutting out competing hotels would constitute a pooling arrangement. As such, every pooling arrangement constitutes a *per se* violation of the Sherman Act, even though the total activities of pool members do not create or threaten to create a monopoly.

20. 15 U.S.C. secs. 1–7, 12–17, 13–13a, 16 (1976 & Supp. V 1981).

21. *United States v. Socony-Vacuum Oil Co.,* 310 U.S. 150 (1940).

22. *American Motor Inns, Inc. v. Holiday Inns, Inc.,* 521 F.2d 1230 (3d Cir. 1975). The franchisor may act *individually* to protect his or her legitimate business interests free of restraint under section 1 of the Sherman Act. The franchisor commits no *per se* violations. The rule of reason must be applied to determine whether the franchisor exerts or threatens to exert monopoly power in the relevant market, under section 2 of the Sherman Act. Economic considerations may properly be introduced by the franchisor as a defense to any such claim of monopoly.

By contrast, the franchisees in *combination* violate section 1 of the Sherman Act, because they compete with each other and act to exclude the entry of new competition within their market area. It is their combined restraint of trade that the court in *American Motor Inns v. Holiday Inns, Inc.,* found an illegal restraint of trade, without justification on any grounds.

23. *Id.*

24. *Northern Pacific Ry. Co. v. United States,* 356 U.S. 1 (1958).

25. *American Motor Inns, Inc. v. Holiday Inns, Inc., supra* note 22.

26. *United States v. Hilton Hotels Corp.,* 467 F.2d 1000 (9th Cir. 1972), *cert. denied,* 409 U.S. 1125 (1973).

27. See *Siegel v. Chicken Delight, Inc., supra* note 3; *Kentucky Fried Chicken Corp. v. Diversified Packaging Corp., supra* note 8.

12
Forms of Foodservice Organization

Objectives

The purpose of this chapter is to:

1. Examine the basic forms of business organization in the foodservice industry.
2. Compare and contrast the different forms of business organizations available to those interested in starting or entering into a foodservice business within the following framework: (1) supervision and control of business; (2) responsibility for business financing; (3) liability for business obligations; (4) duration of business; and (5) taxation of business income.
3. Outline the legal aspects of purchase, sale, and termination of each form.

Case in Point

Allen and Benny, graduates of a hotel and restaurant school, go into a partnership and open a ski lodge. They build two restaurants: Skis, a fast-food operation, and the Mountain Crest, an evening dining room where wine and some mixed drinks are served.

Seven years later, after achieving great success, they are approached by Mary, who joins the partnership. Benny and Mary subsequently decide that two restaurants are not adequate for the ski crowd and want to open an après-ski bar that will serve most drinks, sandwiches, and appetizers. Allen is opposed, saying the bar will radically change the family atmosphere of the lodge. Benny and Mary outvote Allen and proceed to add the Snow and Slush Tavern.

What remedies are available to Allen? Under partnership law each partner has an equal right to manage the firm business, unless there is a contrary provision in the written agreement. Thus majority rule controls. Allen has the power to dissolve the partnership by withdrawing from it at any time. However, the withdrawal must be made in good faith. Bad faith is illustrated by a withdrawal to take personal advantage of a partnership opportunity, such as the expansion of business voted upon by Benny and Mary. In such a case, the two remaining members could sue Allen for any losses they sustained.[1]

This problem could have been prevented in several ways. One would have been to execute articles of partnership or a partnership agreement that required unanimous consent to expand the business. A second method would have been to create a limited partnership agreement, whereby Mary, as a limited partner, would have no voice in management.[2]

For those deciding to go into the restaurant business, there are several forms of organizations from which to choose.

Each has advantages and disadvantages as to degree of responsibility and liability, rights and duties, and taxation. To make the best choice, all the factors must be weighed.

SOLE PROPRIETORSHIPS— DESCRIPTION

The least complex and historically the earliest form of business organization is the sole or single proprietorship. This business form is very popular in the foodservice industry. It offers entrepreneurs the independence and challenge of complete management accountability. The full responsibility for success or failure of a foodservice operation depends solely on the skills and people-management qualities of the sole proprietor.

In this form the owner is also the active operator of the business. The owner voluntarily creates this form by simply starting to do business. No permission to operate as a sole proprietor is required from the federal, state, or local authorities. No fee need be paid to operate in this form; however, a license or permit may be required to operate a foodservice business. You may need a health permit to operate a restaurant, irrespective of the form of business organization you choose.

Figure 12.1
Advantages and Disadvantages of
Sole Proprietorship

Advantages

Method of creation.   It is often easier and less costly to start a sole proprietorship restaurant than to start any other kind of business. Legal formalities are held to a minimum, and the agreement of others is avoided.

Benefits.   The sole proprietor receives all the profits of the business.

Transferability of interest.   The sole proprietor has total transfer rights.

Duration.   The duration of the business is discretionary with the sole proprietor, but in no event to exceed his or her lifetime.

Management.   The sole proprietor has unlimited management authority.

Taxation.   The sole proprietor escapes corporate income taxation, paying only personal income taxes on profits. However, these taxes are not necessarily lower than those imposed on corporations.

Organizational fees.   No fees to create or maintain the sole proprietorship are required by law.

Disadvantages

Liability.   The sole proprietor has unlimited liability for all obligations incurred in doing business, extending to personal assets as well as business assets.

Burdens.   Entire burden of business, including sole responsibility for losses and mismanagement, rests on a sole proprietor.

Financing.   Financing is limited to personal funds and funds of others willing to loan to the sole proprietor.

Rights, Duties, and Liabilities

As sole proprietor you remain in exclusive control of the business, although you may hire employees to help you operate it. You are liable for (1) your own negligent and intentional acts or omissions; (2) all applicable statutory violations (of building, fire, and safety codes); (3) the negligent or willful misconduct of your employees; and (4) all contracts which you make with vendors, competitors, and employees.

An important note: *Your liabilities are not limited to your business assets, but extend to your personal assets.* In short, you may be personally liable for all debts, losses, and valid claims lodged against the foodservice operation. (For the advantages and disadvantages of this form of business, see Figure 12.1.)

Purchase, Sale, and Termination of Business

As the owner/operator, you determine the kind of operation to run; how, when, and where to run it; and the amount of your investment. You may purchase, sell, give away, or simply stop operating the business at any time. The duration of the business is measured by your own life span. When you die, the business automatically ceases to exist.

Tax Considerations

A single proprietorship is not taxed as a business for income taxes separate from personal taxes.

Sales taxes, if applicable, are levied just as with any other business.

If you employ other people, federal and state withholding for income taxes on wages and salaries and unemployment taxes must be paid, regardless of the form of business you choose.

If alcoholic beverages are to be served on the premises, you must obtain a federal alcohol tax stamp. This stamp is required of all those who sell alcohol.

Figure 12.2
Advantages and Disadvantages of the Partnership Form of Business

Advantages

Method of creation. Nothing more than agreement of the parties is required to create a partnership. This may be oral, though a written agreement is recommended. The costs of drawing up an agreement usually are minimal.

Benefits. The profits of the partnership are pooled and shared equally, unless otherwise provided by agreement.

Financing. The costs of financing may be shared equally or split up by agreement. This reduces the burden associated with the sole proprietorship, and makes it possible to draw upon the financial resources of all of the partners.

Duration. The partnership lasts no longer than the life-span of any one partner or until any one partner decides to sell his or her share.

Taxation. A partnership pays no federal income taxes as a business entity. All profits must be distributed to the partners equally, or as set forth in the partnership agreement. The partners add that income to their personal income. Profits are taxable whether distributed or not.

Organizational fees. No fees to create or maintain the partnership are required by law.

Disadvantages

Liability. Unlimited liability. Each partner is the agent of all the other partners. As such, each partner may be individually liable for any business debts or any liability caused by the negligence of any other partner or any employee of the firm.

Burdens. The losses of the partnership are the individual as well as collective responsibility of all the partners.

Transferability of interest. All partners must consent to the transfer of the partnership interest of any partner.

Management. Each partner is entitled to an equal voice in the management and control of the partnership, irrespective of his or her interest in the partnership. This may be an advantage or a disadvantage depending on the differing skills of each partner.

PARTNERSHIPS[3]

Parnerships are another form of business used in the foodservice industry. A partnership is an agreement between two or more persons to conduct a business for profit. Each partner is a co-owner of the business. The partners have joint operating control over the business and the right to share in its profits. Profit is what distinguishes this form from other forms. The business *must* be set up to make a profit. Obviously this is an ideal form for the operation of a food service. Law aside, the main problem is finding the right partner to assume his or her share of management and financial responsibility.

The partnership agreement establishes the rights and obligations of the partners to each other and to the partnership. The agreement is critical, since the law will look first to the agreement to define these rights and obligations, and will apply general rules of partnership law only when the agreement does not provide an answer. Because of the importance the law attaches to the agreement, it should be reviewed by legal counsel and always be in writing. (Figure 12.2 lists the advantages and disadvantages of partnership.)

Types of Partnerships

A *general* or *full partner* is a partner who has unlimited liability for partnership debts and obligations, who has unlimited management powers, and who shares in partnership profits.

A *silent partner* is a partner who lacks any voice, and takes no part in the business.

A *secret partner* is a partner whose presence in the firm is not disclosed to the public, but who may help manage the operation.

A *dormant partner* is a partner who is both a silent partner and a secret partner.

A *nominal* or *ostensible partner* is one who has consented to be known as a partner whether or not a real partner. In practice the law applies the principle of *partnership by estoppel* to this relationship: Even though not a real partner, a nominal partner is liable to those who extend credit to the partnership in the belief that that person is a partner.

A *trading partnership* is engaged in buying and selling for profit; foodservice operators belong in this category. A *nontrading partnership* is engaged in providing a service, such as the practice of law or medicine.

Who May Create a Partnership

Any individual or group of persons may create or enter into a partnership. Any number of people can form a partnership. A minor as well as an adult may become a partner, even though a minor may disaffirm such a contract and withdraw at any time until he or she reaches legal age. This is a possibility in the restaurant industry, where family operations may expand.[4]

A corporation and a limited partnership may join a partnership.

The Law Governing Partnerships

Historically, partnership law developed on a case-by-case basis in the form of common law rules developed by the courts in each state.

The Uniform Partnership Act (UPA) was adopted in 1914 to create uniformity and clarity in partnership law, as well as to put into a workable statutory form the many common law court decisions. Only Louisiana and Georgia have not adopted the UPA.

How the UPA Defines a Partnership

The UPA says that (1) the receipt by a person of a share of the profits is evidence that he or she is a partner; (2) there must be demonstrated *intent* to form a partnership; (3) a partnership must *carry on business* for a reasonable period of time; and (4) the business *must* be set up to make a profit.

The purpose, *to make a profit,* distinguishes a partnership from not-for-profit or nonprofit entities, even though the kind of business carried on may be considered identical. A private membership club is not a partnership, even though the club furnishes meals and beverages comparable to those served in public restaurants catering to the same patrons.

The agreement may divide up assets and management responsibilities. Otherwise, in the absence of an agreement, each person in a partnership shares equally in the profits and losses of the business, according to his or her ownership rights and rights to manage the operation.

The following case illustrates that lack of a written partnership agreement can result in problems for both partners as well as time in court.

Barbet v. Ostovar
Superior Court of Pennsylvania
273 Pa. Super. 256, 417 A.2d 636 (1980)

Facts.

> Daniel Barbet (plaintiff) brought an action . . . against Kurosh Ostovar and his wife, Marjorie

Ostovar (defendants), seeking specific performance of an oral partnership agreement and an accounting.

Kurosh Ostovar was a professor at Pennsylvania State University. Barbet had been trained as a chef and had been engaged in the restaurant business all of his life. He met Ostovar when he married Ostovar's cousin. Ostovar wanted to establish a French-type restaurant in State College, Pennsylvania. He asked Barbet to assist him. They entered into an oral agreement under which Barbet would participate in the establishment and operation of the restaurant and Ostovar would provide the capital.

A restaurant property owned by the Meyers Corporation became available. Ostovar and Barbet entered into an option agreement in 1973 to acquire all of the Meyers Corporation stock in Marjorie Ostovar's name. They did this because they had been advised (erroneously) that aliens could not legally hold stock in a corporation that held a liquor license. Neither Kurosh Ostovar nor Barbet were American citizens. However, they signed as partners a lease of the premises from the corporation. They both participated actively in the business, while Marjorie's activities were limited to helping Kurosh keep the books.

In May 1976 Barbet and Kurosh Ostovar met with the attorney and accountant for the Meyers Corporation for the purpose of completing the purchase of the stock. Barbet and Kurosh Ostovar were represented as the real parties in interest in the restaurant business and as partners. At that time they agreed that Barbet owned one half of the stock. Shortly thereafter, however, the relationship between Barbet and Ostovar deteriorated rapidly. On June 30, 1976, Ostovar had the locks on the restaurant changed to exclude Barbet, who was then "dismissed from his employment."

Barbet filed suit, claiming that he was a partner and seeking the transfer to him of 50 percent of the stock of the corporation and an accounting. At the trial Barbet testified as follows: "It was a very simple agreement. Dr. Ostovar was supposed to invest for this business, and I was supposed to set up the business for him, to supervise it. For disbursement of the profit, Dr. Ostovar was supposed to get his money out of the business, plus an interest on his money in the same amount that the bank would pay for the same—for interest, OK? After that, the profit would be shared on an equal basis."

The decree granting specific performance of oral partnership agreement and an accounting was upheld by an equally divided court.

Reasoning.

It is entrenched in the law of the Commonwealth that the existence of a partnership depends upon the intentions of the parties as to being partners and that no formal or written agreement need be executed in order for a valid partnership to exist. As the Pennsylvania Supreme Court has recently opined:

"There is no requirement that partnership agreements be in writing. They may be orally or may be found to exist by implication from all attending circumstances (i.e., the manner in which the alleged partners actually conducted their business, etc.)."

We find that the evidence supports the Chancellor's conclusion that Barbet satisfied his burden of proving that in 1972, he and Ostovar formed a partnership with the intention of owning and operating a restaurant in State College, Pennsylvania, and said partnership continued in existence until he [Barbet] was "locked out" in June 1976.

The Ostovars contend that the terms of the 1972 oral agreement between Barbet and Ostovar demonstrate, at most, an agreement between them to become partners in the future, but only upon the happening of certain conditions . . . those conditions . . . being the repayment to Ostovar of his capital investments, with interest, and Barbet's resolution of his immigration problems.

We do not agree.

Our examination of the record leads us to conclude that Barbet and Ostovar had unequivocally entered into an oral partnership. This is very clear. They further agreed that profits were not to be distributed until Ostovar had been repaid his original investment, plus interest, and that Barbet would receive a stock certificate representing a 50 percent interest in the corporation once he became a United States citizen. The foregoing were merely conditions governing the operation of the partnership business. They were not conditions precedent which had to be fulfilled before the partnership came into existence.

The repayment of capital investments before distribution of profits is an essential element of every partnership agreement, implied as a term thereof by law.

Conclusion. The Pennsylvania Superior Court applied the common law principle that a written partnership agreement is not a precondition to creating a valid partnership. As long as all the credible oral evidence establishes all the necessary elements of a partnership, a partnership exists until one of the partners withdraws or is wrongfully prohibited from participating in the partnership business. The court stressed that there was adequate proof of an *intent to carry on a business for profit as co-owners,* further supported by the oral agreement to repay capital investments (return invested capital) before any distribution of profits.

The evenly divided reviewing court in this case illustrates the risk you take by not drawing up a written partnership agreement. Everything rests on the credibility of the opponents when a dispute arises. Each party is at the mercy of the subjective evaluation by a jury or judge of his or her testimony against that of the opponents.

Rights, Duties, and Liabilities

Most partnership matters, including how management decisions will be made, should be included in the agreement for the partnership. Generally each partner has the power to make independent decisions in the normal business of the partnership. Usually partners will consult each other before making management decisions involving borrowing money, hiring new employees, altering the premises, and the like.

In the absence of contrary agreement, the vote of a majority of the partners controls such decisions, regardless of the partnership share of each partner. By agreement, the majority may delegate management of the business to one partner, or may delegate management of certain defined activities of the partnership to one partner. For example, if one partner is a financial whiz and another likes to be in the kitchen, an agreement may informally divide up these responsibilities. If partners are on fairly equal footing in terms of skills, a joint decision on each major issue might be best.

Any major change in the nature of the partnership business or in the partnership location, such as a decision to purchase the assets of an existing business or to move the restaurant downtown, would require the unanimous agreement of the partners. The test to determine whether such a vote is required is whether the change would substantially alter the risks or financial liability of the partnership.

Each partner is an agent of the partnership, and the partnership relationship is one of trust and confidence. Partners owe each other the highest degree of loyalty and good faith in all partnership matters.[5] This duty is imposed by law and need not be specifically stated in the partnership agreement. Nor may a partner be relieved of this duty by the partnership agreement or any other contract.

A partner is liable to the other partner(s) if he or she (1) uses partnership property for personal purposes without obtaining the approval of the other partner(s); (2) misappropriates partnership funds;[6] (3) makes a secret profit out of the transaction of partnership business;[7] (4) engages in a competing business without the knowledge and consent of the other partner(s);[8] (5) accepts a secret commission on partnership business;[9] or (6) uses information gained as a partner to the detriment of the partnership.[10]

Every partner owes the partnership a duty to exercise reasonable care in the conduct of partnership business. No partner should exceed the authority granted that person under the agreement. Every partner is liable for losses resulting from his or her negligence in handling partnership business and for losses resulting from unauthorized transactions negotiated in the partnership name.

Each partner is entitled (1) to see the partnership book and records; (2) to a formal accounting of the business; and (3) to be reimbursed for expenses from personal funds for proper partnership business. Each partner is also required to account for his or her use of partnership funds and property, as well as for any benefit received by the partner without the consent of the others. A partner may not sue a partner or the partnership for damages or failure to receive profits. A partner's only recourse is to obtain a court-ordered accounting and distribution of profits and monies owed.

Partners are called *tenants in partnership* of all the firm's assets. No single partner has any right to sell, assign (transfer), or in any manner deal with any partnership property as a sole or exclusive owner.

A partner may not sell or convey partnership property unless he or she does so in the regular course of that firm's business. Thus a partner in a real estate partnership could sell real estate on behalf of the partnership, but a partner in a restaurant business could not. Why? Because a transfer of the land on which the restaurant operates would affect the ability of the business to continue. In that case, all of the restaurant partners would have to agree to the transfer.

Among other business actions that require unanimous consent of each partner are the sale of goodwill, which is actually the sale of public reputation and the right to use recognized product names and identity; an assignment (transfer) of partnership property for the benefit of creditors; any act which would make it impossible to continue the business in the usual way (for example, the sale of the entire food and beverage inventory); a guarantee of the debt of another party; paying or assuming an individual debt of a partner; and providing free services.

Partners are not normally entitled to compensation (salary and wages) for conducting partnership business. Why? Because each partner is entitled to a share of the profits of the firm. Only a surviving partner is entitled to compensation for winding up the affairs of the firm. *However, the partnership agreement may provide for compensation or wages for one partner to run the business.*

Partnership liability differs from sole proprietorship liability in that any legal judgment against the partnership is first discharged out of the assets of the partnership and not from individual income or assets. The personal assets of all general partners are subject to such claims only if the partnership assets are insufficient to satisfy the claims. Individual partners, like sole proprietors, can be personally liable for partnership debts, *but only if the partnership itself is unable to pay the debts.* The law recognizes this dual responsibility to pay by requiring a creditor of a partnership having a legally enforceable claim to exhaust the right to recover against partnership property before going after the personal property of the partners.

Partners are *jointly liable* (meaning that they are collectively liable; all *must* be sued) on partnership contracts and *severally liable*—individually liable—for torts (legal wrongs) committed in the course of partnership business.[11] The partnership is itself liable for contracts and torts, and most states permit the partnership to be sued in its own name.[12]

The crimes of a partner normally do not impose liability on the partnership or other partners, unless those partners participated in the criminal conduct, and the crime was committed in the course of partnership business.

Modern criminal codes do make the partnership liable as a separate entity for partnership crimes, so that upon conviction the partnership must pay a criminal fine.

Partners, *in their relations with third parties,* act as agents of the partnership in the transaction of normal business. Apparent authority is sufficient to bind the entire partnership in its dealings with third parties, unless the third party had knowledge of the partner's lack of authority. The partnership must state any lack of authority to third persons, say suppliers, with whom it deals in the normal course of its business.[13]

New Partners

The admission of a new partner or partners causes the original partnership to dissolve according to law, as in the case of a withdrawal of a partner. The partnership agreement usually provides for this contingency by permitting the new or remaining partners to continue the partnership business. Nevertheless, in law a new partnership is created. The debts of the dissolved partnership carry over to the new partnership, and creditors of the original entity are creditors of the new partnership.

No single partner may transfer his or her interest in the partnership (large share of profits earned and return of capital invested after dissolution and winding up) to another and thereby make that person a partner in the firm. The consent of all partners is required to admit a new person.

Termination

A partnership terminates at the end of the agreed-upon term or when the partnership objective has been attained. Without agreement on duration or objective, any partner

can, by withdrawing, dissolve a partnership. Dissolution by withdrawal is effective, even though it may violate a partnership agreement. A partner who wrongfully withdraws, causing dissolution, is liable to the remaining partners for damages and may not participate in any profits resulting from termination of the partnership.[14] In addition, such a partner loses any claim to the value of partnership goodwill.

The death or personal bankruptcy of a partner automatically dissolves a partnership.

A court may order dissolution if, for example, the partners are at loggerheads and the partnership is unable to function.[15]

A partner may be *expelled* for cause. For example, if one partner uses funds from the restaurant to pay personal gambling debts, the other partners may be justified in expelling that partner. The agreement should state specific practices that may result in expulsion, since, unless the activity is downright illegal, the law may not be on the side of the remaining partners. Liability could result from a wrongful expulsion.

When a partnership is continued by the surviving partners and/or newly admitted partners, the original partners remain liable for all original partnership debts.[16] A newly admitted partner assumes responsibility for all previous partnership debts.[17] For example, in a restaurant dissolution, the partnership assets equal $50,000. A new partner is admitted. The new partner is liable only for his or her share of $50,000, the value of partnership assets. If there were three partners, the new partner would be liable for one fourth of the $50,000.

If dissolution is for just cause, and the business continues, the noncontinuing partner is entitled to first claim to his or her partnership interest due at the time. The agreement may specify that the other partners have the right to buy the interests of the departing partner so they can continue as a partnership. Upon the retirement or death of such a partner, that partner or his or her legal representative can elect to receive either interest on the value of that partner's interest in the partnership or that partner's share in the profits on business conducted after dissolution and wind-up but before termination.[18]

Tax Considerations

Federal Requirements

Each partner in a partnership is taxed on his or her own share of partnership income, whether it has been distributed or not. Accumulated earnings are taxed under this rule. The partnership files an information return only. Capital gains and losses are taxed proportionately to each partner, as are other forms of partnership income. Partners are not taxed on exempt interest received from the firm, such as interest earned on tax-free municipal bonds.

Partners are not eligible to participate in an exempt pension trust. The firm cannot deduct pension payments for its partners under a Keogh (self-employed pension) Plan. Partners are not subject to social security taxes but must often pay a self-employment tax. The Internal Revenue Code does not provide any tax exemption for the payment of death benefits to partners' beneficiaries, excluding those provided by insurance.

State Requirements

Many states exempt partnerships from the payment of income taxes. However, every partnership must pay applicable state sales taxes and unemployment insurance taxes.

Limited Partnerships

In this type of partnership, a degree of limited liability is exchanged for a lack of management of or control over the partnership business. A limited partner who engages in management or asserts control over the business loses the limited liability status and is treated by law as a general partner thereafter, irrespective of the language of the limited partnership agreement.[19]

For example, the fact that Harry Lewis permits the use of his name in a restaurant's business is viewed as a representation to those dealing with the partnership that Harry is a general partner, with all accompanying rights and liabilities. Great care must be exercised by anyone wishing to use a limited partnership as an investment opportunity. Under no circumstances must the limited partner attempt to manage or represent himself or herself as managing the partnership business.

This partnership form is very popular, because unlike a general partner, a limited partner is not fully liable for partnership obligations in the event the partnership is unable to pay them. Rather, the limited partner is liable only up to the amount of his or her investment in the business.

Unlike partnerships and related forms, the limited partnership is not created by agreement but by permission of the state in which the partnership is to be created. The partnership is required to submit its partnership articles or applications for approval and to disclose the names of all of the partners.

Every limited partnership must have at least one general partner whom creditors and governmental bodies may hold responsible for debts, payment of taxes, and failures to meet legal requirements.

As long as the limited partner does not engage in management, that partner's personal assets or estate are not subject to liability beyond the original amount invested.

The Uniform Limited Partnership Act

The Uniform Limited Partnership Act, adopted in the District of Columbia and the Virgin Islands and in all states except Delaware and Louisiana, is the law governing limited partnerships. The limited partnership form is created by legislation and not simply by agreement as in the case of a general partnership. The Act normally governs partnership activities not covered in the agreement.

Joint Ventures

This specialized form of business organization is an offshoot of the partnership. In this form two or more persons agree to join in a *single* business enterprise or activity, sharing profits and losses according to the value of the money or services contributed by each. A joint venture differs from a partnership, which is formed to carry on a business over a continuous, indefinite time period.[20] The joint venture may be formed to start a restaurant, and then later may dissolve or re-form into a partnership.

A party to a joint venture is not an agent of the group and does not have authority to bind the others to individual decisions. However, a court may find that authority to bind them does exist.[21] The management and operation of a joint venture are often placed by agreement in the hands of one member. Some states require that one person have authority and be accountable for actions on behalf of the venture. Unlike with a partnership, the death of one party does not automatically dissolve the joint venture.

One member may sue the joint venture or one or more joint venturers to recover damages in a dispute. This differs from a partnership. Otherwise a joint venture is treated as a partnership and is governed by the law of partnerships.

Unlike a partnership, the joint venture has no legal existence separate from its members. This means that a creditor cannot sue the joint venture in its own name, but must sue all the individual members. Some states have laws that authorize partnerships to be sued and held liable, and these laws may apply to joint ventures. In these states the joint venture may sue and be sued, collect debts, file for bankruptcy, and convey property. Likewise, creditors may be allowed to collect judgments against the joint venture in its own name, rather than its individual members.[22] Persons in a joint venture are taxed the same as persons in a partnership.

CORPORATIONS[23]

A widely used form of organization is the corporation. Although the corporate form is normally associated with a large, complex business, numbers are *not* a legal criterion for incorporation. A relatively small number of persons, varying from one to three, may do so, and still receive the benefits of corporate organization. State laws usually say how many people may form a corporation.

Private corporations should be distinguished from *public corporations*. Public corporations are owned by the public through the purchase of shares. These include utility companies. Private corporations are the type usually found in the foodservice industry.

Private corporations are established for the benefit of their owners. They include both business, or stock, corporations and nonprofit, membership corporations. A typical foodservice corporation is a stock corporation organized for profit. The business corporation is organized to distribute profits in the form of dividends to its owners, called *shareholders*. Business corporations may be *publicly held* (public issue) corporations, which issue stock to the public, or they may be *closely-held*, owned by a family or another company.

The basic idea behind a corporation is to pool the assets of the shareholders into a fund to manage the business, make a profit, and in

Figure 12.3
Comparison of Partnerships and Corporations

Key Elements	Partnership	Corporation
Creation	By agreement of the parties	By statutory authorization or state approval of charter
Entity	Dissolved by bankruptcy or withdrawal of a partner	May be perpetual
Liability	Partners subject to unlimited liability for contracts, debts, and torts (legal wrongs) of other partners	Shareholders not liable for contracts, debts, and torts of the corporation in excess of their investments
Transferability of interest in organization	Interest of a partner in the partnership not transferable without consent of all of the other partners	Shares of corporate stock freely transferable
Management	Each partner entitled to an equal voice in management of the partnership	Management of corporation governed by a board of directors elected by shareholders. Directors establish policies and appoint officers
Taxes	Each partner liable for pro rata share of income taxes on net profits whether or not distributed	Two-level tax imposed. Corporation pays corporate income tax on net profits, including dividends; shareholders pay income tax on dividends received and interest received on corporate bonds
Cost of organization annual fees	No costs or fees are required. Exception: A limited partnership must pay an organizational fee	All costs and fees must be paid
Multistate transaction of business	Generally none	Must qualify and obtain certificate of authority to do business in other states

turn repay the shareholders for their investments. This may offer a business a larger pool of capital to operate, thus spreading the liability a little thinner than in a partnership, although normally a board of directors is accountable for wrongdoing, as is a chief operating officer. Further, banks and other lending institutions are more likely to lend money to a corporation than to a sole proprietorship, since the corporate form may have a stronger financial base—one which does not rely on the management skills or the funds of one person.

This form may be attractive to an entrepreneur who may wish to expand an idea or restaurant concept at a later point. Figure 12.3 compares the corporate form with the partnership form of organization.

The main features of a corporation are its perpetual existence and the fact that the liability of its owners, called shareholders, is limited to their individual investments, or stock purchases. Like limited partners, shareholders or stockholders are generally not responsible for the debts of the corporation beyond their own investments.

A board of directors, elected by the shareholders, actually supervises the managerial policies of the corporation. The board, in turn, employs officers to operate the business on a day-to-day basis.

Neither the directors nor the officers of the corporation need be shareholders unless the corporate articles or bylaws require stock ownership.

The Law of Corporations

The Model Business Corporation Act (MBCA), a model act prepared by a committee of legal experts in 1946 and revised in 1969, has been adopted by the majority of states, either totally or in part.[24] It governs all aspects of corporate formation; powers, duties, and rights and responsibilities of directors, officers, and shareholders to each other and to the corporation; and corporate dissolution.

Doing business as a corporation is governed by statute and not by agreement among the parties, and all states have some laws on this subject. These statutes are usually comprehensive and govern most corporate activities. Only when the statutes do not apply to particular corporate actions do the corporate charter and bylaws and the common law of corporations provide the law for court decisions.

Primary Characteristics of a Corporation

The essential features of the corporate form of business organization, as contrasted with the single proprietorship and partnership, are (1) an independent existence as an entity separate from its directors, officers, and shareholders—that is, it is not affected by their deaths or normal withdrawals; (2) the right to sue and be sued in the corporate name; (3) the right to acquire, hold, manage, and sell property for corporate purposes in the corporate name; and (4) the right to make bylaws.

The separate legal existence of a corporation means that contracts made by the corporation's agents in their corporate capacity *do not bind the members personally.*[25] Likewise, acts of members in their individual capacity do not bind the corporation.

Members may work in a representative capacity and still avoid individual liability. The common law of agency provides that they must *disclose* their representative or corporate capacity when signing contracts on behalf of a corporation with a third party, such as a vendor.[26]

To illustrate, you are a buyer and board member for the Alpha Corporation, which operates a popular restaurant. A wholesale food and beverage distributor, Omega Foods, approaches you to arrange for the sale of next month's meat, poultry, and frozen food staples. Omega's representative, Abbott, draws up and presents you, Costello, with a written purchase order. Assume that both Abbott and you have authority to conclude the deal. How do you, Costello, sign the agreement as a representative of Alpha? The safest form of execution is to sign:

Alpha Corporation
by: Richard Costello, Buyer

This discloses your corporate representative capacity: that you are signing *for Alpha Corporation,* and not for yourself.

By contrast, if you had merely signed "Richard Costello," the law presumes that you and you alone are contracting to buy from Omega Foods, unless Abbott knew that you were signing for Alpha Corporation. This fact may be disputed,[27] and you may suffer the consequences. The same analysis applies to Abbott's method of signing the order on behalf of Omega.

Board Members

Rights, Duties, and Liabilities
of Board Members
Under the MBCA the board of directors of a business corporation is authorized, among other things, to adopt initial bylaws, declare dividends, fill vacancies on the board, elect and remove officers, sell and lease mortgage assets of the corporation in the normal course of business, and propose to the shareholders major changes affecting the corporation that require shareholder approval. The last includes amendments to the articles of incorporation; merger or consolidation; sale, lease, or mortgage of major corporate assets other than in the normal course of business; and voluntary dissolution of the company.

The following are duties of the board of directors: (1) to protect assets and other interests of the owners (shareholders) of the corporation; (2) to ensure continuity of the corporation; (3) to ensure sound corporate management; and (4) to make nondelegable decisions, such as the payment of dividends.

An *individual board member* has no management duties other than possible appointment as a corporate agent by the board. A director has the right to inspect corporate books in order properly to carry out responsibilities as a director to the board and the corporation.

Although not agents of the corporation by operation of law, as are partners of a partnership, board members are required to (1) act within the authority granted by the corporation, (2) act with diligence and reasonable care in conducting corporate affairs, and (3) act in good faith for the benefit of the corporation and maintain loyalty to the corporation.

A director who exceeds the authority granted by the MBCA and the corporate bylaws is liable to the corporation for any resulting harm.[28] A director is also liable for losses incurred by the corporation resulting from his or her negligence or failure to carry out corporate responsibilities.[29]

A director is liable for injury to the corporation arising out of any self-interest activity. A director may not profit at the corporation's expense, or direct corporate opportunities to his or her own use.[30] For example, Peter, acting on behalf of his corporation "Salads to Go," comes upon a prime land deal for a new unit. However, during negotiations for the company, he decides to take a cut of the deal himself. He is no longer acting on behalf of the corporation but in his own self-interest, and may profit at Salads' expense. Peter negotiated a real estate deal that directed a corporate opportunity to his pocket, and may be liable to Salads for his cut.

Corporate Officers

Rights, Duties, and Liabilities
of Corporate Officers
Officers are agents of the corporation, and derive their rights from the company bylaws and from the board of directors. In addition, officers have authority to do those tasks necessary to carry out the duties assigned to them. The president of the board does not, simply by virtue of the office, have any power to bind the corporation. However, if the president is appointed chief executive officer (CEO) with general supervision and control of the company, then as CEO he or she is vested with broad apparent authority to make contracts

and otherwise act in conducting the ordinary business of the corporation. The CEO may hire foodservice managers, handle the budget, and purchase foods and supplies.

The corporate secretary usually keeps the corporate minutes of director and shareholder meetings. The secretary has no other authority.

The treasurer has custody over corporate funds and has authority to receive and use the funds for authorized purposes. The treasurer, standing alone, has no authority to borrow money or issue commercial paper (promissory notes or warehouse receipts, for example).

Officers are personally liable for any willful or intentional misconduct, either under tort law or under an appropriate criminal code. If the misconduct falls within the doctrine of *respondeat superior,* where the employer must account for the actions of employees, the corporation is also held responsible. For example, if an officer acts as an agent in signing a banquet contract the company cannot fulfill, the corporation may be responsible.

Normally officers are not themselves liable for the unintentional negligence of corporation employees unless they authorized or participated in such negligence.

Criminal liability is imposed on a corporation where the board of directors authorizes the wrongdoing or the officer performing or committing the crime is a high-level officer.[31]

Corporate Shareholders

Rights, Duties, and Liabilities of Shareholders

Common shareholders have an interest in (1) corporate net earnings, (2) control of the corporation, and (3) corporate net assets. They are not truly owners of corporate assets, since the corporation, as a separate entity, owns its assets.

Net earnings are dividends on shares of common stock held by each shareholder. Payment of dividends is up to the board of directors, and rests upon that body's reasonable business judgment. Only flagrant abuse of that judgment will cause a court to order a dividend payment in the face of board refusal to do so.[32]

Control of the corporation means the right to vote shares of stock. Each shareholder is normally entitled to one vote for each share held. Voting rights are based on the statutes of the state of incorporation and the corporate articles and bylaws.

Usually the common stock of a corporation carries voting rights, and each shareholder is entitled to one vote per common share owned. Voting rights are extremely important, since they enable the shareholder who has a majority of shares to elect the corporation's board of directors and to change its ownership structure, a not unheard of phenomenon in the restaurant industry.

The following proposals are subject to stockholder approval: (1) to merge the existing corporate business with another with only one of the corporations continuing to exist, or (2) to consolidate the corporate business, where two or more corporations combine, with neither surviving and a new one emerging. The proportion of stockholder approval necessary (two-thirds of all eligible shareholders, three-fourths of all such holders, or a mere majority) is determined by state law.

The quality of management is determined in large measure by the intelligent use of voting rights. The shareholders have the right to vote existing management out of office. A merger or consolidation may drastically affect old management policies, and shareholders are free to pool their voting rights by nominating and electing a particular slate of candidates to sit on the board of directors.

Under most state laws shareholders have the right to amend the articles of incorporation, or the corporate charter. Such a change might involve expanding the types of businesses the corporation was originally set up to transact. Shareholders have few responsibilities. They elect and remove the directors and they vote on extraordinary transactions.

Because shareholders have so few powers and duties compared with board members and officers, their potential liabilities are not as great. Their major protection against creditor claims is their limited liability for corporate obligations: This limited liability translates into no liability beyond their total investment (the cost of the shares purchased). Illegal dividend payments received by shareholders are recoverable by the corporation, if the shareholder knew of the illegality. Shareholders may be held liable for corporate debts if the corporation piled up debts before completing legal requirements for incorporation.

Purchasing and Selling Corporate Assets

The use of a corporation as a vehicle to buy or sell a business permits greater flexibility than does the purchase or sale of a partnership. The purchase and sale of a majority of the shares of stock of a corporation are sufficient to obtain control. The sale of a majority of shares of a corporation does not normally affect the existence of the corporation. Only consolidation creates a new corporation.

Such alternatives as merger, consolidation, and purchase or sale of assets are readily available to a corporation.

In general, corporate stock represents ownership rights. On the basis of the number of shares owned, each stockholder may transfer those shares either by gift or sale to another person, partnership, or corporation, as well as to nonprofit organizations. If the number of shares owned by any one person or entity exceeds 50 percent of the total number of shares of stock issued by the corporation, the buyer acquires a controlling interest in the corporation. This enables the buyer to elect a board of directors and thus manage the corporation.

Closely-Held Corporations[33]

A closely-held corporation, also called a close corporation, is an exception to the general rule that corporate stock is freely transferable by sale or gift. Such a corporation is one whose shares are held by members of a family or a few individuals. It is particularly useful to the small operator starting up a restaurant, because the stockholders are limited in number and the transfer of shares is subject to some restrictions involving sales to third persons.

In many cases the corporation may not offer its securities to the public. This means that shareholders wishing to sell must first offer their shares to the corporation, the other shareholders, so that they may buy up the shares and maintain control within the group. If the stockholders fail or refuse to buy out the selling shareholder, the seller may offer the shares to any other person or institutional buyer. The right of first refusal by existing shareholders might be contained in the corporation's bylaws.

There are statutory restrictions on the number of shareholders a close corporation may have, so this type resembles a partnership rather than a corporation. The shareholders usually *always* know each other personally and work closely in managing the corporation. Typically, a family or group of close friends would not wish control to be transferred outside, since this would destroy the rapport and close working relationship. The closely-held form is treated as a corporation, with all of the rights and responsibilities of that form.

There is one substantial risk involved in the use of the closely-held corporate form of organization. When the corporation is legally formed by a single person or two or three family members, *it is essential that the status of the corporation stay separate from the personal affairs of its individual owners.* Restaurant corporations run by family members can become battlegrounds focused on family problems if caution is not exercised. Typical potential problem areas include combining into one account corporate and personal funds, failing to record in proper form what goes on at board meetings, and shareholder use of corporate property for personal purposes.

Any conduct which seems abusive of corporate privileges for personal benefit or the use of the corporation to blend personal and corporate activity may result in a court "piercing the corporate veil." The court may hold the owner personally liable to creditors for corporate obligations not fulfilled as a result of such activity. This legal doctrine permits courts to disregard the corporate form when it is used to commit wrongdoing, shield fraud, or evade legal responsibility.[34] The activities of each stockholder will be studied with more care, since the possibility for wrongdoing exists to a greater degree because of the greater control of the corporation than is true in a publicly-owned business.[35]

The following scenario will help show you how the courts may view an action by a corporate stockholder.

Albert lent money to his close corporation, Eats Inc., to finance the purchase of a fast-food franchise. Albert took as collateral a deed to the land he owned on which the franchise would operate. Later Eats Inc. became insolvent, and general creditors of the franchise sued to set aside the loan and recover the land collateral. They did this to make the land available as an asset of the corporation against which they could satisfy their claims.

Normally Albert's loan to the company (his own) would give him the status of a preferred creditor, who would be entitled to satisfy *his* loan out of the sale of the land ahead of and in preference to the general creditors.

The court ruled that the loan was not taken out to benefit Albert at the expense of the corporation, and that he had demonstrated good faith and fair dealing in this case and was entitled to preferred creditor status.[36]

However, if Albert had taken the loan out to finance his racing car, which had nothing to do with Eats Inc. or the fast-food franchise, the court might have taken a different view. The following case illustrates that view.

Platt v. Billingsley
California Court of Appeals
234 Cal. 2d 577; 44 Cal. Rptr. 476 (1965)

Facts.   Billingsley, Grimm, and two other persons bought all of the stock in a restaurant corporation. At the time the corporation had a deficit of $51,972. The stockholders did not contribute new money to the corporation. Later Billingsley and Grimm each sold half of his stock to Button for $17,925. (They did not have a "consent to transfer stock," as required by the California Commissioner of Corporations.) Platt, the contractor, entered into an agreement with the corporation to remodel the building as a Polynesian restaurant. He finished the job at a cost of $12,000. At first Platt was paid regularly, but then checks started to bounce. Platt was assured he would be paid. When he was not, he filed suit and attached $7999. He released $4000 when Button and Billingsley told him they would give him a chattel mortgage on restaurant equipment, which turned out to be worthless because of tax liens against the corporation. Platt initiated action to disregard the corporate entity and hold the three personally liable for corporate debts; he won. Billingsley and Grimm appealed.

Reasoning. The court found that they were personally liable as they had disregarded the corporate entity by the following actions:

> First, Billingsley and Button retained personal control over the funds which were never deposited in the corporation account and never became subject to claims of corporation creditors. Second, $17,925 of the money came from the sale of part of appellants' corporate stock. They did not risk their own capital; rather, they sold Button stock in an undercapitalized venture and risked Button's money in an attempt to bolster a faltering business.
>
> Third, use of the money to pay debts of the corporation violated representations appellants made to the Corporation Commissioner in seeking permission to sell half of their stock to Button. Appellants represented to the commissioner that: "none of the proceeds from the sale of said shares will be used directly or indirectly for the benefit of said corporation, but are for the personal, individual benefit of the undersigned."
>
> Other acts of appellants that support the trial court's decision to pierce the corporate veil include (a) Billingsley's promise to protect respondent by a chattel mortgage on kitchen equipment, a representation upon which respondent relied in releasing $4000 of a $7999 attachment of corporate assets; (b) an offer by Billingsley and Grimm to pledge their corporate stock, their personal property, to secure the corporate obligation; (c) operation of the corporation with only two directors, a violation of the bylaws of the corporation and of California Corporations Code section 800, requiring that: ". . . all corporate powers shall be exercised by or under authority of, and the business and affairs of every corporation shall be controlled by a board of not less than three directors."

The court said that the corporate veil may be pierced to *prevent* fraud and unjustness, and the action does not depend on the proof of fraud. The court agreed with the trial court that:

> At all relevant times, the corporation was influenced, dominated and controlled by defendants, Billingsley, Grimm, and Button, and there existed such a unity of interest and ownership that the individuality and separateness of these defendants and the corporation ceased.
>
> That if the acts of the defendants, Billingsley, Grimm, and Button are considered those of the corporation alone, an inequitable and unjust result will follow.

Conclusion. The corporate form is not set up to shield its members against legal action or as a cover for wrongdoing. Members may be held liable for corporate debts if their actions are irresponsible and disregard the corporate entity. Another common example of wrongdoing is for members of a corporation to take huge salaries and not obtain capital for the corporation to meet debts. A corporation is not a fund-raising venture for its members but an entity that requires that some profits be channeled back into the corporation so that it remains solvent.

Advantages

The close corporation might be the vehicle most suitable to the typical foodservice operator. This form (1) provides limited liability to its owner shareholders and yet retains more centralized ownership and control, and (2) permits greater financial incentives to investors than either the general partnership or corporate form.

Disadvantages

The major drawback is the difficulty of obtaining needed financing from banks in times of very high interest rates, since the close corporation may be prohibited from selling shares to the public without losing its status. Initial institutional financing or possible refinancing later may require reorganization of the foodservice business as a general business corporation.

The limited liability of the close corporation form does not always exist in practice, particularly for a new corporation. A bank may be unwilling to lend funds to a small corporation, if it is new and without any established financial track record, unless the stockholders co-sign the loan as individuals. This means that each stockholder agrees to be personally responsible for repayment of the loan. Here the limited liability rule normally available to shield stockholders from personal responsibility for corporate debts does not apply because they have assumed repayment responsibility voluntarily. Business necessity in obtaining bank financing may cause corporate shareholders to trade off their legal right to be shielded from personal liability to obtain the corporate loan.

Tax Considerations

For federal income tax purposes, the corporation is treated differently than a partnership. Because the corporation is a separate legal entity, it is required to pay *corporate income taxes.*

Corporate income is taxed and payable *by the corporation,* which must file a corporate return. Additionally, stockholders are taxed on distributed dividends and interest on corporate bonds or loans. Earnings due but not distributed are not taxed. However, excessive accumulations may result in the corporation paying a penalty.

Corporate capital *gains and losses* are taxed and payable by the corporation. Sales of corporate securities owned by individual shareholders are taxed to the shareholder, with capital gains and losses available to the individual.

Unlike in a partnership, all corporate employees and officers who are stockholders can be beneficiaries of a pension trust. The corporation can deduct any payments made into the trust on behalf of both groups. Corporate employees and shareholder beneficiaries can receive tax shelter benefits up to $5000 per person from the corporations.

Whereas partnerships are not required to pay income taxes in many states, corporations are usually subject to state income tax, with the corresponding right to deduct the payments on federal returns.

Subchapter S Corporation

Ideally some corporations would like to have the tax advantages of a partnership while retaining the limited liability that the corporation offers. The Subchapter S corporation is a tax option authorized by the Internal Revenue Code. It permits those corporations that qualify to be taxed as if they were partnerships. Qualifying corporations file only an information return that spreads income among the shareholders regardless of dividend distributions. All corporate income taxes are avoided. The shareholders are not taxed twice. However, unlike other corporations, the amount of income the Subchapter S corporation can transfer to tax-sheltered pension plans is restricted.

Major Requirements to Qualify under Subchapter S

A number of requirements must be met to qualify for Subchapter S. The most important are:

1. The corporation must be chartered under federal or state laws.
2. The corporation must not be affiliated with any other group of corporations.
3. The shareholders of the corporation must be individuals, estates, or trusts completely owned by the creator of the trust. Corporations and partnerships may not be shareholders.
4. The corporation must have no more than 35 shareholders.
5. The corporation can issue only one class of stock. This means that all shareholders have equal voting rights.

6. The corporation may not receive more than 25 percent of its gross income from investments that the company did not actively generate. This means the company may not receive income from securities of other companies held by it in excess of one-fourth of its gross receipts.
7. The corporation may not receive more than 80 percent of its total income from sources outside the United States.
8. The corporation may not issue shares of its stock to nonresident aliens.

The Subchapter S corporation is tailored to meet the needs of the small restaurant business that fits the definition of a closely-held or family corporation. In addition to other advantages, the Subchapter S corporation is particularly attractive when the individual shareholders are in a lower income tax bracket than the corporation itself. In this case all shareholder income is taxed in the lower income bracket, whether it is distributed or not. This treatment permits the corporation to accumulate more funds than a non-qualifying corporation.

Also, the Subchapter S corporation may select a taxable year other than the normal dividend distribution year and thereby defer some shareholder taxes. Why? Because undistributed earnings are not taxed to the shareholder until after the close of the corporation's taxable year.

To illustrate, Alpha, under Subchapter S, declares but does not distribute a stock dividend from its restaurant profits. Its taxable fiscal year runs from January to January. A shareholder, Beta, uses the calendar year for tax purposes. Beta does not have to include the dividend until after January of the following calendar year. The Subchapter S corporation can offer some tax-free benefits not available to other corporations, such as pension plan contributions and death benefits. The fact that they may be restricted still yields some federal tax savings to shareholders.

NOT-FOR-PROFIT AND NONPROFIT ORGANIZATIONS

Not-for-profit and nonprofit organizations are organized as membership corporations or cooperatives, and do not have stock or other certificates of ownership that are designed to profit the members or owners.

These entities often operate for religious, charitable, educational, fraternal, or civic purposes. They are formed under state statutes that usually provide for different formation and operation policies than for stock companies. If stock certificates are issued to members, no dividends may be paid to the member holders.

Profits from operations are permitted, but the profits must not be distributed to members but left with the corporation.

Normally nonprofit and not-for-profit organizations are exempt from income taxes, and are able to reinvest a greater share of earned income than is the case with business or stock corporations.[37] In other respects the nature of the businesses they operate is similar to that of corporate entities set up to make a profit.[38] A private luncheon or country club might be organized as a nonprofit membership corporation.[39] Trade associations also might qualify for exempt income tax status, so long as they do not engage in excessive lobbying activities.[40]

CHOOSING THE RIGHT FORM

This chapter has explored the choices of business organization available to you when you decide to establish yourself in business, either alone or with others.

You must weigh the advantages and disadvantages of each form. Keep in mind (1) your personal objectives, (2) the costs of organizing your business, (3) the need to share control with others, (4) the amount of outside financing you may require, (5) whether you wish others to continue the business on your retirement or death, (6) how much personal liability you will assume, and (7) how and to what extent your business income will be taxed. *No one form will contain all the advantages you wish without corresponding disadvantages.* Therefore, you must try to list your priorities in the order of their importance and select the form that comes closest to giving you the most pluses and the least minuses. Your goal should be to exercise your best business judgment as to what business form would satisfy your objectives.

Future economic and financial circumstances may cause you to alter your business organization. For example, if your sole proprietorship operation becomes so successful that you wish to operate more than one unit, you may wish to consider forming a partnership or corporation. Delegation of authority may be more easily implemented by a partnership or corporation where supervision of geographically separated units is involved. The partnership and corporate forms may also make it easier to raise the outside financing needed to expand the business. You have the right to change your form of organization to meet future needs.

The form of organization that you may wish to consider adopting if you seek a high degree of internal and external control over decision-making and protection against full personal liability for business debts, but with the sharing of financing and other responsibilities, is the close corporation. This form survives you. The restriction on stock sales to the public minimizes a take-over by outsiders through the purchase of shares. The limited liability of corporate owners/shareholders is preserved, and if the corporation qualifies for Subchapter S treatment, corporate income is treated as partnership income, with no double taxation. The one limitation on the close corporate form is the possible need for outside financing through public stock sales if financing by lending institutions becomes prohibitively expensive. Also, you must take great care in selecting your close corporate shareholders, since you will have to work with them. A high degree of personal ownership interaction will be needed, since very important decisions, such as securing major outside financing to open new units, will require unanimous approval.

Whatever your choice of business organization, the decision to adopt one or another form is yours alone to make. The risk of bad judgment rests with you. The law cannot correct the results of a poor choice of organization. The law does permit you to alter your form of organization as your business needs change.

SUMMARY

There are several forms of business used in the foodservice field to start and maintain restaurants and other operations.

The sole proprietorship is a popular form in the foodservice industry. It offers independence and control to the entrepreneur interested in running the whole show. It also offers unlimited liability and risk. The owner may sell or give away the business at any time.

The partnership is another popular form. It divides up the responsibility and the liability. The personal assets of each partner may be taken to satisfy creditor claims if debts cannot be paid out of partnership funds. Other partnerships may be for partners who want the profits, but do not want to help manage or who want their membership in the operation kept from the public. The Uniform Partnership Act is the source of law for this form of business. The partnership agreement is the basis for the partners' rights and obligations.

A joint venture is a type of partnership formed for a single business purpose, which usually dissolves when the business does.

The corporation is a form of business in which the assets of the owners or shareholders are pooled to manage the business. The liability is spread among the shareholders. The business is usually run by a board of officers elected by the shareholders, who in turn appoint an executive to handle the day-to-day operations. Each of these parties has rights and duties to each other and to the corporation.

A closely-held corporation adopts the same general rules as the corporation, except that the members are usually either members of the same family or are well known to each other. Shareholders in this type of corporation usually want ownership and control to stay within the group, and generally do not offer shares to the public.

Corporations are required to pay corporate income taxes and shareholders' dividends are also taxed. Corporations may also be subject to state income taxes.

The Subchapter S corporation is a form of business that is run like a corporation but taxed like a partnership.

QUESTIONS

1. Tom Sanders wants to start a restaurant. He likes to work alone as far as supervision and management activities go. He doesn't want to have to deal with separate taxation forms for personal and business taxes. Tom has no children interested in continuing the business. He wants to be able to sell the business when he's ready. What business form might be best for Tom? Why?
2. What are some of the characteristics of a closely-held corporation?
3. Which business form do you think would be best for you? Explain your answer.
4. What is the main difference between a partnership and a joint venture?
5. How is a corporation taxed twice?

NOTES

1. See generally *National Biscuit Co. v. Stroud*, 249 N.C. 467, 106 S.E.2d 692 (1959) (grocery store).
2. See *Vidricksen v. Grover*, 363 F.2d 372 (9th Cir. 1966) (auto agency).
3. Unless otherwise noted, the materials to follow are derived from the Uniform Partnership Act of 1914 (UPA), as amended.
4. A conflict exists among the courts as to whether a minor may recover the full amount he or she invested or must bear a proportionate share of partnership losses, not to exceed his or her total investment. The courts agree, however, that a minor may not recover contributions of capital until all creditor claims have been satisfied.
5. *Waagen v. Gerde*, 36 Wash. 2d 563, 219 P.2d 595 (1950) (commercial fishing business).
6. *Clement v. Clement*, 436 Pa. 466, 260 A.2d 728 (1970).
7. *Starr v. International Realty, Ltd.*, 271 Or. 396, 533 P.2d 165 (1975) (real estate venture).
8. *Woodruff v. Bryant*, 558 S.W.2d 535 (Tex. Civ. App. 1977) (finance company).
9. *Starr v. International Realty, Ltd.*, *supra* note 7.
10. *Estate of Witlin*, 83 Cal. App. 3d 167, 147 Cal. Rptr. 723 (1978) (health center).
11. *McBriety v. Phillips*, 180 Md. 569, 26 A.2d 400 (1942) (tavern).
12. *Phillips v. Cook*, 239 Md. 215, 210 A.2d 743 (1965) (automobile dealership); *Vrabel v. Acri*, 156 Ohio St. 467, 103 N.E.2d 564 (1952) (tavern).
13. *National Biscuit Co. v. Stroud*, *supra* note 1.
14. Where the partnership itself is illegal, the courts will not assist in its dissolution, and will not enforce the rights of any of its partners. *Williams v. Burrus*, 20 Wash. App. 494, 581 P.2d 164 (1978) (tavern).
15. *First Western Mortgage Co. v. Hotel Gearhart, Inc.*, 260 Or. 196, 488 P.2d 450 (1971) (motel and restaurant).
16. *McClennen v. Commissioner*, 131 F.2d 165 (1st Cir. 1942) (law firm).
17. *Wolfe v. East Texas Seed Co.*, 583 S.W.2d 481 (Tex. Civ. App. 1979); *Ellingson v. Walsh, O'Connor & Barneson*, 15 Cal. 2d 673, 104 P.2d 507 (1940) (law firm).
18. *McClennen v. Commissioner*, *supra* note 16.

19. *Vidricksen v. Grover, supra* note 2. Cf. *Frigidaire Sales Corp. v. Union Properties, Inc.,* 88 Wash. 2d 400, 562 P.2d 244 (1977) (real estate firm).

20. See *Travis v. St. John,* 176 Conn. 69, 404 A.2d 885 (1978) (real estate investment).

21. *Misco-United Supply, Inc. v. Petroleum Corp.,* 462 F.2d 75 (5th Cir. 1972) (oil lease venture).

22. *Id.*

23. Unless otherwise noted, the materials to follow are derived from the Model Business Corporation Act (MBCA).

24. These states are Alabama, Alaska, Arkansas, Colorado, Connecticut, Georgia, Illinois, Iowa, Kentucky, Louisiana, Maine, Maryland, Massachusetts, Michigan, Mississippi, Montana, Nebraska, New Jersey, New Mexico, New York, North Carolina, North Dakota, Oregon, Rhode Island, South Carolina, South Dakota, Tennessee, Texas, Utah, Vermont, Virginia, Washington, Wisconsin, and Wyoming; also the District of Columbia.

25. *Harris v. Stephens Wholesale Bldg. Supply Co.,* 54 Ala. App. 405, 309 So. 2d 115 (1975).

26. *Id.* See also *Rosen v. Deporter-Butterworth Tours, Inc.,* 62 Ill. App. 3d 762, 379 N.E.2d 407 (1978); *Dinkler Management Corp. v. Stein,* 115 Ga. App. 586, 155 S.E.2d 442 (1967) (hotel management corporation).

27. See *Henderson v. Phillips,* 195 A.2d 400 (D.C. App. 1963) (plumbing contract).

28. *Star Corp. v. General Screw Prods. Corp.,* 501 S.W.2d 374 (Tex. Civ. App. 1973).

29. *Neese v. Brown,* 218 Tenn. 686, 405 S.W.2d 577 (1964) (bank).

30. *Morad v. Coupounas,* 361 So. 2d 6 (Ala. 1978) (medical laboratory); *Lincoln Stores, Inc. v. Grant,* 309 Mass. 417, 34 N.E.2d 704 (1941); *Patient Care Services, S.C. v. Segal,* 32 Ill. App. 3d 1021, 337 N.E.2d 471 (1975); *Aero Drapery of Ky., Inc. v. Engdahl,* 507 S.W.2d 166 (Ky. App. 1974); *Hartung v. Architects Hartung/ Odle/Burke,* Inc., 157 Ind. App. 546, 301 N.E.2d 240 (1973).

31. *United States v. Park,* 421 U.S. 658 (1975) (criminal liability of CEO of national retail food chain for FDCA violation).

32. *Miller v. Magline, Inc.,* 76 Mich. App. 284, 256 N.W.2d 761 (1977) (defense contractor).

33. Lusk, Hewitt, Donnell, Barnes, *Business Law and the Regulatory Environment,* 503–19 (5th ed. 1982).

34. *Valley Finance, Inc. v. United States,* 629 F.2d 162 (D.C. Cir. 1980), *cert. denied,* 451 U.S. 1018 (1981) (Tongsun Park, Koreagate scandal). See also *Felsenthal Co. v. Northern Assur. Co. Ltd.,* 284 Ill. 343, 120 N.E. 268 (1918) (criminal fraud–arson).

35. *Intertherm, Inc. v. Olympic Homes Systems, Inc.,* 569 S.W.2d 467 (Tenn. App. 1978).

36. *Id.*

37. I.R.C. sec. 501(a) *et seq.* require the organization to qualify for tax-exempt status independently of state incorporation statutes that otherwise confer nonprofit status. Clubs organized and operated substantially for pleasure, recreation, and other nonprofit purposes are eligible organizations. I.R.C. sec. 501(c)(7); Treas. Reg. sec. 1.501(c)(7)–1.

38. Unrelated business income, meaning business income that does not contribute importantly to the accomplishment of the exempt purpose of the organization, is subject to taxation.

39. See note 37, *supra.*

40. I.R.S. sec. 501(c)(3) makes such lobbying activities a "prohibited act," which can cause the organization to lose its tax-exempt status.

13
Bankruptcy and Reorganization

Objectives

The purpose of this chapter is to:

1. Examine the purposes of bankruptcy.
2. Compare and contrast the different types of bankruptcy.
3. Explain who may file for bankruptcy, the rights and responsibilities of the parties involved, the procedures, the tests used to determine bankruptcy status, and what debts are most affected by bankruptcy discharge.

Case in Point

Quik-Stop, operator of a serve-yourself vending machine food and beverage outlet, failed to make the required payments on its vending equipment lease with Leaseafoods, and Leaseafoods obtained a court judgment for the total amount due. Afterward Quik-Stop filed a petition to be declared bankrupt, but failed to inform the court of its debt to Leaseafoods or Leaseafoods' identity. The court declared Quik-Stop bankrupt. When Leaseafoods tried to get the bill paid, Quik-Stop argued that the equipment debt was wiped out when the court declared the operation bankrupt. Leaseafoods responded that its debt was not "wiped out" because it was never notified of the bankruptcy court proceedings, and the debt was not given to the court. Which has bankruptcy law on its side?

The reviewing court ruled in favor of Leaseafoods. Every creditor is entitled to challenge a discharge of bankruptcy, and must be given notice of a bankruptcy hearing enough in advance to allow time to prepare for the challenge.[1]

PURPOSES OF BANKRUPTCY

Contrary to popular belief, bankruptcy is not intended to give debtors an open-ended, revolving escape hatch through which to thwart their creditors. If that were truly the case, all credit transactions would virtually end, and our credit-based economy would suffer permanent damage.

Bankruptcy laws serve to protect creditors by permitting an orderly, equal distribution of a debtor's estate. Bankruptcy laws also protect creditors from a debtor's temptation to conceal or "flee with the loot," or to favor one creditor at the expense of the others. Last, bankruptcy proceedings give debtors a new financial lease on life, freeing them from an otherwise endless obligation to pay debts beyond their ability to do so.[2]

In addition to absolute bankruptcy, the law also allows some debtors additional time to pay outstanding debts free of the pressures of creditors.

Viewed realistically, bankruptcy is a rescue device the law establishes to protect creditors *and* debtors from the consequences of circumstances beyond their control, such as accidents, natural disasters, illness, divorce, severe economic problems, and reduction or end of government benefits. Bankruptcy may relieve the severe financial hardship to which these unexpected events can lead.[3]

Both businesses and individuals can file for bankruptcy. As a businessperson, you should be aware that there are options that can help you stay in the foodservice business.

FORMS OF BANKRUPTCY

The Bankruptcy Reform Act of 1978 includes three forms of bankruptcy available to businesses. The most common is straight bankruptcy, or Chapter 7 bankruptcy, with any assets distributed to creditors by a bankruptcy trustee.

Chapter 11 bankruptcy allows the businessperson to reorganize under a repayment plan, assembled by a trustee and approved by a creditors committee.

Chapter 13 allows for a voluntary repayment plan by the debtor.

We will examine each in detail and present the advantages and disadvantages of each.

WHO PETITIONS FOR BANKRUPTCY?

All bankruptcy proceedings are started by the filing of a petition. Filing for bankruptcy can be done in one of two ways: (1) a *voluntary* petition is filed by a debtor, or (2) an *involuntary* petition is filed by a creditor or creditors of the debtor.

Individuals, corporations, and partnerships may file a *voluntary* petition. (However, a partnership petition does not protect the individual partners. To obtain individual relief in bankruptcy, each partner must file an individual petition. Otherwise each partner will be held fully responsible for partnership obligations not satisfied by partnership assets.) Debtors wishing to file a voluntary petition do not have to prove *insolvency,* meaning that their debts exceed their assets. All that is required is proof that the debtor *has debts.*

An *involuntary* petition may be filed by any single creditor having a valid claim exceeding $5000, which does not include security interests or collateral held by the creditor. Three creditors must sign an involuntary petition when the debtor has 12 or more creditors. In an involuntary proceeding, the debtor must be unable to pay debts as they become due, or must have had a court-appointed custodian take charge of his or her property within the previous four months.

This petition can only be used for Chapter 7—straight bankruptcy—and Chapter 11 reorganization. No creditor can file an involuntary petition for a debtor under Chapter 13.

In an involuntary proceeding, the court may permit foodservice debtors to continue to operate if they can establish that they do not intend to dismantle the business or sell the assets at less than fair market value. An involuntary petition may not be filed against nonprofit organizations.

This is usually a last resort for creditors when large sums of money are owed. If you are a creditor, you may be forced to use this against a debtor against whom you have a large claim. Still, you should try to settle out of court if possible. Advantages notwithstanding, it is not the most ideal remedy for creditors or debtors.

JURISDICTION

Congress gave exclusive jurisdiction—court power to hear and determine bankruptcy cases—to all United States district trial courts. Only federal bankruptcy judges have the power to hear bankruptcy petitions.[4]

Every debtor may file a petition in the judicial district in which, for the longest portion of a 180-day period before the filing, the debtor had either (1) a residence, (2) a domicile (a person's true, fixed home, to which he or she always intends to return), (3) principal assets, or (4) a principal place of business.[5] These four locations for filing are called *venue,* that is, where you file your petition. All federal district courts can hear bankruptcy petitions, but the right choice of a particular federal district court depends on the four tests of venue.

For *individuals* and *corporations,* venue is the place where the individual or corporation resides. Corporations may file in any federal district in the corporation's state of incorporation or the district where the company's principal assets or principal place of business is located.[6] An independent operator must file in the place where the restaurant business and assets are located.

Partnerships and *unincorporated associations* must file in the district where their principal place of business or their principal assets are located.[7] Once a partner has filed an individual petition in one district, all other partners may file their petitions on behalf of the partnership in that district. Likewise, a filing in one district on behalf of a partnership permits all general partners to file individual petitions in that district.[8]

What happens when you file in the wrong federal district? That court has the power to transfer your petition to the correct district or to hear and determine your petition in spite of the wrong filing, called *improper venue.* The court choice is made in the interests of justice and the convenience of the parties.[9]

STRAIGHT BANKRUPTCY

For foodservice businesses that are seriously in debt, straight bankruptcy may be the only route. The end result of straight bankruptcy, however, is that the business usually terminates, and any remaining assets are distributed to creditors by a court-appointed *trustee*. Straight bankruptcy, as common as it is, should nonetheless be the last resort for businesspersons.

Straight bankruptcy may be voluntary, if filed for by the debtor, or involuntary, if filed by the creditor(s). Either way, if a straight bankruptcy petition is granted, the foodservice operator may be effectively out of business. Even if the debtor could start up again, the inability to obtain credit after a straight bankruptcy, with the resulting need to pay cash up front, would present a serious cashflow problem.

The main advantage of straight bankruptcy is that it results in a "clean slate" for the debtor. The debtor is freed of the requirement to pay the debts erased under the bankruptcy petition, and the creditors are paid—more or less—since bankruptcy laws allow only so many cents to be paid on each dollar owed.

When a bankruptcy petition is filed, the bankruptcy court must decide whether to grant or deny relief. Relief is automatic when a voluntary petition is filed or the debtor does not contest the filing of an involuntary petition. Should the debtor argue against the granting of an involuntary petition, the court will hold a trial to decide whether a declaration of bankruptcy is appropriate. Relief of this kind will be granted only if the debtor is unable to pay his or her debts as they become due, or in the event a trustee was appointed within four months of the filing.[10]

The court will require the bankrupt to file a list of assets, liabilities, and creditors, and a statement of his or her current financial condition. The debtor must list *all* of his or her creditors on the schedule required by law, or face the likelihood that an unlisted creditor will successfully move to revoke the discharge. The court will then call a creditors' meeting. At that meeting the creditors may elect a committee or appoint a trustee to manage the bankrupt's estate. The court must approve this appointment. The debtor must appear at the meeting and answer questions about his or her financial circumstances.[11] One of the most frequently asked questions is whether the debtor has concealed or wrongfully disposed of assets.

The court-approved trustee takes charge of the debtor's property and has it appraised for value. The trustee sets aside those items of the debtor's property that are exempt from distribution under state or federal bankruptcy laws. In some cases the trustee has temporary authority to operate the debtor's business.[12]

The trustee evaluates creditor claims and objects to those he or she thinks improper. All secured and exempt property is segregated from unsecured property. Unsecured property is sold and the proceeds held for the benefit of creditors in the name of the bankrupt's estate. All money received by the trustee must be deposited in that account, which the trustee must keep and report to the creditors. The trustee must make a final accounting report to the creditors at their last meeting.[13]

At this point, unless the bankrupt files a waiver of the right to a discharge, he or she is entitled to a *discharge in bankruptcy*. The debtor is released from obligation for the debts involved. An individual must wait six years from the last discharge he or she received to be eligible for another discharge. Corporations are not eligible for a discharge in bankruptcy.[14] They are eligible for reorganization under bankruptcy laws, whereby they remain in business and pay off their debts gradually.

Criteria for Grant or Denial of Bankrupt Status

Eligibility for discharge of a bankrupt is not the same thing as *granting* a discharge in bankruptcy. All creditors with allowable claims, the trustee, or a United States attorney may file objections to any pending discharge. A final hearing will be held to determine whether or not a discharge should be granted. A discharge will be denied if the debtor fails to appear at the hearing, or refuses to submit to questions of creditors at a creditors' meeting called by the court.[15] Additionally, the court must decide whether the bankrupt has committed any act that is a legal obstacle to discharge, or creates a bar to discharge.

A *bar to a discharge* is intended to prevent dishonest debtors from using bankruptcy as a means of benefiting from their own wrongdoing. Acts that bar or require the court to deny bankruptcy are: (1) intentionally falsifying, concealing, or destroying debt records; (2) falsifying statements of financial condition to obtain credit or extensions of credit; (3) fraudulent transfers, removals, or concealment of property to hinder, delay, or defraud creditors; (4) failure to account satisfactorily for assets; and (5) failure to obey court orders or to answer questions the court approves of and directs the debtor to answer.[16]

Is it possible to repay debts after they have been discharged in bankruptcy? Yes, *reaffirmation agreements* are allowed. Before a discharge is granted, the creditor needs to negotiate an agreement with the debtor and get the court to approve the agreement. The reaffirmation agreement is allowed as long as the debtor does not cancel within 30 days of the date of court approval.[17]

Debtor Rights and Responsibilities

Every debtor has rights and responsibilities in bankruptcy proceedings.

Exemptions

Certain items of property are not considered debtor assets and are exempt from court disposition, which means that they may be kept by the debtor free and clear of creditor claims, unless the debtor conceals or fraudulently transfers such property in violation of law. Federal and state laws govern such exemptions.[18]

Federal exemptions include: (1) real or personal property used as a residence not to exceed $7500 in value; (2) one motor vehicle not to exceed $1200 in value; (3) household goods, furnishings, wearing apparel, appliances, books, animals, crops, or musical instruments primarily for personal, household, or family use of the debtor or dependents, not to exceed $200 in any one item; (4) personal or family jewelry not to exceed $500 in total value, and used by the debtor or dependents; (5) implements, professional books, or tools of trade not to exceed $750 in total value; (6) life insurance contracts; (7) medically prescribed health aids; (8) any other property of the debtor's choosing not exceeding $400 in value; and (9) social security, disability, alimony, and other benefits reasonably necessary for the support of the debtor or the debtor's dependents.

Liens[19]

Liens are legally created rights that certain creditors may use to seize and sell a debtor's assets. Debtors may avoid certain liens that would otherwise apply to defeat or impair their legal exemptions, such as life insurance contracts. Such voidable liens are court-ordered liens or nonpossessory, nonpurchase money security interests in property exempt under (3), (4), (5), and (7) of the federal exemptions noted above.[20]

Surviving Obligations

The federal Bankruptcy Act makes certain obligations or debts nondischargeable under Chapter 7, meaning that the debtor remains liable to pay them even though the bankruptcy court has discharged all other allowable, provable claims. These surviving obligations are:[21]

1. Federal, state, and local fines or taxes.
2. Any obligations arising out of obtaining money by false statements, pretenses, or representations.
3. Obligations arising out of willful or malicious injury to a person or to that person's property.
4. Alimony and child-support obligations.
5. Obligations created by the debtor's criminal misconduct, such as larceny (theft) or embezzlement (wrongful taking of property of another entrusted to one's care), or fraud committed by the debtor in a fiduciary or trust capacity, such as wrongful use of money entrusted to a debtor as trustee for another person or party.
6. Certain types of educational loans that come due within five years prior to the filing of the bankruptcy petition.
7. Obligations not included in the bankruptcy petition in time, because the creditors involved did not have enough notification of the proceedings even though the debtor knew that he or she owed them money.

Prohibited Practices

Every debtor is prohibited from the following practices:

Preferential Payments[22]
A preferential payment is a voluntary payment made by a debtor to one creditor over other creditors. This preference means that one creditor receives more than his or her fair share of the foodservice debtor's assets, over remaining creditors. A debtor may not distribute his or her assets to a few chosen creditors to the injury of other creditors. A preferential payment is defined as one made within 90 days of the filing for bankruptcy, and enables the "favored" creditor to obtain a greater percentage of a debt than is obtained by the other creditors. The fact that the creditor was unaware of the debtor's bankruptcy petition makes no difference.

A one-year period rather than 90 days applies to a payment to an "insider," a relative of an individual debtor, or an officer, director, or advisor of a company debtor. Such payments can be recovered from the favored creditor by the bankruptcy trustee for redistribution to other debtors.

Preferential Liens
The same definition and recovery procedures apply to preferential liens, since they too, seek to create preferential legal rights for one creditor and are unfair to all other similar creditors.[23] A preferential lien is a preferential transfer by the debtor of assets, either in cash or property, by prior agreement with a creditor. The lien may be in the form of a prior security interest in the property, such as collateral for a bank loan. In other words, a debtor may give a bank the right to sell a pizza delivery truck if he or she fails to repay the loan. However, if the debtor goes bankrupt, the trustee will seize the truck to help repay all the creditors. The lien may take the form of a judicial lien, meaning the right of a judgment creditor, one who has recovered a court judgment against the debtor, to be paid out of that judgment before other creditors are paid.

Fraudulent Transfers
Under the federal Bankruptcy Act, a fraudulent transfer is any gift, sale for less than fair market value, or other disposition of a debtor's property with the intent to hinder, delay,

or defraud creditors. Such a transfer is voidable, meaning that the bankruptcy trustee may take the transferred property for distribution to all creditors. For example, if the owner of Quik-Stop, the debtor in our Case in Point, made a transfer of vending machine foods and beverages to his wife for $50 when the fair market value of the inventory was $500, the purpose being to remove the inventory from the reach of Quik-Stop's creditors, that sale could be voided and the wife forced to return the inventory to the bankrupt's estate.

Bankruptcy Crimes

The Bankruptcy Code defines the following bankruptcy crimes, which are felonies (serious crimes) punishable by a fine of not more than $5000 or imprisonment of not more than five years, or both:

1. Knowingly and fraudulently making a false statement under oath.
2. Knowingly and fraudulently presenting or using a false claim.
3. Knowingly and fraudulently giving or receiving a bribe.
4. Knowingly and fraudulently withholding records.

These criminal acts are in addition to the court's blocking or refusing to discharge debts involving any debtor's own bankruptcy case.

Do these provisions of the Bankruptcy Act prohibit a debtor from continuing a foodservice business? No. The debtor may use his or her remaining available funds to stay in business. Once the bankruptcy court authorizes the debtor to use current funds to buy poultry, meats, and vegetables to carry on the operation, that person is in business. The total assets are not being reduced. The debtor is merely trading current cash for current inventory and supplies, and not building up debts he or she cannot pay.

Creditor Rights and Responsibilities

Creditors also have certain rights and responsibilities under the federal Bankruptcy Act:

1. Every creditor whose debt is not secured by collateral or property of the debtor has the right to file a proof of claim, usually within six months after the first meeting of creditors. When the collateral or security is insufficient to satisfy the entire debt, the secured creditor must file a proof of claim for any unsecured portion of that debt.[24]
2. Merely filing a claim does not automatically entitle the creditor to share in the distribution of the debtor's assets. The claim must be valid, meaning that the trustee must allow the claim. Any legal defenses that the debtor could have made against the creditor may be used by the bankruptcy trustee to reduce or eliminate the claim.[25]

   For example, if Quik-Stop could argue that Leaseafoods breached a warranty of fitness in the sale to Quik-Stop of its vending machines and inventory, that breach of warranty would be available to the trustee, and Leaseafoods might be denied a portion of all of its claim. In this sense, the bankruptcy trustee steps into the shoes of the debtor. Otherwise creditors could obtain a remedy to which they were not legally entitled, simply by filing a petition for involuntary bankruptcy. The Bankruptcy Act is intended to do no more than give creditors a square deal, not to enrich them unjustly.
3. A secured creditor has a preference to receive payment, but only if the creditor's claim is legally enforceable.[26] Creditors cannot have their cake and eat it too. Every creditor must prove a claim before any payment is made.
4. Certain creditor claims are given priority whether or not they are secured by collateral. These claims include: (a) expenses

and fees required to administer the bankrupt's estate; (b) $2000 worth of wages for each wage earner for wages earned 90 days before the filing of the bankruptcy petition; (c) contributions to employee benefit plans arising out of work or services performed within 180 days of the filing of the petition; (d) $900 worth of claims for each individual debtor for deposits made on goods or services for personal use not delivered or provided; and (e) taxes.[27]

5. The creditor is entitled to sufficient notice of a debtor's bankruptcy claim. This is so because the creditor must be allowed time to challenge the discharge or to have equal access with other creditors to debtor assets. A creditor who fails to protect himself or herself after such notice cannot share in the bankrupt's estate.

6. The creditor may not continue to harass or use other methods to obtain payment once a debtor has been granted bankruptcy.[28]

The order of payment gives all allowable secured claims priority, but only to the extent of the security or collateral, over the priorities mentioned above. Afterward all unsecured creditors are paid. Obviously unsecured creditors receive very little, if anything.

Any loan made to someone else should be secured by property or other debtor assets that can be used to reduce or wipe out that debt if the debtor is unable to pay. Otherwise the lender stands to lose any real chance of repayment.

What advantage, if any, does a creditor whose obligation is nondischargeable have over other creditors? A creditor with nondischargeable debts has the right to recover the balance of the debts in full, as well as to share with other creditors in the distribution of the debtor's estate.

CORPORATE REORGANIZATION UNDER CHAPTER 11[29]

Individual, partnership, and corporate debtors in the foodservice field are eligible for reorganization of their businesses by filing voluntarily for such relief or by having a creditor petition the debtor into involuntary bankruptcy under Chapter 11.

Bankruptcy courts will order relief for a properly filed petition. Once this is accomplished, the court will normally appoint a committee of unsecured creditors, a trustee, and a committee of corporate shareholders, who would also be involved in the case of a corporate bankruptcy.

The trustee may run the debtor's foodservice business as well as develop a plan for disposing of the claims of creditors and shareholders. The plan may include refinancing the business with existing treasury shares (shares held by the corporate debtor), or exchanging shares for debts held by creditors. All reorganization plans require that creditors be divided into classes, explain how each class of creditor claims will be handled, say which claims may receive less than full satisfaction, and provide equal treatment for all creditors in each class, unless those creditors agree otherwise. The plan is then submitted to all creditors for approval.

Approval usually requires the yes votes of creditors holding two-thirds in amount and one-half in number of each class of claims receiving less than full satisfaction (full dollar value of claims submitted). The court must then confirm the plan as approved. The debtor is then charged with responsibility for carrying out the reorganization plan.[30] If the total amount of claims is $1200, the yes votes are needed for $800 of the total debt and they must be one half of the number of creditors. If there were 100 creditors, 50 of them would have to vote yes on the plan. The following case is a Chapter 11 bankruptcy and illustrates how the court dealt with one creditor's objections to the plan.

In re Nite Lite Inns and Grosvenor Square Restaurant
U.S. Bankruptcy Court, S.D. California
17 Bankr. 357 (1982)

Facts.   In this Chapter 11 reorganization proceeding involving three hotels and a restaurant located immediately alongside the San Diego hotel, a creditors committee (the Burke Investors) strongly objected to a plan of reorganization submitted to the bankruptcy court by the debtor for confirmation. The bankruptcy court conducted a confirmation hearing to accept or reject the plan of reorganization. The plan of reorganization—which included the three hotels, the restaurant, and individual stockholders of the corporate debtors who had guaranteed payment of corporate obligations—was accepted.

Reasoning.

> At the hearings on confirmation, Burke Investors objected to confirmation of the plan on the grounds that it is not feasible . . . not fair and equitable . . . not proposed in good faith . . . provides for an improper classification . . . does not provide this creditor with property of a value that is not less than the amount such holder would receive if the debtors were liquidated . . . and lastly that consolidation of the cases is not in the best interests of creditors. Burke Investors also moved to block the use of some $300,000 on deposit pending a final determination as to whether Burke Investors is entitled to such sums. This opinion is filed to deal with each of Burke Investors' objections and to determine whether the debtors' . . . amended plan should be confirmed.

In answer to Burke's claims that the debt would not be satisfied in the event of liquidation, the court said the sale of the properties *would* satisfy the debts. Therefore, the plan was *feasible.*

The court said that the *good faith* requirement was met by the reorganization plan. The court found the plan fair and equitable.

The approval of the plan was in effect a *cram down.* In other words, since (1) most of the creditors agreed to the plan and (2) the plan met all the legal requirements, the plan would be approved over Burke's objections. Regarding this, the court said:

> Without "cram down" it is questionable whether many plans would be confirmed where there are disputes between creditors and the debtor. The presence of the "cram down" provision actually facilitates settlement in many cases, while at the same time it allows for confirmation where a settlement cannot be reached. Having already determined that the plan meets the applicable requirements of 11 U.S.C. sec. 1129(a) and that the plan does not discriminate unfairly, the court must only determine whether the plan is fair and equitable.

Conclusion.   Chapter 11 permits a debtor to continue in business, either with or without the supervision of a court-appointed trustee. Chapter 11 differs from straight bankruptcy in that the debtor is (1) not forced to terminate operations, (2) not required to liquidate remaining assets, or (3) not required to distribute the proceeds to existing creditors.

1. A plan of reorganization will not be confirmed if it is likely that the debtor cannot make payments to creditors under the plan without going into straight bankruptcy (liquidation). In this case the San Diego hotel would be sold if the debtor failed to pay creditors. This sale was determined to be more than enough to cover all outstanding debts owed all creditors.

2. A reorganization plan submitted by a debtor in *good faith* may be confirmed. Good faith means that the plan is prepared to achieve a result consistent with the purposes of the federal bankruptcy law. Here

the debtors were making an honest effort to keep the San Diego hotel operating to benefit all the creditors as well as themselves. This was sufficient proof of good faith to reject the creditors' objection.

In an interesting moment of reflection, the court noted a basic fact of bankruptcy: "In any bankruptcy case there are seldom any winners, just survivors." We might add: A major objective of a bankruptcy proceeding should be to remain in business and attempt to reorganize. You may be fortunate to come out a business survivor.

DEBT ADJUSTMENTS UNDER CHAPTER 13[31]

Chapter 13 permits individual debtors to pay their debts in installments with court protection against attachments—seizure and sale—of property by the creditors. The debt ceilings fixed by the federal Act are individual liquidated (acknowledged), unsecured debts of less than $100,000, and secured debts of less than $350,000 for each individual and his or her spouse.[32]

Sole proprietors of businesses and individuals may apply for Chapter 13 protection.

Unlike either Chapter 7 or Chapter 11 proceedings, Chapter 13 permits voluntary debtor petitions only. No creditor may petition a debtor into involuntary debt adjustment. Debtors may petition for either a composition of debts or an extension of debt payments, or both, out of future earnings. A *composition* is a reduction of total indebtedness. An *extension* gives the debtor a longer period of time in which to pay debts in full. Usually, in filing for such relief, the debtor provides a list of creditors as well as assets, liabilities, and contracts not yet performed by the debtor.[33]

Once a petition is filed, the court will hold a meeting of creditors, and then review proofs of claim filed by each. The court questions the debtor, who then submits a payment plan. The plan is submitted to the secured creditors for their approval. If they accept, and after finding that the plan was made in good faith, meets legal requirements, and adequately protects all creditors, the court approves the plan.

Next the court appoints a trustee to administer the plan. All payment plans require repayment in three years or less, unless the court approves a longer period of time. In no case may the court approve a plan scheduling repayment beyond five years from the date of its approval.[34]

If the plan is approved, the creditors may not later force the debtor involuntarily into straight bankruptcy. Under Chapter 13 the court may order a discharge of the bankrupt even though the bankrupt has failed to meet all required payments within three years, if the court finds that the debtor's failure to do so was due to circumstances beyond that person's control. However, if the debtor fails to file an acceptable plan, or fails to pay for unjustified reasons, the court may dismiss the Chapter 13 proceeding.[35] Then creditors may petition for involuntary bankruptcy and require a total liquidation of the debtor's assets.

The following foodservice bankruptcy example will illustrate the procedures and criteria for obtaining a petition of bankruptcy. Chapter 13, the Debt Adjustment for Individuals with Regular Income, is chosen because it is the most favorable form of bankruptcy discharge for the independent foodservice operator.

Chapter 13 bankruptcy is only available to a single proprietor, not corporations or partnerships. However, this does not disqualify a husband and wife team, if they are not operating a foodservice partnership or corporation. Our operators, John and Lois Evans, run the Devon Park Restaurant.

John and Lois file a voluntary petition together. Only they can file for bankruptcy. No creditors can petition for their involuntary bankruptcy under Chapter 13.

John and Lois submit a list of all creditors, including their names and addresses, and *schedules*. There is a filing fee that must be paid. An original plus three copies of the petition are filed.

Two schedules are filed, Schedule A and Schedule B. The schedules are lists of all assets and liabilities of the restaurant.

Schedule A contains a list of creditors, including priority secured creditors and unsecured nonpriority creditors. Priority creditors include those providing administrative services, and claims for wages, contributions to employee benefit plans, consumer deposits, and taxes, in that order. Secured creditors are those holding security interests in collateral owed by the single proprietor, either John or Lois, or creditors with judicial liens against the restaurant. Unsecured, nonpriority creditors are the remaining creditors.

Schedule B contains separate lists of John and Lois' real property (home or other real estate), personal property, and property claimed by them as exempt.

It is very important for John and Lois to file the petition for bankruptcy as soon as possible, even without Schedules A and B. These schedules can be filed within 10 days after the petition is filed, if a list of the names and addresses of all creditors has been furnished. An additional 10 days or more may be granted by the court for good cause.

Providing accurate schedules is of vital importance. Carelessness or negligence on John or Lois's part may be viewed as an attempt to falsify information, with very severe criminal penalties, not to mention that the claim of the creditor will be omitted from any discharge granted.

The automatic stay or hold on debt collection and lien enforcement by creditors protects John and Lois. However, the stay only suspends collection temporarily. It does not permanently excuse John and Lois from payment of those debts. Moreover, the stay applies only to debts that John and Lois plan to pay off *in full* at a later date, and not to debts they want to pay only in part. For example, John and Lois owe Joe, the vegetable vendor, $1000. If they submit a debt-adjustment plan to pay off only $700 in full later, Joe can take immediate steps to recover the $300 difference. Joe's request to the bankruptcy court to do so will probably be granted.

One special advantage under Chapter 13 is that John and Lois can continue to operate the restaurant themselves. Usually no trustee will be appointed to run the business.

Trustees are given certain duties in Chapter 13 proceedings, such as investigation of financial condition and the operation of any debtor's business. The court always has the right to order that the restaurant be operated by a trustee, when the trustee's investigation reveals mismanagement, incompetence, dishonesty, or other business irregularities.

The heart of every Chapter 13 case is the repayment plan. Only John and Lois may file a repayment plan. A plan may not be forced on them by their creditors, as is true under Chapter 11 reorganization or under Chapter 7 liquidations. The creditors may challenge the plan, however. Failure to file on time gives any interested party the right to ask the court to dismiss the petition or to convert the case to a liquidation under Chapter 7.

The role of the trustee is only to advise John and Lois to help them keep the restaurant open without breaking themselves financially.

Three provisions *must* be contained in John and Lois' repayment plan:

1. Provision for submission of all or a portion of future earnings or income to the trustee to execute the plan. All other income remains with John and Lois to support themselves and their dependents.
2. Provision for the payment in full of all priority claims listed on Schedule A.

3. Provision for equal treatment of all creditors if the plan classifies creditors.

A confirmation hearing on the repayment plan will be held only if a creditor or other interested party objects to the plan. Only the trustee need appear at the hearing.

Confirmation under Chapter 13 does not give unsecured creditors the right to vote to accept or reject John and Lois's plan. Nor does Chapter 13 confirmation require a finding that either John or Lois is not guilty of any bankruptcy act that would otherwise cause an objection to their discharge.

The Bankruptcy Code under Chapter 13 requires John and Lois's plan to meet six requirements as conditions of confirmation. The plan must:

1. Comply with the Bankruptcy Code.
2. Allow for payment of fees and charges.
3. Be a good faith proposal.
4. Provide for some distribution to all unsecured creditors.
5. Treat secured creditors equally.
6. Be feasible.

The effect of confirmation of the repayment plan makes it binding on John and Lois and all creditors, whether or not the creditor claim is provided for by the plan and whether or not the creditor has objected to, accepted, or rejected the plan. However, *under Chapter 13 John and Lois are not discharged until the plan is fully carried out.* Under Chapter 13 reorganization, confirmation results in an immediate discharge of debts and their replacement with new debts as spelled out in the plan.

USING BANKRUPTCY

One stark reality confronts those who wish to avail themselves of bankruptcy protection. Bankruptcy is not a painless legal escape from one's debts. Bankruptcy stigmatizes those who

use it. How? It does so by requiring anyone discharged in bankruptcy to state that fact on any future application for credit, and thus face the likelihood of having the credit application legitimately rejected. The federal Act does not require such disclosure, but any potential creditor is permitted to ask that question.[36] However, in most states a creditor need only call the local credit bureau to get a credit record, which includes any adjudication of bankruptcy.

A discharge in bankruptcy necessarily makes the debtor a less than worthy credit risk. Therefore, straight bankruptcy should be used only as a last resort, when no other viable means of settling debts is available.

Although a reorganization under Chapter 11 or consumer debt adjustment under Chapter 13 does not carry the same mark of shame as does straight bankruptcy, it still may cause a creditor to place your credit application in a less desirable category. Naturally this result can worsen your business as well as personal financial prospects.

Most creditors and suppliers want to avoid the prospect of a debtor's straight bankruptcy or some other plan as much as you do. This is true because they usually receive so much less of your dollar in straight bankruptcy than in other forms, or through their own payment plan. To avoid this, creditors will usually accept a voluntary repayment plan without court supervision. A reasonable, mutually agreeable repayment plan has two advantages: (1) it avoids the badge of shame associated with bankruptcy; and (2) it gives the creditor more assurance of total repayment than would be likely under federal and state bankruptcy laws.

As a businessperson you may be eligible to reorganize your foodservice business under Chapter 11 or Chapter 13 of the federal Bankruptcy Act. These procedures will allow you to stay in business rather than close your doors and liquidate your assets to satisfy creditor claims. You should consider using these less drastic procedures whenever possible, since a reorganized business is often better than no business at all.

In contemplating bankruptcy don't look at it as a debtor's haven, but use it only as a last resort when all other avenues of voluntary settlement of debts are off limits.

If you are a creditor who seeks to compel bankruptcy of a debtor, you must be aware that if your debts are not secured by other assets, you stand little chance of recovering anything. As a prudent foodservice businessperson, you must carefully check the credit standing of any potential debtor *and* obtain security from the debtor as a hedge against unforeseen economic circumstances. Otherwise you stand to suffer severe losses yourself. Figure 13.1 lists the advantages and disadvantages of all three forms of bankruptcy.

SUMMARY

There are three forms of bankruptcy foodservice operators may use. Chapter 7 bankruptcy is straight bankruptcy, with any assets distributed to creditors by the trustee. Chapter 11 is designed for a businessperson who wants to stay in business. It allows for reorganization of the business, which is supervised by a trustee and must be approved by a majority of creditors. Chapter 13 bankruptcy allows for a voluntary repayment plan by the debtor.

Petitions for bankruptcy may be filed for *voluntarily* by the debtor, or involuntarily by creditors for Chapter 7 and Chapter 11.

Jurisdiction for bankruptcy proceedings rests in the federal courts. The debtor must file in the district in which the food service is located.

Bankruptcy is not granted automatically. The person must first be eligible for discharge. Then creditors have time to object to

the discharge. Dishonest acts such as fraudulent transfers or false information will usually bar a discharge.

Debtors have rights as well as surviving obligations. Debts such as alimony and taxes survive a discharge of bankruptcy.

Creditors also have rights to protect claims and courts will usually decide which claims have precedence over others. It is not up to debtors to decide how any assets will be distributed.

QUESTIONS

1. Norman and John Sweeny have owned and operated the Courtyard Inn as a corporation for 10 years. Some major equipment purchases made at the same time that the interior of the restaurant was remodeled have put them in severe debt and they cannot continue to operate until their debts are erased. They had planned to run the restaurant for five more years before turning it over to their children. Assuming they would like to stay in business, which form of bankruptcy would you recommend? Explain your answer.

2. Miriam Duffy is going through bankruptcy proceedings. She files on September 3. On November 1 she pays the full amount to one of her creditors, Bucky's Wholesalers, whose debt is discharged along with those of the other creditors. Has she done anything wrong? What could be the result of this? Explain.

3. Name several obligations that cannot be discharged in bankruptcy.

4. List three criteria or tests according to which a bankruptcy court may deny a discharge in bankruptcy to an otherwise eligible debtor.

5. How does Chapter 13 bankruptcy of the federal Bankruptcy Act differ from a straight bankruptcy proceeding? Who may file?

Figure 13.1
Advantages and Disadvantages of Types of Federal Bankruptcies to Debtors

Advantages	Disadvantages
Voluntary Liquidation under Chapter 7 (Straight Bankruptcy)	
May be sought voluntarily by debtor. Provides most complete relief to widest types of debt. Six-year discharge rule does not prevent filing of bankruptcy petition, proceeding as debtor, and obtaining orderly liquidation of assets. Debtor receives automatic stay (hold) on debt collection and enforcement of liens by creditors.	Discharge (forgiveness of debts) available only to individual debtors, not to partnerships, corporations, or unincorporated associations. Discharge may be opposed and denied—discharge not automatic. (a) Discharge application within six (6) years of prior discharge. (b) Fraudulent transfer of assets within previous year. Certain debts survive discharge. (a) Federal income taxes. (b) Alimony and child support. Assets of debtor must be sold and distributed to creditors. Usually results in very poor credit rating.
Reorganization under Chapter 11	
Primarily available to businesses, both small (sole proprietors, partnerships, and unincorporated associations) and large (corporations): Anyone that can file a voluntary petition for complete liquidation is eligible to file under Chapter 11. Permits businesses to continue operating, thus minimizing unemployment and waste of business assets. Makes better use of business assets: It enables use of assets for intended purpose, rather than forcing sale of assets at depressed prices. Debtor normally remains in control of business (as a debtor in possession), with same powers as that of court-appointed trustee. Debtor receives automatic stay (hold) on debt collection and enforcement of liens by creditors. Debtor can rehabilitate without terminating the business.	Creditors may petition for involuntary reorganization of debtor, using same procedures established under Chapter 7. Debtor must perform functions and duties of trustee. (a) Preferences. (b) Fraudulent transfers and obligations. (c) Executory contracts (contracts not yet performed that are burdensome to debtor). Individual debtor not discharged from federal income tax obligations and alimony and child support. When liquidation is granted by Chapter 11, confirmation of the plan will not discharge the debtor. This means that corporations and partnerships otherwise entitled to liquidate will not be discharged.

Figure 13.1
Advantages and Disadvantages of Types of Federal Bankruptcies to Debtors (*Continued*)

Advantages	Disadvantages
Reorganization under Chapter 11 (*Continued*)	
Authorizes confirmation of reorganization plan by court, preventing creditors from blocking plan by failure to approve plan unanimously.	
Unlike Chapter 7, corporations and partnerships are entitled to discharge in bankruptcy.	
Discharge is not refused by reason of fraud, or willful misconduct of debtors, making such debts nondischargable under Chapter 7.	
Tax claims of corporations and partnerships are discharged under Chapter 11.	
Liquidation is authorized under Chapter 11.	
Debt Adjustment for Individuals* with Regular Income under Chapter 13 **Applies to sole proprietors and employed persons.*	
Debtor is free from many debts not exempt under Chapter 7.	Only available to natural persons with regular income.
Debtor may not need to make periodic payments on old debts, as required under Chapter 7.	The pay-off of old debts may be required, which would be avoided under Chapter 7.

Debts not otherwise dischargeable (willful injury, fraud, income taxes) can be reduced and then paid off in installments. This procedure is not available under Chapter 7.	Debt ceiling limits use of Chapter 13 to small businesspersons:
	    Less than $100,000 of noncontingent, liquidated *unsecured* debts.
	    Less than $350,000 of noncontingent, liquidated *secured* debts.

The six (6) year discharge rule does not apply to Chapter 13, as it does under Chapter 7.	(Noncontingent means not subject to some future event. Liquidated means not disputed. Unsecured means lacking collateral. Secured means backed by collateral. Ed.)
The stigma attached to Chapter 13 debtor is not as severe as under Chapter 7, since no liquidation and complete discharge is provided.	
Chapter 13 encourages debtor to pay as a moral duty.	
For small business persons, creditor approval of a Chapter 13 debt adjustment plan is not required.	
Simpler, more flexible procedure than under Chapter 7.	
The individual debtor cannot be compelled to use Chapter 13 by creditors.	

NOTES

1. *Moureau v. Leaseamatic, Inc.,* 542 F.2d 251 (5th Cir. 1976).

2. Article 1, Section 8, Clause 4 of the United States Constitution grants Congress the power to establish uniform bankruptcy laws throughout the United States. The Bankruptcy Reform Act of 1978, Pub. L. No. 95–598, 92 Stat. 2549 (1978), created a new Bankruptcy Code, giving bankruptcy courts broad powers to hear and determine all controversies affecting debtors or their estates.

    The Code is found in a new Title 11 of the U.S. Code, 11 U.S.C. sec. 1 *et seq.* (1976 & Supp. IV 1980 & Supp. V 1981). The states are permitted to enact bankruptcy laws as long as they are not in conflict with federal law. This chapter will deal exclusively with federal bankruptcy law.

3. Lusk, Hewitt, Donnel, Barnes, *Business Law and the Regulatory Environment* 932–33 (5th ed. 1982).

4. Bankruptcy Reform Act of 1978, 11 sec. 201(a), amending 28 U.S.C. See 28 U.S.C. secs. 151, 1471 (Supp. IV 1980). In *Marathon Pipeline Co. v. Northern Pipeline Constr. Co.,* 12 Bankr. 946 (D. Minn. 1981), the bankruptcy court held section 1471 unconstitutional because of the extensive jurisdiction (power) over regular civil actions granted to judges who lack lifetime appointments to the federal courts. The Supreme Court of the United States affirmed that ruling on appeal. 102 S. Ct. 2858 (1982), stayed 103 S. Ct. 199 and 200.

5. 28 U.S.C. sec. 1472(1) (Supp. IV 1980).

6. *Id.*

7. *Denver & R.G.W.R.R. v. Brotherhood of R.R. Trainmen,* 387 U.S. 556 (1967), interpreting prior federal bankruptcy law (Chandler Act of 1938). No case has yet interpreted the new code on this question.

8. 28 U.S.C. sec. 1472(2) (Supp. IV 1980).

9. *Id.* sec. 1477(a). See also Bankruptcy Rule 116(b)(2).

10. 11 U.S.C. secs. 301, 303(h) (Supp. V 1981).

11. *Id.* secs. 343, 521(1) (Supp. V 1981); Bankruptcy Rules 204(a)(2), 205(b).

12. 11 U.S.C. sec. 303(g) (Supp. V 1981) governs the appointment of an interim trustee by the bankruptcy court until the creditors elect a permanent trustee, subject to court approval. The powers of the interim and permanent trustee to take charge of and appraise the debtor's property are the same. Normally, however, this is done by the interim trustee prior to the confirmation of a permanent trustee by the court. *Id.* secs. 544(a)(1), (2), 721 (Supp. V 1981).

13. *Id.* secs. 363(a), (c)(4), 544(b), 1106(a).

14. *Id.* sec. 727(a)(1), (8).

15. Unlike prior law, the Bankruptcy Code permits a debtor to refuse to testify or answer questions on the ground of the constitutional privilege against self-incrimination. *Id.* sec. 727(a)(6)(B).

16. *Id.* sec. 727(a)(2), (4)(A), (4)(D), (5), (6).

17. *Id.* sec. 524(c).

18. The states are permitted to establish bankruptcy laws not in conflict with the federal Bankruptcy Reform Act of 1978, the latest major revision of the 1938 Chandler Act.

19. Liens given this protection are defined as *statutory liens* under 11 U.S.C. sec. 101(38) (Supp. V 1981), and must be distinguished from *security interests* created by the parties under sec. 101(27). *Id.* sec. 101(27).

    A typical security interest is a bank's interest in restaurant tables and chairs you purchased by means of a bank loan. The interest is protected by giving the bank a *lien* or right to seize and sell the tables and chairs in the event you fail or refuse to pay back the loan in the manner agreed upon with the bank.

    An example of a *statutory lien* is a *tax lien* to ensure the payment of federal or state taxes due, or a *mechanic's lien* created by law to protect a contractor by giving the contractor the right to sell your restaurant if you do not pay for work the contractor performed for you, such as installing a new kitchen floor.

    A *judicial lien* is created by a court order giving the court a right to sell your property to pay a money judgment rendered against you by the court.

20. Federal law permits a bankruptcy trustee to avoid statutory liens, otherwise recognized, in three situations: (1) Liens that first become effective upon financial disaster. 11 U.S.C. sec. 545(1) (Supp. V 1981). (2) Liens that do not meet a hypothetical *bona fide* purchaser test. The test requires the lien to be perfected or enforceable against a *bona fide* purchaser who purchases the property at the time the bankruptcy case is commenced, that is, when the bankruptcy petition is filed. The purchaser need not actually exist; only the lien need be perfected. If this test is not met, the lien is not valid in bankruptcy. *Id*. sec. 545(2). (3) Landlords' liens to secure the payment of rent. *Id*. secs. 545(3), 545(4).

21. *Id*. sec. 523(a) *et seq*.

22. *Id*. sec. 547.

23. For example, a preference may take place where a creditor (bank) obtains a judicial lien on your restaurant tables and chairs by getting a court order of execution and levy (the right to seize and sell) upon those assets after you have filed for bankruptcy. Your giving the bank a mortgage on your restaurant, land, and building would also create a preferential transfer by you as a debtor in bankruptcy. See generally *Glessner v. Massey-Ferguson, Inc.,* 353 F.2d 986 (9th Cir. 1965), *cert. denied,* 384 U.S. 970 (1966).

24. 11 U.S.C. sec. 501(a) (Supp. V 1981). Under the Bankruptcy Code, the filing of a claim is not required. However, in order to share in the liquidation of a debtor's estate or in a Chapter 13 debt adjustment, a creditor must file a proof of claim with the bankruptcy court. *Id*. sec. 502.

25. A presumption exists that every claim that is filed is valid, placing the burden on the bankruptcy trustee to object. *Id*. sec. 502(a), (b)(1); Bankruptcy Rule 306(b).

26. 11 U.S.C. sec. 506(a) (Supp. V 1981).

27. *Id*. sec. 507(a)(1), (3)–(6).

28. *Moureau v. Leaseamatic, supra* note 1.

29. 11 U.S.C. sec. 1101 *et seq*. (Supp. V 1981).

30. *Id*. secs. 1102(a)(1), 1104. The appointment of a trustee is not mandatory. In appropriate cases the bankrupt may continue in business, as a "debtor in possession," during reorganization, *id*. secs. 1101(1), 1102(a)(2), 1106(a)(5) (plan), 1108 (operate business), 1122(a), 1126(c), 1128(a). The statutory requirements for confirmation are set forth in sections 1129(a), 1129(d), and 1141(b).

31. *Id*. secs. 1301–1330.

32. *Id*. sec. 109(e).

33. *Id*. secs. 303(a), 103(a).

34. *Id*. sec. 1322(c).

35. *Id*. sec. 1328(b). Section 524(d) requires the bankruptcy court to hold a discharge hearing at which the debtor must appear in person. Absent the granting of a hardship discharge under section 1328(b), a debtor's failure to complete payments will cause the court to dismiss the application for discharge.

36. Chapter 13 adjustment cases do not require an individual debtor to make an adequate disclosure statement. Chapter 11 reorganization cases require such statements. See *id*. sec. 1125.

14
The Court System and Out-of-Court Settlement

Objectives

The purpose of this chapter is to:
1. Outline the United States court system.
2. Explain less costly methods of settling disputes, short of going to court.

Case in Point

Bob Baker is the sole owner of Bob's Beef-steak and Brew, a high-volume, fast-food operation situated on private property adjoining Powtochie Park, a park operated by the U.S. Park Service. Bob is a resident of Wyoming, where his restaurant is situated. One day Bob is served with a U.S. Government notice that the government is going to acquire a portion of his private parking area so as to widen a federal highway that adjoins it. The government offers Bob an amount he considers too little to compensate him for the taking of his land. Moreover, the taking will cut off existing access to his premises from the federal highway, and the government's offer does not include adequate provision to build an alternate access road. Negotiations with the federal Highway Administrator do not resolve the dispute.

Bob decides to sue. Which court, a federal or state court, will have jurisdiction over his case? As a citizen of Wyoming, Bob can sue the federal government in the federal district court for the District of Wyoming. Bob satisfies the requirements of federal jurisdiction.

COURT TRIAL

Most legal disputes are settled out of court by negotiation between the parties. A court trial is usually a last resort, when all other efforts to resolve a dispute have been unsuccessful. Why? Because going to court is expensive, time consuming, and uncertain as to the outcome. You may have a good case as to the law, but if the jury or judge does not believe your version of the facts, you may not recover if you sue, or may be found liable to pay a damage judgment if you are sued.

Our trial system is an *adversary* system. The object of a trial is to present the case in such a way as to persuade the trier of the facts (the jury or a judge in a court sitting without a jury) that one side is right and the other is wrong.[1]

The judge hearing a case to be decided by a jury plays an impartial role, and does not actively take sides, but is actually a mediator. The court makes rulings on the admission of evidence and instructs the jury on the law.[2] The court may also dismiss a case if it does not justify a legal remedy, or there is insufficient evidence to prove it.[3] The court may even render a judgment in a person's favor in spite of a contrary jury verdict if the judge finds the evidence insufficient to support the jury's verdict.[4]

Otherwise the court functions as an umpire, permitting each side to plead, prove, and persuade: (1) the jury (or court sitting without a jury) of the truth of the facts, and (2) the court of the sufficiency of its legal arguments.[5]

Court Systems

There are two major court systems in the United States: federal and state courts. Each state has its own court system. The federal government has a court system as well, with different types of jurisdiction.

State Courts

In a typical state court system, courts are divided into a triangular group (Figure 14.1). At the bottom of the triangle, and supporting the rest of the court structure, are *trial courts* of *general* or *limited jurisdiction,* the latter also called *special inferior courts.* Trial courts are the courts in which all controversies are first heard. The phrase "having one's day in court" means having an opportunity to have a dispute resolved by the first series of courts having the power to do so. Most foodservice lawsuits would originate in a trial court.

Figure 14.1
State Court System

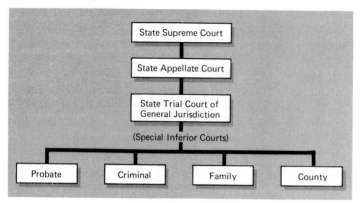

*Reprinted by permission from Frascona, Joseph L.,
Business Law: Text and Cases, The Legal Environment,
2nd ed. p. 26, fig. 2.1. Copyright 1981, 1984 by Wm. C.
Brown Publishers, Dubuque, Iowa. All Rights Reserved.*

What is the difference between general and limited jurisdiction? *General jurisdiction* is the power to hear all cases under state law, such as corporate law, contract law, agency law, and tort law, often without regard as to the money value of the case being heard.

Courts of general jurisdiction may exist within each county of the state, and in large cities. A county that is too small to qualify for a trial court of general jurisdiction will be served by a court from a neighboring county, provided by state law. A state judge may be assigned to hear cases in each county at specified times of the year.

Limited jurisdiction means that a court has power to decide only certain types of cases. Jurisdiction can be limited to specific subjects, such as family matters or landlord-tenant cases. These courts are also called state inferior courts.

Jurisdiction can also be limited by the amount of money the party suing seeks to recover. Small claims courts typically have a monetary ceiling for jurisdiction of between $250 and $1000, which is set by state law. This means that if the amount the claimant seeks to recover exceeds the state ruling, the small claims court cannot hear the case.

The next level of courts is called *intermediate appellate* or reviewing courts; their jurisdiction lies between that of trial courts and of the highest state court. Each state has at least one reviewing court. Most heavily populated states also have intermediate appellate courts, as well as a court of last resort or a supreme court. Less populated states may have only trial courts and one court of appeals or supreme court.

The reviewing courts sit to hear appeals—they never function as trial courts. The courts primarily decide only questions of law. Questions of law refer to errors of the trial court claimed by the party that appeals. A typical error is an improper or erroneous charge to the jury on the law made by a trial judge. If the error is serious, the reviewing court has the authority to send the case back for a new trial. If the error is harmless, the court has the authority to uphold the judgment given by the trial court.

Figure 14.2
Federal Court System

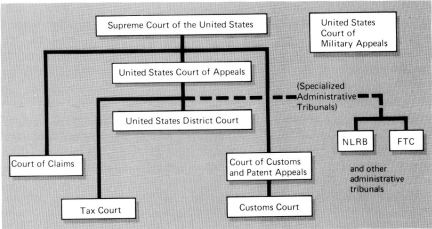

Federal Courts

Like the state courts, federal courts are divided into trial courts, intermediate appellate courts, and a court of last resort (Figure 14.2). There is more specialization in federal courts, including administrative tribunals for various federal regulatory agencies.

Trial courts of general jurisdiction are called district courts. Trial courts of limited jurisdiction include bankruptcy courts, tax courts, customs courts, courts of claims, and a court of customs and patent appeals. All of these trial courts are located in federal judicial districts established by the Congress, and vary in size and number from state to state.

The federal system has intermediate courts of appeals. This is a change from the state court system, where such courts are optional. Why? Because there is only one Supreme Court of the United States, and that court could not function if it were required to hear all appeals from each of the 50 states. The federal courts of appeals, found in 11 judicial circuits, each with a fixed number of states,

operate in much the same way as state reviewing courts. These courts review decisions of the federal district courts within their geographical circuits, and decisions of federal administrative agencies, such as the Food and Drug Administration.

The United States Supreme Court sits at the top of our federal court system. Because it is the only court of last resort within the federal system, appeals to this High Court are heard and decided with permission of that Court by a procedure called a petition for *certiorari*. Only the most important matters are accepted and heard by the Supreme Court.

Why do we have a system of state courts and federal courts? Would not one court system be sufficient to handle all legal controversies? The answer is this: Each state is sovereign, an independent political body, over all of its citizens in their activities and conduct within its borders. Each state court normally lacks the power to settle controversies that affect citizens of other states that arise in another state.

The federal court system was created to fill this void in the state court system. The federal courts under the federal Constitution have two sources of judicial power or jurisdiction: (1) the power to settle federal questions, meaning controversies totally or partially involving the United States Constitution, a treaty, or a federal law; and (2) the power to decide controversies involving *diversity of citizenship*. Diversity of citizenship means a case involving (a) citizens of different states; (b) a foreign country suing citizens of a state, or different states; and (c) citizens of a state and citizens or subjects of a foreign country. *Citizens* has been interpreted to mean corporations as well as persons.

In both federal questions and diversity jurisdiction cases, the amount in controversy must exceed $10,000. Only when the defendant is the federal government or a federal employee is the jurisdictional amount eliminated.

In our Case in Point, Bob's legal right to sue is based on the federal Constitutional requirement that the federal government adequately compensate U.S. citizens for land acquired for legitimate federal purposes. The dispute does not question the government's *right* to acquire Bob's parking area. It instead centers on the adequacy of the compensation by the government for the exercise of that right.

After trial the district court will issue a money judgment for Bob. If either Bob or the government is dissatisfied with the amount of the award, either party may appeal to the federal Court of Appeals for the Tenth Circuit, which includes Wyoming. That court will review the adequacy of the district court's findings on which the award was based. If the findings are clearly erroneous, the Court of Appeals may send the case back for a new trial, or may increase or decrease the award, modifying the judgment of the district court.

At this stage either party may petition for a *writ of certiorari* to the Supreme Court, asking for further review. In all likelihood the petition will be denied. Why? Because the High Court usually reserves review for important federal questions; to resolve conflicts of law interpretation between federal courts of appeal; and to review cases which can only be resolved by the Supreme Court, such as interpretation of a federal treaty with a foreign government. In such cases the federal Court of Appeals is really the court of last resort. Bob's controversy does not fit any of the necessary criteria.

Jurisdiction

Jurisdiction is a very important factor in a legal case. Courts are, of course, limited in jurisdiction by geographical location, but there are other limitations related to the case and procedure used by both parties.

Jurisdiction refers to the power of a court to decide a case. If a court lacks jurisdiction over the parties or over the subject of the case, the court cannot make a binding determination of the dispute.

Jurisdiction over the parties means that the parties are all properly before the court. Parties to a lawsuit are "properly before the court" either because they voluntarily appear or because they have been served with legal *process* (legal papers such as a summons, complaint, or petition). The service of process gives the court the power to act in the dispute even if the party served fails or refuses to appear.

Jurisdiction over the subject of the case means that the court has the power to decide the controversy before it. Not all courts have the power to decide all controversies brought to them for determination. For example, a bankruptcy court can only hear and determine bankruptcy cases. It has no power over, say, a liquor liability lawsuit. A family court has no power to resolve a dispute in a management contract case.

Jurisdiction can also involve the money value of the claim or case. Minor courts, such as small claims courts, cannot hear cases involving a sum greater than that fixed by each state, even though they have the power to hear the controversy itself. In the complaint the party suing must state the amount of money he or she wishes to recover from the other party. If the amount claimed in the complaint exceeds its ceiling for jurisdiction, the court must either dismiss the case or transfer it to the proper court.

GOING TO COURT

At some point you may enter into a dispute that can only be settled in court. If you do, remember that there are procedures for court trials that can pave the way for you to win your case, or at least ensure you a fair trial. These steps are usually handled by your lawyer on your behalf, but knowing them will help you monitor his or her progress.

A trial seeks to resolve disputes by finding for or against one of the parties on the *facts* and the *law*. Facts are presented to the jury, which decides to accept or reject them. The law is explained to the jury by the judge at the end of the case, to enable the jury members to apply the facts they found to the law and to enter a *verdict* in conformity with the law. A verdict is the jury's decision.

Both the plaintiff and defendant have basic rights in United States courts. Each has the right to have an attorney represent him or her in court, to gather evidence, to participate in jury selection, to make opening statements, to call friendly witnesses, to dispute evidence given by the other side, to examine and cross-examine witnesses, and to give closing arguments. The right to a jury trial is limited in some states by the amount of damages in dispute.

A wronged party has the right to sue if another party has committed a legal wrong that affected the plaintiff, and for which damages are due. It is up to the judge to determine whether these factors exist, and if they do not, he or she may dismiss the suit.

Small Claims Courts

Going through a court trial with a lawyer can be complex, time consuming, and costly.

To meet the criticism that the traditional court systems do not address the needs of the "average person," *small claims courts* have been established in most major cities. These courts, usually part of the city or municipal court system, were created to provide justice quickly, conveniently, and inexpensively in cases not requiring a lawyer.

The following are the major features that distinguish this special court from other courts.

1. The procedures used by small claims courts are very informal. A simple form of *summons* and *complaint* is issued by the clerk of the court, which may be served by any adult person other than the plaintiff. A simple answer by the defendant is then filed, and the case is immediately set for trial. No discovery procedures or interrogatories before trial are used, nor are pretrial motions permitted. On the trial date the plaintiff tells his or her version of the case, and the defendant gives his or her side. Usually no lawyers take part, although in some cases they may represent clients as in regular court proceedings. No objections to evidence or other trial maneuvers are allowed because the case is heard by a judge without a jury. At the end of the testimony, the judge makes a decision from the bench.

2. The monetary jurisdiction of small claims courts is limited, and the ceiling amount varies according to state law. The court has

no authority to issue injunctions—court orders halting a labor dispute, for example—or to order specific performance of a contract, such as the sale of a house. These jurisdictional limits are intended to keep the disputes simple and to provide prompt relief.

3. Normally no appeals from small claims judgments are allowed. This is so because no record of testimony or of the proceedings is kept by small claims courts for review by a higher court. Where an appeal is permitted, it takes the form of a new trial.

4. The small claims judge functions more as an arbitrator than a trial judge. In some states the judge is not elected or appointed, but is an attorney assigned to hear the cases and sits part-time. As an arbitrator the judge tries to protect the interests of both sides to the controversy, since attorneys are not usually present to perform this function. Once satisfied that he or she has heard enough testimony to reach a decision, the judge does so.

5. Small claims courts have certain *advantages:* (a) They are accessible to more members of the public, since an attorney need not be hired. (b) They hear cases sooner, with much less formal pre-trial and trial procedure than is true in most other courts. (c) They are cheaper to use, since the small claims judge acts as a legal arbitrator for both sides. (d) They render immediate decisions, which in most cases are final, because they are nonappealable.

6. Small claims courts have *disadvantages:* (a) They are set up to handle minor disputes, and can issue only money judgments. (b) They are unable to deal with other than small money disputes, which compels most parties to hire an attorney to take their case to a regular court. The money ceiling on cases heard means that only a small fraction of the total cases filed can be heard by small claims courts. (c) They lack the power to provide anything other than money relief. (d) They deprive the parties of an opportunity to appeal an unfavorable judgment. The losing party has little choice but to accept the decision given.

Small claims courts have attempted to simplify the process of resolving minor disputes to avoid expensive, formal, and time-consuming court trials. Small claims courts provide "homespun" justice without the legal niceties of procedure normally used before and during a full trial. They are available to food-service operators as well as foodservice patrons and should be considered as part of your legal checklist of useful methods of settling disputes.

OUT-OF-COURT SETTLEMENT OF DISPUTES

The process of trial and appeal of court cases is costly and lengthy, and may be disappointing. As a method of settling business disputes, going to court should be viewed with caution and used only as a last resort.

It is true, we must defend ourselves against lawsuits others bring against us. But even in such cases thought should be given to resolving the dispute out of court. Why? (1) By doing so you have more control over the outcome of the dispute than by leaving matters in the hands of a trial judge and/or jury. You do not run the risk that the jury will not believe your testimony and will give a verdict in favor of your opponent, or that the judge may not like your case and unconsciously make those feelings known to the jury. (2) It is better to settle for less now than run the risk of paying more later. (3) An out-of-court settlement saves time and energy needed to manage your foodservice business. (4) Settlement may preserve the goodwill of the person or party suing or being sued.

What disadvantages are there in settling a dispute out of court? (1) You may be tempted to settle a case just to get rid of the dispute even when no settlement is warranted. This gives your opponent the opportunity to take advantage of you. Your opponent may be encouraged to do so repeatedly, knowing that you will settle rather than go to court. (2) Settlement will deprive you of the opportunity to test a legal theory or rule that should be, and might be, changed by the courts in your favor. (3) Settlement may work a hardship if the dispute involves costly and permanent economic harm. You may not be able to recover sufficient money in an out-of-court settlement to make up for the long-range costs to you. (4) Settlement can deprive you of the opportunity to pursue an unscrupulous person who will only settle under the threat of a pending lawsuit. Settlement presumes that both parties have something to gain by settling out of court. When your opponent has everything to gain and nothing to lose by refusing to settle, then the prod of a lawsuit may be needed to persuade that person to change his or her thinking.

Compromise, Arbitration, and Mediation

There are different types of out-of-court settlements.

Compromise

Compromise is another word for a voluntary settlement of a dispute by the disputing parties among themselves, without the aid of third parties. An out-of-court settlement is a compromise of a dispute. For example, in a contract dispute with a vendor, you may want to reach a negotiated settlement. Keep one thing in mind: Vendors are rarely out to cheat you. Honest mistakes can be remedied without going into court.

Arbitration

Arbitration differs from compromise in that an arbitrator is a third party selected by the disputing parties to *decide* the issue or issues of the dispute. An arbitrator's decision *is binding* on the parties, and is enforceable by the courts. The parties to an agreement may select those issues that will be left to arbitration.

The major advantage of arbitration is that it keeps certain issues out of court for the sake of a timely and less costly settlement. The major disadvantage of arbitration is that once a decision is made by the arbitrator, it will be enforced by the courts without any review of its soundness or sufficiency.

The following case was decided by an arbitrator, and the decision is consistent with legal principles. This is a labor case, and many such employer/union cases are decided either by arbitration or through mediation. Both parties were represented by attorneys here, but it is not normally necessary.

A San Diego, California, restaurant, which offered European cuisine, required its cocktail waitresses to wear classically styled gowns reminiscent of the Roman or Grecian mode and to wear their hair blond and upswept. Management believed that this requirement was consistent with its image of fine European dining. The appearance rule, in existence for over 18 years, had become a citywide trademark, according to the restaurant, and had been instrumental in its receiving numerous national awards for fine European cuisine, elegant decor, and superior service.

One waitress, who had dyed her hair blond in order to get her job, and had been forced to purchase two blond wigs at a cost of $60 each when she decided to return her hair to its natural color, charged that the restaurant's policy was unreasonable and that, in any event, the restaurant should pay the cost of purchasing and maintaining her wigs.

Award: The restaurant's hair rule is reasonable, according to Arbitrator Thomas Christopher, who concludes that it has been applied in a fair and consistent manner and without violating any express or implied term of the collective bargaining contract. Thomas finds that the waitresses' appearance is a significant component of management's business concept, while the rule itself is not an unreasonable restriction on the employees' appearance, since an employee who does not wish to dye her hair may wear a wig and thus have her appearance off the job remain unaffected. Although the arbitrator concludes that he is without authority under the contract to order the restaurant to pay for the purchase and maintenance of wigs, he asks the restaurant to consider proposals outlined by the union for relieving the waitresses of some of the costs of complying with the hair rule (Mister A's Restaurant, 80 LA 1104).

Discussion: Arbitrator Christopher agrees that management has the fundamental right unilaterally to establish reasonable work rules that are not inconsistent with law or the collective bargaining contract (55 LA 306, 54 LA 942, and 54 LA 129). However, he notes that work rules must be reasonably related to a legitimate objective of management (55 LA 283). In this situation, the record established that the restaurant had achieved an outstanding reputation for its elegant and distinctive dining atmosphere in part because of the appearance of its waitresses. Although Thomas believes that any rule governing the appearance of employees must consider the impact the rule may have on employees' freedom of expression, he points out that where the sales of the business "are highly sensitive to the image portrayed, . . . the balance tends to weigh heavily in the favor of the employer." (56 LA 597)

Although the arbitrator was barred by contract from forcing the employer to pay the waitress for the cost and maintenance of the wigs, he noted:

> Nevertheless, this case does raise some equitable considerations and the arbitrator will therefore request that the Company consider the proposals outlined by the Union in its post-hearing brief for relieving the waitresses of some of the

costs of complying with the hair rule. The proposals are: (1) The Company could purchase the wigs and contract for their upkeep at probably a discount rate. To insure their longer use, the wigs could be stored on the Company premises. (2) For waitresses who dye their hair, the Company, at no cost to itself, could make an arrangement with a particular salon to provide a discount to the waitresses if a certain number of them regularly patronize the salon.

(Reprinted by permission from *Labor Relations Reporter,* copyright 1983, by the Bureau of National Affairs, Inc., Washington, D.C.)

The major plus of arbitration is that the decision is final and binding. There are no appeals. Out-of-court settlements in liability cases may be the result of arbitration. It is generally less costly and time consuming than court trials.

Mediation

Mediation is the action of a third party, usually agreed to by the parties in a dispute, to encourage opposing sides to come to agreement. The mediator makes no decision for the party, but rather acts in the role of a neutral expert to help the parties to continue their own efforts to resolve the problem. The mediator issues recommendations, which are not binding on the parties. *Conciliation* is another term for mediation.

Mediation falls between compromise and arbitration. Mediation is less costly in time and expense, but does not force the parties to settle. The settlement of the dispute rests solely with the parties.

RESOLVING LEGAL DISPUTES

You may find it necessary to resort to litigation to resolve disputes either as a plaintiff or as a defendant. Normally you will settle controversies with your patrons, your suppliers, your competitors, and the government at all levels by negotiation and compromise. Litigation should be used only when all other methods of settlement have failed.

Whether you settle out of court or after court trial and appeal, you must *always* make a written record of every major dispute. This is essential for a number of reasons: (1) It will enable those responsible for a settlement (lawyer, judge, jury) to know the nature of the dispute, how it occurred, why it occurred, and how frequently it has occurred. In this way you may not only settle the current dispute, but, wherever possible, be able to plan ahead to prevent or minimize future disputes. (2) You will be able to locate and summon people involved if litigation should prove unavoidable. (3) You will be able to use your insurance coverage better as a hedge against insurable risks and thereby effectively control your insurance costs. (4) You will be maintaining all records required by law to establish your rights with greater certainty in the event of a government agency investigation and possible court action. Disorganized records can destroy an otherwise winnable court case. (5) It will demonstrate that you are professional in your business transactions and merit the confidence and respect of all who do business with you. This objective alone may result in fewer lawsuits and a better business climate.

If you decide to bring a lawsuit against someone, you must be prepared to state and prove your case. This burden is normally on the plaintiff. You not only must produce concrete facts, rather than hypothetical theories, but you must consult your attorney to determine whether your facts are legally sufficient to justify court action. If they aren't, then you know that you must settle the case out of court.

Your physical time, effort, and financial resources are not inexhaustible, and you must, as in your other business dealings, weigh the costs of litigation against the benefits that you may receive. In court cases where a jury is involved (that is, cases not decided on the law alone), you cannot predict the outcome. Even if successful in court, you may find that the costs of litigation are too high to justify a favorable judgment. You can only make such a critical business judgment by understanding the basic judicial process.

SUMMARY

Our trial system is based on an adversary justice system. Each side endeavors to prove that that side is right and the other is wrong. To accomplish this usually requires, in addition to a competent lawyer, witnesses and evidence. Obtaining these can be costly.

The states and the federal government have a trial system that functions according to which courts have jurisdiction geographically, or over the subject, or as to the amount of damages (money) involved.

Courts of general jurisdiction hear all types of cases within a geographic jurisdiction. Courts of limited jurisdiction deal only with certain subject matter such as bankruptcy or tax law.

Small claims courts exist in major cities to settle disputes involving damages set by each state. These courts do not require lawyers and involve fewer procedures than regular courts.

Out-of-court settlements are always preferable to a trial. Relevant methods include compromise, mediation, and arbitration.

QUESTIONS

1. Mort Quentin of Mort's Delicatessen chain is declaring bankruptcy in Arizona. Will the federal or the state court have jurisdiction over this case? Why?

2. What is the difference between a trial court and an appellate court?

3. Who usually has the burden of proof in a trial, the plaintiff or the defendant?

4. Karl Kemp ordered $300 worth of potatoes for his first-class steak restaurant and specified Idaho baking potatoes. When his shipment arrived, it consisted of Wyoming potatoes suitable for frying. Now Karl has potatoes he cannot use and is out $300. What, if any, legal steps should Karl take to get his money back from the supplier? Explain your answer.

5. Compare and contrast compromise, mediation, and arbitration from the standpoint of advantages, disadvantages, and the degree to which each is binding.

NOTES

1. Lusk, Hewitt, Donnell, Barnes, *Business Law and the Regulatory Environment* 21–24 (5th ed. 1982).

2. Throughout the trial of a case, the trial judge rules upon or determines questions of law. The trial judge is not bound by legal arguments made by opposing lawyers. The trial judge is free to disregard those arguments and interpret the law independently, subject to review if one or the other side makes an appeal, claiming an error of law committed by the trial judge.

3. *Wallace v. Shoreham Hotel Corp.,* 49 A.2d 81 (D.C. App. 1946) (complaint by patron, alleging hurt feelings inflicted by defendant's dining room waiter, insufficient; only hotel guest entitled to courteous and considerate treatment); *Buck v. Del City Apartments, Inc.,* 431 P.2d 360 (Okla. 1967) (hotel guest fell on icy walkway; risk of fall within knowledge of guest; demurrer to guest's evidence affirmed).

4. *Apper v. Eastgate Assoc.,* 28 Md. App. 581, 347 A.2d 389 (1975) (*res ipsa loquitur* doctrine applied to overturn directed verdict in favor of motel keeper in case involving defective bathroom shower handle). See also *Haft v. Lone Palm Hotel,* 3 Cal. 3d 756, 478 P.2d 465, 91 Cal. Rptr. 745 (1970) (reversal of trial court verdict, notwithstanding the jury verdict for the motel keeper, in a motel pool drowning death).

5. Lusk *et al., supra* note 1.

15
Choosing and Managing Your Attorney

Objectives

The purpose of this chapter is to:

1. Outline the legal rights of a client in selecting and using legal services.
2. Suggest practical procedures for selecting and working with a lawyer.

Case in Point

Tom and Sue Clinton hired Darren Varney to represent them in a case in which they were being sued for liability for injuries caused by a patron's fall. The patron maintained that the Clintons failed to provide proper railings on the staircase leading to the rest rooms and that he had fallen as a result.

Tom and Sue failed to tell their attorney that they had been warned a week before by the building inspector that the railing on the right side might come loose because of the way in which it was bolted to the wall. They were given 10 days to have it fixed or the safety department would close the restaurant. They had already contacted and scheduled a carpenter to repair the railing. Varney had asked the Clintons at their first interview if they had ever been warned or cited for any violation, and they both said no. During the trial Varney was "surprised" by the warning, courtesy of the opposing attorney. Varney had prepared no defense for this factor, although the 10-day rule might have been sufficient.

They lost the case.

Can the Clintons sue Varney for negligence because he had no defense for the warning issue? Hardly. Their own failure to provide this information when asked was just that—their failure. Allowing the attorney to be surprised in court by something that could have been clarified, and possibly defended, was their negligence, not Varney's.

CHOOSING A LAWYER

You are very likely to require the assistance of a lawyer at some time during the course of your foodservice career. No one is immune from the possibility of a lawsuit brought by a patron, competitor, or the government. In a more positive sense, you will need legal guidance in the organization and operation of your foodservice business, and in those situations where you may wish to bring a lawsuit against a patron, a competitor, or the government. The fact that your operation may be small in no way alters the importance to you of competent, unbiased legal advice at reasonable cost.

The choice of a lawyer depends first on finding one who is willing and able to work with you and represent you.

Finding a Lawyer: The Advertising Factor

Unlike other businesses, the legal profession has traditionally frowned on public advertising of legal services or the cost of such services as being unbecoming to the profession. What advertising was permitted in the past was limited to professional announcements for lawyers or lists maintained primarily to benefit other lawyers. Such advertising was virtually unavailable to the public. Lawyer referral lists maintained by local bar associations (associations of lawyers in a particular geographical area who are supervised by the highest court in that area) were seldom publicized, with the result that potential clients had to rely on word-of-mouth recommendations.

The absence of public advertising often deprived the potential client of adequate legal services simply because the lawyer recommended might not practice business or commercial law of the sort the client required. Another referral to the right lawyer was possible, but meant loss of time, effort, and money.

The traditional policy of forbidding public advertising of legal services was eventually overturned by the United States Supreme Court in 1977.[1]

However, in denying state bar associations the right to prohibit any advertising of legal services directly to the public, the Supreme Court did not outlaw state bar regulation of such advertising. Reasonable regulation was approved.

Since advertising has been allowed, however, neither the larger, well-established firms nor storefront law offices have rushed out to buy the services of major advertisers. The advertising, as such, is still mainly low-key, and you will probably have to do your own research.

Generalists versus Specialists

Another factor that affects public knowledge of the availability of legal services is the great degree of specialization that has developed in recent years. Jack-of-all-trades lawyers are being replaced by lawyers who specialize in narrow legal areas. These specialists tend to be in lucrative areas such as real estate, tax, or contract law, or in business fields where the type of business generates more legal work at higher fees.[2]

Lawyers who specialize exclusively in foodservice law are still a minority, mainly because foodservice law does not command the higher fees in terms of legal effort that other businesses do. Lawyers who do practice in this field usually represent big business interests, fast-food franchisors, or other corporate clients who are better able to pay hefty legal fees.

The types of problems that your small business generates are better suited to the general practitioner. This is true because your needs are likely to be more varied and numerous than those generally served by the specialist.

One thing you should keep in mind when searching for and working with your lawyer is that law schools may not teach either general business law or foodservice law. This means that any lawyer willing to help but lacking practical exposure to foodservice management may have to learn the ropes at your expense.

In spite of these problems, you owe it to yourself to get the best legal advice you can afford. There are plenty of lawyers available to help you, and media advertising makes finding them somewhat easier than before.

Practical Guidelines to Choosing Your Lawyer

The following are some guidelines to follow in choosing a lawyer.

1. Seek the recommendations of trusted business and personal friends who have or have had problems *similar to your own.* But beware of the "my brother-in-law the attorney" trap. Make sure people know that you're seeking a competent attorney who has had experience in handling small business problems.
2. Contact your local bar association, usually located in your county seat or the city where your trial courts are situated. Ask for the client referral office. Explain your needs as specifically as you can.
3. Go to your public library and verify the list of attorneys provided by the bar association office by checking the *Martindale-Hubbell Legal Directory.* This directory comes in a series of volumes, broken down by states. Locate the volume for your state. Look in the front of the volume to see if any of the lawyers from your bar referral list are listed there. If so, check to see if the lawyer or law firm with which he or she is associated has a separate listing in the back of the volume. These listings include the type of law practiced by all partners, and biographical information about all partners and senior associates.

Martindale-Hubbell carefully screens all attorneys listed in each volume. *However, Martindale-Hubbell does not guarantee the competence of the lawyers who are listed. They merely provide a list of lawyers who meet their high screening standards.* A Martindale-Hubbell lawyer listing is a fairly reliable recommendation of that lawyer, however.

4. Make appointments to see those lawyers, three if possible, who pass muster on the criteria given in paragraphs 1, 2, and 3.

5. At each interview briefly outline your legal problem and let the lawyer ask you questions. Ask yourself: Do I feel comfortable with this lawyer? Can I divulge my needs fully and frankly, without hesitation? What is my gut reaction to the way the lawyer conducts himself or herself? Am I receiving a song and dance, or am I getting an honest, objective initial opinion?

Lawyers are generally cautious and conservative in their professional relations with clients. Do not be put off by this. Lawyer flattery and overconfidence in the initial interview ought to be viewed skeptically. Remember that you are purchasing honest, objective, and competent legal advice. A lawyer who appears more anxious to please you than to perform usually is trying to cover a lack of experience, of competence, or both. Such a lawyer may not serve your best interests.

6. Make no final decision on your choice of a lawyer until you have had an opportunity to review your reactions to all three interviews. Watch out for a legal fee that seems too good to be true, or promises of results that sound like pie in the sky. *Do not allow any attorney to force you into signing a retainer* (a contract for services) *agreement at the first interview.* Give the matter careful thought to ensure a good choice.

Advertising by lawyers does not guarantee the competence of legal services. It is still necessary to evaluate the legal services of any lawyer you wish to employ. State and local bar association referral lists are also no guarantee of competence, since some states require *all licensed attorneys to join.* However, limited competence of licensed attorneys (those who passed the bar) can be assumed because of the rigors of legal education and the passing of a bar examination as required by virtually all states. Some bar associations are better than others for referrals. Bar associations are not required by law to establish and maintain referral lists. Even so, you are advised to contact your local bar association for assistance. Most bar associations do list lawyers who will volunteer to meet with you at a reasonable initial fee. These lists are usually broken down into legal specialties to help you locate a lawyer competent to serve your particular needs.

THE LAWYER AS A BUSINESSPERSON: PROFESSIONAL FEES

The practice of law is a business, as well as a licensed profession. The object of every businessperson in our private enterprise system is to make a reasonable living. Every lawyer's professional fees reflect this fact of economic life. However, a lawyer has an ethical obligation to put your interests above his or her own interests in setting the price of legal services. The legal profession is a branch of the administration of justice and not a mere money-making trade.

Fee Schedules

Legal fees can and do take various forms. There are voluntary fees and scales for certain types of services, such as writing a will. Generally you will have to negotiate with your lawyer. There are four general methods that attorneys use to fix fees.

By the Hour

Lawyers work by the hour as a general rule. This means that your lawyer's fee may be made up of an hourly rate plus expenses for writing a foodservice employment contract or handling a foodservice real estate contract. This is the normal method of payment for legal work other than courtroom representation.

Courtroom Trials and Appeals

Lawyers usually charge by the day for courtroom trial and appeal work. Such a fee usually consists of a per-day (per diem) amount times the number of trial days. An appeal is usually heard during part of one day, and the fee charged includes preparing and filing the records on appeal and legal briefs. This preparation time is lengthy. Filing appeals is costly, making them available only to those foodservice operators who have the means to afford what is actually only a review of the original decision.

Contingent Fee

Lawyers may work on a contingent fee basis, meaning that their fee is a percentage of any favorable judgment or award, with no fee paid if they are unsuccessful. These contingent fees are often controlled by court rules to prevent lawyers from taking the entire award and leaving you empty-handed. Lawyers who handle liability cases are more likely to enter into this type of arrangement.

Retainer Agreement

Lawyers enter into retainer agreements for services of a general kind over a longer period of time. Here you pay a fee for having the services of a lawyer. A written retainer agreement is a contract which states your rights and responsibilities to your lawyer and his or her rights and responsibilities to you. It outlines the legal advice or services you may request of that lawyer or law firm. Essentially the retainer agreement includes what is to be done, when it is to be done, and how much the work will cost you. Retainer agreements are used to provide general advice, and the fee reflects this by usually being less than for a single case or problem. Very large foodservice operations, or operators getting into franchising or other areas of the foodservice business, may use this arrangement. It is of questionable value to small businesspersons with only sporadic needs for lawyers.

WORKING WITH YOUR LAWYER: YOUR RIGHTS AND RESPONSIBILITIES

Once you have selected a lawyer, it behooves both of you to interact in a cooperative, effective, and efficient manner. Some major points require attention.

1. You have the right to receive timely, honest, competent, and confidential advice, and you are entitled to know the cost of that advice from the beginning. Although it is not yet possible to shop for legal advice as you would shop for an automobile or house, you have the right to compare the costs of legal services.

2. You have the right to obtain independent legal advice, without conflict of interest or a biased viewpoint that might cause your lawyer to be less than totally committed to serving you. You have the right to receive competent legal advice. Your lawyer may not deceive you about professional skills and experience or take on a case he or she is not competent to handle. A lawyer may not limit responsibility to you for his or her own malpractice, or disclaim that responsibility by prior agreement.

3. Your lawyer has the right to expect truthful answers to questions, your cooperation in meeting court and other deadlines, and the freedom to exercise his or her best professional judgment in providing you with legal advice. Your lawyer has the right to payment within a reasonable time, or according to your agreement.

Both you and your lawyer have the right to terminate the relationship at any time, either as per the agreement or for just cause. If this is done, the lawyer is entitled to receive the reasonable value of services provided to date, and you are entitled to the return of any papers or other documents you gave to the lawyer.

Getting on the Right Track with Your Lawyer

The following practical tips will help to create a mutually beneficial working relationship with the lawyer you select:

1. *At the first interview or meeting,* state clearly, concisely, and honestly your needs, what you expect of the lawyer, and how much you can afford to spend. If you need to employ a lawyer on a long-term basis, to cover all types of problems, a written retainer agreement may be negotiated, to be signed later. A lawyer retained by you should charge you less overall than a lawyer you employ to solve a one-shot problem.

   If you need to employ an attorney for one-time or nonrecurring advice, then obtain an agreement on a fee for that advice and a commitment letter indicating the type and duties of service.

2. Before signing a retainer agreement or a commitment letter, decide how you feel about developing a close working relationship with the lawyer. Do you feel comfortable giving very private information to the lawyer? Remember that your lawyer will be one of your closest advisors. You may reveal matters to a lawyer you withhold from family members. The relationship may expand from business matters to personal matters. Any doubts you may have should be thoroughly aired with the lawyer up front.

3. Explain your particular legal needs in the context of your *foodservice operation,* not just in terms of a small business. Thoroughly explain not only what happened, or what you want to happen, but *why.* This will enable your lawyer to tailor the right legal remedy to your problem or to prevent a legal snarl.

Don't be afraid to mention what you know about foodservice law. This is especially useful regarding local regulations that other small businesses do not encounter. The foodservice industry is somewhat unique in the scope and amount of local regulation, and your lawyer may not be aware of this.

4. Acquaint your lawyer with outside foodservice experts who can help on specific issues. For example, you may know that your local restaurant association has an expert in security prevention, financial management, credit controls, or real estate. Names of such people should be given to your lawyer.

5. Encourage your lawyer to contact specialists who teach at major schools of hotel and restaurant management and have published books or articles in your problem area. They can be of invaluable assistance to the general practitioner.

6. When your legal problem involves an insured risk, always provide your lawyer with the name of your insurance carrier. This step should be taken even though the legal defense as well as the claim may be covered by that carrier. Cooperation between your lawyer and your carrier's legal staff is needed to prevent future risks as well as to defend claims against you.

7. Be candid and truthful with your lawyer. Holding back information because it is unpleasant or personally damaging is shortsighted. Doing so will only throw your lawyer off the track, cause surprise during negotiations or at trial, and make both you and your lawyer lose credibility with opposing counsel, the court, and a jury. Knowing the worst of your problem will enable your lawyer to meet that problem, and not be caught by surprise without adequate time to deal with it.

The following guidelines should help you *maintain* a good working relationship with your lawyer:

1. Always reach a definite understanding of what you want to discuss before calling or seeing your lawyer. Frequent, unnecessary telephone calls or visits are time consuming, expensive, and accomplish little. Set aside enough time and be prepared to discuss important matters. Being unprepared wastes valuable time, for which you are paying.

2. Set a reasonable timetable for results, with appropriate lawyer deadlines. Monitor the deadlines and the results promised by your lawyer.

3. Always meet deadlines imposed by your lawyer. Otherwise he or she will be unable to perform any assigned tasks properly.

4. Always document the length of telephone calls you make to your lawyer, so you can verify any fees for the calls.

5. Require your lawyer to give you a detailed statement supporting each bill for professional services. Examine each statement against your original agreement for accuracy. Check to see that all fees are within your fee agreement, and that any overcharges are correct. Do not hesitate to question your lawyer about fee statements. It is your money, and you deserve to pay only for the services you agreed to, at the rate agreed on.

6. When you feel that your lawyer is deliberately trying to take advantage of you, such as by billing you for fictitious services, or serving you and another person interested in the outcome without informing you, you should notify your state or local bar association. Each bar association has the power to investigate violations of its professional codes and to discipline guilty attorneys. You have the right to expect honest as well as competent legal representation.

7. You must be able to discipline yourself as well as your lawyer to act as a team, not as contestants in a battle of wits as to which of you is right or wrong. You are the team captain, responsible for making all business decisions. Your lawyer is your advisor, not your superior. Properly used, your lawyer will hear you out, give you his or her best legal judgment on the pros and cons of your plans, and offer alternatives to accomplish your goals that can stand muster legally, should that be necessary.

You are free to disregard your attorney's advice and to use your own best business judgment instead. Your lawyer has no power to override your decision, but may wish to terminate his or her association with you if your decision in any way violates the law.

Ultimately you, and you alone, must take responsibility for the consequences of your decisions. Your lawyer is your agent, and is not liable to you or to others for your mistakes or lapses of judgment.

You have the right to expect that your lawyer will follow the proper legal procedures to protect you, or carry out specific promises made to you. You have the right to check periodically to see that your lawyer does so, or gives you a reasonable explanation as to why it was not done.

Good management of your lawyer means reasonable and periodic inquiries on progress on your case. It does not mean badgering your lawyer with unnecessary calls for which you may be charged an additional fee.

Judge your lawyer by results obtained, not by the quality of his or her manner. Remember that no lawyer can guarantee a favorable outcome. What a competent, trustworthy lawyer *can do* is to promise to use his or her best efforts to ensure the best possible result, or to tell you honestly that your chances of success are slim. Be wary of the lawyer who is too quick to promise you perfect results. Such a lawyer is either ill-informed, dishonest, or both.

Two Recurring Problems

A final word of warning is needed in choosing and working with any lawyer.

First, you must make certain that the lawyer you select is free of any *conflict of interest.* For example, you retain lawyer Jones to represent you in the purchase of land for your new foodservice business. Jones operates as a real estate agent (which Jones may do as an attorney in some states), and owns a parcel of land and a building that fit your needs. Jones is under an ethical and legal duty to tell you that, or disqualify himself from representing you in the purchase of his own property. However, you also should make independent inquiry of Jones as to any interest in the property you're thinking of buying, so that any concealment or false statement Jones may make can be used to deny Jones any legal fee, and also to bring Jones up on charges of professional misconduct.

Second, all lawyers are bound under the rules of professional conduct not to disclose any communications you make to them in their role as lawyers, without your approval. This duty is called the *attorney-client privilege.*

For example, you hire Jones to represent you in a liquor license revocation hearing, where you are accused of selling liquor to minors. You tell Jones that you were found guilty of selling to minors in another state some years ago. Jones, without your knowledge, casually mentions this information to a friend at dinner. The friend calls the local newspaper, and the following day the morning edition contains a lead article titled, "Convicted Restaurateur Martin Again Up on Charges of Selling Liquor to Minors." That unauthorized disclosure by your attorney of damaging information is a violation of the attorney-client privilege, whether the information is true or not. Jones could be professionally disciplined for the disclosure. You in turn could sue him for malpractice for any damages you suffer as a result of his disclosure.

PROBLEMS WITH YOUR LAWYER

At some point during your relationship with your lawyer, as with any business relationship, you may have a problem. Most problems businesspersons have with their attorneys can be traced to breakdowns in communication. If you follow the guidelines in this chapter for establishing and maintaining good communication with your attorney, you should have few problems. You must be able to differentiate between a problem caused by your own failure to provide critical information, or to notify your lawyer of necessary deadlines, and a lawyer's negligence, willful misconduct, or incompetence in handling your case.

The American Bar Association's (ABA) Code of Professional Responsibility and Canons of Legal Ethics establish rules of conduct for all lawyers, which each state bar association or disciplinary board is urged to follow when reviewing individual cases of misconduct (Figure 15.1). The overall aim of the code is to establish and maintain honesty and fairness among lawyers in their dealings with the government, other lawyers, and their clients. The ultimate penalty for professional misconduct is disbarment, or revocation of the guilty person's license to practice law.

What happens if a lawyer injures you by acting negligently, failing to act properly, or intentionally misrepresenting your interests? Is your only recourse to complain to the local bar association? No. You may sue the lawyer to recover compensation for any losses the misrepresentation or negligence caused you.

Figure 15.1
American Bar Association Canons
of Legal Ethics

1. A lawyer should assist in maintaining the integrity and competence of the legal profession.
2. A lawyer should assist the legal profession in fulfilling its duty to make legal counsel available.
3. A lawyer should assist in preventing the unauthorized practice of law.
4. A lawyer should preserve the confidences and secrets of a client.
5. A lawyer should exercise independent professional judgment on behalf of a client.
6. A lawyer should represent a client competently.
7. A lawyer should represent a client zealously within the bounds of the law.
8. A lawyer should assist in improving the legal system.
9. A lawyer should avoid even the appearance of professional impropriety.

You would sue for *malpractice,* or for the negligence or misconduct. For example, Ed Conley employs a lawyer, Sam Smith, to appeal a ruling of the Zoning Board. The Board turned down his application for a variance he needs to build a restaurant on land he's contracted to buy. Conley's purchase contract requires he obtain a variance within six months or forfeit his down payment. Smith, who knows of this requirement, negligently fails to file the appeal within the required time limits. Unless Smith can prove that his failure to do so was beyond his control or was otherwise justified, he may be liable for Ed's loss of the down payment. As in other negligence actions, Conley would be required to prove the existence of a legal duty, a breach or violation of that duty, and proximate cause and damages.

To protect the public further when a lawyer cannot make good a client loss, some states have created state-administered client compensation funds whereby lawyer licensing and registration fees may be used to purchase insurance against such risks. Lawyers often insure themselves by purchasing professional liability insurance, but it is not required.

Your lawyer is only liable for injuries inflicted on you by his or her own willful misconduct or negligence in the handling of your legal affairs. The law differentiates between injuries caused by your lawyer's failure to act and injuries caused by your lawyer's exercise of legal judgment, a discretionary act. Failures to act, such as not filing a legal complaint in time to satisfy the statute of limitations, may constitute malpractice. Exercises of professional judgment, however poor they may seem afterward, do not constitute malpractice, unless the advice given is known to be false or is made intentionally to injure you.

The Code of Professional Responsibility requires every lawyer to deal fairly and truthfully with his or her clients. An ABA Disciplinary Rule prohibits lawyers from intentionally making false statements as to their skills or experience. Every lawyer is a *fiduciary,* meaning in a position of special trust, in dealing with clients. A violation of that trust makes a lawyer subject to reprimand (censure), or even disbarment in very serious cases.

The following attorney-client-attorney case is unique in that the client encountered problems with two attorneys. The malpractice suit against the second attorney for negligence is the subject here.

Basic Food Industries, Inc. v. Grant
Court of Appeals of Michigan
107 Mich. App. 685, 310 N.W.2d 26 (1981)

Facts.   This is a legal malpractice lawsuit for negligence brought by Basic Food, a corporate foods producer, against its lawyer. Basic Food accused the attorney of negligence in defending the company against a lawsuit for legal fees by another lawyer. That previous lawsuit resulted in a jury verdict against Basic Food in the amount of $25,000. The judgment was affirmed by the Court of Appeals.

Basic Food then started this lawsuit for malpractice, arguing that Grant's failure to obtain the sworn statement of the chairman of the board of Basic Food for use at the trial despite repeated written promises to do so, to investigate or ascertain the facts so as to establish a defense to the attorney fee lawsuit, and to engage in any pre-trial discovery whatsoever resulted in a judgment against Basic Food in an amount greater than that for which Basic Food properly should have been held liable.

The judgment of the trial court based on a $5000 jury verdict for Basic Food was upheld.

Reasoning.   The court evaluated the following criteria in coming to its decision:

> In an action against an attorney for negligence or breach of implied contract, the plaintiff has the burden of proving: (1) the existence of the attorney-client relationship; (2) the acts which are alleged to have constituted the negligence; (3) that the negligence was the proximate cause of the injury; and (4) the fact and extent of the injury alleged . . .

The court reached the following conclusions:

1. The defendant's contention that Basic Food had to prove that it would have won the case had it not been for his negligence, was

not required in this case. The court said, "Rather, the attorney's liability, as in other negligence cases, is for all damages directly and proximately caused by the attorney's negligence." That the attorney's negligent conduct maximized the chances of Basic Food's prior opponent led to a higher damage award than would otherwise have been returned by the jury.

2. The attorney's defense that he had made errors of *professional judgment,* which are not grounds for a malpractice suit, was held to be insufficient in this case. The court found the errors too serious to be classified as errors of professional judgment.

3. The court found that the evidence which Basic Food presented at the lower court trial again was sufficient to justify that court's decision for the plaintiff.

4. The court also pointed out that a challenge by the defendant that he was entitled to a new trial because of the previous trial judge's failure to charge the jury properly could not be substantiated, and that it was up to the trial court to determine whether the defendant was entitled to a new trial.

Conclusion.   This case illustrates a number of legal rules regarding the suing of a lawyer for malpractice (negligence) resulting in injury to a business.

1. A lawyer is bound to use reasonable care, skill, and judgment in the conduct and management of legal affairs entrusted to him or her.

2. There are two types of cases relevant to this malpractice suit, and Basic Food either could have sued only on the basis that it was prevented from filing on time *or* on the basis that the filing caused Basic Food to be liable for a larger settlement than otherwise might have been decided. A lawyer's negligence is a *proximate cause* of your injuries if the value of the judgment rendered against you may not have been set if the lawyer had performed properly,

not whether you lost because you were prevented from suing or filing an appeal within the required time. In the second type of case, you must prove that you would have won your case, or won your appeal. In the first case, illustrated here, Grant was found to have caused Basic Food to suffer a higher jury award than would have been decided had Grant done what he was supposed to do in his representation of Basic Food.

3. A lawyer's defense that he or she merely made errors of judgment, which would otherwise excuse liability, does not apply to *very serious* errors. Grant's negligence in not even offering any defense at the trial was very serious.

MANAGING YOUR LAWYER

Manage your lawyer's services with the same vigilance as you would manage any other professional person you employ, such as a certified public accountant, architect, or engineer. This means that you are entitled to have all services agreed to performed on schedule, or with an explanation and reasonable alternatives provided if the services are delayed or must be changed. You are *not* entitled to supervise the methods your lawyer employs in his or her professional capacity, but merely the accomplishments of the promised result.

Be wary of a lawyer who guarantees all results. You are entitled to his or her best professional effort on your behalf. You are not entitled to a guarantee of success unless the lawyer makes one. Such guarantees should not be relied upon. The honest attorney knows better than to guarantee services against all risks.

Successful management of your lawyer requires maintaining good communication throughout your association. Good communication means knowing when to contact your lawyer and when to leave your lawyer alone.

Good communication rests on a foundation of mutual trust and respect.

Legal success or justice cannot always be assured. Your ultimate decision as to whether to retain the services of a lawyer should rest on the quality *and* honesty of his or her performance.

SUMMARY

You should know how to choose an attorney. This means more than just finding an attorney. It means finding an attorney able, willing, and experienced enough to provide you the best service per dollar you can afford to spend.

Increasingly lawyers specialize in areas such as tax law or real estate. Since small business operators such as restaurant owners may encounter a variety of legal problems, a general practitioner might be the best choice.

Although advertising is allowed for lawyers, it is still uncommon, but there are more varied sources of information about legal services currently available than in past years. *First,* there is the traditional word-of-mouth referral by a family member or friend. *Second,* the referral services of your local or state bar association should be explored. *Third,* mass media advertisements are now available. *Fourth,* the local chapter of your state restaurant association may be able to refer you to local or national foodservice law specialists. In each of these cases, you must remember that the referral is not a guarantee of successful performance, but only notice that the lawyer is available for consultation.

You must next determine whether the attorney you find through any of those sources is personally compatible, and is willing to meet your specific needs and to work for you at a fee you can afford to pay. It is critical that *you* know what your needs are, that *you* communicate your needs to your attorney, and that *both of you* agree on all essential terms and conditions. To avoid misunderstandings later, it is to your advantage to draw up a letter of commitment.

There are four methods lawyers use to fix fees. They may charge by the hour, or by the day for courtroom trials or appeals. They may accept contingent fees—percentages of awards, or be paid according to a retainer agreement, usually drawn up by the lawyer.

Both attorney and client have rights under the law. The attorney has the right to expect honest answers and cooperation. The client has the right to expect competent service, free of any conflict of interest.

There are a number of guidelines in this chapter for working with lawyers to obtain the best results. The objective is not to interfere with or direct an attorney's work, but to monitor the work, document expenses, and cooperate.

It is important to ensure that an attorney does not have any conflicting interest in the outcome of your case and will not violate the attorney-client privilege.

If a lawyer acts unprofessionally or incompetently, or violates a client's trust, the client may have the option both to sue the attorney and to complain to the local bar association. Generally the misdeed must be very serious before a lawyer is disbarred or loses a malpractice suit.

QUESTIONS

1. List three sources of information available to you in selecting a lawyer for the first time.
2. What type of lawyer would you want to help you with the legal areas of running a foodservice operation—a general practitioner or a specialist? Explain your answer.
3. What steps should you take to manage your lawyer's services after hiring one?
4. The Donaldsons are buying land on which to build a restaurant. They have decided on some land owned by the local school board and they hire attorney Richard Killian to help them with the contract. He is also one of five attorneys representing the school board. Is there a problem with this? If so, what should the Donaldsons do?
5. When should you consider complaining to your state or local bar association about your lawyer's misconduct?

NOTES

1. *Bates v. State Bar of Arizona,* 433 U.S. 350 (1977).
2. Additionally, some states are planning to certify legal specialists, meaning that these states will license lawyers as specialists. As yet, most states have not adopted this certification procedure. Moreover, the special practice areas are limited in those states that have done so or are moving in this direction.

Appendixes

The various state-by-state charts
included in these appendixes
are meant to provide a quick reference
to state positions on specific legal issues.
They do not take the place of a lawyer.
As states add to, repeal, or rewrite laws,
it is wise to consult an attorney
regarding a specific issue.

Appendix A
Federal Acts Affecting Foodservice Operators

Age Discrimination in Employment Act (1967)
Prohibits discrimination against job applicants and employees between the ages of 40 and 70.

Bankruptcy Reform Act of 1978
Resulted in clarification of alternatives to straight bankruptcy for businesses and individuals, simplified procedures, and changed the previous court and trustee system.

Civil Rights Act of 1964
Prohibits discrimination in employment and public accommodations on the basis of race, color, religion, or national origin. Sex and pregnancy are covered in the employment section.

Clayton Act of 1914
Antitrust law which prohibits exclusive-dealing contracts, tying arrangements, and stock acquisitions designed to lessen competition.

Economic Recovery Tax Act of 1981
Provides accelerated recovery deductions for depreciation of buildings and equipment.

Equal Employment Opportunity Act (1972)
Prohibits discrimination based on race, color, religion, sex, or national origin. Amended Civil Rights Act of 1964.

Equal Pay Act
Requires employers to provide employees of both sexes equal pay for equal work.

Fair Labor Standards Act
Establishes requirements for minimum wages, work time, overtime pay, equal pay, and child labor, and enforcement of such requirements.

Federal Insurance Contributions Act
Source of federal payroll tax law, especially regarding Social Security.

Federal Unemployment Tax Act
Source of tax law for unemployment compensation.

Hart-Scott-Rodino Antitrust Improvement Act of 1976
Empowers states' attorneys general to sue businesses that violate the Sherman Act.

Internal Revenue Code
Major source of tax laws. Regularly amended.

Labor Management Relations Act
(a.k.a. Taft-Hartley Act)
Regulates employee and employer actions regarding unionization.

Model Business Corporation Act
Regulates all aspects of corporation formation and dissolution, and rights of directors, shareholders, and officers.

Robinson-Patman Act of 1936
Prohibits price discrimination designed to lessen or injure competition, or to create a monopoly.

Sherman Act of 1890
Prohibits contracts, combinations, or conspiracies to restrain trade among the several states or with foreign nations.

Truth-in-Lending Act
(a.k.a. Consumer Credit Protection Act) (1969)
Regulates extension of credit in the absence of similar state legislation.

Uniform Commercial Code (UCC)
Sweeping law covering all commercial transactions, particularly aimed at sales of consumer products.

Uniform Limited Partnership Act
(adopted 1961; revised 1976)
Source of law for setting up and dissolving limited partnerships. It is the law only in states that allow limited partnerships.

Uniform Partnership Act (UPA) (1914)
The law regulating partnerships, adopted in most states.

Vocational Rehabilitation Act (1973)
Prohibits discrimination against job applicants or employees because of mental or physical disabilities. Applies only to those who contract or subcontract with the government.

Appendix B
Alcohol Beverage Control Laws Concerning Minimum Age Requirements

State	Minimum Drinking Ages			State	Minimum Drinking Ages		
	Distilled Spirits	Wine	Beer		Distilled Spirits	Wine	Beer
Alabama	19	19	19	Montana	19	19	19
Alaska	21	21	21	Nebraska[d]	20	20	20
Arizona	19	19	19	Nevada	21	21	21
Arkansas	21	21	21	New Hampshire	20	20	20
California	21	21	21	New Jersey	21	21	21
Colorado	21	21	21[a]	New Mexico	21	21	21
Connecticut	20	20	20	New York	19	19	19
Delaware	21	21	21	North Carolina	21	21[e]	19
District of Columbia	21	21[b]	18	North Dakota	21	21	21
Florida	19	19	19	Ohio	21	21	19
Georgia	19	19	19	Oklahoma	21	21	21
Hawaii	18	18	18	Oregon	21	21	21
Idaho	19	19	19	Pennsylvania	21	21	21
Illinois	21	21	21	Rhode Island	20	20	20
Indiana	21	21	21	South Carolina	21	18	18
Iowa	19	19	19	South Dakota	21	21	21[f]
Kansas	21	21	21[a]	Tennessee	19	19	19
Kentucky	21	21	21	Texas	19	19	19
Louisiana	18	18	18	Utah	21	21	21
Maine	20	20	20	Vermont	18	18	18
Maryland	21	21	21	Virginia	21	21	19
Massachusetts	20	20	20	Washington	21	21	21
Michigan	21	21	21	West Virginia	19	19	19
Minnesota	19	19	19	Wisconsin	19	19	19
Mississippi	21	21[b]	21[c]	Wyoming	19	19	19
Missouri	21	21	21				

[a]*Age 18 for 3.2 percent beer.*
[b]*Age 18 for light wine.*
[c]*Age 18 for beer not over 4 percent alcohol by weight.*

[d]*Age 21 effective January 1, 1985.*
[e]*Age 19 for light wine.*
[f]*Age 19 for beer not over 3.2 percent alcohol by weight.*

Appendix C
Accuracy in Menus

REPRESENTATION OF QUANTITY

Proper operational procedures should preclude any concerns with misinformation on quantities. Steaks are often merchandised by weight, and the generally accepted practice of declared quantity is that prior to cooking.

Obviously, double martinis are twice the size of the normal drink, and if jumbo eggs are listed it means exactly that—as "jumbo" is a recognized egg size. Petite and supercolossal are among the official size descriptions for olives. However, the use of terms such as "extra large salad" or "extra tall drink" may invite problems if not qualified. There is no question about the meaning of a "three-egg omelette" or "all you can eat." Also remember the implied meaning of words—a bowl of soup contains more than a cup of soup.

REPRESENTATION OF QUALITY

Federal and state standards of quality grades exist for many restaurant products including meat, poultry, eggs, dairy products, fruits, and vegetables. Terminology used to describe grades include Prime, Grade A, Good, No. 1, Choice, Fancy, Grade AA and Extra Standard.

Care must be exercised in preparing menu descriptions when these words are used. In certain uses, they imply certain quality. An item appearing as "choice sirloin of beef" connotes the use of USDA Choice Grade Sirloin of Beef. One recognized exception is the term "prime rib." Prime rib is a long established, well understood and accepted description for a cut of beef (the "primal" ribs, the 6th to 12th ribs) and does not represent the grade quality, unless USDA is used in conjunction.

Because of our industry's volume use of ground beef, it is well to remember the USDA definition: Ground beef is just what the name implies. No extra fat, water, extenders or binders are permitted. The fat limit is 30 percent. Seasonings may be added as long as they are identified. These requirements identify only product ground and packaged in Federal or State inspected plants.

REPRESENTATION OF PRICE

If your pricing structure includes a cover charge, service charge or gratuity, these must be appropriately brought to your customer's attention. If extra charges are made for requests such as "all white meat" or "no ice drinks" these should be so stated at the time of ordering.

Any restrictions when using a coupon or premium promotion must be clearly defined.

If a price promotion involves a multi-unit company, clearly indicate which units are participating.

REPRESENTATION OF BRAND NAMES

Any product brand that is advertised must be the one served. A registered or copywritten trade-mark or brand name must not be used generically to refer to a product. Several examples of "brand" names of restaurant products are:

> Armour Star Bacon, Sanka, Log Cabin Syrup, Coca-Cola, Seven-Up, Swifts Premium Ham, Pepsi-Cola, Starkist Tuna, Ry-Krisp, Jello, Heinz Ketchup, Maxwell House Coffee, Chase & Sanborn Coffee, Kraft Cheese, Tabasco Sauce, Ritz Crackers, Seven and Seven, Miracle Whip.

Your own "house" brand of a product may be so labeled even when prepared by an outside source, if its manufacturing was to your specifications. Containers of branded condiments and sauces placed on a table must be the product appearing on the container label.

REPRESENTATION OF PRODUCT IDENTIFICATION

Because of the similarity of many food products, substitutions are often made. These substitutions may be due to non-delivery, availability, merchandising considerations or price. When such substitutions are effected, be certain these changes are reflected on your menu. Common substitutions are:

Maple syrup and maple flavored syrup

Boiled ham and baked ham

Chopped and shaped veal pattie and veal cutlet

Ice milk and ice cream

Powdered eggs and fresh eggs

Picnic style pork shoulder and ham

Milk and skim milk

Pure jams and pectin jams

Whipped topping and whipped cream

Turkey and chicken

Hereford beef and Black Angus beef

Ground beef and ground sirloin of beef

Capon and chicken

Standard ice cream and french style ice cream

Cod and haddock

Noodles and egg noodles

Light meat tuna and white meat tuna

Pollack and haddock

Flounder and sole

Cheese food and processed cheese

Cream sauce and non-dairy cream sauce

Bonita and tuna fish

Roquefort cheese and blue cheese

Peanut oil and corn oil
Beef liver and calves
  liver
Cream and half & half
Margarine and butter
Non-dairy creamers or
  whiteners and
  cream

Tenderloin tips and
  diced beef
Mayonnaise and salad
  dressing

REPRESENTATION OF POINTS OF ORIGIN

A potential area of error is in describing the point of origin of a menu offering. Claims may be substantiated by the product, by packaging labels, invoices or other documentation provided by your supplier. Mistakes are possible as sources of supply change and availability of product shifts. The following are common assertions of points of origin.

Lake Superior
  Whitefish
Idaho Potatoes
Maine Lobster
Imported Swiss Cheese
Puget Sound Sockeye
  Salmon
Alaskan King Crab
Imported Ham
Colorado Beef
Long Island Duckling

Bay Scallops
Gulf Shrimp
Florida Orange Juice
Smithfield Ham
Wisconsin Cheese
Danish Blue Cheese
Louisiana Frog Legs
Colorado Brook Trout
Florida Stone Crabs
Chesapeake Bay
  Oysters

There is widespread use of geographic names used in a generic sense to describe a method of preparation or service. Such terminology is readily understood and accepted by the customer and their use should in no way be restricted. Examples are:

Russian Dressing
New England Clam
  Chowder
Irish Stew
Country Ham
French Fries
Danish Pastries
Russian Service
English Muffins
Swiss Cheese

French Toast
Country Fried Steak
Denver Sandwich
French Dip
Swiss Steak
German Potato Salad
French Service
Manhattan Clam
  Chowder

REPRESENTATION OF MERCHANDISING TERMS

A difficult area to clearly define as right or wrong is the use of merchandising terms. "We serve the best gumbo in town" is understood by the dining-out public for what it is—boasting for advertising sake. However, to use the term "we use only the finest beef" implies that USDA Prime Beef is used, as a standard exists for this product.

Advertising exaggerations are tolerated if they do not mislead. When ordering a "mile high pie" a customer would expect a pie heaped tall with meringue or similar fluffy topping, but to advertise a "foot long hot dog" and to serve something less would be in error.

Mistakes are possible in properly identifying steak cuts. Use industry standards such as provided in the National Association of Meat Purveyors *Meat Buyer's Guide.*

"Homestyle," "home made style" or "our own" are suggested terminology rather than "homemade" in describing menu offerings prepared according to a home recipe. Most foodservice sanitation ordinances prohibit the preparation of foods in home facilities.

If using any of the following terms, be certain you can qualify them.

Fresh daily	Corn fed porkers
Fresh roasted	Slept in Chesapeake
Flown in daily	Bay
Kosher meat	Finest quality
Black Angus beef	Center cut ham
Aged steaks	Own special sauce
Milk fed chicken	Low calorie

REPRESENTATION OF MEANS OF PRESERVATION

The accepted means of preserving foods are numerous, including canned, chilled, bottled, frozen and dehydrated. If you choose to describe your menu selections with these terms, they must be accurate. Frozen orange juice is not fresh, canned peas are not frozen and bottled apple sauce is not canned.

REPRESENTATION OF FOOD PREPARATION

The means of food preparation is often the determining factor in the customer's selection of a menu entree. Absolute accuracy is a must. Readily understood terms include:

Charcoal broiled	Deep fried
Sauteed	Barbecued
Baked	Smoked
Broiled	Prepared from scratch
Roasted	Poached
Fried in butter	

REPRESENTATION OF VERBAL AND VISUAL PRESENTATION

When your menu, wall placards or other advertising contains a pictorial representation of a meal or platter, it should portray the actual contents with accuracy. Examples of visual misrepresentations include:

- The use of mushroom pieces in a sauce when the picture depicts mushroom caps.
- The use of sliced strawberries on a shortcake when the picture depicts whole strawberries.
- The use of numerous thin sliced meat pieces when the picture depicts a single thick slice.
- The use of five shrimp when the picture depicts six shrimp.
- The omission of vegetables or other entree extras when the picture depicts their inclusion.
- The use of a plain bun when the picture depicts a sesame topped bun.

Examples of verbal misrepresentation include:

- If a waiter asks "sour cream or butter with your potatoes" when in fact an imitation sour cream or margarine is served.
- A waitress' response—"the pies are baked in our kitchen" when in fact they are a purchased prebaked institutional pie.

REPRESENTATION OF DIETARY OR NUTRITIONAL CLAIMS

Potential public health concerns are real if misrepresentation is made of the dietary or nutritional content of food. For example "salt free" or "sugar free" foods must be exactly that to assure the protection of your customers who may be under particular dietary restraints. "Low calorie" or nutritional claims, if made, must be supportable by specific data.

Appendix D
State Laws Prohibiting Discrimination in Places of Public Accommodation

State	Sex Based	Sexual Preference	Physical Handicap	Mental Handicap
Alabama				
Alaska	X			
Arizona				
Arkansas				
California	X	X	X	
Colorado	X		X	
Connecticut	X		X	X
Delaware	X			
District of Columbia				
Florida	X		X	
Georgia				
Hawaii				
Idaho	X			
Illinois				
Indiana				
Iowa	X			
Kansas	X		X	
Kentucky	X			
Louisiana	X			
Maine	X			
Maryland				
Massachusetts	X			
Michigan				
Minnesota	X		X	
Mississippi				
Missouri				
Montana				
Nebraska	X			

State Laws Prohibiting Discrimination in Places of Public Accommodation

State	Sex Based	Sexual Preference	Physical Handicap	Mental Handicap
Nevada				
New Hampshire	X		X	X
New Jersey*	X	X		
New Mexico	X			
New York†	X		X	
North Carolina				
North Dakota				
Ohio				
Oklahoma				
Oregon	X		X	X
Pennsylvania	X		X	
Rhode Island				
South Carolina				
South Dakota				
Tennessee				
Texas				
Utah	X			
Vermont				
Virginia				
Washington			X	
West Virginia	X		X	
Wisconsin	X		X	
Wyoming				

*By Supreme Court interpretation of Civil Rights Act, public accommodations section [Seven Eleven Wines and Liquors v. Division of ABC, 50 N.J. 329, 235 A.2d 12 (1967)].

†The state of New York prohibits discrimination based on marital status.

Appendix E
State-by-State Adoption of UCC 2–318

Alabama *Section 7–2–318*
Omits words "who is in the family or household of his buyer or who is a guest in his home."

Alaska* *Section 45.02.318*
No change.

Arizona *Section 44–2335*
Alternative A adopted.

Arkansas *Section 85–2–318*
Alternative A adopted.

California
Section 2–318 not adopted.

Colorado *Section 4–2–318*
No alternative chosen. Language adopted reads: "A seller's warranty whether express or implied extends to any person who may reasonably be expected to use, consume or be affected by the goods and who is injured by breach of the warranty."

Connecticut *Section 42a–2–318*
No alternative chosen. Language adopted reads: "This section is neutral with respect to case law or statutory law extending warranties for personal injuries to other warranty."

Delaware
Not adopted.

District of Columbia *Section 28–2–318*
No change.

*In states where no alternative or language is adopted, the courts are free to apply the appropriate alternative.

Florida *Section 672.318*
No alternative chosen. Language adopted reads: "A seller's warranty whether express or implied extends to any natural person who is in the family or household of his buyer, who is a guest in his home or who is an employee, servant *or* agent of his buyer if it is reasonable to expect that such persons may use, consume or be affected by the goods and who is injured by breach of the warranty. A seller may not exclude or limit the operation of this section."

Georgia *Section 2–318*
No alternative chosen. Language adopted reads: "No privity is necessary to support an action for a tort; but if the tort results from the violation of a duty, itself the consequence of a contract, the right of action is confined to the parties and privies to that contract, except in cases where the party would have had a right of action for the injury done, independently of the contract, and except as proved in Code section 109A–2–318. However, the manufacturer of any personal property, sold as new property, either directly or through a dealer or any other person, shall be liable in tort, irrespective of privity, to any natural person who may use, consume or be affected by the property and who suffers injury to his person or property because the property when sold by the manufacturer was not merchantable and reasonably suited to the use intended and its condition when sold is the proximate cause of the injury sustained; a manufacturer may not exclude or limit the operation thereof."

Guam *Section 2–318*
Alternative C adopted.

Hawaii *Section 490: 2–318*
Alternative C adopted.

Idaho *Section 28–2–318*
Alternative A adopted.

Illinois
Not adopted.

Indiana
Not adopted.

Iowa *Section 554.2318*
Alternative C adopted.

Kansas *Section 2: 318*
No alternative adopted. Language adopted reads: "A seller's warranty whether express or implied extends to any natural person who may reasonably be expected to use, consume or be affected by the goods and who is injured in person by breach of the warranty."

Kentucky
Not adopted.

Louisiana
Not adopted.

Maine *Section 2: 318*
No alternative adopted. Language adopted reads: "Lack of privity between plaintiff and defendant shall be no defense in any action brought against the manufacturer, seller or supplier of goods for breach of warranty, express or implied, although the plaintiff did not purchase the goods from the defendant, if the plaintiff was a person whom the manufacturer, seller or supplier might reasonably have expected to use, consume or be affected by the goods."

Maryland *Section 2–318*
Alternative A adopted. Language adopted reads: "or any other ultimate consumer or user of the goods or persons affected thereby," added following "home."

Massachusetts *Section 2: 318*
Alternative A adopted. "Lack of privity between plaintiff and defendant shall be no defense in any action brought against the manufacturer, seller, lessor or supplier of goods to recover damages for breach of warranty, express or implied, or for negligence, although the plaintiff did not purchase the goods from the defendant, if the plaintiff was a person whom the manufacturer, seller, lessor or supplier might reasonably have expected to use, consume or be affected by the goods. A manufacturer, seller, lessor or supplier may not exclude or limit the operation of this section: Failure to give notice shall not bar recovery under this section unless the defendant proves that he was prejudiced thereby. All actions under this section shall be commenced within three years next after the date the injury arose."

Michigan
Not adopted.

Minnesota *Section 336.2–318*
Alternative A second sentence reads: "A seller may not exclude or limit the operation of this section."

Mississippi *Section 75–2–318*

Alternative A adopted. Language reads: "In all causes of action for personal injuries or property damage or economic loss brought on account of negligence, strict liability or breach of warranty, including actions brought under the provisions of the Uniform Commercial Code, privity shall not be a requirement to maintain said action." Mississippi Code 11–7–20

Missouri

Not adopted.

Montana

Not adopted.

Nebraska

Not adopted.

Nevada

Alternative A adopted.

New Hampshire *Section 382–A: 2–318*

No alternative adopted. Language adopted reads: "Actions of (sic) Warranties against Manufacturers, Sellers or Suppliers of Goods. Lack of privity shall not be a defense in any action brought against the manufacturer, seller or supplier of goods to recover damages for breach of warranty, express or implied, or for negligence, even though the plaintiff did not purchase the goods from the defendant, if the plaintiff was a person whom the manufacturer, seller or supplier might reasonably have expected to use, consume or be affected by the goods. A manufacturer, seller or supplier may not exclude or limit the operation of this section."

New Jersey

Not adopted.

New Mexico

Not adopted.

New York *Section 12: 318*

No alternative adopted. Language adopted reads: "A seller's warranty, whether express or implied, extends to any natural person if it is reasonable to expect that such person may use, consume or be affected by the goods and who (sic) is injured in person by breach of the warranty. A seller may not exclude or limit the operation of this section."

North Carolina

Not adopted.

North Dakota *Section 41–02–35*

Alternative C adopted.

Ohio

Not adopted.

Oklahoma

Not adopted.

Oregon

Not adopted.

Pennsylvania

Alternative A adopted.

Rhode Island *Section 6A–2–318*

No alternative adopted. Language adopted reads: "A seller's or a manufacturer's or a packer's warranty whether express or implied including but not limited to a warranty of merchantability provided for in 6A–2–314 of this chapter, extends to any person who may reasonably be expected to use, consume or be affected by the goods and who is injured by breach of the warranty. A seller or a manufacturer or a packer may not exclude or limit the operation of this section."

South Carolina *Section 36.2–318*
No alternative adopted. Language adopted after "natural person" reads: "who may be expected to use, consume or be affected by the goods and whose person or property is damaged by breach of the warranty."

South Dakota *Section 2–318*
No alternative adopted. Language adopted in first sentence of the section reads: "A seller's warranty whether express or implied extends to any person who may reasonably be expected to use, consume or be affected by the goods and who is injured by breach of the warranty."

Tennessee *Section 37–2–318*
No alternative adopted. Language adopted reads: "In all causes of action for personal injury or property damage brought on account of negligence, strict liability or breach of warranty, including actions under the provisions of the Uniform Commercial Code, privity shall not be a requirement to maintain said action."

Texas *Section 2.318*
No alternative adopted. Language adopted reads: "This chapter does not provide whether anyone other than a buyer may take advantage of an express or an implied warranty of quality made to the buyer or whether the buyer or anyone entitled to take advantage of a warranty made to the buyer may sue a third party other than the immediate seller for deficiencies in the quality of the goods. These matters are left to the courts for their determination."

Utah *Section 70A–2–318*
Alternative C adopted.

Vermont *Section 2–318*
No alternative adopted. Words "who is in the family or household of his buyer or who is a guest in his home" omitted.

Virgin Islands
Not adopted.

Virginia *Section 8.2–318*
No alternative adopted. Language adopted reads: "Lack of privity between plaintiff and defendant shall be no defense in any action brought against the manufacturer or seller of goods to recover damages for breach of warranty, express or implied, or for negligence, although the plaintiff did not purchase the goods from the defendant, if the plaintiff was a person whom the manufacturer or seller might reasonably have expected to use, consume or be affected by the goods; however, this section shall not be construed to affect any litigation pending on June twenty-nine, nineteen hundred sixty-two."

Washington
Not adopted.

West Virginia *Section 46–2–318*
Alternative A adopted.

Wisconsin
Not adopted.

Wyoming *Section 34–21–235*
No alternative adopted. Language adopted reads: "A seller's warranty whether expressed or implied extends to any person who may reasonably be expected to use, consume or be affected by the goods and who is injured by breach of the warranty."

Appendix F
State Dramshop Acts

Alabama

Title 7, Section 120: A parent, guardian or party responsible for a minor may sue any person who sells liquor to the minor if the seller knew or was legally responsible for knowing that the recipient was a minor. The jury determines damages.

Title 7, Section 121: Any person injured in any manner, including means of support, by any intoxicated person, or in consequence of the acts of an intoxicated person, may sue the seller or donor of the alcoholic beverage which caused the intoxication if the sale or gift was illegal.

Title 7, Section 122: The injured party, or his personal representative if he is dead, may sue the intoxicated person or the provider of the liquor separately or jointly.

Alaska

No dramshop act.

Arizona

No dramshop act.

Arkansas

No dramshop act.

California

Section 25602.1: A cause of action may be brought against a licensee who furnishes alcoholic beverages to an obviously intoxicated minor if the minor causes the person injury or death.

Colorado

Section 41–2–3: Any person injured in any manner, including means of support, by any intoxicated person, or in consequence of the intoxication of any person, may sue the seller or donor of liquor who caused the intoxication of an habitual drunkard by the sale or gift of liquor, provided that the seller or his employees have been given prior written or printed notice not to serve the habitual drunkard from the husband, wife, child, guardian, or employer of the habitual drunkard. This illegal sale or gift shall cause a forfeiture of all rights of the lessee or tenant under any lease or contract of rent upon the premises.

Connecticut

Section 30–102: A seller or seller's agent who sells liquor to an intoxicated person who injures the person or property of another due to his intoxication shall be liable to each injured person for damages up to $20,000 and to each group of persons injured by the same drunkard up to $50,000. To recover, the injured persons must notify the seller in writing of the intent to sue under the act within 60 days after the injury. Any lawsuits under this section must be filed within one year after injury.

Courtesy of the National Restaurant Association.

Delaware

Title 4, Section 711: The person in charge of licensed premises is not liable to an individual for damages arising from the refusal to sell liquor to an intoxicated person.

Title 4, Section 716: A licensee who sells liquor to a person classified as an habitual drinker under Section 715(a)(6), and after being notified of the classification by the state, shall be liable in a civil action for damages and may be sentenced to pay not more than $500 by way of exemplary damages to the person appealing.

District of Columbia

Section 25–121: A licensee shall not be held liable for damages resulting from the refusal to sell or deliver liquor to a minor or a person who appears to be intoxicated.

Florida

Section 562.51: A person selling or furnishing liquor to another person may not be held liable for injury or damage caused by or resulting from the intoxication of that person. *However,* any person selling or furnishing liquor to a minor may become liable for injury or damages by that minor.

Georgia

Section 105–1205: The father, or the mother if the father is dead, may sue any person furnishing liquor to his or her minor without the said parent's permission.

Hawaii

No dramshop act.

Idaho

No dramshop act.

Illinois

Chapter 43, Section 135: Any person who is injured in any manner, including means of support, by an intoxicated person can sue the seller or donor who caused the intoxication of the person causing the injury. Any person owning, renting, leasing or permitting the use of the premises for the sale of liquor or for other purposes and who knowingly permits the sale of liquor shall also be liable for damages done by the intoxicated person. The illegal sale or gift of liquor creates a forfeiture of the rights of a tenant or lessee of the premises. No judgment for injury to the person or property of any one person shall exceed $15,000. Recovery for loss of support resulting from death or injury of another person perpetrated by the intoxicated person shall not exceed $20,000.

Indiana

No dramshop act.

Iowa

Section 123.92: Any person injured in person, property, or means of support by an intoxicated person or resulting from the intoxication of such person, can sue a licensee or permittee who serves liquor to any intoxicated person or serves a person until he gets intoxicated. Every liquor control licensee and class "B" permittee must furnish proof of financial responsibility either by a liability insurance policy or by posting bond.

Section 123–92: The injured party must give written notice of intent to sue the licensee, permittee, or the insurance carrier within 6 months after the injury. An extension of time is granted if the plaintiff is incapacitated or unable to discover the name of the licensee, the permittee, or the party causing the injury.

Section 123.92: A liquor control licensee or beer permittee can avoid civil liability under the dramshop act by establishing that the intoxication did not contribute to the injurious action.

Kansas

Prior dramshop act, Section 21–2150, was repealed by Section 41–1106.

Kentucky

No dramshop act.

Louisiana

No dramshop act.

Maine

Title 17, Section 2002: Any person injured in person, property, or means of support by an intoxicated person, or because of the intoxication of any person, may sue anyone selling, illegally selling, or giving away alcoholic beverages who thereby causes or contributes to the intoxication of the person causing the injury. The owner, lessee, or person renting or leasing the property with knowledge of the illegal sales may also be liable in conjunction with the seller or distributor.

Maryland

No dramshop act.

Massachusetts

No dramshop act.

Michigan

Section 436.22: Any person injured in any manner by a visibly intoxicated person and whose injury was proximately caused by the illicit sale of liquor to the inebriate may sue the seller or donor of the liquor and/or the principal and surety of such seller. The injured party may recover actual damages of at least $50 in each case in which the judge or jury decides that intoxication was the proximate cause of injury or death. All suits must be brought within two years of the injury.

Minnesota

Section 340.95: Any person injured in any manner, including loss of means of support, by an intoxicated person or by the intoxication of any person, can sue any persons for all damages resulting from such person's illegal sale or other distribution of liquor which caused the intoxication of the party in question. No recovery shall be had in any action(s) in excess of $250,000 for all damages to one person and $500,000 for all damages to two or more persons arising out of a single instance of the illegal sale or barter of intoxicating liquor. All suits must be brought within one year of injury.

Mississippi

No dramshop act.

Missouri

No dramshop act.

Montana

No dramshop act.

Nebraska

Prior dramshop acts repealed, Laws 1935, chapter 116, page 430, Section 107.

Nevada

No dramshop act. Prior statute repealed in 1969.

New Hampshire

No dramshop act.

New Jersey

No dramshop act.

New Mexico

Section 41–11–1: Civil liability shall be predicated . . . in the case of the licensee who: (1) sold or served alcohol to a person who was intoxicated; (2) it was reasonably apparent to the licensee that the person buying or apparently receiving service of alcoholic beverages was intoxicated; and (3) . . . knew from the circumstances that the person buying or receiving service of alcoholic beverages is (was) intoxicated. Furthermore, . . . no licensee is chargeable with knowledge of previous acts by which a person becomes intoxicated at other locations unknown to the licensee . . . (that) as used in this section, "licensee" means a person licensed under the provisions of the Liquor Control Act and the agents or servants of the licensee . . . A licensee may be civilly liable for the negligent violation of Sections 60–7B–1 and 60–7B–1.1 NMSA 1978. The fact-finder shall consider all the circumstances of the sale in determining whether there is negligence such as the representation used to obtain the alcoholic beverage. It shall not be negligence per se to violate Sections 60–7B–1 and 60–7B–1.1 NMSA 1978.

New York

New York General Obligations Law Section 11–101: Any person injured by an intoxicated person or as a result of the intoxication of a person, whether or not the person dies from intoxication, may sue anyone who illegally sold or procured liquor for the intoxicated person. The survivors of a deceased intoxicated person may also sue. Where parents are entitled to sue, only one parent may successfully sue and recover damages.

North Carolina

General Statutes, Chapter 18B, Article 1A: An aggrieved party has a claim for relief of damages against a permittee or local Alcoholic Beverage Control Board if: (1) an alcoholic beverage was negligently sold or furnished to an underage person; *and* (2) the consumption of the alcoholic beverage caused or contributed to, in whole or in part, an underage driver's being subject to an impairing substance at the time of the injury; *and* (3) the injury that resulted was proximately caused by the underage driver's negligent operation of a motor vehicle while so impaired.

However, no permittee or his employee may be held liable for damages resulting from the refusal to sell or furnish an alcoholic beverage to a person who fails to show proper identification or who appears to be an underage person.

Additionally, no permittee or his employee may be held civilly liable if he holds a customer's identification documents for a reasonable length of time in a good faith attempt to determine whether the customer is of legal age to purchase liquor, provided the permittee or employee informs the customer of the reason for his actions.

North Dakota
Section 5–01–06: Any person injured in person, property, or means of support by an intoxicated person or in consequence of intoxication, may sue the person who caused the intoxication for all damages sustained if intoxication resulted from the illegal dispensing of alcoholic beverages.

Ohio
Section 4399.01: Any person injured in person, property, or means of support by an intoxicated person or in consequence of the intoxication of a person after the issuance of the Department of Liquor Control order prohibiting the sale of intoxicating beverages to such a class of intoxicated persons (Section 4301.01 of the Revised Code), can sue the person responsible for the illegal sale or gift of liquor which caused the intoxication.

Section 4399.02: The owner or person leasing or renting a building or premises who knows that illegal sales of intoxicants occur on the premises or, if rented for other purposes, knowingly permits illegal sales of intoxicants which cause the intoxication of a person, as described in Section 4399.01 (above), shall be liable for damages to the same extent as the person who sells the intoxicants described in Section 4399.01.

Oklahoma
Prior statute, Title 37, Section 121, repealed by Title 37, Section 501, effective 1959.

Oregon
Prior statute, Title 3, Section 30.730, repealed by chapter 801, Laws 1979.

Chapter 801, Section 1: No licensee or permittee is liable for damages incurred or caused by intoxicated patrons off the licensee or permittee's business premises unless the patron was served alcoholic beverages while visibly intoxicated.

Chapter 801, Section 2: No private host is liable for damages incurred or caused by an intoxicated social guest unless the guest was served alcoholic beverages while visibly intoxicated.

Chapter 801, Section 3: No licensee, permittee or social host may be liable to third persons injured by persons under 21 years of age who obtained alcoholic beverages from the licensee, permittee or social host unless it is demonstrated that a reasonable person would have determined that identification should have been requested or that the identification exhibited was altered.

Pennsylvania
Title 47, Section 4–497: A licensee is liable to third persons for acts of customers off the premises only if the licensee sold or furnished liquor to the customer while the customer was visibly intoxicated.

Rhode Island

Section 3–11–1: Any person injured by an intoxicated person may sue both the intoxicated person and the person who supplied the intoxicated person with alcoholic beverages if the liquor was illegally supplied.

Section 3–11–2: The husband, wife, child, guardian, parent or employer of a habitually intemperate person may give written notice to another person requesting the other person not to sell or deliver intoxicants to the habitually intemperate person. If within 12 months after delivery of the notice, the other person sells or delivers intoxicants to, or permits the loitering on the premises of, the habitually intemperate person, the person who gave notice may sue the other person for damages.

South Carolina

No dramshop act.

South Dakota

No dramshop act.

Tennessee

No dramshop act.

Texas

No dramshop act.

Utah

Section 16–6–13.1: Any person who illegally gives, sells, or provides liquor to another and causes the intoxication of the other person will be held liable for injuries in person, property, or means of support to any third person resulting from the intoxication.

Vermont

Title 7, Section 501: Any person injured in person, property, or means of support by an intoxicated person, or as a consequence of a person's intoxication, may sue the persons who caused the intoxication, in whole or in part, by the illegal supplying of liquor to the intoxicated person. If the liquor was supplied in a rented building and the owner or owner's agent knew or had reason to know of the illegal sales or storage, then the owner would also be liable for damages.

Virginia

No dramshop act.

Washington

No dramshop act.

West Virginia

No dramshop act.

Wisconsin

Section 176.35: Any person, injured by or in consequence of the intoxication of a minor or habitual drunkard, has a right of action against any individual who sold or gave liquor in disregard of a written notice or request not to sell or give liquor to that minor or drunkard.

Wyoming

Section 12–34: Licensees or permittees who sell or give alcoholic or malt liquor to a minor or habitual drunkard after having received written notice from a court, parent, or guardian, in the case of a minor, or from a spouse or dependent, in the case of a habitual drunkard, are liable to an action for actual and punitive damages.

Appendix G
State Equal Opportunity Laws

State	Civil Rights	Sex Based	Marital Status	Sexual Preference	Age	Physical Handicap	Mental Handicap
Alabama						X	
Alaska	X	X	X		X	X	
Arizona	X	X			X		
Arkansas		X				X	
California	X	X	X		X	X	
Colorado	X	X			X	X	
Connecticut	X	X	X		X	X	X
Delaware		X			X		
District of Columbia	X	X	X	X	X	X	
Florida	X	X	X		X	X	
Georgia		X			X	X	
Hawaii		X	X		X	X	
Idaho		X			X		
Illinois	X	X	X		X	X	X
Indiana	X	X				X	
Iowa	X	X			X	X	X
Kansas	X	X				X	
Kentucky		X			X (40–65)		
Louisiana		X			X	X	
Maine	X	X			X	X	X
Maryland	X	X	X		X	X	X
Massachusetts	X	X			X		
Michigan	X	X	X		X		
Minnesota	X	X	X		X	X	
Mississippi							
Missouri	X	X				X	
Montana	X	X	X		X	X	X
Nebraska	X	X	X			X	

State Equal Opportunity Laws

State	Civil Rights	Sex Based	Marital Status	Sexual Preference	Age	Physical Handicap	Mental Handicap
Nevada	X	X			X	X	
New Hampshire	X	X	X		X	X	X
New Jersey	X	X	X		X	X	
New Mexico	X	X			X	X	X
New York	X	X	X		X	X	
North Carolina		X			X	X	
North Dakota		X			X		
Ohio	X	X			X	X	
Oklahoma	X	X					
Oregon		X	X		X	X	X
Pennsylvania	X	X			X	X	
Rhode Island	X	X			X	X	
South Carolina	X	X			X		
South Dakota	X	X					
Tennessee	X	X			X		
Texas		X			X (public)	X	
Utah	X	X			X		
Vermont		X			X	X	X
Virginia		X				X	
Washington	X	X	X		X	X	X
West Virginia	X	X			X	X	
Wisconsin	X	X		X	X	X	
Wyoming	X	X		X	X	X	
Puerto Rico		X			X		
Virgin Islands		X			X		

Note: All states not adopting employment opportunity laws are covered by the Federal Civil Rights Act, Title VII [Race, Color, Religion, National Origin, Sex, Pregnancy, Equal Pay, Age, or Handicap (government contractors)].

Appendix H
Polygraph Laws

There are 20 states that, in some way, have banned the use of the polygraph in matters of personnel administration. The following lists those states and indicates, in each instance, the limitations that prevail.

State/Date	No employer may " . . . " any employee or prospective employee to take a polygraph test.
1. Alaska (1964)	"request or suggest"
2. California (1963)	"demand or require" (but may request or permit)
3. Connecticut (after 1966)	"request or require"
4. Delaware (1966)	"require, request, or suggest"
5. Hawaii	"require"
6. Idaho	"require"
7. Maine (1979)	"require, request, or suggest"
8. Maryland (1966)	"demand or require"
9. Massachusetts (1959, amended 1963)	"subject or cause"
10. Michigan	Cannot discharge for refusal
11. Minnesota (1973)	"request or require"
12. Montana (1974)	"require"
13. Nebraska	"require" as a condition of employment; may ask if certain rules are followed.
14. Nevada	"require" Employer must advise that employee has the right to refuse if incriminating or degrading. No questions referring to politics, religion, sex, or labor activities permitted.
15. New Jersey (1966)	"influence, request, or require"
16. Oregon	"require" Refusal to take cannot be basis for denying or terminating employment.
17. Pennsylvania (1969)	"require"
18. Rhode Island (1964)	"require, subject, or cause"
19. Washington (1965)	"require"
20. Wisconsin	"require" or administer to determine honesty

At present 21 states have laws providing for the licensing of polygraph operators: Alabama, Arizona, Arkansas, Florida, Georgia, Illinois, Kentucky, Massachusetts, Michigan, Mississippi, Nevada, New Mexico, North Carolina, North Dakota, Oklahoma, Oregon, South Carolina, Texas, Utah, Vermont and Virginia.

Courtesy of the National Restaurant Association.

Glossary

Abandoned property Property that is deliberately discarded by the owner.

Abandonment When a tenant vacates the rented premises before the lease term expires, without the landlord's consent.

Acceptance In contracts, agreement by the recipient of an offer to the terms of an offer.

Accession An increase in property by production of the property or by actual addition to property.

Accessory use Property use that is incidental to the main use for which an area is zoned.

Administrative law Laws created and often administered and enforced by federal, state, and local agencies.

Adulteration Contamination of food products as a result of unsanitary handling during preparation, packing, or storage.

Adverse possession A method of acquiring property without a voluntary transfer by the owner. This method requires the possessor to occupy the property, openly and visibly, for a period of time fixed by state statutes.

Affirm In an appeal, the appellate court may *affirm* or uphold the lower court's decision rather than reverse or remand it.

Affirmative defense A response by the defense that attacks the legal right of the plaintiff to make a claim, caused by a plaintiff act or failure to act that may entitle the defense to a favorable judgment.

Affixation Attachment of property to real estate with the intention to make the property a permanent fixture.

Agreement Essential contract element that requires that all parties agree to the terms of an offer and accept the offer.

Air rights Legal rights to the air space above land.

Alcoholic One who is addicted to liquor. In legal/foodservice terms this is relevant when the server knew or should have known the patron was an alcoholic.

Alien Any person who is not a U.S. citizen. The person may be a *legal* or an *illegal* alien.

Answer The first response by the defense to the plaintiff's charge or complaint.

Antitrust Actions taken by businesspersons that violate laws designed to prevent monopolies.

Appeal (1) A request, usually by the loser in a lawsuit, for an appellate court to review a trial court decision. (2) The actual trial of an appeal.

Appellate court Intermediate review courts at the federal or state level. These courts are between the trial and supreme courts in terms of review authority.

Appraisal right The right to redeem shares of stock at fair market value.

Arbitration A method of settling disputes whereby an arbitrator decides the case. This method binds all parties to the decision.

Assault Any act or threat that creates a reasonable risk of physical harm to a person.

Assignee The person to whom another person assigns rights and interest in real property.

Assignment A transfer of interest and rights in real property.

Assignor The person who assigns rights and interest in real property to the assignee.

Assumption of risk A legal defense that is used when the plaintiff should have known about the risk and voluntarily assumed it.

Attachment (1) An enforceable security interest in property. (2) The physical act of seizing property by the sheriff, as ordered by a court.

Attorney-client privilege The duty all lawyers owe clients not to disclose information given them in their role as lawyers.

Bailment A voluntary transfer of goods from one person to another for safekeeping.

Bankruptcy A federal procedure that enables a person or business to escape nonexempt debts when circumstances make the debtor incapable of meeting them.

Battery An act that physically harms a person.

Bilateral contract A contract in which both parties are expected to perform because a promise has been exchanged for a promise.

Bill of lading A document, issued to the shipper of goods by the carrier, that lists the goods accepted for transport.

Blacklisting In franchising, a *per se* antitrust violation where franchisees boycott a supplier's business for refusing to fund a promotion of the franchised product.

Blue laws State and local laws prohibiting conducting certain business operations on Sunday.

Board of directors The governing body of a corporation.

***Bona fide* occupational qualification** In the Civil Rights Act of 1964, an exemption to the rule of equal employment opportunity may be created if the difference in treatment is justified because of the requirements of the job.

Breach of contract Nonperformance of contract terms by one of the parties.

Breach of warranty Nonperformance according to the terms of a warranty of sale.

Brief A summary of facts of the trial of a case given on appeal.

Burglary The breaking and entering of a building with the intent to steal at a time when the business is unoccupied or very few people are present.

Capacity In contracts, the legal capacity to enter into and perform a contract, including the emotional maturity and mental competence to comply.

Case law Law created by judicial decision by the highest court to act on an issue. Also called *common law.*

Casualty insurance Insurance designed to protect property from risks other than fire, such as strikes and robberies.

Causation The direct relationship between a legal harm and the alleged cause.

Caveat emptor Let the buyer beware.

Caveat vendor Let the seller beware.

Certificate of occupancy A certificate issued by local building inspectors after the building has been approved for business use.

Certiorari Permission by a court saying it will hear a case. The request to the court is called a *petition for certiorari.*

Chapter 11 bankruptcy A bankruptcy procedure for individuals, partnerships, and corporate debtors whereby they apply for reorganization of financial structure.

Chapter 7 bankruptcy Straight bankruptcy whereby all nonexempt debts are absolved.

Chapter 13 bankruptcy A form of bankruptcy that permits the debtor to pay debts according to a plan agreed to by the creditors.

Child labor laws Laws designed to protect minors from unfair and exploitative labor practices.

Civil rights laws   Federal, state, and local laws that prohibit discriminatory practices against members of particular racial or minority groups.

Civil unrest   Disturbances caused because of riots or politically motivated terrorist activity.

Class action suit   A suit brought on behalf of a group of people who have an interest in the outcome.

Closely-held corporation   A family-owned corporation or one owned by a few close individuals. Also called a close corporation.

Closing arguments   Arguments presented at a trial by attorneys for both the plaintiff and the defendant, after they have rested their cases.

Collateral   Personal property that may be held as security for a loan or other extension of credit.

Commercial zoning   Allocating land use to businesses.

Common law   Law created by the highest court to deal with an issue. This law remains in effect until changed by statute. Also called *case law.*

Communication   In contract law, the offer to contract that limits the offer to specific persons.

Comparative negligence   A defense to liability claims, which basically assigns a percentage of any judgment against the defendant to the plaintiff. Also called *contributory negligence.*

Compensatory damages   Damage awards not intended to punish the defendant in a lawsuit, but only to compensate the plaintiff for injuries or losses.

Complaint   The first pleading in a lawsuit, which notifies the parties involved of the purpose and facts of the case.

Compromise   A voluntary settlement of a dispute between the parties, without recourse to lawsuits or third parties.

Concealment   A failure to give information relevant to an insurance claim that might cause the carrier to deny that claim.

Conciliation   Another term for *mediation,* which is the action of third parties who try to settle a dispute.

Confiscation   A taking of private property by the government for public use.

Confusion   A mixing of the property of two persons.

Consequential damages   Damages that arise from the results of a breach of contract, but were not part of the contract terms.

Consideration   Money or other compensation that is given by one party to a contract to the other party in exchange for something of value.

Constructive eviction   Conditions that force a tenant to move, such as the presence of vermin.

Contempt of court   An action or refusal to act that obstructs a court's work or undermines its dignity.

Contingent fee   An attorney's fee based on a percentage of a favorable award or judgment.

Contract   A legally enforceable agreement between two parties, in which each agrees to perform according to the terms of the agreement.

Contract law   The body of laws that enforce legal contracts.

Contract of sale   A contract for the purchase and transfer of goods from seller to buyer.

Contributory negligence   A defense to liability suits where the plaintiff is partially responsible for the illness or injury, and the court assigns a percentage of the award or damages to the plaintiff. Also called *comparative negligence.*

Conversion   Use of another's property without legal justification.

Copyright   A method of protecting literary and audiovisual works.

Corporation   A form of business created by statute that allows a group of persons to work together for profit.

Counterfeit   Not the real thing. When applied to money, the difference may be hard to detect.

Counteroffer A rejection of a contract offer that causes a new offer to be made, except in the case of a firm offer.

Credit A delay of payment through mutual agreement.

Creditor The person to whom money is owed.

Criminal trespass Presence on private property of persons who intend to commit a crime.

Cross-examination Examination, at a trial, of an opponent's witnesses or the opposing party.

Damages Physical or economic harm that requires a court to require the person who caused the harm to compensate the victim. The compensation is also called damages.

Debt Money owed by a debtor to a creditor.

Debtor The person who owes money to a creditor.

Deed A document of title to property. Legal rights to property are contained in the deed.

Defamation A false statement that injures a person's reputation.

Defamation by computer False information attributable to a company that owns or distributes computer printout information.

Default A failure to perform a legal duty. A failure to comply with any of the procedural requirements of a trial may result in a *judgment by default*.

Defendant The person or entity against whom legal action is taken.

Definiteness In contract law, terms must be specific and firm enough for a court to enforce.

Delivery The actual transfer of property from one person to another.

Demolition lien A legal claim by which a regulatory body may demolish a building, and then seek compensation from the owner.

Demurrer A response to a complaint filed by the plaintiff in a lawsuit.

Department of Justice Federal cabinet department that enforces antitrust laws, and is the legal arm of the White House.

Depositions Sworn testimony in a trial, which is taken down by a court stenographer.

Derivative shareholder action A lawsuit to defend the rights of the corporation.

Destination contract This requires the seller to deliver the goods to a specific place.

Disaffirm In contract law, to set the contract aside or refuse to perform according to the terms.

Disbarment A process by which a lawyer's right to practice law is taken away.

Discharge (1) In contract law, a contract may be discharged by performance or by mutual agreement of both parties. (2) In bankruptcy law, a person is released from debt through a discharge in bankruptcy.

Disclosure statement In franchising, a statement that includes the financial condition of the franchisor as well as terms of the agreement. The FTC requires that the franchisor furnish prospective franchisees with this statement.

Discovery In a lawsuit, the process of gathering evidence before the trial.

Dismissal A court order that removes a lawsuit from the authority or action of the court.

Disorderly conduct Fights, noise, or other conduct that threaten the peace and safety of an area.

Disparagement of goods False, libelous statements about someone's product, business, or property. Also called *slander of title*.

Doctrine of unconscionable conduct A legal doctrine that protects the victim of a contract or legal proceeding from being denied fair treatment because of unreasonable terms.

Document of title A document that gives the owner rights in the property the document covers.

Dormant partner A silent partner who does not participate in management, and also a secret partner, not known to the public.

Dramshop acts State acts that define liability for liquor sales to patrons who injure or kill third persons.

Dramshop liability Liability to third parties created by the sale of alcohol to a patron who injures another person.

Economic strike A union employee strike related to hours, wages, and working conditions disputes.

EEOC Equal Employment Opportunity Commission.

Eminent domain Government power to take private property for public use.

Encumber To put up land as security to finance improvements.

Equal Employment Opportunity Commission (EEOC) Federal enforcement agency for the employment section of the Civil Rights Act of 1964, the Age Discrimination Act, and the Equal Employment Opportunity Act of 1972.

Equitable risk distribution According to the Uniform Commercial Code, retailers can sue growers or producers of food products for losses caused by their negligence.

Equity (1) The value of interest in property. (2) Fairness.

Equity of redemption The right to prevent foreclosure.

Evidence Information presented at a trial.

Examination During a trial, questioning of a witness or party to the case by either attorney.

Excess liability policy An insurance policy that protects the insured in the event the basic policy does not cover a liability claim.

Exclusion In insurance, situations the carrier refuses to cover.

Exculpatory clause An unenforceable, illegal contract clause whereby one party conditions the offer on the other party's waiver of legal rights related to the contract.

Executed contract One not fully performed by both parties.

Executory contract One not completed by one party.

Express contract One in which all of the terms and conditions are fully stated.

False imprisonment A personal tort that interferes with a person's right to move freely.

FDA Food and Drug Administration.

Featherbedding Paying employees for work not done.

Federal Trade Commission (FTC) Enforcement agency with broad enforcement powers over federal trade and commerce laws, including such foodservice areas as food labeling, franchising, and advertising.

Fee simple A form of ownership without any restriction on estate disposal or use.

Fee simple absolute Same as *fee simple*.

Fidelity insurance Insurance that bonds an employee and protects the employer from losses arising out of employee actions, including criminal misconduct.

Fiduciary One in a position of trust.

Fiduciary duty The duty owed a client by a lawyer. The client has the right to expect that the lawyer can be trusted with personal and business information.

Fire insurance Insurance to protect premises from fire and other related hazards.

Firm offer In contracts, an offer that is good only for a specified time period.

Fixtures Anything attached to land or a building that is not readily removable.

Food and Drug Administration (FDA) Federal enforcement agency that controls the manufacture, distribution, and sale of food and drug products. This agency is the source of regulations and model standards.

Foreclosure   A process that legally ends a person's rights in property. If the mortgage is not paid, a bank will usually take back the property to sell it.

Foreclosure lawsuit   A lawsuit to take property back when the mortgage debt is not paid off.

Foreign or natural test   A test applied by the courts in food liability cases that determines liability for food fitness based on whether or not the matter that caused the illness or injury was natural to the food item.

Foreseeable risk   A risk or hazard that is visible and could be prevented.

Forged check   A check that is genuine except that the signature of the actual owner is imitated.

Formal contract   A tangible, negotiable instrument.

Franchise   A license from the owner of a trademark or service name giving another the right to sell the product and use the name in advertising.

Franchise disclosure rule   An FTC rule that requires franchisors to disclose certain information to a prospective franchisee.

Franchisee   The person who has bought into a franchise and has the right to use the products and trade names of the franchisor.

Franchisor   The person or corporate entity that owns trademark product names exclusively, but licenses those rights to others to distribute the products.

Fraud   Deceit; in legal terms, behavior designed to cheat another out of legal rights.

Fraudulent transfers   A gift or sale for less than fair market value with intent to delay or defraud creditors from obtaining legitimate claims.

Freehold estate   An estate that may be held indefinitely.

FTC   Federal Trade Commission.

Full partner   Same as *general partner*. See that term.

Function contract   A foodservice contract that reserves a specific space and an exact time for a special event.

Future interests   The rights of a future owner of property.

General partner   A full partner in a partnership who has unlimited liability and management powers and shares fully in the profits.

General warranty deed   A property deed that conveys the largest number of rights.

Genuineness of assent   A legal phrase that means a contract must be fully negotiated by both parties.

Gift   A method of acquiring or transferring real property whereby the owner voluntarily gives it away.

Grading   Federal evaluations of meat products that enable buyers to select standardized products.

Grandfather clause   A clause contained in local building codes that allows existing buildings to be exempt from the newer requirements.

Grand larceny   Theft of property or money of a value over a certain amount set by law.

Gross lease   A type of lease in which the tenant's sole responsibility is to pay rent.

Ground lease   A type of lease in which the landlord rents out vacant land and the tenant agrees to erect a building, which the tenant may, in turn, mortgage.

Guarantor   The person or entity who assures a creditor that the debt will be paid.

Home rule   Power granted by the state to certain cities or counties to regulate certain areas.

Hot cargo clause   A clause as part of a labor agreement whereby the employer agrees not to deal in another's products.

House rule   A rule or set of rules foodservice operators use to maintain the class and type of an operation.

Implied contract One in which the terms and conditions are implied by the conduct of the parties.

Implied warranty An unspoken guarantee by a seller that a product is fit for sale.

Improper venue A wrongful filing of a claim in a jurisdiction unable to hear the case.

Incompetent A person who is legally defined as lacking sufficient mental capacity to understand the consequences of his or her acts, particularly regarding contracts.

Informational picketing Union representatives distributing literature outside a business.

Inheritance A method of obtaining property. A will transfers specific property to a person or party.

Insanity Recognized mental incompetence that is judicially declared and can render the person's contracts void.

Insolvency When debts exceed assets.

Insurable interest A legally recognized interest in whatever is to be insured.

Intangible damage Damage that is not physically apparent, such as harm to one's reputation.

Intangible property Property that has no physical substance, but represents rights or interest in property.

Intentional tort A legal wrong by which the wrongdoer wants to harm another.

Interrogatories A form of discovery used before a trial in which the person is given a written set of questions and responds with written answers.

Interstate commerce Trade between the states.

Intestate succession When an owner of property dies without a will.

Intoxicated Legally drunk or incapable of being in complete control of one's actions.

Intrastate commerce Trade within a state.

Invasion of privacy Use of a person's name or picture for commercial purposes, or disclosure of private facts without permission.

Involuntary petition A petition for bankruptcy filed by the creditor or creditors of the debtor.

Joint venture A form of partnership in which two or more persons agree to enter into a single business enterprise.

Judgment N.O.V. A judgment notwithstanding the verdict.

Jurisdiction The power of a court to hear and decide a case.

Jury A panel of private citizens who are assigned to decide which side is right or wrong in a court case.

Kosher Food that is prepared in the Orthodox Jewish manner.

Landlord A person or entity who owns and leases land and/or a building.

Landmark A site or property declared by a local commission to be of historical value and in need of preservation.

Larceny Theft.

Law merchant A common law system of rules used by sellers.

Lease A contract to use land, a building, or part of a building for a specific time period.

Legal duty The legal responsibility one person owes another, and which is enforceable in court.

Legality In contract law, a contract must not violate any laws in order to be enforceable.

Letter of intent Letters that announce *intent,* such as to make reservations for a special function or space available for a function, and are not generally accepted as contracts.

Liability   The enforceable responsibility one person has to another.

Liability insurance   Insurance designed to protect foodservice operators from losses resulting from patron liability claims.

Libel   Written defamation of a person's reputation.

Lien   A legal claim against property, or interest in property, that entitles the bearer to take over the property, or part of it, in the event the debt is not settled.

Life estate   A form of ownership in which owner rights are for life only.

Life tenant   Non-owner occupier of land.

Limited partnership   A form of business in which the limited partner has limited liability in exchange for lack of management control.

Liquidated damages   A provision included in a contract that provides for compensation in the event of a failure of one of the parties to perform.

Listing contract   A real estate broker's agreement.

Mailbox rule   A rule governing contracts which requires that an acceptance of an offer be properly posted and mailed.

Majority   The legal age to form contracts, vote, drink, or go into business. Set by state law.

Malicious mischief   Intended injury to real or personal property of another.

Malpractice   Misconduct or negligence by a professional in the process of handling another's business. Used here to apply to lawyers.

Manifestation of authority   In franchising, representation of control or authority given to patrons through advertising.

Mediation   A method of settling disputes by which a third person aids in negotiating by moderating and making recommendations that are not binding.

Mental distress   An intentional tort that causes emotional harm.

Merger   The union of two or more companies, where one becomes a part of the other.

Minor   A person who has not reached legal age, or majority, as set by state law.

Misbranding   False and misleading advertising, usually on the product label.

Misdemeanor   A lesser criminal offense than a felony, punishable by a fine or a brief jail term.

Misrepresentation   A tort that involves false statements or concealments of facts for personal gain.

Mixed zoning   Local zoning that allows both residential and commercial use.

Monopoly   Illegal control over the manufacture, sale, distribution, or price of a product.

Mortgage   A method of putting up land or buildings as security for a loan or to finance improvements of land.

Mortgagee   The lender in a mortgage plan.

Mortgagor   The person taking out a mortgage on land or a building.

Motion   In a trial, a request by either party that the judge must act on or dismiss.

Mutual mistake   In contract law, a mutual misunderstanding on one of the terms of a contract.

National Labor Relations Board (NLRB)   Enforcement board created by the National Labor Relations Act, which enforces union and employer labor practices.

Natural persons   In law, refers to persons rather than artificial entities such as corporations.

Negligence theory   A liability theory that requires the injured person to prove negligence on the part of another.

Negotiable instrument   A promise to pay.

Negotiation   Discussion of contract terms to obtain the best deal.

Net lease   A lease in which the tenant assumes incidental costs, such as utilities, insurance, or taxes.

Nominal damages Small compensation, awarded by a court to one party to a contract for its breach by the other party.

Nominal partner A partner in name, who may be liable under certain circumstances.

Non compos mentis Describes the state of mind of a person who is unable to understand the legal consequences of his or her actions or abilities to contract.

Nonconforming use A form of zoning in which a businessperson applies for permission for special use when an area has been restricted to one use, such as for residential purposes.

Non-freehold estate Restricted estates that may be held for a specific time.

Nonprofit An organization not engaged in a profit-making activity, or classified as such for tax purposes.

Nontrading partnership A partnership that provides a service rather than a product.

Not-for-profit A tax classification covering businesses not engaged in profit-making activities.

Objectionable conduct Misbehavior or conduct that is offensive to others.

Objective appearance test Use of observation of an individual to determine sobriety.

Occupational Safety and Health Administration (OSHA) Federal agency assigned to enforce regulations pertaining to the on-the-job health and safety of workers. OSHA is the source of laws and standards regarding worker safety.

Offer To make a proposal. The first step in a contract.

Open-end mortgage Form of mortgage whereby money may be borrowed at different times under the same agreement.

Opening statement Statement given by attorneys for both sides in a trial, which presents what it is they will attempt to prove.

Operation of law In contract law, circumstances that result in automatic termination of an offer.

OSHA Occupational Safety and Health Administration.

Ostensible partner Same as *nominal partner.* See that term.

Overrule (1) A high court may overturn the decision of a lower court by overruling it. (2) A judge may refuse to acknowledge an objection during a trial by overruling it.

Partial performance Incomplete performance of contract terms.

Partnership A form of business organization in which two or more persons agree to conduct a business for profit.

Partnership by estoppel A legal principle that may make nominal or ostensible partners liable if customers act on the belief that the person is a full partner.

Patent A government grant giving an inventor the exclusive right to manufacture, use, and distribute a product for 17 years.

Penalty clause A contract clause that requires a penalty to be charged to the party who violates the contract.

Per diem Per day. During a trial, an attorney may charge for each day of the trial.

Perfection Protection of a security interest through attachment.

Per se **violation** Antitrust violations that cannot be justified by proper motive, absence of intent, or economic necessity.

Personal property Movable property.

Petition of certiorari Request by a party to a lower court trial that a higher court review the lower court's decision.

Petit larceny Less serious theft.

Plaintiff   The person bringing suit.

Police power   A government's right to enforce laws.

Policy   An insurance contract between the carrier and the insured, which provides the coverage conditions.

Polygraph   Lie detector. Mechanical device run by an operator, and used to determine whether or not a person is telling the truth.

Possession   Simple ownership of property.

Possessory   Form of landholding where the occupier has certain rights in, but does not own, real estate.

Preemptory challenge   A challenge of a juror by the attorney for either side. The court must comply with these challenges, but their number is limited by law.

Preferential liens   A prohibited transfer of cash or property by the debtor in a bankruptcy proceeding.

Preferential payment   A prohibited payment made by a debtor to one creditor in preference to the others.

Preliminary negotiations   Negotiations that precede actual contract offers. Accepting a bid is an example.

Premium   Payment for insurance coverage. This charge is not a set fee and may be based on a number of factors.

Preservation zoning   Zoning designed to preserve historical landmarks.

Pre-trial hearing   A conference held between the parties and the judge before a trial to settle any disputes, and to determine the length of the trial, the number of witnesses that may be called, and any special requirements.

Price fixing   Setting the prices of products by franchisees or franchisors to harm competitors.

Prima facie   On the face of it. A fact will be held true, unless evidence disputes it.

Private corporation   A corporation established for the benefit of its owners, as distinguished from a *public* corporation.

Privity of contract   A direct relationship between the parties to a contract.

Prohibition   Historical period in the United States when it was illegal to make or sell alcoholic beverages.

Property   In law, legally protected rights in or ownership of anything having recognized value.

Proximate cause   The actual cause of an illness or injury. In liability cases, this is a requirement.

Proxy   A piece of paper representing a shareholder's right to vote.

Proxy fight   A corporate voting battle between existing management and those seeking to control the company, in which shareholder votes are sought.

Public corporation   One owned by the general public through issues of shares.

Publicly-held corporations   Private corporations that issue some stock to the public.

Punitive damages   Money awarded to a person who has been harmed by another's malicious or deliberate act. Distinguished from *compensatory damages*.

Purchase   Method of obtaining property by ordering it from the seller and paying for it.

Purchase money mortgage   Where the seller of real property finances the buyer's purchase in exchange for the mortgage.

Purchase order   A simple contract form that contains a promise to pay, a description of the goods, and the place to which they are to be shipped.

Quantum meruit   Compensation for work done.

Quasi-contracts   Duties imposed by a court on one party to a contract in order to correct an injustice.

Quiet enjoyment   The right to peaceful and undisputed use of real property.

Quitclaim deed   A property deed, which provides the buyer only with those rights the seller has at the time of the sale, and includes any limitations.

Raised genuine check Same as *forged check*. See that term.

Ratification Performance of a voidable contract, obliging the other party to perform.

Reaffirmation agreement An agreement between the creditor and the debtor whereby the debtor agrees to repay debts that would otherwise be discharged in bankruptcy. The agreement must be approved by a court.

Real estate Property that is immovable, such as land or a building.

Real property Same as *real estate.*

Reasonable care In tort law, the standard of care expected of a reasonable person by another in a particular set of circumstances.

Reasonable expectations test A test applied by courts in food liability cases that determines liability for food fitness based on whether one might reasonably expect to find the matter that caused the injury or illness in the final, processed item.

Reasonable person test A test used in liability for safety cases, used to determine whether the accused party exercised ordinary care to protect patrons against unreasonable risks of harm.

Rebuttal Disputing evidence presented by the opposition in a trial, by presenting contrary evidence.

Recovery deduction A depreciation allowance allowed by the Economic Recovery Tax Act of 1981, which accelerates the time in which purchases may be written off.

Re-direct examination In a trial, the plaintiff's re-examination of a witness, after the defendant's attorney has examined that witness, to restore his or her credibility or address any damaging evidence brought out during the examination.

Reformation Revision of a contract by a court to express the real intentions of the parties.

Remand To send back. A higher court may send a case back to a lower court with instructions as to how the latter is to look at it again.

Request for admissions A motion by either side in a trial to obtain specific facts from the other party.

Rescission The right to cancel a contract because of fraud, duress, mistake, or failure of consideration by the other party.

Reservation contract In foodservice law, a contract involving the use of an establishment's tables where a specific table or tables are reserved in advance for the patron for a specific date and time, without payment or deposit.

Residential zoning Local restriction of land use to residential purposes.

Res ipsa loquitur "The thing speaks for itself." In liability law, the use of circumstantial evidence of negligence to impose liability.

Respondeat superior A legal rule that makes the employer liable for an employee's conduct when that conduct occurs in the course of employment and is intended to benefit the employer.

Restitution The return of each party to a contract to the position occupied prior to the contract.

Restoration In a contract between a seller of majority and a buyer who is a minor, if the seller fully performs and the minor avoids performance, the minor must restore the goods or services received to the seller. The minor is not required to compensate the seller for any damage caused.

Retainer The agreement to employ an attorney.

Reversal A higher court rejection of a lower court decision on a case.

Reverse discrimination When a member of a group not normally the object of discrimination is discriminated against.

Riot A violent, uncontrolled public disorder.

Robbery A felony in which property is taken from the person of the victim or in the victim's presence by means of force, violence, or threat of same.

Rule-of-reason violation Violation of antitrust laws involving marketing activities that create monopolies. The conduct may be justified by proof of economic necessity.

Sale and leaseback A real estate transaction in which the seller sells land for full value and the buyer agrees to resell the land to the seller.

Sale on approval A transaction in which the goods are delivered to the buyer, who does not assume title or risk of loss until approval or acceptance of the goods.

Sale on return A transaction in which the buyer assumes risks of loss and holds title unless he or she returns the goods.

Secondary boycott An illegal union boycott of a neutral employer to force the latter to harm the employer with whom the union has a dispute.

Secret partner In a partnership, one whose presence in the firm is not known to the public but who may manage the business.

Secured creditor A creditor whose claim is legally enforceable and secured by collateral.

Security interest A protected claim on property, usually secured by collateral.

Separate but equal A civil rights doctrine which predated the Civil Rights Act of 1964, and which held that accommodations for white and nonwhite people could be separate as long as they were equal in quality.

Service contract A contract to secure professional services.

Service mark A mark used to indicate and distinguish the services of one person from another.

Services Work performed by one party in return for payment.

Sex discrimination Action or treatment meant to deny rights or fair treatment to a person on the basis of sex.

Sexual harassment Treatment of women employees designed to demean them by lewd comments, suggestions, or demands for sexual favors as a condition of employment.

Sexual preference Sexual orientation.

Shareholders Owners of a corporation.

Shipment contract A contract specifying that the seller deliver goods to a carrier.

Shortchange An action where a cashier may be cheated out of correct change by quick, deliberate action on the part of a patron.

Silent partner In a partnership, a person who does not take part in managing the business.

Slander An oral defamation of a person's reputation. Proof of damage to the victim is usually essential.

Slander of title A defamation of goods, which consists of false statements about a person's product, business, or property.

Small claims courts Municipal courts set up to decide on cases not requiring an attorney and for an amount of money not higher than set by the state.

Sole proprietorship A form of business organization with one owner who runs it and has sole liability for the business.

Special warranty deed A property deed in which the seller guarantees he or she will not diminish the value of the land.

Specific performance Court-ordered correction of a breach of contract where one party is required to perform the duties specified in the contract rather than pay damages to the other party.

Spot zoning A form of zoning granted by special request where a landowner requests that a single property be exempt from regular zoning. The special zoning must benefit the surrounding community.

Squatting The attempt to take property merely by occupation. This is illegal unless the rightful owner creates a lawful tenancy.

Statements of intention Promises to make a future contract. Not an offer.

Statute of limitations Period of time set by law during which a claim can be decided or a legal wrong corrected. Once this period runs out, the claimant has no recourse to the courts.

Statutory law Law formed by elected officials at the local, state, or federal level.

Straight bankruptcy Complete bankruptcy, where all nonexempt debts are discharged and remaining assets are distributed to creditors by a trustee.

Strict liability A common law liability theory that assigns liability regardless of proof of negligence or breach of warranty.

Subchapter S corporation A tax option form of incorporation that permits corporations that qualify to be taxed the same as partnerships.

Sublease An agreement whereby the tenant gives up part of the lease to another tenant.

Subpoena ad testificandum A requirement that case-related documents be brought to court by the person in charge of them.

Subpoena duces tecum A court order requiring a person or company to provide documents for a trial.

Substantial performance Contract performance adequate for the provider to recover payment.

Subsurface rights Rights to soil below the surface of land and other natural material on it or under it.

Summary judgment A judgment in favor of one side before the trial ends, based on a motion filed by that side.

Summons A notification of a lawsuit or legal action against a party, which directs that party to answer the complaint.

Sustain A court agreement to a point made by either the attorney for the plaintiff or the attorney for the defendant.

Tangible damages Damage that is visible and easily verifiable, such as physical injury.

Tangible property Property that has physical substance.

Tenancy at sufferance Occupying land, or squatting. This form of tenancy is not recognized by law.

Tenancy at will One created by the landlord for as long as he or she desires.

Tenancy for years One in which the duration is specified in the lease.

Tenancy from period to period One that does not specify the duration of the lease, but requires that rent be paid at a certain time.

Tenant The person who occupies and leases land and/or a building from a landlord.

Tenants in partnership Ownership in common of a partnership. None of the parties has the exclusive right to handle partnership business without consulting the other parties.

Tender (1) An offer. (2) When the seller performs the requirements of a contract.

Terrorism Hostile, violent activities designed to frighten, intimidate, or harm a person or group of people.

Theft of services Using a stolen or canceled credit card to obtain services *or* intentionally avoiding payment by misrepresentation of fact or by avoidance.

Tip credit Tips added to the cash wage in order to meet the federal minimum wage scale.

Title (1) Ownership right to goods. (2) A document showing ownership in goods.

Tort A civil wrong arising out of a legal duty owed by one person to another.

Totally fabricated check A check that is not drawn on a real account *and* has no real owner.

Trade fixtures Personal property installed on property as part of a lease permitting use for a specific purpose.

Trade-mark A mark that is fixed on tangible goods to identify and protect the product registered by the owner.

Trading partnership One engaged in buying, selling, or trading goods and services for profit.

Transcript The official, typed record of a court proceeding.

Trespass Wrongful entry onto privately owned property.

Trespass to land Wrongful entry onto privately owned land.

Trial court   The first court to hear a case.

Trial *de novo*   A retrial of an entire case before a reviewing court.

Trustee   (1) In bankruptcy, the person appointed to distribute the assets of the bankrupt. (2) A fiduciary, or person in a position of trust.

Truth-in-menu   Government guidelines and laws specifying truthful advertising of products on a menu.

Tying contract   An agreement required by a franchisor specifying that franchisee purchases of certain items must be made from the franchisor.

Unforeseeable cause   The direct cause of an injury that could not be foreseen by the defendant in a negligence suit.

Unilateral contract   An agreement whereby one party promises to perform only in exchange for an act by another party.

Unilateral mistake   A misunderstanding of contract terms where only one party makes the mistake.

Unintentional tort   Negligence or a wrong committed by one person which injures the person or property of another.

United States Department of Agriculture (USDA)   Federal cabinet department that enforces laws relating to farming and is the source of regulations in this area.

Unjustified act   Malicious mischief not provoked by another's conduct.

USDA   United States Department of Agriculture.

Variance   A legal permit issued by local government to allow a property owner to use land for other than the specified zoned use.

Venue   The area in which a case may be tried or in which the court has jurisdiction.

Verdict   A decision on a court case by a jury.

Voidable title   Ownership that cannot hold up in court because the "owner" has no real title.

Void title   Term meaning the seller had nothing to sell.

Voluntary petition   A petition by a debtor requesting that the debtor be judged a bankrupt.

Walkout   A customer who leaves a business premises without paying.

Wanton act   Malicious mischief committed in total disregard of the consequences.

Warranty of seisin   The right to exclusive title and the right to convey the property.

Wildcat strike   An illegal strike not called for by a union.

Workers' compensation   (1) Insurance required by federal law to cover workers for on-the-job injuries. (2) The federal law requiring such insurance.

Writ of certiorari   A petition asking a high court to review a case.

Zoning   Use of police power to regulate local land use.

Index